Excavation

Fieldwork in archaeology has been transformed over the past three decades. Drawing on a wealth of experience in excavating some of the most complex, deeply stratified sites in Britain, Steve Roskams describes the changes that have taken place in the theory and practice of excavation. He then provides a clear account of contemporary techniques, covering pre-excavation reconnaissance and site evaluation, the preparations for full excavation, the actual process of excavation, and the recording of photographic, spatial, stratigraphic and physical evidence. A final chapter discusses the future of excavation. This manual will be welcomed by the professional excavator, the academic researcher, students and the interested amateur.

STEVE ROSKAMS is Lecturer in Archaeology at the University of York.

CAMBRIDGE MANUALS IN ARCHAEOLOGY

Series editors

Don Brothwell, *University of York*
Graeme Barker, *University of Leicester*
Dena Dincauze, *University of Massachusetts, Amherst*
Priscilla Renouf, *Memorial University of Newfoundland*

Cambridge Manuals in Archaeology is a series of reference handbooks designed for an international audience of upper-level undergraduate and graduate students, and professional archaeologists and archaeological scientists in universities, museums, research laboratories and field units. Each book includes a survey of current archaeological practice alongside essential reference material on contemporary techniques and methodology.

Already published

J. D. Richards and N. S. Ryan, DATA PROCESSING IN ARCHAEOLOGY
Simon Hillson, TEETH
Alwyne Wheeler and Andrew K. G. Jones, FISHES
Lesley Adkins and Roy Adkins, ARCHAEOLOGICAL ILLUSTRATION
Marie-Agnès Courty, Paul Goldberg and Richard MacPhail, SOILS AND MICROMORPHOLOGY IN ARCHAEOLOGY
Clive Orton, Paul Tyers and Alan Vince, POTTERY IN ARCHAEOLOGY
R. Lee Lyman, VERTEBRATE TAPHONOMY
Peter G. Dorrell, PHOTOGRAPHY IN ARCHAEOLOGY AND CONSERVATION (2ND EDN)
A. G. Brown, ALLUVIAL GEOARCHAEOLOGY
Cheryl Claassen, SHELLS
William Andrefsky Jr, LITHICS
Elizabeth J. Reitz and Elizabeth S. Wing, ZOOARCHAEOLOGY
Clive Orton, SAMPLING IN ARCHAEOLOGY

EXCAVATION

Steve Roskams

CAMBRIDGE
UNIVERSITY PRESS

PUBLISHED BY THE PRESS SYNDICATE OF THE UNIVERSITY OF CAMBRIDGE
The Pitt Building, Trumpington Street, Cambridge, United Kingdom

CAMBRIDGE UNIVERSITY PRESS
The Edinburgh Building, Cambridge CB2 2RU, UK
40 West 20th Street, New York, NY 10011-4211, USA
10 Stamford Road, Oakleigh, VIC 3166, Australia
Ruiz de Alarcón 13, 28014 Madrid, Spain
Dock House, The Waterfront, Cape Town 8001, South Africa

http://www.cambridge.org

© Cambridge University Press 2001

First published 2001

Printed in the United Kingdom at the University Press, Cambridge

Typeface Monotype Times 11/13pt   *System* QuarkXPress™   [SE]

A catalogue record for this book is available from the British Library

ISBN 0 521 35534 6 hardback
ISBN 0 521 79801 9 paperback

This book is dedicated to the memory of my Mum.

My world is a much lesser place since her death, and no longer what it once seemed to be.

CONTENTS

PLATES

FIGURES

ACKNOWLEDGEMENTS

The thoughts and ideas expressed here have been influenced, inevitably, by many other people. These include the first supervisors I worked for who had to put up with endless queries such as 'But *why* do sections have to be vertical?' and 'Why take the photograph *now* rather than after the next occupation layer has been removed?' (I never got a straight answer to these, or most other, questions.) Later there were fellow excavators in full-time units with whom I discussed improvements in excavation techniques during site tea-breaks, that time long acknowledged as the most productive part of the working day. Recently there have been the students at York who have had to sit through seminar discussions on anything from site safety to questions such as 'What is a phase?', or even more philosophical issues such as 'What are data?' I have borrowed ideas from them all, knowingly or otherwise.

There are several individuals who deserve more specific mention. A long time ago, in Cirencester, Richard Reece showed me that excavations could be not only physically enjoyable but intellectually demanding, and further that it was not necessary to act as Adolf Hitler in order to supervise them effectively. Henry Hurst, during our work at Carthage, let me into the secret that post-excavation analysis was not just a necessary evil which made you pull your hair out (though it certainly does this) but also a creative activity in its own right. Later, in London, Annie Upson and Friederike Hammer opened up my eyes to new aspects of site recording, especially its graphic representation. More recently, Phillip Rahtz and Martin Carver of this Department have set me straight on different conceptions of the archaeological record and tolerated my argumentative interventions into their seminars, whilst Mark Whyman has discussed various issues with me and so demonstrated on many occasions that research students give much more to their academic 'supervisors' than they receive. Finally, Martin Jones and Tracy Wellman in Algeria showed me that collaboration in a team really was the best way to work and to learn in archaeology (and in many other areas besides). If I take full responsibility for the biassed views, incoherences and mistakes in this manual, it is all the excavators who have worked with me who are to blame for stimulating me into writing it.

Finally I would like to thank Jessica Kuper of Cambridge University Press for her encouragement during the long time this book has been in preparation and thus allowing it to see the light of day.

INTRODUCTION

'Why did *you* get involved in archaeology?' People have a variety of responses to this question. Some answer in ways which attempt to justify why we study the past at all, perhaps in order to defend the expenditure of resources on archaeology rather than another activity: phrases such as 'our past is vital' and 'it is part of our heritage' come to the fore. Others list the particular causes which have stimulated them, as an individual, to get caught up in the subject: 'I saw a television programme, tried a local dig and caught the bug' or 'I have always been interested in local history and archaeology seemed to offer me a way of getting more directly involved.'

Yet, whatever type of answer they give, many people will find that their involvement leads them, at some stage or another, to be actively engaged in gathering data in the field, rather than just using information obtained by other people. In archaeology, such data-gathering can take a great variety of forms, for example studying artefact collections in museums, analysing aerial photographs, surveying standing buildings and field-walking. These activities already play a significant role in augmenting the material base of the subject and, given current trends, will probably become increasingly important in the future. However, the material culture of past societies which archaeologists might wish to examine is not all stored in museums, and the occupation areas and artefacts related to them are not always accessible on the earth's surface. Sites and finds have become buried by a variety of mechanisms including the activities of construction, occupation and destruction by humans, together with accumulations due to natural agencies (of which the most extreme case would be 'burial' underwater, such sites requiring their own specialist approaches and techniques: Green 1990). Hence remote sensing, field-walking or building surveys each have their limits. At this point excavation, meaning the disturbance of the ground in archaeologically controlled conditions, may be needed to reverse the burial process.

Of course, it must be emphasised that excavation, although central to *this* manual, is not the only, or even the most desirable, way in which the discipline of archaeology acquires new data. Fowler (1980), for example, has argued that field surveys have a primary role, both historically and in terms of present cost effectiveness. However, it must also be acknowledged that excavation has become, in practice, the main way of capturing much of our data. Indeed, for certain questions, excavation is presently the only viable way for research to

1

proceed, even given the recent developments in more sophisticated techniques of remote sensing. In short, it seems likely that digging will remain central to archaeological fieldwork for the foreseeable future. The aim of this manual is to provide a coherent framework for understanding both general approaches and the practicalities of the digging process itself, together with some of the principles which underpin the subsequent stratigraphic analysis of the data created.

The book is aimed at a variety of audiences. First, there are those involved in excavation at the purely practical level. This includes both unit-based and independent field-workers, whether engaged full-time or part-time. Second, there are those interested in the excavation process because they use the resulting data in their analytical work. This embraces a great range of people, from the individual with a great interest and expertise in a particular artefact-type, right down to the polymath professor heading a university archaeology department – jack of all trades, master of none. Finally, there are those many people who have encountered excavations, either in a busy high street or intruding into the peace of a country walk, and wondered not just 'Have they found anything interesting?' but also 'How do the diggers go about their task?' and 'What do they do with all the records once they have finished?' (or, to be more realistic and accurate, the many people who wonder 'Why don't they stop all that writing, measuring and drawing, and get on with actually *finding* things?').

This is obviously a very large group of people to accommodate. Where there is a conflict of interest, I have erred on the side of looking in detail at the problems faced by the first category, the person working in the field at the cutting edge of excavation practice, rather than talking merely of general approaches and principles. This is presumably in keeping with the concept of a *manual* of archaeological excavation. It has also been designed to allow those with particular interests to dip into it at various points and look for solutions to their problems (e.g. 'What photographic and planning policy must be designed for our needs?' – 'See page such-and-such'). Thus I have endeavoured to provide practical responses to the problems which arise on excavations, as well as a theoretical overview of the whole process.

The manual attempts to give a description of the present 'state of the art' in excavation techniques. But, as anyone with an interest in the past would agree, that present situation can only be understood properly in terms of its previous development, not viewed in isolation. So these techniques are first set in context with a discussion of the recent history of their evolution. It is my belief that historical development is more comprehensible when explained in its material context than in terms of the activities of a particular genius in the field or, for that matter, of technological advances external to the discipline, for example in computer hardware. Most archaeologists readily acknowledge that an undue focus on known figureheads, or simplistic notions of technological determinism, are of limited use when looking at past societies: we should remember this lesson when looking at our own, present practices. Thus Chapter 1 concentrates on the institutional and organisational background of excavation practice and the general economic and political context in which the subject exists. In doing so, it contrasts somewhat with those descriptions of methodological developments phrased in terms of the inventions of the 'great women and men' of field archaeology.

The conduct of excavations requires both a general perspective and specific arrangements. It thus involves a consideration of theoretical approaches and practical preparations. The former is considered in Chapter 2, where I have outlined my views on the 'total excavation versus research design' debate, favouring decisively the latter. My conclusion here is that what I would call perspective in site recording, and opponents would no doubt call bias, is something to be welcomed rather than worried about or shunned. The difficulty comes in devising an excavation strategy, and doing so in an explicit form, whilst at the same time retaining the fluidity of response which all such work requires. Though not all readers will agree with my conclusion, the issue itself is important, both in its own right and because the approach then colours the content, and provides the structure, of the remainder of the manual. However, I hope that those who do not concur will still find what follows of use.

If it is necessary to have particular perspectives when approaching any excavation, this implies the use of previous knowledge when structuring research objectives. Whilst the preceding chapter noted the need for interdisciplinary research at the most general level, it is the application of more directly *archaeological* methods which is required to gain sufficient information before constructing a detailed research strategy. In Chapter 3 I therefore outline what is required to discover sites and to evaluate their potential before full-scale excavation takes place.

The next chapters detail the practical preparations which any modern excavation involves. Most archaeological endeavour is engendered by a need to throw light on past societies – it is questions, whether related to general issues or specific off-the-cuff enquiries, which stimulated most of us to get involved in the discipline in the first place. However, much of any excavator's time, and certainly most of that of the site director, is really spent not on sophisticated academic thoughts but on organisational matters: it is all very well pondering on what your site is saying about the changing nature of Roman imperialism but this doesn't actually help to get the Elsan rota organised. Chapter 4 therefore looks at background preparations such as finance and administration, without which no project stands a chance of success; staff and their support facilities, site workers being the most important asset of any excavation; and general site safety plus special situations, safety being a fundamental responsibility of anyone organising an excavation. Chapter 5 then considers the more detailed issues which arise when excavation proper starts. This includes site clearance using mechanical methods, the establishing of site survey grids, and then spoil removal, shoring, de-watering and finds retrieval systems. Difficulties during the excavation itself will be minimised if sufficient effort has been put in at this planning phase, even though continuous monitoring and modifications will then be needed at all later stages.

A central message of the foregoing discussion is the need to have an organised approach to the excavation as a whole, and to data gathering on site in particular. To reinforce these messages, Chapter 6 gives an itinerary for the recording and excavation of a stratigraphic unit: a day in the life (and death, usually) of a typical layer. This is not meant to be a definitive statement of what process should be followed in every conceivable situation. It has been said long ago by Wheeler (1954: 1), and is worth repeating here, that there is no right way to dig but there are many wrong ways. However, what is put forward is *one* way of creating a full record which fulfils the more abstract requirements of the subsequent chapters. It also makes the point that a structured approach to recording can usually be translated into an equally clearly ordered sequence of operations in the field, thus greatly simplifying the learning of such methods. One of the biggest battles on excavations, a battle more often lost than won in my experience, is to demystify the recording process. The itinerary presented here may help in achieving this.

The meat of the book is provided by a discussion of site recording in the remaining chapters, their order following the itinerary mentioned above. Chapter 7 considers the photographic record, an essential component of nearly every project but one whose role is rarely discussed, either in itself or in relation to the rest of the record. It gives details of recording systems and describes methods of cleaning for photography, followed by particular photographic techniques and finishing with some specialist uses. Correspondingly, Chapter 8 looks at the spatial record, starting with a discussion of drawing techniques and necessary equipment. Spatial information is still gathered mostly by hand-drawn plans and sections, although this is an area in which increased use of sophisticated surveying equipment and computer technology is starting to have a significant impact. For example, such hardware can greatly increase the efficiency with which individual finds can be measured-in, generating corresponding developments in the degree of detail which forthcoming research agendas might require in terms of artefact positioning.

Chapter 9 is concerned with the stratigraphic record, again an area which has undergone substantial change in recent decades. It considers the types of relationships which might be recorded; how they can be represented with the use of sequence diagrams, notably the 'Harris-Winchester' matrix; and a variety of systems which have been devised for calculating stratigraphic relationships and for checking the accuracy of the record presented in this diagrammatic form.

The next chapters examine the descriptive record of the physical characteristics of any stratigraphic unit. Chapter 10, prefaced with a discussion of who actually produces that record and at what stage of the excavation of the unit, then proceeds with a résumé of approaches to deposits description – colour determination, particle size of soil matrix, compaction, inclusions and surface detail. Correspondingly, Chapter 11 considers masonry and brick features, timbers, skeleton recording, cut features and finds groups. Then Chapter 12 discusses a variety of other matters concerning finds recovery and the mechanics of soil removal. Here the need for an explicit sampling strategy is stressed, followed by a detailed discussion of methods of trowelling, still the most common way of removing archaeological deposits in controlled conditions, and of the vexed issue of how to decide where one unit ends and another starts. The completion of the record and the need to check the accuracy of the whole process is outlined finally.

No excavation manual would be complete without a consideration of the implications which both the general approaches and specific strategies outlined above have for manipulating excavated data. Hence, in Chapter 13, I discuss the stratigraphic analysis which takes place after the excavation has finished. Developments in excavation since the 1970s have ensured that data are gathered in a much more controlled and consistent fashion than previously. But this increased sophistication is rarely matched by the processing of that data. Finally, in Chapter 14, I speculate on how archaeological excavation might develop in the coming decade, based on a consideration of the intellectual, technical and organisational trends currently visible in the field.

Some people will find difficulties with the tenor of the manual. Archaeological excavation, by its very nature, is such that not all of the problems which arise can be predicted and catered for in advance. In addition, it could be said that nearly all such fieldwork now takes place under less than ideal circumstances, in rescue and salvage conditions ahead of modern redevelopment. So the idea that one has time to plan the work systematically, test alternative approaches, discuss results, etc. may be seen as hopelessly idealistic. To this it might be added that the whole topic is now so large that uniform coverage in a single book is not just increasingly difficult, which it clearly is, but actually impossible and can only mislead. Finally, it is inevitable that my own views will be biassed, for instance by my own political perspectives on what is wrong with this world and how we might change it. They will also be limited, for example by being derived from experience of only the last twenty years, mainly on urban sites in London and North Africa, and then concerned with recording layers, pits and structures rather than artefacts and ecofacts. Thus it would be true to say that this manual will be even less of a final word on its subject than many others in the Cambridge University Press series, and will become outdated more quickly than attempts from previous decades to discuss excavation techniques. On balance this is, no doubt, all to the good, and anyway an inevitable product of a modern world which reinvents itself at increasingly shorter intervals. However, though accepting this, I would make two additional responses.

First, in an attempt to defend myself from a charge of undue parochialism, I have endeavoured to remedy my own lack of breadth by reading directly what others have written about archaeological excavation techniques, and between the lines of many of the more significant publications of site-work in Britain and abroad. I have also discussed the issues involved in a variety of forums and drawn on the ideas of those with different, and often greater, experience than myself. Despite this attempt to 'broaden my mind', the case studies and illustrations will still seem to be drawn from a limited range of projects. Here I would argue that the deeply stratified, complex sites with which I have been mainly involved provide an advantageous starting point for discussing techniques as a whole. Droop suggested a long time ago that 'to be able to dig a stratified site well is to have attained to the highest and most remunerative skill in this particular work' (1915: vii). Even if such a claim is somewhat excessive, I have found it far easier to take the procedures involved with such sites and apply them to those with shallow stratigraphy, or with no stratigraphy at all, than to go in the opposite direction.

Second, to answer the charge that ideas and techniques expressed below are 'all very well for pure research but largely irrelevant to commercial work', I would note that my own knowledge of excavation practice derives almost entirely from sites concerned with rescue work in its various guises on which a mainly professional workforce was engaged. To me, that experience suggests, very clearly, that the pressures of the real world are better catered for by understanding basic principles and approaches, then cutting one's cloth accordingly, rather than adopting the seemingly more simple, but ultimately less useful, strategy of just rushing in and doing one's best with whatever has been made available. Thus I have set out in detail how things might be done in each sphere of recording but noted in passing some shortcuts, together with the impact that these will have on data quality and thus the questions which the fieldwork might be expected to answer. Such a sequence is essential if one is to put projects into practice, yet retain a hold over what any one piece of archaeological fieldwork can realistically hope to deliver in terms of data which are useful to future researchers.

In short, this manual cannot expect, and does not pretend, to be a complete guide to excavation practices and may seem, at first glance, to be a 'very British' book in terms of style, examples and terminology. Yet it is my belief that, with a little effort on the part of the reader, the general points of principle which I endeavour to draw out of it are relevant to the wide range of situations which excavation directors face in many parts of the world on a day-to-day basis. Any such attempt to present the underlying theory and logic of the excavation process in this way will be of direct relevance to many people in the field and of some interest to those nearer its fringes – or so I hope!

HISTORY OF DEVELOPMENT OF TECHNIQUES

Introduction

The discipline of archaeology has a long history, even if it has only recently been accepted by most people as an important and vibrant research subject. However, the point in time at which it might be defined as a distinct discipline varies, depending on whether one chooses as its central focus simply the *collection* of material culture from past societies, which took place at an early stage; the *classification* of this material, starting in a later period; or the *interpretation* of data, which occurred later still. None the less, by any definition, the subject has existed for at least a century and, naturally, it is not difficult to find authors who have charted the trajectories of its overall development. For the British audience, Daniel's various works (especially 1975) may take pride of place. Klindt-Jensen (1975) has provided a corresponding description of Scandinavian traditions, and Willey and Sabloff (1974) of American developments. Thus, the general history of the discipline is well known and easily accessible.

Publications which focus specifically on the nature of archaeological fieldwork and its history of development are less numerous. Initially such matters either were discussed by oblique reference within excavation reports, for example those of Pitt-Rivers (1887), or occurred in more general works on aims and methods within the discipline, as with Petrie (1904). Even where a book was centrally concerned with digging up the past, it might still contain very little on the actual recording of excavations (Woolley 1930). Later, this situation changed. Specialist authors such as Atkinson (1953) and Crawford (1953) discussed fieldwork *per se*, the latter admittedly being more concerned with surface configurations than digging. For excavation itself, Wheeler has pride of place, not just in his well-known book *Archaeology from the Earth* (1954) but, more importantly, in his 'technical papers' (1945 and 1946) on the use of a grid of excavation boxes.

Publications by Alexander (1970), Coles (1972) and Webster (1974) discussed the direction of excavation projects and endeavoured to set them in a more general institutional and organisational context. Even so, it must be said that each, and especially the last, has very little to say on detailed matters which are a central concern of this manual, for example the descriptive criteria which might be applied to archaeological strata. Furthermore, any recording methods which are mentioned are mostly unsystematised and vague in their application. Finally, Barker has had the most recent word, both on techniques in particular (1977) and on the philosophy behind excavation in general (1986).

From these and other studies, it is possible to chart the progress of archaeological fieldwork. This might be seen as starting in the middle of the first millennium bc with interventions in the city of Ur, or with work by Greeks in Hippias Major, mentioned by Plato, which involved using material remains to write *archaiologia*. The latter term might be best understood as involving 'stories' about the past, rather than purported historical accounts drawing on evidence, in the way a modern reader might understand. Whether in Sumerian or Greek contexts, such activities arose not simply out of human inquisitiveness, but rather from social need. Recovering archaeological remains was part of the drive to extend a city's origins into the past, thus legitimating its position within the region, and when undertaken by particular families this would reinforce their own importance and authority. In this sense, such investigations were intimately bound up with the needs of maintaining citizenship within the ancient world.

These initial steps were followed by Roman interest in past societies, which included a strong focus on what would be now called anthropology, as is clear from the writings of authors such as Tacitus. Again the main objective was not simply knowledge for its own sake but, with the vast expansion of the Empire, either to contrast the tribal peoples which the legions encountered with their own, Roman 'civilisation', or to see them as 'noble savages' who became soft when they took on an urbanised lifestyle. Roman involvement extended to the collection of material remains, particularly in Italy, even though this often amounted to little more than glorified looting.

After the fall of the Roman Empire, attitudes towards the past developed in different directions within Europe. Islam, with its greater respect for academic learning, retained an interest in Latin authors and protected their works from the excesses of destructive Christian zeal when possible. By the same token the Byzantine Empire, where 'Roman rule', in some sense of the word, might be seen as lasting until the fifteenth century, continued to facilitate the archaeological work of such scholars as Cyriac of Ancona. The contrast between Islamic and Byzantine spheres and Western Christendom is clear, the latter being more often concerned to lay waste or marginalise earlier monuments than to protect or investigate them. Yet, even within Christianity, particular events should not go unremarked. Thus the monks of Glastonbury excavated to uncover their links with Arthur, and in the process legitimate the holiness of their foundation and promote its economic power. Equally intriguing, though problematic, is the suggestion (Clark 1978: 198) that Geoffrey of Monmouth may have made use of a Roman antiquity in the twelfth century to elaborate his story of the life of Cadwallo, king of the Britons.

The birth of Renaissance movements in Europe, concentrated in Italy but with reverberations far beyond, prompted a renewed contact with Antiquity. Those at its epicentre, where Roman buildings often remained visible above ground, responded most forcefully. The pope, for instance, took the opportunity to excavate large areas of Pompeii in the late sixteenth century. However, even countries which had been on the margins of the Roman Empire, such as Britain, or entirely outside it, as with Scandinavia and much of Germany, became deeply involved. Antiquarian interest generated huge collections of objects derived from ancient cultures, initially from within home countries and then, with colonial expansion, from increasingly accessible sites abroad. Such collecting created a demand which could be best served simply by looting, an activity with a long, and in some ways venerated, history which continues in many parts of the world up to the present.

These huge numbers of artefacts in antiquarian collections were eventually classified into typological sequences, a process augmented by the concept of the three-age system. This, plus other general developments such as the notion of *biological* evolution later expressed in Darwin's *Origins*, was a product of the more general notion of 'progress' abroad in a society responding to the Scientific Revolution. Such forces led, understandably, to the use of archaeological material to elucidate *social* evolution. Arguably the late seventeenth century was a critical turning point in this respect, the time when the term archaeology, with its Latin root, was used by Jacob Spon to describe the activity of antiquarians studying objects and monuments with the explicit objective of shedding light on past societies. The questions raised in the process of this intellectual enquiry required, in turn, further fieldwork to furnish not just more artefacts, but also the structural and topographical information which would give such finds a meaningful context. Thus controlled excavation to provenance finds became, increasingly, the order of the day: it remains a requirement which field-workers in the twenty-first century still endeavour to satisfy (and, in my opinion, are becoming increasingly expert at achieving).

The objective of this chapter is not just to provide the above brief outline of these developments, but to consider the dynamic behind them. Some have portrayed the process as being driven forward by the dynamism of particular individuals (described in **1.1** below). Such terms of reference, though allowing convenient descriptions, ignore social forces. If we wish to understand the sequence of development more fully, we have to consider the three elements of intellectual framework, available technology and organisation of fieldwork, and to understand the way in which they react on, and interact with, each other. Thus the subsequent sections will consider the ideological background within contemporary society which both constrained and promoted new forms of explanation (**1.2**); the technical, usually technological, developments outside archaeology which the discipline then incorporated to mutual benefit (**1.3**); and the social and economic context in which archaeological excavation took place (**1.4**). In particular, recent professionalisation (**1.5**) has turned the excavator into wage labour and thus transformed the way in which fieldwork is practised. The content of this manual is largely a product of attempts to cope with this new and challenging context.

The order in which these ideological, technical and organisational factors are discussed below reflects my own view of how change takes place in human society in general. Ideas are clearly *one* of the driving forces (see 1.2), but only develop in circumstances composed of a historically specific combination of technological and organisational factors (see 1.3 and 1.4 respectively). Thus fieldwork activity itself, in the techniques which it employs, and in the way people use these techniques and the organisational context in which they find themselves, constitutes the real motor for change in excavation practice. In short, the practice of archaeology underpins its ideological development (or, as Marx famously once put it, the material world precedes consciousness).

1.1 The role of dynamic individualism

The brief historical outline given above demonstrated that humans have long been interested in 'the past' and have often become involved in archaeology as a result. Indeed, such curiosity is seen by many commentators as a natural phenomenon evident in every social formation (or at least as far back as those for which we have documentary evidence to demonstrate conscious human intention, for example in the writings of the earliest classical authors). Yet that résumé also shows that, even if such interest is seen as part of human nature, curiosity is expressed in different ways in different societies, and that it changes through time. How are we to comprehend such diversity of response and evolutionary process?

As already noted, some commentators suggest that all intellectual enquiry passes through a similar sequence of development which starts with the collection of material, moves on to classification to impose order on chaos, then proceeds towards the explanation of any patterns derived. This process, they maintain, is visible in various disciplines including, most pertinently, archaeology. Hence, it could be said that early antiquarians gathered artefacts (the 'collection' phase); archaeologists in the eighteenth and nineteenth centuries imposed typological systems on them ('classification'); and twentieth-century scholars specified dynamics to facilitate the move from typological arrangement to interpretation ('explanation'). By the same token, when we consider specifically work in the field, early practitioners can be seen as collecting monuments, at least to the extent of noting their existence in particular places (Plate 1). Monuments were then classified into different types and their positions plotted on maps to elucidate distributions. However, in order to move towards interpretation, one had to know whether any patterns were 'real' or simply a product of intensity of fieldwork and/or visibility of the monument concerned.

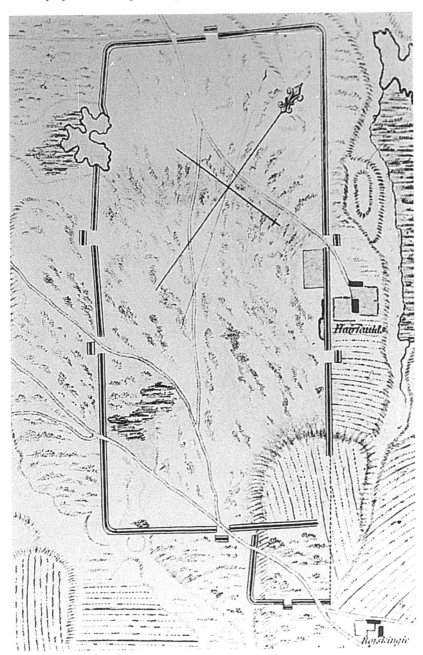

Plate 1 Drawing by William Roy of the plan of the Roman camp at Kirkboddo, published in his 1773 work *The Antiquities of the Romans in North Britain*. In effect, the fieldwork which underpinned such books 'collected' monuments in the landscape and, as here, then began to classify them by cultural period.

Only then could one assess their significance. Hence it became necessary to dig to augment the data-base and to confirm or deny the historical reality of a class of monument and its distribution. Only then could one start the difficult job of moving from recognition of architectural form and spatial distribution to interpretation of the social process which produced it.

Yet there is a problem with the above characterisation. Although archaeology can be seen as developing along broadly similar lines to other disciplines such as botany and geology, in the process of moving from a hobby to an intellectual enquiry in its own right, these developments took place at different times and were stretched over different periods. Even if the change from vague, quirky interest of the few, to scientific endeavour supported by the many is an inevitable one, how are we to explain different rates of progress? One way forward has been to avoid the question by simply associating new developments with particular, named archaeologists. Hence individualism provides, albeit implicitly, the dynamic of change.

Thus, in Britain, one might start with Leland (1506–52), Camden (1557–1623), Aubrey (1626–97) and Stukeley (1687–1765), who form a nearly overlapping sequence of antiquarian observers. After this one might note the more intensive intervention in the nineteenth century of excavators such as Colt-Hoare (1758–1838) in Wessex, Petrie (1853–1942) in the Near East and Pitt-Rivers (1827–1900) in southern England. In the twentieth century, Wheeler and Kenyon can be seen as promoting advances in Britain and abroad, to be followed by Barker and others more recently. Corresponding 'histories' could, no doubt, be provided for other countries.

Such descriptions, using individuals as exemplars of best practice at particular points in time, are a convenient mechanism for narrative accounts but can hardly be portrayed as coming to grips with the forces at play behind the changes. On the one hand, they pass over the diversity of techniques employed at a specific time. On the other hand, they fail to explain the way in which any one approach spreads to other field-workers (unless one assumes that everyone else simply learnt from that person designated as 'the master' – and this is often provably *not* the case). Thus, even if one considers developments within archaeology in isolation, let alone if one seeks a wider social context, such discussions remain intellectually dissatisfying.

Taking these two criticisms in order, let us consider first changes which occur at the same time in different places under the direction of different individuals. Colt-Hoare, who dug many sites, especially barrows, on Salisbury Plain and made one of the first uses of the archaeological section of Wansdyke, was drawing conclusions from stratification in the late eighteenth century. His projects were paralleled in broadly contemporary work in America by Jefferson, who noted stratigraphic relationships in the context of employing a consciously formulated research design on early burial sites. We have no reason to believe that the one learnt from the other, so is the correspondence a simple coinci-

dence? Equally, Petrie's work in Egypt and then the Near East gave more structure to excavation practice and the impetus to 'record everything'. To offer
explanation of why this approach developed, beyond the individual and parochial, we must set it beside the work of Schliemann in the same era, who was
digging for explicit research reasons and with attention to method.

Secondly, as well as correspondence, we must account for diversity of
response, both between different people and within the same individual. For
example in the late nineteenth century Petrie was roundly criticising inadequate
techniques abroad and General Pitt-Rivers was advancing meticulous excavation and publication at home, emphasising the importance of common items
over spectacular treasure, perhaps influenced by the anthropological interests
expressed in his large ethnographic collections (Bowden 1991). None the less,
during the same decades, Greenwell and Mortimer continued to open barrows
on the Yorkshire Wolds at a vast rate, sometimes using methods considered
rudimentary, even by contemporary standards (Marsden 1974). In addition,
even the meticulous General could use a vertical section to record relationships
at Cissbury in 1875, yet forget the technique when recording Mount Caburn
two years later (Bowden 1991: 94). By the same token, and coming into the
twentieth century, Wheeler advocated box-excavation and attention to
sequence, promoting strict control of stratigraphy and, indeed, of all other
activities on site. The excavation process thus took on the appearance of a military operation, including separate teams each with its own leader, an NCO, in
each box, and Wheeler, of course, as the overall commanding officer. Even so,
Wheeler himself utilised, for good or ill, very different techniques on other
occasions, for example wall-chasing at Stanwick, or narrow trenches across the
defences of Maiden Castle alongside box excavation in the entrance area and
the exposure of large, 'open areas' in the centre of the same hillfort (Plate 2).

In recent years, many archaeologists may have moved away from Wheeler's
paradigm and towards the techniques advocated by Barker (1977), involving
the exposure of sites in large, open areas and adding further precision to site
drawing. Barker's own work at the Roman city of Wroxeter and the medieval
castle at Hen Domen was preceded by the rural excavations of Steensberg in
Denmark, whose influence is explicitly acknowledged. Barker then influenced
the work of other excavators who had a formative role in British developments.
For example, Brian Hope-Taylor (1977) developed new techniques of recognising colour differences in separate deposit types and in recording inclusions at
the early medieval 'royal' centre of Yeavering. He was able to make sense of the
evident patterns only by viewing them *in extensio*. Similarly, excavations at
Cheddar by Philip Rahtz revealed complete structures over 20m in length, the
scale of building suggesting to him that they should be interpreted as Saxon
and medieval palaces (Rahtz and Hirst 1979).

Yet this move towards larger excavations is far from universally applied. For
example, although many excavators in Britain are now critical of Wheeler's

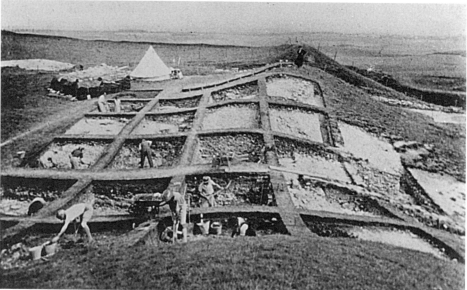

Plate 2 Wheeler's excavations at Maiden Castle used a variety of techniques: slit trenches to investigate defensive ditches (*top*) and box-excavation in the fort entrance (bottom), alongside open areas to investigate central occupation zones.

boxes and favour open areas, a manual based on US experience (Joukowsky 1980: 139) still recommends the principles developed by Wheeler and Kenyon and thus discusses grid squares as if they are the only legitimate way to excavate. Indeed, what might be called excavation 'trenches' in a British context are likely to be termed 'squares' in America, even if they are often rectangular in shape. In short, fieldwork practice develops in different ways, and at various speeds, in different places. One can only understand this diversity of response, as well as any general trends, by looking beyond individuals and towards underlying dynamics. To do so requires distinguishing between three forces – intellectual developments, technical changes and organisational contexts. Each will be discussed below.

1.2 Ideological factors

An interest in the past can be driven by intellectual curiosity or emotional necessity. Nevertheless, as argued above, whether, when and how such demands are met is decided within a living society. The past may be used to foster nationalist feelings, give a sense of cultural identity, promote revolutionary fervour or whatever, but always subsists in an intellectual context, a framework produced by the ruling ideas in society. Approaches to archaeological research provide a good illustration of this relationship (see Trigger 1989 for proper detail, giving his usual range of stimulating insights into this complex interaction).

In coming to terms with the Age of Reason, archaeology moved from inductive and pre-scientific approaches, where antiquarian collections were valued for aesthetic reasons and the objects used, at best, to illustrate the margins of documentary history, to a discipline requiring scientific endeavour. Ideas of *biological* evolution, developed and then used within a capitalist system itself undergoing progressive transformation at an ever-increasing rate, brought the issue of *social* evolution firmly to the surface. The world at large thus demanded explanations of the phenomenon from the anthropologist and, especially, the archaeologist. At the same time economic and political development was increasingly tied to regionally located units of capital – nation states – which required the creation of national identities. The ideological justification for such structures was facilitated by 'the invention of tradition' (Hobsbawm and Ranger 1983) and archaeologists reflected these changes in their emphasis on culture history. Thus evolutionary and culture-historical paradigms, though apparently contradictory, were really opposite sides of the same coin emerging from a single social and political context.

Of course, change in past societies was conceived and explained in different ways by different people. Some favoured the notion of the survival of the fittest, underpinned by the idea that competition was inherent in human beings and the driving force behind all social development. This no doubt appeared as a reasonable, 'common-sense' conclusion, given that competition is indeed integral to the functioning of capitalism, the system under which they lived: all dominant systems endeavour to portray their own dynamic as inherent and inevitable, as part of 'human nature'. Alternatively other commentators, at pains to gloss over emerging conflicts within society, played down competition and argued that collaboration was central and that all humans were essentially one. From here it is only a short step to structuralist perspectives, or at least the notion that each individual was linked to those of the same nation or race.

Unfortunately, explanations in terms of either an essentially competitive human nature or the psychic unity of humanity both raised the problem of how to explain diverse social trajectories. This difficulty became increasingly apparent as anthropology provided fuller indications of such diversity, a result both of an inductive reaction which gave a greater role to evidence, and of the vastly increased amount of data gathering which followed the increased professionalisation of anthropology. None the less, despite these weaknesses, the central requirement of archaeology remained the formulation of explanations of social evolution.

A driving intellectual need is one thing: the way in which ideological structures fulfil it is another. At any particular time, ideology is constructed within a society riven with contradictions, and thus itself contains contradictory perspectives. In a changing world, prevailing ideas will act both to constrain answers to newly emerging questions, and to promote them. Thus bourgeois revolutions may have sounded the death knell of a feudal ruling class, first in Britain and Holland in the seventeenth century, and later elsewhere. All the same, their ushering in of a new emphasis on rational explanation did not mean that earlier Christian belief systems then disappeared, to be replaced at a stroke by the Age of Reason. In reality, both paradigms had a continuing influence, and this is particularly clear within archaeological interpretation.

Hence, on the one hand, the discipline of archaeology still had to overcome theological reservations on the antiquity of the earth, and human activity thereon, in order to progress. Previously, it had been acceptable to study the past in the terms presented by classical authors, as long as it did not proceed beyond 4004 bc. Prehistory, at least, remained shackled by the church. In the same way, geological interpretation was bound up with recognising a biblical flood as a fixed point in the sequence of natural development. However, perplexing evidence was accumulating from Europe and from pre-Columban sites in the New World. These data, although irreconcilable with biblical accounts, could not, eventually, continue to be simply ignored. Thus when, in 1800, Frere wrote tentatively to the Society of Antiquaries of London to describe observations of flint artefacts in strata overlain by deposits containing extinct animals at Hoxne in England, his letter provoked little initial reaction. Even so, by 1859 Evans, an archaeologist, and Prestwich, a geologist, were reporting to the Royal Society the validity of similar findings of Boucher de Perthes in France.

The notion of the antiquity of man, confusing and even unacceptable at first, had become undeniable by mid-century (in fact by the very year in which, by an understandable coincidence, Darwin's *Origins* was published).

The tendency of current ideologies to constrain explanation is mirrored, on the other hand, by its role in breaking through barriers. In the case of archaeology, this often involved the incorporation of perspectives from outside the discipline. In relation to the above debate, it was possible to collect objects, and in a sense therefore lifestyles, from periods preceding the available documentary sources and thus implicitly question what was theologically 'given'. Nevertheless, lacking any real notion of time depth and how to quantify it, alternative explanations remained fanciful and, mostly, mythological. The development of the concept of stratification, borrowed from geology, changed all that.

The idea of stratigraphy had appeared at an early stage with the work of George Owen and his *History of Pembrokeshire* of 1570 (interestingly, only formally published in 1796) and Nicolaus Streno in the *Prodromus* in 1669. Yet it was the publication in the 1830s of Lyell's *Principles* which consolidated the learning and allowed the development of a proper discipline of geology. His arguments against catastrophist explanations first set out there have a clear parallel with the effect of Darwin's ideas on the notion of creation (although the latter was no 'naive gradualist': short-term change is not, in itself, incompatible with an evolutionary perspective, as the many, engaging papers by Gould (1978 onwards) clearly demonstrate).

Geological notions of stratification were soon adopted by archaeologists concerned with human society, influencing the observation and illustration of sections by Rudbeck at Uppsala in 1680s (Klindt-Jensen 1975: 30), and of Stukeley in 1723 in Britain. Geologists described the creation of basins in land surfaces which became filled as deposits took the line of least resistance. Humans could be portrayed as just another agency of erosion and deposition, moulding nature and creating their own basins in which, or upstanding features against which, material then accumulated. The parallel between human and natural processes can be, and has been, taken too far, but the description of natural agencies creating stratigraphic accumulations does have a resonance with the sequences seen on archaeological sites, and the concept of a stratigraphic sequence has been, perhaps, the single most important influence on fieldwork practice during the past century.

Hence Thomsen's idea of a 'closed finds group' (e.g. the finds from a grave), which allowed the construction of the three-age system, is an accepted concept today but rests on the notions of context and stratification, to which Worsaae could only give validity by seriation following his investigation of the layers in Danish peat bogs. Later, the move in archaeology from an evolutionary perspective to culture-historical interests required a tightening of chronology – hence Pitt-Rivers' greater attention to stratigraphic relationships (although

this did not lead him to differentiate deposits and actually excavate them stratigraphically – Bowden 1991: 78). Then the work of Wheeler at Segontium,
Verulamium and Maiden Castle on the features and their boundaries seen in
baulk sections added further detail to the stratigraphic record in the field. This
was accompanied by corresponding developments under Kenyon which transformed work abroad (although Kidder (1924: fig. 8) seemingly developed
similar ideas in the US with less lasting impact on excavation technique there).
Finally, recent developments such as Harris matrices to represent and manipulate stratigraphic sequences (Harris 1989), and Schiffer's work on the formation and transformation of archaeological deposits (Schiffer 1987), both
central discussion points in the present book, are clearly predicated on a
concept of stratification.

As discussed, ideological frameworks can constrain or liberate the operation
of any discipline. Yet, in the case of archaeology, the ultimate result was never
in doubt, given an increasing emphasis on scientific explanation in society at
large. Thus theological notions of time were overcome and the geological idea
of stratification was incorporated as a key concept to help understand social
evolution. At every stage since, our fieldwork has owed a debt of gratitude to
geology. The academic perspectives which were engendered have allowed the
change from a focus on monuments exposed in a frozen moment, to landscape
features created in successive stages, to sites with periods of construction, use
and demise visible in section, to complex structural evolution in large, open
areas. Today we are still working with, and working through, the implications
of the concept of stratification.

Fieldwork developments were described above in terms of the influence of
changing ideologies, yet this can only be part of the story. Ideas, however bril-
liant and innovative, can be put forward but then fail to transform practice
because material conditions are inappropriate. Conversely, when new perspectives do have an effect, it is because they find an audience, some people ready
to listen. For instance, the breakdown of medieval belief systems and their
replacement with 'scientific' rationalism happened, not because people lacked
the intelligence to think in such ways before, but because society was then in a
state of flux. The changing balance of class forces, notably with the emergence
throughout Europe of an increasingly powerful bourgeoisie who first chal-
lenged, then overthrew, the pre-existing feudal social order, created the circumstances in which these new perspectives developed.

Clearly the material context in which ideas operate at any particular time is
critically important in understanding why they take hold. Dynamics operating
within the real world can be divided between technical factors – those who do
the work and the tools they use – and the changing social context in which
people live and are exploited. This division, between the forces and relations of
production, was initially put forward and elaborated by Marx. The first set of
factors is discussed next.

1.3 Technical factors

The technological developments which have promoted change within archaeology in general, and excavation practice in particular, have nearly always occurred first outside the subject, to be then incorporated into our processes of data gathering, data manipulation or dissemination of results. The discipline has been transformed as a result of such intrusions, both immediately in the way we do things, and in the longer term because the possibilities opened up have created wider horizons and a more sophisticated set of research directions. To see the effect of technological change, one can look as far back as Camden in the seventeenth century whose book, *Britannia*, had a formative influence on the subject. It is not the brilliance of its content but the fact that it could be printed, in contrast to the previous histories of authors in the ancient and medieval worlds, which ensured such wide dissemination of his information. Indeed, it might be argued that the printing press is the single most important mechanism which led, albeit only eventually, to the creation of a whole new set of intellectual disciplines which have transformed society.

On other occasions, the effect of changes in technical conditions was more a matter of a coincidence. The way in which geology had to overcome ecclesiastical constraints in order to progress has been described above. Part of this process was related to the sheer amount of new raw data which had accumulated and now demanded explanation. Yet this data mountain was not the product of gradual accretion through the centuries but the result of an explosion. Geological observations of Lyell and others were greatly facilitated by the progress of the Industrial Revolution which disturbed the ground for factory building and made visible a large number of strata in a multitude of railway cuttings. The mid-nineteenth century was also the period when major drainage schemes in historic cities allowed pioneer field archaeologists such as Wellbeloved in York and Roach-Smith and Hodge in London to take part in some of the earliest 'salvage' work (Plate 3). In carrying out their work, they produced records which are still useful to those writing-up recent excavations (Marsden 1987; Milne 1992). Thus specific material conditions were of central importance in the creation of pools of geological and archaeological data.

With the greater speed of development in the twentieth century, itself a product of the increasingly frantic needs of capitalism, the relationship between technological advance and fieldwork method has become even clearer. Carbon-14 and dendrochronological techniques, each again coming from outside archaeology, have totally changed our dating of stages within prehistory. Further, in the case of the latter technique, it may allow us to identify 'marker dates' in a sequence (Baillie 1991) which result from traumatic events such as volcanic eruptions and can then be used to interpret site development. Such precision may even require a reassessment of the relationship between documentary history and archaeology: if it really becomes possible to date the

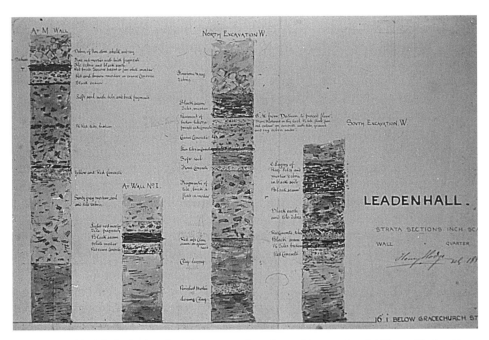

Plate 3 Scale-drawings, in water colour, by architectural artist Henry Hodge. In the last decades of the nineteenth century he recorded building elevations (*top*) on the site of what was later shown to be London's forum and basilica. He also drew some of the first annotated sections through Roman strata (bottom).

construction of a timber waterfront to the nearest year, and even the season within the year, the question of correlations between archaeological evidence and, for example, political events arrives on the agenda in a more forceful way than was possible previously.

Looking at fieldwork practice more specifically, air photographs have transformed the process of finding sites in the landscape, for example increasing estimates of the population of Roman Britain by a factor of five. If we were still flying only kites and balloons rather than aircraft, the impact would have been significantly less. By the same token, ground-based remote-sensing equipment has greatly augmented the ability of archaeologists to understand below-surface site configurations before formal excavation takes place. Indeed, in geophysics, we may even begin to see the start of a reverse process, flowing from our discipline outwards. The diversity of the features which archaeologists investigate, the subtlety of their physical characteristics and the difficulties of their differential survival mean that hardware can be tested in these demanding conditions and then employed more effectively elsewhere – 'if it can work on an archaeological site, it can work anywhere'. Remote sensing and careful excavation to help with police investigations, or Radar to help construction engineers find cracks in buildings or geologists water in deserts, are some of the hoped-for outcomes.

Lastly, and most obviously, the revolution in information technology allows us to manipulate data in ways which would have been previously impossible and to communicate it to increasingly diverse audiences (see Scollar 1982, Gaines 1984, Richards and Ryan 1985 for commentaries at a formative period, Richards 1998 and refs. for more recent work). Further, the use of computers does not just provide answers to old queries more quickly, and perhaps with proven statistical significance, but also leads to our asking new types of questions: technological development generates intellectual change. Computers have the added advantage of forcing us to order our data in such a way that its hierarchical relationships are explicitly acknowledged and, if necessary, reorganised. The development of formalised languages for describing stratigraphic units and the designation of set systems for effective work on site, central to the discussion in this manual, are partly a product of IT developments.

1.4 Organisational factors

Taking the above discussion to its (il)logical conclusion, one could be forgiven for adopting an entirely 'technologically determinist' view of the evolution of fieldwork techniques, in which the gradual accumulation of technical expertise leads to inevitable progress. All the same, this would fail to do justice to the diverse rates and ways in which changes are promoted and implemented in society. To take a simple example, aircraft were invented and technically refined, not out of the blue or gradually over decades, but in particular circumstances on the ground, notably in the course of two world wars. In addition, the production of a profusion of air photographs for archaeologists later on was related, in part, to the type and amount of flying taking place during the Second World War. After 1945, when the post-war boom allowed greater input from the white heat of technology and thus the construction of cheaper aircraft plus wider access to their use, the employment of air photography in archaeological research was further promoted. Again, this was not automatic. Social circumstances had to be right for resources to be allocated to the pilots who created the widespread and intensive coverage of the landscape which archaeologists now have in so many areas.

Similar examples abound, not least because conflict, now open, now hidden, drives so much of capitalist development. Thus the Second World War promoted advances in radar, now employed increasingly within archaeology, while the later, more subtle 'cold war' involved a space race which generated major spin-offs in computer technology. Archaeological survey by air (Gould 1987) has employed military procedures derived from search-and -rescue (SAR – and presumably could use lessons from search-and-destroy actions, SAD). Even the statistical software packages archaeologists employ with their computers were borrowed from social sciences not even defined as distinct disciplines, let alone invested in, until the decades after 1945. Technological development is necessary, but not sufficient, to guarantee widespread change and social context is vital for its comprehension. Unfortunately few authors have seen fit to discuss the history of archaeology explicitly in social terms, let alone to understand fieldwork developments (Hudson 1981 is one exception, together with specialist studies of Marsden (1974) and Levine (1986)). To see the relationship more clearly, we can return to the history of antiquarian involvement outlined previously around the figures of Leland, Camden, Aubrey and Stukeley.

The first worked as the official King's Antiquary, touring England and Wales. Although Leland concentrated on documents and genealogies, he also described sites of interest, including prehistoric monuments. His very appointment was no doubt closely related to the attempts of the Tudor dynasty to create a national consciousness by listing 'their own' monuments (how far down society this ideology of nationalism did, or was intended to, spread has been much debated). Next Camden, the Elizabethan antiquary seen by many as laying the foundations of modern fieldwork, focussed most of his efforts on Roman epigraphy. This would have been a quite natural emphasis in a society with a perceived need to integrate Britain with the rest of Europe. A common inheritance, that of the classical world, came readily to hand. Third, Aubrey was an acute observer and illustrator of monuments such as Stonehenge and Avebury. But he also felt the need to classify artefacts and sites, and such an impetus must have owed much to his relationship with scientists in the Royal Society in the era when polymaths were still allowed. Finally, Stukeley, who not only added detail to the same monuments but discussed them with a vivid imagination, signalled the move from classification as an end in itself to the process of interpretation. This is exactly what one might expect of a person living on the cusp between a society bound up with classical architecture and one about to indulge in the excesses of a Gothic tradition: fanciful links between Druids and Christianity come as no surprise.

Of course, amongst the people concerned, social context influenced, but did not dictate, development, and anyway there were diverse individual backgrounds to accommodate. For instance, in the nineteenth century, Pitt-Rivers, part of the landed gentry with an inheritance and time on his hands, and Schliemann, an industrialist increasingly liberated from factory management, had very different class origins, an example of the contrast between trajectories of capitalist development in Britain, the first nation to experience a bourgeois revolution, and other countries on the continent such as Germany and France. However, they did have in common the fact that their position not only allowed them to transcend feudal beliefs on the origins of humans without fear of ostracism but, equally important, gave them the freedom and time to travel, and the material circumstances to organise fieldwork projects.

In addition, it must be remembered that the Renaissance, although centrally an intellectual process generating a renewed interest in things Roman and, later, a new spirit of rational enquiry, must be set beside the imperial expansion of Western Europe, requiring increasingly direct contact with other civilisations in newly colonised areas. The later 'Grand Tour', with resulting artefact collections then donated to public museums, was a product of this empire-building. Shared colonial aspirations and real imperial conquests dictated the similar intellectual frameworks adopted by German and Austrian archaeologists in Greece, and by British, French and Italian archaeologists in the Far East, the Middle East or North Africa. Common material circumstances also explain how these archaeologists managed to get the resources and permissions to organise fieldwork in the countries on which they impinged. In the process, as we know, they often denuded the conquered regions of their cultural heritage, just as other colonialists decimated their natural resources and their political and social organisation.

1.5 The professionalisation of fieldwork and its implications

Finally, rather than consider only general political contexts in the rather distant past, it is necessary to end this chapter by focussing on the way in which working conditions have influenced recent fieldwork development, a topic of particular relevance to the content of this manual. A second World War was needed to bring the world economy out of the recession of the 1930s, to be followed by the boom years of the 1950s, 1960s and into the 1970s. The threat which this economic growth posed to our material heritage called forth a response from the archaeological community. Studies from various countries (Barley 1977) show that, even though the timing of destructive construction programmes varied between different parts of the Western Bloc, and solutions to these threats took different forms in separate countries, the problem was a very widespread phenomenon. In Britain, for example, it ushered in the rescue movement and the setting up of RESCUE! (Rahtz 1974), an independent organisation formed in 1971 in order to pressurise the government into putting in place financial resources, organisational structures and legal provisions to allow archaeological material to be either protected or investigated before being destroyed by modern development.

In general terms, the organisational reaction to reconciling archaeological work with new growth was in line with much that was going on in the rest of society, in particular in relation to a new role for the state. Late-capitalism has seen a considerable growth in state planning, particularly after, and to some extent as a result of, World War II. In certain spheres this even took the form of concrete intervention in social developments, for example in health and education services, and by nationalising industries in certain segments of the economy. Such development generated a series of material changes (for example in the design of the buildings in which we live) linked to intellectual changes (for example the development of social sciences in general, and sociology in particular). Thus architectural developments such as the high-rise blocks of council housing were associated with the sociologist predicting how much washing line and leisure space each 'family unit' within would require. Hard on their heels came philosophical changes, in particular the notion that the methods of hard science should be applied to society in general – that we could, indeed should, model human activity, test the models, refine them, etc., the better to predict the future.

How these changes affected archaeological theory, most obviously in the development of 'New Archaeology' and an emphasis on hypothetico-deductive approaches, is well known. Yet, equally striking, though not usually linked in so directly, is the way in which state planning on a much wider scale created a new institutional structure for archaeological practice. As part of this process, the legal rights and duties of the discipline had to be more fully defined or, where appropriate, redefined. Some even thought it possible, and desirable, to define a code of ethics for the profession (Smith 1974). In addition, if archaeological impact was to be accepted as a material consideration in decision-making, archaeologists had to be drawn into the workings of both local and central government to a greater degree than before, not just left in universities and museums. Furthermore, field-workers had to relate to commercial organisations and pressures in ways which would have seemed quite alien in previous decades.

Thus archaeologists were employed in central government to help phrase legislation and to issue guidance which, though it sometimes lacked the force of law, was often listened to, both by other archaeologists (the issuing authority often held the purse strings) and by private developers (ignoring government advice would simply invite formal legislation in its place soon thereafter). At the local level, councils began to employ archaeologists so that the planning process could include an archaeological perspective. Their advice might then be used either to protect sites or to twist the arms of commercial developers into paying for investigation ahead of destruction. In Britain, the emerging relationship between archaeologists and the property business was signalled by the issuing of a code of practice between both parties (British Archaeologists and Developers Liaison Group 1986 – though the detail has not been taken up universally). Similar links are evident around the globe (Cleere 1984, 1989).

The development of professional fieldwork from the mid-twentieth century was not, of course, a straightforward, automatic or immediate process. For example, teams in Britain and Germany rescuing cities threatened by rebuilding after the Blitz were usually hopelessly underfunded and muddled through, frequently to very good effect, in much the same way as they had done before the war. However, as the pace of redevelopment increased, the rescue demand came from all sides, both town and country. Urban renewal was related not so much to war damage as to economic boom in Western Europe and America. The white heat of technology employed in towns demanded their extensive redevelopment, whilst motorway schemes to link these expanding centres scarred many rural landscapes. The organisational and financial requirements to accommodate such rescue projects demanded professional teams of archaeologists working together all year round.

In Britain such demands generated the 'circuit digger', moving from project to project. Then, from about 1970, and at an increasing rate during the next five years, archaeological units were set up with regional or specific urban responsibilities to organise the field teams. In line with the wider changes described above, these organisations were expected to be, and succeeded in being, supported by the state. The fieldwork professional had truly arrived (Plate 4).

Similar developments were evident in the rest of Europe. The professional units which were put in place in many major towns and regions have allowed a fruitful interchange of personnel over the past two decades. Equally, on the other side of the Atlantic, salvage and contract archaeology became commonplace (Wilson 1987). Thus the terminology used and the sites concerned may differ but the processes of Cultural Resource/Heritage Management and the economic position, rights and duties of crews/teams of archaeological fieldworkers have been subjects for heated debate everywhere in the last decade. The threats are international, and common problems have often led to similar organisational solutions. In 1953 Crawford could write that field archaeology was 'an essentially English form of sport' (1953: 208). Today it is neither exclusively English (if it ever was), nor seen by those involved as a sport. In most

Plate 4 Professional site staff celebrating the end of another excavation. This group, at the GPO site in the City of London, were described by Hudson (1981) as 'paid graduate professionals. All are under 30 and most under 25 . . . older people with family responsibilities could not exist on the wage offered.' To him, they represented 'a small army under the control of the site supervisor'. As the supervisor in question, I can now reveal that many pictured were graduates only of 'the university of life', that some would have been pleased to be thought of as in their twenties, and that most would have resented anything resembling 'military' control. None the less, Hudson is essentially correct in stressing their professionalism and defining their institutional position as waged labour. He was also right about the low level of those wages!

developed countries, salvage and rescue work is the main driving force behind excavation, and it is contract archaeology which now generates the vast majority of data used by our discipline.

The change to units staffed by full-time, paid professionals, had considerable and sometimes traumatic effects on field-workers, in particular divorcing them from an academic community which none the less continued to spawn a good proportion of the profession as archaeology graduates. Equally, because archaeology remains, in essence, a research discipline with an abiding appeal to interested sections of the general public, further trauma is evident in the lively, and sometimes acrimonious, debate on the competing rights, privileges and status within archaeology of, on the one hand, 'professionals' and, on the other, 'independents' or 'volunteers'. This has been promoted in Britain by Selkirk (1986), though whether the ensuing discussion has generated real understanding or just unnecessary division is another matter. The tension bubbling below the surface is produced by the organisation of the discipline, not out of thin air by the protagonists. The changes in archaeology may be regretted by some and decried by others, but much field archaeology today must be seen as a proper profession (or even, as I would prefer, a job).

On balance, I believe that this increased professionalisation is all to the good, and in any case fairly inevitable, as are the implications of such changes. The workforce in the field is portrayed by most archaeologists, quite correctly, as our biggest asset, more important than any single site or project will ever be. When these people are employed full-time, they constitute wage labour whose interests are radically altered as a result. As paid workers, they can only protect their individual wages and conditions of work by acting collectively. By the same token, only collective action on their part can protect the standards of fieldwork which are now, rightly, demanded by those using the data. The proliferation of unionisation amongst archaeologists in Britain in the 1990s was the logical outcome, as is a closer alliance with other paid workers whose material problems and political solutions they share. Of course, joining unions is not a guarantee of protection in itself, as redundancies within some of the largest, most organised units show. However, if not sufficient, it is generally a necessary condition of successful defence and has at least meant that archaeology has become linked to wider strata within society.

So much for the plus side. At the same time, these employment conditions tend to result in the severing of some links with elements of the rest of the archaeological community. Such a distancing can mean that universities provide training which falls behind technically, and thus produce less useful graduates. Within the profession itself, an excavator whose whole career is in fieldwork will have some different interests from a weekend volunteer on site, no matter how well the two get on, either individually or on a group-to-group basis. More important, divisions with the upper end of the spectrum will also appear. Thus organisations such as the Institute of Field Archaeologists in

Britain, developed on the premise that all archaeologists have something in common, will see this common purpose increasingly obscured when one IFA member, who happens to head an archaeological unit, attempts to throw other IFA members out of work because of a financial crisis. Even initial designs for a code of ethics (Smith 1974) had to acknowledge that the specific content of any such charter might be different depending on whether it applied to the general archaeologist, commercial sponsor, site supervisor or all the other excavation staff. Similar tensions are evident in different institutional contexts around the globe as the field-worker looks more readily to workers employed in similar circumstances, but less readily to those who, though still within archaeology, are situated above or outside that context.

As a final twist in the tale, we have seen, most recently, another development on both sides of the Atlantic. The mid-1980s up to the present has been the era of increased 'privatisation' and withdrawal of state support for certain services. Whether presided over by so-called Socialist or Democratic parties of the left, or those from Conservative or Republican backgrounds on the right, the net result has been the creation of a large, sometimes fragmented, private labour market, frequently working with short-term contracts on projects funded by commercial developers. It is these workers who now do the vast majority of archaeological data gathering in the field. Paradoxically, the attacks on wages and working conditions since the 1980s have been so widespread that they also encompass the university sphere. The increased number of academics working on fixed-term contracts, without tenure or other security, means that they now find themselves in very similar positions to the rescue field-worker. Perhaps this will help to heal the rift between the two spheres which opened up in the course of the 1970s.

The final result of these changes in conditions of employment, and the most pertinent for present purposes, comes from the fact that the jobs of waged, full-time field-workers have to be defined much more exactly than hitherto, in order to justify a specific economic reward. Hence positions and responsibilities must be carefully delineated. In addition, if fellow professionals were to integrate their activities effectively, they required a common language and designated systems of work. This was true of the large, state-supported organisations of the 1970s, but no less needed with the more mobile working conditions forced on the professional excavator since then.

A spate of publications on excavation recording spawned during that period have attempted to service the needs of these teams or crews. Although general books (Barker 1977, Dever and Lance 1978, Fladmark1978, Joukowsky 1980, Hester *et al.* 1981, Hester *et al.* 1997) have their own important perspectives and insights, in Britain it is the book*lets* (Hirst 1976, Jefferies 1977, Boddington 1978) which show how fieldwork recording has developed (indeed, the same is apparent in pottery research – see Orton *et al.* 1993 and Kunow *et al.* 1986, the latter putting the case for systematisation in three languages to show that it's serious). Further manuals were issued subsequently for use within units such as Essex County Council, Exeter Museums Archaeological Field Unit, Humberside Archaeological Unit, the Scottish Urban Archaeological Trust, the Trust for Wessex Archaeology and York Archaeological Trust. Their authorship, by organisations rather than individuals, may be the clearest indication of a changed emphasis, away from the site-director and polymath, and towards professional team members.

The present manual has been written by an individual who is now, perhaps inappropriately, an ex-unit worker. Although it covers wider ground than most of the unit publications (or at least the same ground over more pages!), it comes out of a very similar tradition, part of the same response to increased professionalisation. This hopefully gives it a current relevance.

2

EXCAVATION IN THEORY

Introduction

The foregoing chapter charted the way in which approaches to archaeological fieldwork have changed throughout preceding years, reflecting developments in ideological structures, available technologies and organisational systems adopted by various societies at different times. However, underlying these chronological and geographical differences is a fundamental, and vital, debate concerning the relationship between the past and present. For the archaeological excavator the essential problem might be put as follows: when we carry out our fieldwork, does the past speak directly for itself through its material remains (thus 'The spade cannot lie')? Or do we impose present-day perspectives on that past to make sense of it when excavating? How one answers this question has influenced archaeological practice in all periods and contexts.

The first standpoint, that the past is directly revealed to us in the field, usually leads to an emphasis on the need for total excavation – if one can expose all of a site, and treat it with sufficient care by using the best techniques, then it will offer up its secrets. Hence 'the only valid questions to ask of a site are "What is there?" and "What is the whole sequence of events on this site from the beginning of human activity to the present day?"' (Barker 1977: 42). On the other hand, if the job of archaeology is to impose perspectives on the past, excavation projects require specific research objectives. Data are not gathered passively but produced by active intervention of the archaeologist. The excavator proposes academic questions, decides which sites and what types of data are needed, and creates an appropriate structure for capturing the data. Such work would necessarily operate within a more focussed framework than that provided by Barker's 'What is there?' question.

These different conceptions of the excavation process also have implications for how post-excavation work is characterised and carried out. If one sees excavation as communing with the past, and records every scrap of evidence given up by the earth, work afterwards just requires an open mind and some lateral thinking (Barker 1977: 193). In contrast, if field-workers impose perspectives, structuring and constraining data capture accordingly, they will have to employ formal analytical procedures afterwards to create meaning from those data.

In this chapter I will tackle this debate by considering various critiques of total excavation, in terms of its being morally unacceptable, unattainable in practice, unattainable in theory and an internally incoherent conception (see **2.1** below). I believe that only the last of these has any force, but this is sufficient to demonstrate that the alternative approach, requiring problem orientation, must be central to all excavation practice (**2.2**). When constructing a meaning-ful research agenda to give such focus, other disciplines must be used alongside archaeology (**2.3**), thereby generating a positive cycle of research (**2.4**). These conclusions provide the structure for the remainder of this manual.

Before proceeding with the argument, it is necessary to remove a misconcep-tion. Many commentators seem to believe that the dichotomy portrayed above can be reduced to that of research versus rescue excavations. This leads to the simple opposition of total excavation, open areas and research projects, on the one hand, versus problem orientation, small trenches and rescue work on the other. However, such amalgamation is mistaken. For instance, some rescue workers see themselves as digging without particular questions in mind, and have portrayed the lack of problem orientation as advantageous in that it allows their data to be employed by anyone and everyone in the future (see, for example, Carver's view (1979a) that 'in rescue work, it is data, not models, which are threatened. We are primarily in the business of data collection – we build models for pleasure. Our rescue projects should be those which yield the most data, not those which are designed to check existing models', perhaps stung by Renfrew's criticism (1978: 157) that rescue work amounts to 'little more than the unthinking collection of raw data'). Whichever view is correct, clearly both see rescue work and problem orientation as strange bedfellows. Conversely, many directors of research excavations believe themselves to be problem solvers, not total excavators. Figure 1 provides some quotes which one might expect the various viewpoints and circumstances described above to generate.

In what follows, it is important to separate two issues. One refers to contin-gent facts about archaeological practice – whether an excavation takes place in a research or a rescue setting. The other involves the fundamental nature of any archaeological investigation – whether the past speaks for itself and excavators just listen, or whether every interpretation is a product of today's imposed per-spectives. Only the second, deeper matter is relevant in this chapter.

2.1 A critique of total excavation

The concept of 'total excavation' might be criticised on four grounds. Some have suggested (Olsen 1980) that to remove all strata when excavating a site is morally unacceptable because it is totally destructive – if we excavate only a part of the site, future generations can dig what remains in order to test the initial conclusions. In response to this accusation, three points should be made. First, strictly speaking, adjacent excavations can neither prove nor disprove earlier work. All material remains are a product of diverse human activities,

	PAST SPEAKS FOR ITSELF	**PERSPECTIVES ARE IMPOSED**
RESCUE	*'We are simple, humble diggers who just rescue the data and put it in what, we hope, are secure archives. It is up to cleverer people, such as those writing in the columns below, to decide later on what it all means. Even if they never actually do so, at least we have fulfilled our commitment to the past by achieving our archive objective.'*	*'We can't do anything about the inadequate resources available to us. So we will concentrate on the Roman forum, to make sure that this, at least, is properly understood. If that means digging away the medieval layers because time and money are in short supply, then it may be a sad commentary on the modern world, but so be it.'*
RESEARCH	*'I am fortunate with this unthreatened, deserted Roman town. There is all the time in the world to throw every available evaluation and excavation technique at it, and so not miss a single bit of information. Even if we only get through "Horizon One" in my life time, that is a small price to pay for doing things properly.'*	*'I have chosen this site for good, academic reasons, gaining financial support because our research group is at the cutting edge of studies of Neolithic flint production. Thus, clearly, I must design a research strategy which does justice to that specific objective (satisfying our sponsors and enhancing my own academic reputation to boot).'*

Figure 1 Rescue versus research projects cross-referenced with different approaches to the past – some (fictitious) quotes.

and one area may be very different from another. Later work can, at best, only strengthen or weaken previous conclusions.

Second, the logic of Olsen's argument would be to dig a still smaller area next time, with a *reductio* of working, ultimately, in infinitesimally small trenches. Droop noted long ago (1915: 1) that, when one area was investigated and the remainder 'preserved for posterity', the understanding of the dug sector, and perhaps the potential interest of the non-dug sector, was necessarily diminished, as the relative position of find and features in each area was unknown.

Finally, and most seriously, this criticism misses the point. Total excavation prescribes what should happen once one has decided to intervene in the ground, but is not concerned with the *earlier* argument about preservation versus investigation. The two principles – that sites should be left, where possible, as future archive but, when investigation is unavoidable, total excavation is mandatory – are mutually consistent. Total excavation is not, *per se*, a licence to dig everything and forget about preservation.

Next there is the notion that total excavation is practically unattainable: 'We never have enough time and resources and should just get on with the job as best we can: other approaches are simply irrelevant philosophising.' This argument is wrong on two counts. First, such a policy of despair would probably prevent any energy going into developing new techniques. Second, it suggests that resource allocation is *totally* beyond our control, and that we have no archaeological criteria for deciding how to divide up what is available. A valid response is that we must aim to get as close as possible to total excavation whilst demanding more time and resources. Telling someone to 'live in the real world' should not be an injunction to leave it completely unchanged.

A third school proposes what seems a more radical critique, that total excavation is theoretically unattainable because techniques are always improving (this is usually stated, not illustrated). Thus what constitutes total excavation today will be considered inadequate tomorrow, paradoxically because today's investigations throw up new problems, and hopefully new solutions, and so techniques advance. The riposte here is straightforward. Of course total excavation is advocated only *for a given level of technology*, especially by someone like Barker, who has been at the forefront of advances.

Yet the fourth, and most fundamental, criticism, that the objective of totally excavating a site is actually incoherent, cannot, I think, be countered. Three problems must be considered. First, how is one to define the limits of the site itself? Archaeologists doing surface surveys in the field have found the concept of 'a site' of limited use and hence have defined it in terms of degrees of concentration of artefacts (Gallant 1986) or soil phosphates (Cavanagh *et al.* 1988). Others have even dispensed entirely with the concept and carried out siteless surveys (Dunnell and Dancey 1983). Yet similar problems of definition exist in excavation. For example, if one exposes a complete building, not just some of its rooms, does this constitute the total excavation of the site? Clearly it will not include all the buildings in the street, still less all those in the settlement, and it avoids any contact with the surrounding hinterlands used by the occupants of the building. If 'the site' cannot be defined in absolute terms, how can we talk of its total excavation?

Second there is the issue of selecting excavation techniques. If total excavation means excavating as large an area as possible – the more you excavate the more you are likely to know – it is difficult to disagree but hardly a profound theoretical point. Something more is usually implied, that one should have sufficient time and resources to employ all available techniques to the excavated area. Yet such a requirement is clearly not achievable. To excavate in one way is to dismiss many others, not just because of practical limitations of time and money, or because techniques may improve in the future, but of necessity. For example, allowing vegetation growth over winter may help distinguish occupation zones within a structure but the intrusion of these same modern plants may prevent the recovery of uncontaminated environmental samples. Equally, to provide information on site formation processes, the micromorphologist may need to see soil interfaces in elevation, yet setting out such baulks across the site may militate against recognising ephemeral timber buildings.

Sometimes compromises are possible, but often they are not. At this point, advocates of total excavation fall silent. They are unable to provide guidelines on which tools to take from the tool-kit, and which to avoid, because any selection would be a step away from their ideal.

So there is incoherence at the heart of the idea of total excavation, which stems from seeing fieldwork as the use of all available techniques to unravel the details of a 'unique site in an unrepeatable experiment'. True, every archaeological site will be a unique combination of particular environmental, cultural and chronological factors, but each component could be investigated either as a discrete entity, or in relation to the others. Equally misleading is the underlying notion of the unrepeatable experiment, in apparent contrast to the hard sciences: after all, even physicists do not actually crack the same atom. Of course an archaeological site is a lot more complex than the humble atom, its structure involving a combination of many more factors because it is a product of a far more complex totality, human society. In addition, the archaeologist does not work in controlled, laboratory conditions. Hence a variety of factors may explain particular patterning in the excavated record, and conversely the importance of a single factor may be masked by its being linked with changing combinations of other determinants. So many data sets are needed to understand any component, as with most studies of human behaviour. Sampling in excavation thus become a much more difficult and complex (and, for the same reasons, more interesting) activity than in hard sciences. It will use a greater range of methods, and it requires greater fluidity of response, than laboratory work. However, the two spheres are not, ultimately, qualitatively different in terms of the unrepeatability of their experiments.

In accepting that investigation of a site involves selecting some factors for analysis and ignoring others, the criticisms of total excavation discussed above can be resolved. The decision as to what defines 'the site' depends on settling what you want to do there: it is neither a choice with an absolute, timeless validity nor a purely subjective guess, but a decision based on research objectives. By the same token, the techniques applied are neither simply all those available at the time, nor the 'best ones' given practical constraints of time and resources: they are chosen because of their ability to create data relevant to stated research objectives.

Field-workers have clung so tenaciously to the inductive approach of total excavation because the alternative is seen as a rigid and constraining hypothetico-deductive method, conjuring up outmoded Popperian ideas of falsification by critical experiments. However, the sharp dichotomy between pure induction and hard deduction is unnecessary. The objective of our fieldwork should be wide-ranging explanation of human activity, not stultifying prediction. By rejecting both camps, we can enter a research cycle which will allow us to judge not the truth or falsity, but the superiority or inferiority, of a particular set of interpretations of past society.

2.2 Problem orientation

The point which emerges from the foregoing discussion is that field-workers do not dig up evidence. We dig up earth, stones, etc. and, in the process of making observations about their appearance and configurations, turn them into data. Hence data are *produced* in excavation, not lying around dormant on the ground waiting to be discovered, and their production involves the active intervention of the excavation team. Subjecting such data to post-excavation analyses then allows interpretation, giving them meaning. This is the route by which physical material is turned into data, and data are turned into evidence – evidence *of* social processes.

This argument leads to the conclusion that problem orientation in excavation is not just an unfortunate result of insufficient time and resources, or a necessary evil because we do not live in an ideal world, but a fundamental aspect of the process of archaeological investigation. Imposing present-day research objectives on sites, and by implication on the societies which produced those sites, presents us not with a problem but with a potential. This relationship with the present makes the site relevant to today, and forms a fundamental part of the rationale for society to spend money on archaeological digging as well as women's refuges and more school textbooks, or instead of nuclear warheads.

However, there are objections to this view which must be confronted. If excavation is necessarily selective, what about the idea of preservation of the site by record, which forms the justification for many rescue excavations? Second, if excavation is just intervention from the present, does this not make it an entirely subjective product of each director's conception (or misconception) of what is important at the moment? Can excavations never produce anything for posterity? This objection is often connected with a third criticism. If we dig with specific objectives, we will ignore, and thus implicitly dismiss as unimportant, many other matters – we will 'find only what [we] expect to find' (Reynolds and Barber 1984: 96). As we can never be sure of what lies beneath the ground in advance, fluid responses are essential. Problem orientation, in so far as it militates against this fluidity, is undesirable.

In reply, it must be said, first, that the 'archive objective' of rescue archaeology does have limited application: no set of records could answer every subsequent question, any more than they could have answered all the questions which might have been posed when the excavation actually occurred. Yet that is not to say that they can be relevant only to predefined questions. Excavations can be approached in a way which makes them relevant to issues not even phrased, let alone thought to be important, when the fieldwork took place. Importantly, whether a set of old data today is useful for a newly developed issue is best decided if the original research objectives and the data structure which results have been stated explicitly, rather than characterising the project aims as 'preserving the entire site by record in a total excavation'.

Second, if one admits that there is no objective evidence waiting in the ground to be revealed, does this not make all excavations a product of each director's subjectivity? This criticism confuses two different concepts – the objective/subjective category and the relative/absolute category. Thus Fowler (1977: 95) states that there is 'no objective truth buried in the ground waiting to be revealed by the archaeologist: he and his results are creatures of himself, his times and his techniques', thereby neatly counterposing absolute truth and subjective individualism. Yet, from the suggestion that any excavation will be relative to present-day perceptions, it does not follow that those aims are solely a function of the subjective biases of each individual director. What is required is inter-subjective agreement between all parties on aims and methods. Excavation always takes place in a social context and to say 'We must pose questions' is far from maintaining that 'I just assume answers.' However, it *is* to maintain that we must have an idea of what would constitute an answer to our questions – what type of data would have to be produced, how they might be manipulated later. It need not, indeed should not, make any assumptions about what the evidence might actually show. In short, observation is theory-laden but not theory-determined.

The issue of fluidity remains. Does not problem orientation militate against that responsiveness to specific site conditions? And will not standardised recording remove 'any possibility of elucidating further information' (Reynolds and Barber 1984: 98) from a site? The important truth here is that emphasising problem orientation puts greater demands on properly evaluating the nature of the deposits before excavation. No deposit model can predict every eventuality, so one must be reactive as well as proactive. Fluidity is integral to any research designs, even if this limits comparability of data sets, because changes in direction, or of gear, during an excavation are the rule rather than the exception. Yet these necessary alterations are best coped with when working away from an explicit strategy, leaving excavators clear about what they are moving away from, the reasons for doing so and what they are moving towards. Far from being an excuse for a mechanistic approach to excavation, problem orientation should enhance, not reduce, fluidity.

2.3 The need for interdisciplinary research

The above discussion has emphasised the need to define research objectives before starting any fieldwork project. Any such agenda must be constructed on as wide a base as possible, a process in which cooperation between archaeology and other disciplines is often essential. Such relationships are made possible because of the common 'real world' which surrounds all intellectual endeavour, providing a similar organisational context and ideological climate in which research can take place – the academic Ivory Tower stands in less glorious isolation from the rest of society than some would have us believe. Some forms of collaboration with the physical and social sciences and with other humanities are outlined below, and taken up in more detail as the occasion requires in later chapters. However, before doing this, it is necessary to flag up the limitations on interdisciplinary study. These have meant that demands to organise archaeological fieldwork along such lines are, more often than not, honoured in the breach and contributions by other disciplines are either avoided or, at best, marginalised to particular, specialist studies. Hence it is rare indeed to find truly interdisciplinary objectives being developed from the start of a project, in setting out its research agenda.

The reasons for this failing are many and various. Some concern purely organisational matters, for example the sources of funding available to different disciplines, the context in which awards are made, and the timing of applications for support. More fundamental is the intellectual dimension, notably the timescale within which different disciplines work and the levels of resolution which they require. Thus particular, accurately dated episodes, central to a historian's understanding of the past, may be very difficult to set beside archaeological work which seeks to elucidate more general processes of social development. And the timescale over which biological scientists stretch their investigations may be still longer. In this sense, what constitutes 'an event' in each sphere will be quite different. However, neither organisational nor intellectual matters should provide fundamental barriers to collaboration and, perhaps, the underlying reason for the dearth of good interdisciplinary work lies with the socio-political context of academic study. In particular, archaeology is a 'newer' discipline. It is only when it gains more confidence in itself as a real subject in its own right, and thus becomes less defensive about some of the inadequacies of its evidence, that progress will be made and we can start to engage in proper, frank debate with more established disciplines.

Turning now to the detail of the biological and physical sciences, there are myriad specific techniques and approaches which can be applied to all stages of an excavation project, apart from the overall influence of 'the scientific method' on archaeology (Kelley and Hanen 1988). These scientific disciplines might generate initial hypotheses, for example by stimulating an excavation to take pollen columns to aid the reconstruction of a past environment. Or their input may be crucial in finding sites, as with chemical sampling for phosphate analysis or the electronics used in ground-based remote sensing. They can influence the excavation process itself, as when biological knowledge improves the recording and lifting of human skeletons, or helps in the selection of mesh-size to recover particular seeds in sieving operations. Finally, much post-excavation work demands the application of laboratory techniques (Ellis 1982, Phillips 1984). It is now difficult to imagine an excavation project which does not call on the archaeological scientist at some stage of its research cycle, and the earlier this is thought through the better.

Within the human and social sciences, geography and archaeology have had mutual influences in both general approaches and specific models. Previously parallel paths are now beginning to converge (Wagstaff 1987), affecting the way in which archaeologists employ sampling strategies in the landscape, geomorphology in understanding archaeological deposits, and geographical models to interpret the significance of spatial patterns in their data post-excavation. Equally anthropology can provide a fuller understanding of the material residues we excavate (Orme 1981 and Hodder 1982) and the cultural processes embodied in the formation and transformation of archaeological record, essential if we are to integrate artefactual record and structural sequence. Finally, a related field concerned with the use of analogy in archaeological explanation is experimental archaeology (Coles 1979). Reynolds (1978) shows how it might influence strategy and enhance field recording in a variety of ways and certainly could be used more fully and interactively in enhancing some aspects of field recording, for example in a 'smoothness quotient' in cut descriptions to help recognise grain storage pits, or concentrating more fully on the diagnostic position of inclusions in ditch fills when recording of sections after work done in monitoring the degradation of experimental earthworks. Whether we are all sufficiently committed to carefully dissect the fauna from the contents of a modern cess-pit (Osbourne 1983), or to pass un-filleted fish through our own digestive system and systematically collect and analyse the results (described in Wheeler and Jones 1989) is another matter. Which is worse – investigating your own faecal material or excavating the recent output of another individual? At least it's all in the cause of science.

Finally, from within the humanities, the relationship between history and archaeology has been much discussed. Some see mutual benefits, with particularist documents biassed towards upper echelons of society of the former discipline being balanced by archaeological studies giving voice to 'the people without history'. Others see constraints, and maintain that archaeology must do much more than simply flesh out culture history, noting in the process that our sequences are rarely so accurately dated that connections with documented events become feasible. What remains clear is that historical sources can be used to construct period-based activity models for archaeology; that particularly important documentary issues can influence archaeological priorities, for example to dig cemeteries to study known plagues; and that maps, engravings and even oral history can give spatial and architectural details which can both identify excavation sites and give a social context for excavated remains.

The interdisciplinary problems really come from attempting to integrate these different types of evidence after excavation. Do industrial residues from a cellar on a documented property recall the activities of its named, high-status proprietor, or of unrecorded tenants of very different status? Do water-logged seeds from a cess-pit behind a medieval town house relate to the diet of its aristocratic owners, who probably resided on their country estates for much of the year, or to their servants living there all the year round? Of course, the issues which arise when trying to relate archaeological evidence to documentary history are now familiar and, although the relationship between the different disciplines has not always been straightforward and happy, archaeological study in documented periods has generated the whole sub-discipline of historical archaeology (Schuyler 1978 charts its growth), hopefully an indication of future, productive collaboration.

2.4 Conclusions

This chapter has argued that we must define areas of interest in approaching archaeological excavation, rather than attempt the incoherent objective of obtaining data in isolation in a 'total excavation'. It has further suggested that multidisciplinary approaches are vital to planning, carrying out and analysing the data resulting from excavations. These conclusions dictate the framework of the rest of the book. Other disciplines may be important, but it is archaeology itself that influences site discovery and site evaluation, which will be discussed next. The practical preparations for digging, which should logically flow out of, rather than dictate, the research objectives, are then described. These factors combine to create a structure for the excavation data, looked at afterwards, and influence methods of data manipulation described at the end of the volume.

Not everyone will accept fully the positions outlined in this chapter. A variety of opinions on this and all other aspects of fieldwork is inevitable, it being this lack of consensus which gives the discipline its ability to change. But if the subject is to advance, rather than merely change, the various positions must be openly debated, each protagonist showing how their stance relates to, and dictates, particular actions on the site. It is this process of argument which will be pursued in the remainder of the book.

3

PRE-EXCAVATION STRATEGIES

Introduction

If all excavation must be approached by way of present perspectives, as suggested in Chapter 2, then good research design must involve digging in existing areas of knowledge in order to augment, or even transform, them (the 'areas' mentioned here being defined, of course, in conceptual terms rather than as geographic entities). At a general level, frameworks for this knowledge can be drawn from outside archaeology using the multidisciplinary approaches mentioned at the end of that chapter. However, for setting the more detailed agenda, it is necessary to employ more specifically archaeological techniques to demonstrate the existence of sites and evaluate the nature of what survives on them before full excavation commences. (In the following discussion, it should be remembered that separating the techniques used to discover sites from those employed to evaluate them is questionable. For example, it is possible to use test pitting to provide more detailed information about existing sites as well as to find new ones, or to use an auger to turn up new sites in the landscape as well as add detail to a known site at the evaluation stage. Thus the distinction is used here mainly for convenience.)

Each process of identifying a new site, evaluating it after such identification, and then investigating it by selectively recording features and gathering finds in the field, constitutes an exercise in sampling. Thus, not surprisingly, sampling has been central to the discipline of archaeology for some considerable time, albeit initially implicitly. However, with the advent of 'New Archaeology' from the early 1970s, sampling strategies started to be discussed explicitly and in detail. This was first signalled to a wide audience as being a contemporary issue by Ragir (1972), quickly followed by the publication of the proceedings of the San Francisco symposium (Mueller 1975). The latter focussed on regional strategies, in line with the then-conventional wisdom that 'the region' was the most appropriate unit of analysis, being sufficiently general to iron out the vagaries of individual site histories, yet specific enough for the detail of diverse processes of social development to emerge.

The British audience, at this time, had further to travel intellectually before accepting that sampling must be an integral part of archaeological fieldwork. This accounts for the rather more polemical tone of the publication (Cherry *et al.* 1978) of the Southampton conference in the UK, which followed the San

Francisco meeting. The British publication gave a greater emphasis to site specifics and their wider range of contexts, rather than regions. It also included attempts to define strategies on deeply stratified sites although, essentially, this amounted to splitting them into separate chronological horizons and adopting different sampling methods for each period. In the process it thus effectively ignored the essence of such sites, that they evidenced complex, interconnected sequences of development evolving independent of chronological labels such as Roman, Anglo-Saxon, etc.

The point of fundamental importance to emerge from these, and many later, studies is that the choice of sampling method (grid, transect, etc.) and of sampling interval depend, in part, on the size and form of the entities which one is sampling, and how profuse and evenly distributed they might be within the study area. Thus the design of any sampling exercise requires some pre-existing knowledge to characterise the population to be investigated (see below on site evaluation procedures, although the use of 'adaptive' approaches may allow one to develop such strategies in the course of a project). There is insufficient space here to develop discussion further but, fortunately, Orton (2000) covers this ground with more expertise than this author could possibly muster. I will therefore merely note, first, that sampling is not just a technical, mathematical exercise. Any coherent strategy must be constructed on the basis of the research aims of each individual project. Second, the methods adopted will depend on whether one wishes to locate new sites and study their relationships (inter-site patterning) or to enhance the information from a specific area (intra-site sampling). The latter distinction is therefore developed below.

Finding sites in the landscape is an important aspect of archaeological research in its own right, as well as an obvious prerequisite of starting any excavation project. Work may use previous archaeological observation in one area to look for further sites in adjacent ones; or employ techniques such as aerial photography and field-walking in entirely new sectors. A vast quantity of information on techniques of discovery is available, much of it now being brought together both in this country and in North America, there under the heading of remote sensing linked to cultural resource management, conveniently summarised by Lyons and Methien (1980), Ebert (1984) and Scollar *et al.* (1990). The handbook by Lyóns and Avery (1977), backed up by seven supplements, describes the mechanics and illustrates them with a series of case studies.

Turning to the design of sampling strategies at known sites, surveys which aim to chart the differential survival of deposits in a designated area have a vital role to play at a series of levels. At the most general, they can facilitate the setting of priorities, and thus efficient resource allocation, between different settlements of a defined type (see Carver 1983 for comparisons between some English and French towns). Next, within a settlement, they can provide detailed information with which to define the most productive zones for given research objectives. Finally, and most important for present purposes, such surveys give foreknowledge of the configuration of deposits under the ground when selecting sectors for investigation, thus influencing particular excavation strategies and recording techniques. Naturally, such deposit mapping is, in itself, insufficient to structure research priorities completely: one needs not only to find out what survives in an area, but also to decide how important these levels might be for specific academic objectives. However, knowing as much as possible about the depth and characteristics of the deposits beneath the ground is a necessary condition of these objectives being achieved coherently.

Information on deposits can be conveniently structured around the three criteria of preservation, spacing and status (Carver 1987). Thus there will be a need to assess the depth of a deposit and whether it is, or has been, waterlogged or anoxic (Carver's 'preservation'); whether the sequence is inter-cut sufficiently to give stratigraphic relationships, yet not so much that legibility is precluded ('spacing'); and whether strata have a primary relationship with the artefacts which they contain, or include mainly artefactual assemblages redeposited from earlier levels on the site or brought in from elsewhere ('deposit status'). On this basis one can judge which research questions might be answerable at which site; where trenches might be positioned to provide the most useful sets of data; what the structure of the record should be; and what resources will be needed, even including the provision of unusual facilities such as conservation for particular materials. Of course, not everything below the ground is exactly as predictable, but the more energy that goes into getting information at this stage, the more successful any excavation strategy is likely to be.

This chapter therefore discusses a variety of techniques used to give us knowledge of sites prior to full excavation. It is not intended as a complete list, rather a brief statement of the more common methods. Probably the three techniques used most widely to discover sites *de novo* are aerial photography (see **3.1** below), field-walking/pedestrian survey (**3.2**) and shovel test pits or divoting (**3.3**). Orton (2000, ch. 4) provides a background discussion to sampling in this context. After this initial phase, the sources of information needed to map deposits on known sites range from the general and non-destructive to the more specific and interventionist. These are discussed below in the order of the degree of destruction which they involve – hence documentary references (**3.4**), is followed by previous excavations (**3.5**), then ground-based remote sensing (**3.6**), chemical mapping (**3.7**), drilling cores or augering (**3.8**) and digging evaluation trenches (**3.9**). Once again, see Orton (2000: ch. 5) for a general setting.

Of course, these methods are often employed interactively. For example, one might undertake intensive aerial photographic coverage of a landscape, followed by detailed field-walking of selected areas. More accurate finds plotting may then elucidate the character and date of the site, indicate its status and even suggest different activity areas. Finally, ground-based remote sensing can discover lines of structural activity, before specific evaluation trenches elucidate the character and depth of stratigraphic accumulation, and a more general campaign of coring identifies the overall limits of the archaeological deposit – hence the somewhat arbitrary nature of the distinction between techniques used to find sites and those used to chart the extent and character of their deposits. Cumulatively, gathering data from a variety of such operations allows one to create a sophisticated deposit model, which can be set beside a project's research agenda before the main excavation starts (**3.10**).

3.1 Aerial photography

Sites can be recognised from the air by a variety of mechanisms, ranging from the low-flying kite (admittedly usually employed in photographic recording during excavation: Noli 1985), to satellites using sophisticated imaging techniques to record features from vast distances (for example imagery derived from the Landsat Thematic Mapper: Showalter 1993). However, the more conventional technique is that of photography from aircraft, whether to record actual standing monuments, provide indications of underlying features from shadows cast in appropriate light, or register indications from crop or soil marks. Its techniques have been widely discussed and the literature is easily accessible (see Wilson (1982) on the problems of mistaking natural or modern features for ancient features of the landscape, Riley (1987) on recent applications, methods and problems and a basic bibliography for further reading, and Maxwell (1983) for further case studies). More recently, Cox (1992) has shown how satellite imagery and aerial photography can be harnessed in parallel to enhance identification of sites and aid their classification, in this case on lowland wetlands, even though the cost of implementation in terms of time and expertise is considerable, and Spenneman (1987) has demonstrated how one can quickly plot sites onto copies of aerial photographs, with considerable savings in time and accuracy.

Aerial photographic work shows an interesting difference in approach on either side of the Atlantic. The British preference was originally for vertical photographs, working from the monument towards its setting within the landscape, a move from the particular to the general which appears to reflect a cultural-historical tradition. In the US the preference for oblique views suggests a greater emphasis on the landscape itself, and only subsequently on the position of the site within it. Such a focus, on the context in which individual sites subsist, is presumably a product of the closer links between archaeology and anthropology. Thus different conceptions of 'the site', and indeed of the nature of 'landscape archaeology', affect the way in which aerial photographs are taken and interpreted, although the available technology is essentially the same. It will be interesting to see whether increased interaction at a theoretical level closes the gap between the continents.

For sites to be recognised from the configuration of crop marks, it is best to survey densely sown plants growing under stress, for example in the spring or early summer. Soil marks obviously require the soil to be disturbed, usually by tilling, before becoming apparent. Thus, in both cases, recognition depends on the nature of the agricultural regime and the time of year. It also depends on the time of day when the photograph was taken, since the angle of sunlight affects visibility. Coverage of any landscape is therefore a cumulative, if not continuous, process, rather than a matter of a single flight to discover all features. Furthermore, certain areas may be largely inaccessible because over-flying is prohibited, either because it would impinge on military or commercial flight paths or because aerial information on a monument is thought to be undesirable, for instance in the case of a medieval castle reused as a modern prison. However, in the near future, satellite technology may circumvent these problems and further revolutionise the whole sub-discipline.

Given these technical and organisational issues, the use of aerial photography by central authority as a planning tool to identify and thus protect sites, or to dictate excavation priorities, is fraught with danger (Bewley 1993, Palmer and Cox 1993). Sites which show up may be only those which have already been partially destroyed, for instance in the case of soil marks, and thus those least deserving of preservation (Plate 5). Correspondingly, the absence of sites in a region may indicate limited recent disturbance, and thus better preservation, rather than a real absence of occupation. Thus localities where air photographs suggest dense occupation may be a guide as to where *not* to excavate, since all sites are heavily disturbed, rather than suggesting a priority area for investigation.

These problems notwithstanding, when an area is threatened with destructive redevelopment, or is being considered for excavation for other reasons, it is vital to inspect any aerial coverage beforehand. In Britain, photographs will often be available via the holdings of the local Sites and Monuments Record, usually in the care of the County Archaeologist. Failing that, the national record held by the Royal Commission on Historical Monuments, now subsumed by English Heritage, can be consulted. Similar centralised and regional facilities exist in many countries. Sometimes photographs will have been taken and then already scrutinised for indications of occupation, with any features plotted on maps. However, more often, only the photographs will exist. Identification of any features on them may require specialist help, or at least the tutored eye. Whether accurate plotting of apparent features is then needed depends on the use to which the data is to be put. If it indicates activity in an area which is going to be extensively exposed anyway, then it may serve as a useful indicator without further work. However, if the photograph is to be used as a detailed guide to trench location, for example to section linear features of the landscape, then an exact plot will become essential.

Plate 5 Differential visibility, and perhaps survival, of archaeological features at Holbeach in Lincolnshire owing to diverse farming regimes. Droveways, field boundaries and other, smaller enclosures, all probably of Roman date, are visible. Well-preserved earthworks are evident in the central field, under grass, and corresponding alignments in the ploughed field towards the top of the photograph must represent their partially destroyed counterparts there. However, different cropping regimes in further fields above this and to the left show none of the expected features. Here they could have been completely eradicated or the nature of crop growth may limit visibility at this time. Alternatively, and confusingly, their non-appearance may be due to shallower ploughing, and hence much *better* deposit survival here than elsewhere. When adjacent fields have different aerial photographic responses, which zones are most deserving of protection: those which show evidence of archaeological features, or those which show none?

3.2 Field-walking/pedestrian survey

Coming back down to earth, field-walking may be used either to follow up the initial indications of aerial photography or to identify new sites and settlement patterns in its own right (Fowler 1972a; see also Aston and Rowley (1974) on techniques and organisational matters and Taylor (1974) for many useful approaches in Britain; O'Brien and Lewarch 1981, Lewarch and O'Brien 1981, and Wandsnider and Ebert 1988 in the US). Increased awareness of the importance of field-walking is evident in various studies, for example Hinchcliffe and Schadla-Hall (1980), and the methods to be employed and records to be made are well known (see the pamphlet by Fasham *et al.* 1980 and work in Hayfield 1980). Recent surveys from around the Mediterranean basin (e.g. Carrete *et al.* 1995), amongst others, show the huge potential of this work, demonstrating that it can both provide information in its own right, and act as a guide to identifying new sites.

When one is trying to identify archaeological sites in a landscape which is undisturbed by recent farming, and so where surface finds are not recoverable, it may be necessary for the archaeologist to provide such disturbance oneself. Thus an area might be turned over by an agricultural plough (or even a firebreak plough: Bloemker and Oakley 1999) in order to bring cultural material to the surface. However, such a strategy is necessarily destructive if applied to 'virgin' ground, so it is more usual to adopt such a technique only in areas which have been previously ploughed up, but where the ground is not freshly disturbed. The depth to which this new, 'archaeological' ploughing may legitimately proceed can be determined by test pits (see below).

The role of field-walking in site discovery is one thing, its use as a guide to excavation tactics within a particular site another. Sometimes the distribution of artefacts with diagnostic structural information can not only suggest the status of a site, but also show up differences within a building complex. Thus (Figure 2), the distribution of roofing stone shows which range of rooms of a proposed Roman villa site may have been tiled, and that of *tesserae* suggests the position of mosaic pavements. Plotting these distributions against the configuration of underlying features deduced from a remote sensing plot provides information in itself, but can also be an excellent guide to excavation strategy should more destructive intervention be thought desirable.

Yet, clearly, there are complex relationships between tillage, the distribution of artefacts in the plough zone and the underlying archaeological record. These depend on the form of surface disturbance, the nature of the assemblage gathered in the field, the character of the underlying features, and the subsequent transformations of that record. Hence problems will arise when interpreting patterns of artefact distributions on plough-damaged sites in the countryside. How closely do patterns of finds from the topsoil reflect underlying activities?

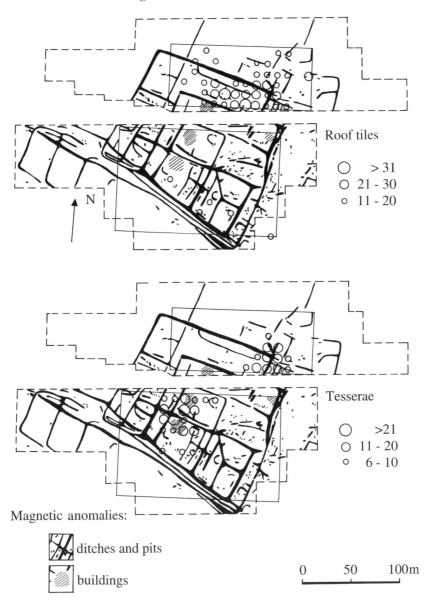

Roof tiles

○   > 31
○   21 - 30
○   11 - 20

Tesserae

○   >21
○   11 - 20
○   6 - 10

Magnetic anomalies:

ditches and pits

buildings

0   50   100m

Figure 2 The distribution of Roman roof tiles and *tesserae* plotted against features indicated by magnetic anomalies from a site near the medieval village of Wharram Percy in North Yorkshire. Clear concentrations of each artefact type indicate ranges of rooms which had better-quality roofing and mosaic floors.

Do particular concentrations indicate actual occupation zones or merely the pattern of former manuring regimes in the landscape which incorporate artefacts from settlements situated elsewhere? Thus it has been argued (Frink 1984) that we can make estimates concerning site size and artefact density, and perhaps set out some experimental laws concerning vertical and horizontal displacement and the vertical distribution of artefacts, but that site function and cultural association may be beyond our grasp.

Since that claim was made, some progress in these matters is suggested as we have moved from studies which simply try to estimate these relationships (Odell and Cowan 1987) to those which use simulation studies to model the processes involved (Boismier 1997). For example, closer inspection of the character of the artefact assemblage itself (e.g., sherd size or abrasion suggesting redeposition) and of the degree of concentration which the finds exhibit may help to decide between manuring and occupation. In addition, size distribution of degradable artefacts such as low-fired pottery can indicate the depth from which material in plough soil assemblages has been disturbed (Dunnell and Simek 1995). Finally, repeated exercises over the same area may allow us not only to monitor the long-term impact of ploughing (Ammerman 1985), but also to get a more accurate picture of the character of the site below (Shott 1995).

These recent developments in analysing the results of field-walking may have been impressive but many such exercises elsewhere remain unsystematic, and indeed unimaginative, underpinned by the assumption that artefacts from topsoil are essentially unstratified assemblages and therefore of little use in understanding buried or destroyed features. Only when the relationship, albeit a complex one, between topsoil finds and associated features is acknowledged, can we start to understand it better. Then the use of field-walking as an accurate predictive tool will increase and, hopefully, we can heed Haselgrove *et al.*'s plea (1985: 2) to move towards an integrated process of plough soil investigation, intervention by selective excavation, and artefactual studies, to allow social reconstruction.

3.3 Shovel test pits/divoting

Where the landscape concerned does not allow the collection of surface finds, for example when working within forested or other heavily vegetated areas, more interventionist methods such as cutting divots or shovel test pits may be used. Such methods are especially important in areas which are spatially extensive but likely to contain only shallow stratigraphy. They involve the excavation of a small volume of soil at regular intervals along survey transects, digging out the deposit and inspecting it for evidence of former human activity such as the presence of artefacts. Turning over small divots will simply expose any material immediately below the turf, whereas shovel test pits will be dug down to, or perhaps just below, the subsoil, though usually without the careful attention to any stratigraphic changes within the pit which only the systematical use of a trowel would allow. Finds recovery can be by eye, with perhaps the position of individual items measured in ('piece-plotting') when they appear, or by use of a screen with a designated mesh size.

Such a technique, employing very small sampling units (typically 0.5m square), means any interpretation must be based on sampling fractions which are minute in areal terms. Obviously its effectiveness depends on the size of the soil samples, their spacing and patterning in relation to any underlying former occupation zone, the artefact density which that area embodies, and the recovery methods used to gather finds (Stone 1981). Detailed methodologies have been developed in the course of recent decades, initially with an understandable focus on probability sampling (Lovis 1976) and regional levels of analysis (Krakker *et al.* 1983), under the influence of processualist explanation in archaeology and its common emphasis on environmental factors. Subsequently, the theoretical perspectives which such research designs embody have been much debated, for example in relation to the issue of 'the site' and siteless surveys, as have the strengths and weaknesses of the methods themselves (Lightfoot 1986, Nance and Ball 1986). This is, in part, a reaction to the suggestion that shovel testing may be of limited utility in discovering sites in the landscape, let alone elucidating their internal configuration (Shott 1985).

However, work by McManamon (1984), comparing shovel testing with coring, augering and divoting in relation to five types of evidence for sites, concluded that, in general, shovel testing was the most effective of the probing techniques. Kintigh (1988) has further outlined the efficiency and effectiveness of various designs of shovel test survey. Although it is clear that one must take account of a large number of pitfalls and biases, and even then may be able to reach only guarded, provisional conclusions, this does not, in itself, demonstrate that such exercises are invalid – nobody said that sampling in archaeology was easy! Hence it is no surprise to find that, recently, certain archaeological curators have felt sufficiently confident of their background knowledge of their region to stipulate quite exact sampling strategies. In Maryland, for example, although acknowledging the need to relate such strategies to the expected size and frequency of a site, curatorial staff propose the use of test pits comprising circular holes dug to the width of a shovel blade (c.35cm) and to the depth of subsoil which is devoid of 'cultural material' (Schaffer and Cole 1994, 20), though continuing for another 10cm through the subsoil to be sure this has been correctly identified. Finds are recovered using a ¼ in. mesh and bagged, etc., and deposit colouration and texture recorded, in the normal way.

3.4 Documentary material

The general relationship between documentary history and archaeological fieldwork was mentioned in the previous chapter. When we come on to the more detailed matter of finding new sites and modelling deposits on known examples, references from a great variety of written sources may be relevant. These range from the intentionally informative history of an area, perhaps describing the monuments which existed there at a particular point in time, to the casual aside, for example that of a medieval legal case which reported flooding, or even deaths by drowning, in a particular sector of a settlement, thus showing its tendency to have a high water table. Similarly, place names, either of whole towns or villages, specific areas, or individual streets or fields can be fed into the equation to elucidate apparent ground conditions and thus help in characterising the deposits one is likely to encounter.

Of course, in using this information, problems arise. Some are the sole concern of the documentary historian, others more wide-ranging: Are we certain that the document is not a fake? How accurately dated is it? How consistent is the use of terminology? Such matters obviously influence whether an archaeologist can predict the location of an event accurately, or have a reasonable expectation that a particular building or type of feature once existed at a site. Further difficulties arise over terminology. Do the terms employed in a document translate into recognisable archaeological features? This is a problem not only with references to legal rights and privileges, as might be expected, but even with documents which purport to refer directly to physical objects (consider the difficulties in correlating the material remains of the Berlin Wall with references to it in newspaper articles from both Eastern and Western blocs before the wall was pulled down, or even afterwards when the Cold War had ended). None the less, desktop studies skimming or trawling through the documents, either from secondary sources or, more reliably, with the primary material held in the local records office, is generally an essential preliminary to any excavation project.

3.5 Previous excavations

Before tackling new sites, any information from previously published archaeological work in the vicinity will obviously have to be taken into account. However, the information must be treated with great care in order not to be misleading, especially with very old observations. The work should include a careful consideration of the recording conditions, the attitude and expertise of the recorder, and the meaning of the terms used and how consistently they were employed – in essence the use of the thought processes followed in any documentary study. Locating earlier work may require searching not only formal publications in local journals and printed ephemera such as local newspapers, but also unpublished materials held in archives at museums or at a variety of less formal establishments. Some areas are fortunate in that the majority of the relevant material has been assimilated into an enhanced sites and monuments record or an implications survey. However, the standard achieved in these studies will vary across any region.

In planning an excavation, it can also be vital to draw on the knowledge of local inhabitants. This is especially useful in relation to recent changes and disturbances of the site or aspects which might influence the character of former occupation, such as a propensity to produce subsidence in present buildings due to underlying features. Here locals may know much about immediate ground conditions which has escaped the notice of statutory agencies. Of course, the use of this type of evidence can raise many problems. An example from my early experience concerns a site in Minchinhampton, Gloucestershire. Here we were told by successive 'informed' villagers looking over the fences around our trenches that the mounds which we were being paid (much to their amazement) to investigate were either part of a modern golf course, glider traps from the Second World War, or medieval rabbit warrens: in fact anything other than the late prehistoric ditches which we hoped for. In the event, the humps turned out to be entirely natural landscape features. This cautionary tale is, of course, a recommendation to be careful, not to suggest ignoring suggestions out of hand.

3.6 Ground-based remote sensing

On the more technical and scientific side, various methods of ground-based remote sensing can be used to elucidate site geometry before excavation. Thus techniques such as infrared photography can be used to register ephemeral features on the surface of a site which are otherwise invisible to both conventional photography and the human eye. However, it is geophysics which has been used more intensively in remote sensing up until now. Indeed, developments here have been at the forefront of applied archaeological science since the 1970s (Aspinall 1992), and examples of specific applications abound, whether in America (Vogel and Tsokas 1993), Britain (Gaffney *et al.* 1991 and English Heritage 1995 plus bibliography) or the continent of Europe (Hesse 1978, Bossuet 1980). Initial work went into the development of hardware, but recent developments in computer technology have promoted a move towards the automation of data capture and hence much larger-scale surveys (Gaffney *et al.* 1998). The two most common methods are resistivity and magnetometry, the latter first as gradiometry, then with a more recent emphasis on magnetic susceptibility.

Resistivity was the first approach to be used, pioneered in Britain from the

1950s by Atkinson (1963) and soon after by Clark (1990: 15ff) and others. A resistivity meter registers changes in the electrical resistance in the ground, itself largely a function of the amount and distribution of moisture within soil. As buried remains affect this (e.g., the stones of a wall may be more resistant to water than the surrounding area, the fills of a ditch less resistant), then patterning in electrical resistance can be indicative of upstanding or intrusive features below the ground.

Magnetometry and magnetic susceptibility survey was promoted from the late 1950s under the stimulus of Aitken and others (Aitken *et al.* 1958) both for dating purposes and to register sub-surface features, using either a fluxgate or a proton magnetometer to register patterning in distortion of the earth's magnetic field. Iron, held in compounds such as magnetite, haematite and maghaematite, can be redistributed or changed into more magnetic forms by human activity. The classic cases of such modification occur with the operation of kilns, hearths, etc., which reach a sufficiently high temperature for the oxides to be completely de-magnetised, then re-magnetised by the earth on cooling. However, much weaker effects can be caused by simply redistributing material when back-filling a ditch or pit. Thus anomalies in the magnetic field can register the below-ground existence of a variety of features. However, as with other ground-based systems, negative results can never be proof of an absence of archaeological features.

Various other methods of ground-based remote sensing have been utilised in archaeological fieldwork. For present purposes, it is useful to mention dowsing, which is probably the most debatable and has the longest history; radar, which has caused a stir in the last few years; and vegetation surveys, which shade into the sphere of aerial photography. Exactly how dowsing works is unclear (indeed, some would maintain that it has not been *scientifically* demonstrated to do so), though the existence of magnetic material in the front of human skulls, as is known from other vertebrates, has been claimed as being of critical importance (Thompson and Oldfield 1986). Whatever the explanation, perhaps the initial scepticism of many commentators can be tempered with a more open-minded approach. Evidence discussed by Bailey *et al.* (1988) has led them to suggest that dowsing is capable of recovering details of construction phases of underground features.

Radar works by transmitting a short pulse of radio energy from an antenna on, or near, the ground which is then partially reflected back to a receiving antenna at some measured delay time. Changes in reflected signal are a function of the electrical conductivity and water content of the ground below. Thus underlying anomalies which result from archaeological features can be recognised (Plate 6). (See Conyers and Goodman 1997, plus refs., for further elaboration.) The development of such techniques has been heralded on many sides, both as a means to discover more information before excavation and to protect important sites from the ravages of modern redevelopment (Batey

Plate 6 RADAR equipment being used to investigate the periphery of a Roman fort at Lambaesis, Algeria. Data, once gathered, were downloaded using equipment set up in the landrover and viewed on screen there. Rather than trying to pick up individual features, the objective here was to chart changes in the 'background noise' of signals in order to understand how general occupation spread beyond the fort walls and along the roads leading from its gates.

1987, Imai *et al.* 1987, Stove and Addyman 1989, Aitkin and Milligan 1992). However, recent trials (Campbell 1991) suggest that more caution is required. Radar may eventually revolutionise the process of remote sensing, particularly for monitoring the condition of standing structures (Tealby *et al.* 1993), but this will take place only after proper testing, the development of new hardware and the creation of new methods of processing and filtering the data derived from the field such as amplitude slice maps (Conyers and Cameron 1998).

The analysis of vegetation patterns on a site before excavation has been used regularly in many projects, but is rarely discussed in more general terms. These work on the same basis as crop marks – that underground features affect plant growth on the surface. In particular, certain types of plant are more likely to take hold after disturbance of the ground by human activity, so charting their distribution can be informative. It would be possible, of course, to sow such plants before excavation in an intentional experiment. However, much more common is to use an existing convenient by-product and survey plant cover above the site before excavation starts. Barker (1977) has drawn attention to intermediate stages on seasonally conducted excavations, where areas which have lain fallow can be inspected for differential plant growth to elucidate the

characteristics of the underlying stratigraphy. Knowledge of the present vegetation can help excavators plan in advance for the destructive effects of root
action, whether as a major cause of possible artefact intrusion in the case of
large tree roots, or more generally destructive of the uppermost deposits in the
sequence due to plants such as bracken (Figure 3). Thus the information
derived can both guide excavation strategy and, given that certain plants are
more destructive of underlying cultural deposits than others, be used as a management tool when designing strategies to protect the site.

The relative strengths and weaknesses of the methods outlined above are an
important area of research which is now starting to receive the attention it
deserves (Weymouth 1986 summarises techniques (Table 6.9), as does English
Heritage 1995 (Table 2); Clark 1990 and Gaffney and Gater 1991 discuss the
issues more generally). Two lessons seem clear. First the different techniques
are effective on different soils and for different types of feature. They must
therefore be used in a complementary way. For example, recent work with radar
suggests that, if used in conjunction with an initial resistivity survey, it can give
greater detail to our understanding of particular features and areas. Second,
experiments to judge the efficacy of different methods must be carried out in
controlled scientific conditions in a variety of well-defined geological and cultural contexts and, if the results are to be really useful, must be followed up by
excavation to validate initial indications. The Sutton Hoo excavations provide
an example of what is possible (Gorman 1985, Carver 1986). Thus the full
exploitation of remote sensing requires interaction, both between different
techniques and in relation to subsequent excavation work, via a nested research
design then completion of the full research cycle to facilitate feedback.

3.7 Chemical mapping

At a slightly more interventionist level, various chemical analyses of topsoil can
inform excavation practice by identifying occupation areas in advance. Trace
metal accumulations (Bintliff *et al.* 1992) are one way forward here which may
become more useful in the near future. However, phosphate sampling is presently much more popular, with awareness of its archaeological use now at least
thirty years old (see Deetz and Dethlefsen 1963), though its potential was
apparently appreciated much earlier, in Egypt in 1911 (Clark 1990: 11). The
technique has been used intensively, for example in Mesoamerica following up
the work of Eidt (1974, 1984). It rests on the fact that naturally occurring phosphate in soils is concentrated by animals, so that the burial of bones, excrement
or food refuse can create particular foci. Phosphate in the soil is usually converted into an insoluble form or fixed to inorganic compounds, so these concentrations can be registered for a long time after the original date of deposition.

Thus high phosphate readings relative to the background noise in the area

Yorkshire Fog and Spring Beauty Yorkshire Fog *(Holcus lanatus)*
Sheep's Fescue *(Festuca ovina)* Moss *(Polytrichum* sp.*)*
Spring Beauty *(Montia perfoliata)* Bracken *(Pteridium aquilinum)*
Exposed sandy soil and Gorse *(Ulex* sp.*)*
Outline of burial mound

N

0   50   100m

Figure 3 A vegetation survey at the Sutton Hoo site, plotted as part of the pre-excavation evaluation. Some plants correlate with mound positions; others cross such boundaries. Growth of particular species could also help to indicate whether underlying disturbance of the site was very recent, took place in the last few decades, or was more ancient.

can indicate the earlier manipulation of soil chemistry, whether through artificial fertilisation or nutrient depletion, and thus the presence of human occupation and perhaps the existence of a site. Further, the distribution of readings within a defined zone can be used to suggest where the more intensively occupied areas might lie (Figure 4). (See also Proudfoot 1976 and, for an

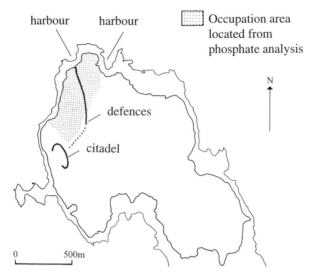

Figure 4 Mapping of phosphates can give a focus to subsequent site work. In the south of the settlement here at Birka, Sweden, there is a significant correlation between the extent of occupation implied by phosphate distribution and the area enclosed by the town's defences but, to the north-east, high phosphate readings extend beyond that defensive line. It was thought either that this was caused by the area being used as a cemetery, rather than occupation *per se*, or that it indicated an earlier settlement area excluded when defences were added in the tenth century AD. However, recent coring has cast some doubt on both hypotheses and further fieldwork will be needed to explain this anomaly.

excellent résumé of methods and brief bibliography, Gurney 1985, plus Balaam and Porter 1991 for a useful case study, and Ball and Kelsay 1992 and Dunning *et al.* 1997 plus refs. for work in central America.) Statistical analyses of results can help further define site boundaries (Hassan 1981) and variations within 'the site' thus defined can be plotted using techniques such as 'Change Point Analysis' (Cavanagh *et al.* 1988).

Other work (Craddock *et al.* 1985) has demonstrated that the phosphate content of even disturbed horizons such as topsoil is a useful indicator of previous occupation, vitally important because aerial photography and field-walking are best at identifying the existence of just such disturbed sites. Experimental work done at Tadworth (Hampton *et al.* 1977) shows that a combination of aerial photography, phosphate sampling and electromagnetic survey produces the most effective results, whilst work in Ecuador (Lippi 1988) has used phosphate sampling in conjunction with systematic soil-coring. Such studies serve to reinforce the idea that the use of a suite of methods will have an exponential rather than just cumulative effect in our ability to predict sub-surface features before any formal disturbance of the ground and, as in the

Ecuador example, may mean sometimes that more destructive interventions can be avoided entirely.

3.8 Coring and augering

In many cases archaeological deposits lie at some depth below the surface, and will not therefore become visible by ploughing or inspecting divots. Here techniques which are still more interventionist than those described so far may be required. Bore holes, originally used to obtain samples for sedimentary dating, are now a common method of site evaluation, their use ranging from the minimalist taking of thin soil cores to the use of much more destructive auger holes. Relevant data may be generated either by cores drilled for entirely commercial reasons, for example to elucidate geological formations to help with designing future building foundations, or by intentionally implemented archaeological sampling strategies (Bailey and Thomas 1987). The importance of coring has been further enhanced by the use of mechanical corers, which are virtually essential for large-scale work (Canti and Meddens 1998). Yet for smaller projects, especially those in less accessible areas or countries with limited resources apart from person power, the hand corer can still be an effective instrument.

Chance bore holes can provide information on the height and character of the natural stratigraphy and an outline of the nature and depth of the cultural accumulation above this. Also finds collected from such operations can give a rough idea of date range. These indications, although fairly general, may directly affect the timetable of work, the resources required, methods of recording, and possibly even the amount of detail that the excavation can realistically aim for. Close-interval cores can then be used to provide more detailed understanding on internal site structure (Hoffman 1993). Similarly, augering data may be used, first, to identify accurately the specific position of buried features and then, perhaps, to sort them into broad functional categories prior to their excavation (Whalen 1990).

However, as already noted in the discussion of sampling strategies in fieldwalking and shovel testing, interpretation of the results of coring, and how they might be used to define excavation strategy, are contested areas (Stein 1986, 1991, Schuldenrein 1991). The issues here revolve around technical, archaeological and intellectual factors. For example, it is obvious one should not expect a simple relationship between auger sherd counts and the real, below-ground assemblages, in terms of either the number of sherds recovered, the proportion of different fabrics, or their size (Howell 1993). Equally there will be variability between archaeological sites in terms of their horizontal and vertical extent, the nature of the remains and their degree of survival. These are factors which most would readily recognise, but sampling strategies must also accommodate a third factor, that research objectives will vary between field projects (Orton

2000: 126). Finally, even when used as part of a proper sampling exercise, the results of coring and augering work may require highly sophisticated and mathematically demanding statistical manipulation to exploit their full potential.

3.9 Evaluation trenches

Whether one uses coring or augering to model deep deposits, or to define site edges, follow features off-site, or provide samples for particular specialists, the results of such work will rarely, of themselves, provide enough information to enable one to develop a full excavation strategy, except in the most general terms (Canti and Meddens 1998). Hence, in order to formulate detailed plans, it will often be essential to use a more destructive component of pre-excavation operations, the recording of various types of evaluation trenches, in advance of the main excavation. Here important evidence can be obtained from sources not focussed directly on archaeological investigation, for example by monitoring commercial trenches dug to test the nature of the foundations of nearby standing buildings to ensure their safety before the archaeologists move in. These operations can be particularly useful in giving basic information on levels of natural strata and obtaining dating evidence from artefacts disturbed in the process, but may even allow more accurate recording in drawn sections on occasion. Also variations in the character and depth of the modern foundations can give vital information on the nature of the underlying stratigraphic accumulation, for example if they are deepened to compensate for unstable strata, and on the type of building techniques adopted.

Second, in more archaeological vein, emptying modern cellars or other recent disturbances can be very informative. This may clarify where double basements, more destructive than single ones, are sited, which can influence trench positions when excavation starts. Looking at cellar plans may even suggest areas where stratigraphy survives to unexpected heights, for example below a modern lane or road providing access between basemented buildings. However, such hints will usually be of a fairly general nature, and much more information can be revealed only if the cellar walls are removed and the strata previously hidden behind them recorded by drawing the extant sections. This can give an extremely detailed picture of the depth, complexity and physical character of the stratigraphic accumulation at that point (Plate 7).

Of course, fortuitous sections, though useful, will not always be available, or may not fall in the most appropriate places. Furthermore, even where such intrusions are numerous (which of course also means a reduction in the amount of stratigraphy available for investigation in the excavation proper), generalising from limited and chance observations to create a deposit model for the whole site is inherently chancy. Pre-excavation work may therefore have to

Plate 7 The removal of a cellar wall allows the extant stratigraphy behind it to be exposed, cleaned and drawn. The record thus contributes to a more detailed deposit model than can be derived from coring or augering.

include preliminary trenching of the proposed excavation area with explicit archaeological objectives. This could take the form, at one end of the spectrum, of a machine-dug trench beneath the planned position of the spoil heap or, at the other, controlled excavation of a series of 2m × 2m boxes carefully positioned in what seem to be critically important areas where preliminary information is entirely lacking. Obviously, the more care that can be taken with these activities, the more useful the results will be in future planning. Also, if the recording system used in this preliminary work is designed both in terms of the information required from evaluation and with an eye to the likely data structure used on the main excavation, then integration of the two data sets will be that much easier.

Even when dug with the greatest care, one can question the ability of sampling trenches to discover features and estimate their overall frequency on a site to known levels of accuracy (Shott 1987). Here the lessons from techniques used in more general surveys might be applied to allow us to estimate more accurately the probability that a site of a certain size and shape will be intersected by transects (Sundstrom 1993). In this way it should be possible to calculate the probability that an evaluation trench of given dimensions will intersect a specific feature-type of predefined form and density.

Clearly, both carrying out this preliminary evaluation work, and then interpreting its output for use in the full excavation, are technically demanding and quite specialised tasks, not to mention often potentially dangerous. It is not, therefore, a job for the inexperienced person who is not up to 'proper' excavation work in controlled conditions. Rather than shoving a novice down a hole with notebook and torch and telling her to do her best (though such equipment may be most vital), it requires the attention of the most experienced fieldworker. Equally, interpretation of results must be done with awareness of all the pitfalls if one is to construct a meaningful excavation strategy thereafter. None the less, when carried out expertly, and interpreted with care, such evaluation can produce at least an outline, and on occasion a very detailed model, of the deposits surviving on the site.

3.10 Conclusions

As shown above, a variety of techniques can be used to discover new sites, and to throw light on their internal configuration and physical character before formal excavation starts. Aerial photography and field-walking remain the two most important ways in which new sites enter the archaeological arena. After this, a perusal of documentary sources, including reports of earlier excavations, may give more detailed information about the particular area, and even about the specific site conditions. This picture can then be greatly enhanced by recording the residual effects of former occupation still sealed beneath the ground, using a variety of ground-based remote sensing equipment and chemical sampling, throwing light on the spatial configuration of features and perhaps indicating differential occupation across the area. Finally, the use of more interventionist techniques such as bore holes and evaluation trenches can produce stratigraphic and chronological knowledge. *In toto*, therefore, the evidence derived from this work allows the archaeologist to create a detailed deposit model of the site before any full-scale excavation takes place. When this model is set beside the pre-existing academic agenda, there can be one of three results: excavation may be deemed inappropriate; work may need to take place immediately; or archaeological investigation may be desirable but only become feasible after some technical development of further field methods.

In the worst case, the deposit model may show that the type of questions being asked simply cannot be answered on this site. For example, strata dating to the high medieval period may have been truncated previously, so the central issue of the project – the change in thirteenth-century society – cannot be elucidated here. Or organic survival may be lacking, so the site will yield none of the precious textile fragments which are thought central to its investigation. Perhaps the stratigraphic accumulation may be insufficiently complex to yield information on those relations between adjacent property holders known from documentary sources. Or it may be so complex that associated artefacts are mainly redeposited and would provide none of the clean finds groups required by the research design, and so forth. Hence further work would be a waste of time and money.

Alternatively, it may be that the questions posed of a site are answerable from the surviving deposit and with the techniques and personnel presently available to gather the data. Even if the evaluation exercise simply confirms one's hopes in this way (and suggests that one might be asking some very boring questions!), this should not be seen as lessening the importance of the preparatory work. First, it is always useful to have suspicions confirmed before expending more resources. Second, the survey is quite likely to suggest that particular parts of the site have more research potential than others and to allow them to be ranked accordingly, thus influencing the position and size of appropriate trenches. In addition, more accurate decisions can be made on the resources required and the personnel needed on the project, in both their number and their expertise. Also it may let one predict a need, and thus plan, for certain specialist facilities such as artefact conservation. Evaluation can then simplify decisions on the form of the archaeological record and, accordingly, aid in the creation of an appropriate, standardised recording system.

Third, evaluation may show that the questions being asked of the site may *become* answerable, but only if strata receive a certain amount of enhancement to yield up their secrets. This may involve anything from the simple use of water sprays which heighten stratigraphic distinctions, to implementing research to invent new techniques, thus requiring time to create the methods and to test them in experiment. A classic example of this process in action was the Sutton Hoo excavation project (see Carver 1986). Here the setting of the Anglo-Saxon research agenda in the most general terms, with its emphasis on socio-economic and religious transformation and early medieval state formation, allowed the creation of an 'activity model' when applied to the specific site itself. This more refined and focussed agenda required the elucidation of burial practices, a type of information difficult to obtain on a sand-site where bones of human skeletons survived only as stains. To make data-recovery possible, new techniques were developed to give a 'visibility model'. Their application then allowed the 'sand men' of Sutton Hoo to make their appearance. In short, the deposit model shows what is in the bank, and the research agenda indicates whether it is worth withdrawing it. If so, and if the keys to the vaults already exist, it is a matter of hiring efficient key turners. If not, keys have to be fashioned beforehand by active research and tested out, people trained in their use, and the vault opened.

The use of a variety of evaluation techniques, especially destructive ones such as small holes in trial work, has come under a certain amount of criticism, for example being portrayed as 'too small for real observation' (Reynolds and Barber 1984: 98). However, this objection rather misses the point. Obviously, the size and shape of the trench needed will vary, depending on the question being asked. Opening up a smaller area will limit the type of information recoverable at that point. However, the real decision is not to choose *in principle* between the open-area excavation and narrow *sondages*; rather the more practical question is how to use a particular set of resources. This depends on the questions being asked, where one is in the research cycle, and the character of the deposits on the site. The above description of evaluation techniques and their application has sought to show that any sophisticated excavation project can only hope to be successful once it has modelled the deposit likely to be encountered on the site in the fullest possible way, utilising a variety of desk-based and field techniques, before deciding whether or not to intervene more forcefully on a larger scale and, if so, how.

4

EXCAVATION IN PRACTICE: BACKGROUND PREPARATIONS

Introduction

In Chapter 2 it was argued that practical preparations for excavation should be a product of research objectives, not a precursor to their being established. Hence any project should, from the start, employ an academic research design to generate the financial support, staff and legal permissions which are an essential preliminary to actually starting on site. Equally, initial site evaluation outlined in Chapter 3 will not only produce a deposit model and thus suggest which area(s) should be dug, but also indicate the extent of the human and material resources required to do this, including any particular specialist facilities and expertise. The organisation of these general resources is the subject of this chapter.

Such preparations should aim to provide finance, set up public relations systems, hire excavation personnel and even accommodate the concerns of local political organisation. Thus it may be necessary to employ simple management techniques such as Gantt charts and critical path scheduling (Bleed 1983). Long (1974) provides a convenient example of the system of overall strategy used on one, fairly large, urban excavation project in Manchester (Figure 5). The inputs–process–output, represented in a flow diagram, is clearly a product of the then prevalent influence of functionalist 'systems theory' in archaeology but serves rather well to make the point that it is essential to plan tasks in a clear and appropriate order, with the relationships between different elements strictly defined. In short, an explicitly structured approach is needed throughout.

Of course, in the real world, things never happen exactly as they are meant to. In particular, full financial backing for the original project may not be forthcoming, so one must cut one's cloth accordingly. However, the cycle of decision-making is worth pursuing, even in this fluid context. For example, the provision of a lower level of funding than originally planned may mean backtracking to see how best to spend what has been made available. Rather than writing off the whole venture or cutting back arbitrarily by a set percentage across the board, it may be possible to modify the original research agenda, or to rerank the research objectives, with excavation areas altered accordingly.

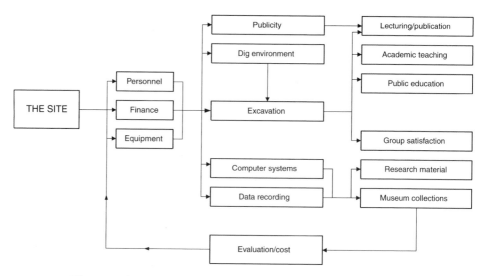

Figure 5 The excavation strategy adopted in an excavation project in Manchester in the mid-1970s. Although the diagram itself, and the language used to express the approach, is very much a product of the then-current 'systems theory' in archaeology, the principles which it expresses are still relevant today.

Although excavations take a great many organisational forms and have a variety of objectives, they all have some general factors, and so certain background preparations, in common. Thus almost all projects need financial support, no matter how minimal, in the form of either real funds or help-in-kind. They also require a system to administer these resources and cover legal and other matters (detailed in **4.1** below). Similarly, all projects need site personnel to work on photographic recording, surveying and excavating. Employing people can only be effective when preceded by the setting up of a variety of support systems concerned with displaying results to visitors, providing environmental and finds processing and conservation facilities, and developing or buying-in computer systems (**4.2**). Furthermore, all staff need a safe environment in which to do their work. This requires an understanding of general legislation, organising insurance cover, catering for problems such as electricity cables or gas supply pipes which remain in use ('live services'), setting up rest facilities on site, providing a safe context for moving about the excavation and for using plant and machinery, and establishing an accident recording system for when things go wrong (**4.3**). Finally, special safety situations bring with them more particular problems, as with salvage work, where one is allowed merely to oversee building operations and record deposits as they are removed only in rudimentary fashion, if at all (a 'watching brief' in British parlance); operating within buildings which are either redundant but still standing, or in need of archaeological recording ahead of internal refurbishment; or uncovering and lifting human burials (**4.4**).

4.1 Finance and administration

Few excavations can work with absolutely no funding, if only money for bus fares to get to the site. The sources of funding for a project are many and various, but no project will even start to be supported unless the team knows what it wants and why. Thus projects with research objectives up front are not only the most logical and academically desirable, but also those which stand the best chance of sponsorship. Presenting a coherent strategy of work will appeal more readily to funding agencies wanting to be assured, above all, that their money is being spent in an effective and proper fashion. Of course, obtaining support for archaeological research is a time-consuming, and often cyclical, process. Thus academic objectives are outlined; some support is gained but not enough to complete the whole agenda; objectives are modified and some slanted in a slightly different direction to link in the interests of a second potential sponsor; another source provides further input, and so forth. With such horse-trading, clear overall objectives becomes even more vital than ever.

Sources of funding can be split into three sections. Government agencies at local, regional or central level can be expected to support some work within their jurisdiction or, on occasion, outside it. Next private institutions, most obviously companies who wish to develop a site, so creating a threat to its archaeological remains, may have to resource excavations by law in order to obtain planning permissions to redevelop, or simply to avoid tarnishing their reputation. Finally, particular individuals, charitable bodies or commercial businesses may have an enlightened view towards 'cultural activities and the arts' or even 'public access to the sciences' (archaeology is fortunate in having a legitimate foot in both camps). They may therefore give donations because they see archaeology as being good for their image, which it undoubtedly is.

In nearly every case, getting sufficient funds will require contact with, if not an in-depth understanding of, local politics. Knowledge of how the wind blows at an early stage, or better still personal contact, often pays unexpected dividends in the longer term. This is not a matter of compromising one's integrity as an archaeologist to achieve results, or even of subverting the democratic process, such as it may be. Rather it's a case of presenting your work in a way that is appropriate and accessible to those who may be interested in supporting it. Fund raising is complicated by the fact that the various types of funding institutions have very different deadlines and lead-in times for applications (there is nothing more depressing than being told that you would have received support for a project if only you had applied before the biannual meeting of the appropriate committee which took place the week before). Matching the deliberations of an academic committee, which meets rarely, with the requirements of a dynamic developer, who offers to fund part of the fieldwork if you can start next week, requires a difficult balancing act.

As mentioned above, procuring funds for a project is usually a cumulative process in which getting support from one area then persuades another sponsor to match this, ECU for ECU or dollar for dollar. It may even be necessary to begin with a certain level of funding, then look for more support once the project has started to prove itself. Such a chancy strategy is best accommodated by a nested research design, which makes successive stages of the work clear and prevents a piecemeal expansion of activities. In fact, this approach may be entirely appropriate and archaeologically respectable. For example, finance may be obtained for site evaluation. Then, when the project is proven to have considerable potential to answer a set of designated research questions, one can begin to search for much larger resources on a more convincing, rational basis. With careful preparation, it is usually possible to find sufficient latitude in the way that funding mechanisms operate to promote, rather than reduce, what is desirable from an archaeological point of view.

Finally, all funding bodies will require feedback on the progress and results of the work, in part to enable them to monitor the spending of their funds. Some, particularly those who give money out of interest in the work itself rather than as a statutory requirement, may need specially organised site tours, lectures, displays, articles for company magazines, etc. Of course, names of sponsors, whether government, private bodies or individuals will have to be carefully recorded, so that their help can be accurately acknowledged in any publications.

Excavation may use not only financial support: **help-in-kind** is equally useful. This can take a variety of forms, including the provision of administrative services (dealing with accounts, providing office space), giving specialist advice (documentary research on the area by a local historian, stone identification from the local university geology department) or lending excavation equipment (dumper trucks from the site developer who is already building elsewhere, chest freezers for storage of water-logged wood on site from the local freezer centre). Sometimes getting such facilities is just a matter of asking for them, sometimes it takes a little badgering. More often than not, the request is met not with refusal but with surprise, because it has simply never occurred to them that archaeologists can provide interim protection for organic materials by freezing them, or that they get paid wages for their work and so need to be linked in to a taxation system. Help-in-kind can be especially useful when working on projects abroad, where it is simply impossible to bring with you all the equipment which you might need.

However, there are dangers in looking around for such resources, which may lead to running a project on a shoestring, and never providing vital equipment from a central source. This not only is undesirable in the short term for the efficient working of the particular project, but may also generate an attitude in the donors that archaeology is an unprofessional, unstructured hobby of a few curious individuals who have to beg, borrow or steal materials to get by. Over time this can only be detrimental to the proper resourcing of excavation projects.

Such difficulties can be guarded against by keeping core equipment centrally supported, and seeing help-in-kind as a very useful addition to a project rather than as fundamental to its running.

It is also important, when accepting such offers, to ensure that what is being donated is exactly what is needed, or at least that it is useful rather than a liability. For example, someone outside the project may decide that what you really require is their largest mechanical digger for a day to quickly remove all that boring overburden and get down to the 'real archaeology' of substantial town-houses underneath. This may not correspond exactly with your research objectives, designed to look for any traces of ephemeral occupation within that apparently featureless, but highly significant, 'overburden' and then to stop, much to your sponsor's mystification, when you reach the good-quality pavements below. It is also important that any equipment lent to the project is safe in itself and can be used by your staff with a level of expertise which matches that of the usual operators.

Finally, if help is being given in order to get publicity for the donor, one must check that this is acceptable in principle and that there are no objections to the particular type of company and its country of origin from those working on the project or from other institutions and individuals already providing support. With these provisos, it is quite clear that many excavations gain greatly from help-in-kind, both directly in reducing their costs, and more generally in making links between archaeologists active in the field and interested parties working in related areas.

On any large project, financial transactions will require a proper **administrative and accounting system** and qualified staff to run it, dealing with wages, taxation, petty cash (especially important if selling pamphlets or charging entrance fees to the site), and the many other money-handling activities which such an excavation brings with it. Such staff may also have a variety of other organisational responsibilities, such as the reconnection of telephone and electricity for computers and lighting, then monitoring usage and bills; creating a system for supplies of materials which designates who is allowed to request what equipment, and who is accountable in obtaining supplies; chasing outstanding orders and paying invoices; and procuring advice on legal matters such as site and workers' insurance and implementing recommendations.

Although much of this work will be the direct responsibility of office administrators, some archaeological guidance will be needed, especially in setting up systems. For instance, particular types of materials may be required from an archaeological point of view, but this may not be apparent from the distance of an office. To take a (?not so) trivial example, a certain type of coloured pencil may have been designated for site drawing because it is long-lasting and therefore an appropriate archive medium. It is important that those ordering equipment know of this requirement, and that it will not be acceptable to have just any old crayon, or the cheapest available. Such communication will be even more vital for larger, or more technical equipment and is best achieved in regular meetings. In my experience, it can be more effective for the administrator working in the office to visit the site and see the problems first hand, rather than have the muddy field-worker coming to them. This can also be a welcome break from their routine inside. So invite them to your site tours, as well as to the financial crisis meetings.

4.2 Staff and support facilities

The human and technical resources needed on an excavation will flow from its research agenda and the site evaluation, set beside the financial and other support actually obtained. Obviously surprises, for example the particularly special find or unexpectedly surviving architectural feature, can alter the types and level of expertise needed on occasion. However, in most cases the character, and sometimes even the approximate size, of the artefactual assemblage which will result from the work can be known beforehand to assist the organisation of finds work; the sampling strategy for ecofactual materials can be constructed in advance with the help of the environmental scientist; the likelihood and degree of water-logging can be estimated to help the conservator decide on whether organic materials will have to be accommodated; the approximate volume of earth to be dissected archaeologically can be calculated to help in organising spoil disposal and in estimating the number of excavators required, and so forth. Having covered the majority of situations, the unexpected can usually be catered for, and is almost a pleasure.

Employing new staff on a project may require advertising and follow-up interviews, though local conditions of employment can affect whether, and exactly how, this is done. Even if only pre-existing core staff are being used on the project, they will still need to be seen either collectively or individually to explain the research objectives and the role of each person within this. Also their expertise and experience will be useful in adding to the running of the project, so these meetings will be an opportunity to get initial reactions and modify the research strategy accordingly.

Indeed, interaction between team members at an early stage has become more essential in recent years. It was argued above (1.5) that the professionalisation of the archaeological workforce has been generally beneficial to all concerned, in terms of the standards achieved and scale of work allowed. Yet there can be a danger in such developments. Either each project can be merely another step in an unending treadmill for the fieldwork professional, the recording system becomes fossilised, and one site is recorded much like the last, i.e the tail (the unquestioned site manual) wags the dog (the, now-unquestioning, worker). Alternatively, site workers can be seen as simple technicians, with the designation of priorities and techniques the responsibility, and therefore the interest, of the project director alone. Thus the diggers in direct contact with the stratigraphy, whose experience is the most vibrant and useful, have no mechanism to feed this back to the higher echelons who make the real decisions. Both tendencies – either the worship of the site manual, or undue reverence to the director and his personalised recording system – are dead-ends for our discipline. Collaboration at the earliest stage helps set the scene and creates an atmosphere in which the ideas of all of the workforce can start to be incorporated, a process which is then more likely to continue during the remainder of the excavation. The types of demands and staff required are discussed below. The order is not arbitrary, being rather the sequence in which such inputs are likely to be needed on the site.

The most fundamental requirement is for a **safe working environment.** For Droop, writing in 1915, the only mention of first aid was in relation to finds: today, we talk of health and safety in the work-place. Archaeological fieldworkers are portrayed by many people, correctly, as being the discipline's greatest asset, so their safety should be of primary importance to any project – the first responsibility of any site director is not, as often stated, to the material remains being excavated, but to the welfare of the workers under her control. This means providing proper facilities, for example when extremes of climate (Plate 8) demand the provision of a staff room and other facilities. It also means generating a level of awareness of safety in all staff and a systematic approach to implementing precautions. Because of its great importance, the issues involved are treated in detail below (4.3, 4.4)

Facilities for **communicating and displaying** the results of excavation work are also essential. The objective of archaeology is to understand the past in order to relate more fully to the modern world. As discussed previously, drawing out such a relationship is made feasible by the fact that we impose perspectives from that present onto the past in the process of excavating sites. Hence the audience for the results of our work is much wider than just other archaeologists. Both during and after any excavation, we must cater for the vast number of interested people on the periphery of the subject, or even wholly outside it. This requirement seems increasingly recognised by the archaeological community, being taken seriously even at the very highest levels. For example, Montagu (1987) outlined some of the British government's organisational arrangements and specific projects for doing this, including the then-embryonic Maiden Castle scheme. Similar responses are evident lower down, no doubt related to the increased responsibilities which come with greater public funding, and will exist in all quarters of the globe.

However, attitudes to the archaeologically interested public vary considerably. Sometimes they are portrayed as coming from an unscientific lunatic fringe, the job being then to 'constructively cope' with them (Cole 1980), presumably by keeping them at arm's length. Somewhat more dismissive attitudes are apparent in Feder (1984), who was moved to caricature the activities of the

Plate 8 A professional workforce is expected to work all year round, not just in a summer season, so section-drawing in the snow becomes part of everyday life. Hence the provision of proper, warm conditions for breaks in work becomes essential.

'pendulum-swinging psychic'. But how different is such activity from dowsing, or even the use of remote sensing equipment, to the uninitiated? Remember Arthur C. Clarke's dictum that 'any sufficiently advanced technology is indistinguishable from magic'! The lesson here is that our audience becomes interested in archaeology from a variety of points of view, and is never a blank sheet to be written upon using the correct archaeological lettering techniques in order to eliminate the disreputable elements. Also the ideas in people's heads, however wild and inaccurate they may be, are rarely simply irrational. The attitudes of the archaeologists cited above to their public seem, to me, to do little credit to the individuals concerned or to the discipline as a whole.

The objective, then, is to build on a person's existing interests, not to dismiss them as peculiar. At the same time, of course, we have a duty to criticise what we think is false and to promote what is true about the past: to maintain that we should listen to what people have to say is not to suggest that all ideas are equally valid or should not be debated. We clearly have a duty to counter some of the more outlandish interpretations of previous societies seen in popular publications, which approach fiction rather than fact. Yet being aware of their starting point can be the most effective way to put over a different message, one which shows that what is revealed by excavation is more relevant, more inter-

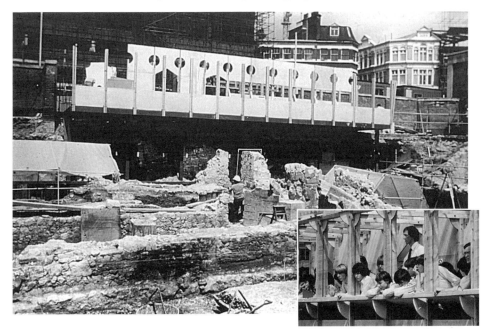

Plate 9 The viewing platform, being erected here with the help of commercial sponsorship, allowed the large, complex excavations at the Billingsgate site in the City of London to be viewed by various audiences. When work was completed, trained guides were able to explain the intricacies of urban archaeology to both school children (*inset*) and office workers.

esting and, sometimes, even more strange than the fictions which aroused their initial curiosity. Developing the public's interest, not showing them who is the intellectual boss, is the main object of any display or site tour.

By talking above of 'the general public', there can be a real danger of appealing only to that section of society already favoured by archaeologists, of preaching to the converted and thereby excluding disabled people, members of ethnic minorities, younger or older age categories, etc. To allow these groups to view the work and come to grips with its results requires practical action and careful consideration of the concepts used in displays and of the language in which they are expressed. Each requires planning, and perhaps allocating some precious finances to employ people who can give talks, produce textual and graphical publicity material, etc. Practical action may be as simple as replacing steps with wheelchair ramps and enhancing the enjoyment of the visually impaired with tactile experiences. However, other visitor access, especially if it involves specialist construction such as viewing platforms, may have considerable implications in terms of structural engineering, legal requirements on visitor safety, and staff to cope with the response (Plate 9).

Often, members of local archaeological groups are best placed to organise such links with the public. They can also make the most appropriate guides, giving visitors undivided attention and being much closer to the types of issues and interests relevant to the local community. Binks *et al.* (1988) have produced a manual of the types of thinking and methods needed. Not everyone will agree with their implicit assumption on the need to package the past as a commodity in order to sell it. However, the book is full of good advice on general aspects of presentation and on the specific wrinkles which turn a good general approach into a viable end product which can attract and then satisfy the (?paying) customers.

In terms of content and language, displays can be used to show how past social development has always involved both sexes and incorporated people from a variety of religious, racial and ethnic backgrounds. It is quite possible to communicate aspects of an excavation successfully using language which avoids talking down to people or cheapening and trivialising the past in the process, provided one targets the audience carefully. An obvious target is young people, if only to guard against archaeology becoming the preserve of the over-40s (Jones 1987). School children, whether in organised groups or as individuals, may need not only special facilities at the excavation but scene-setting and follow-up work. A school visit beforehand, hand-outs on the site in the form of an education pack, and subsequent discussions of areas of misunderstanding or newly aroused areas of interest can ensure that the message gets across. Cracknell and Corbishley (1986) have discussed the many issues relevant to presentation of excavations. After all, a visit to the 'local dig' is that context which embodies, *par excellence*, the immediacy of discovery.

Museologists have been centrally concerned with matters of presentation for a long time and have accumulated a vast body of experience and literature in the process, much of which has yet to be assimilated by archaeological field-workers. The local museum may be the best source of such advice and also provides a route into existing systems and interest groups. The local library is another important point of contact with people, especially since it draws in a more diverse social group than those who would be confident enough to visit an excavation, or even a museum, of their own accord. Lastly, local newspaper columns and radio stations can provide an excellent opportunity to put over our messages to audiences otherwise beyond our reach, such as those house-bound owing to age, disability or child care commitments, or at work in a factory or office during the hours when the excavation is being worked and open for visitor access.

If site information is to be distributed widely using the conventional media of press, radio and television, it is often the site director, or other site personnel, who will be called upon to front these sessions. Sometimes pressure of work dictates that other staff must be used, though be aware that, even though perfectly knowledgeable alternative spokespersons have been provided, some reporters will still demand the direct attention of those at the work-face (O'Connor 1986). It may not be the duty of the director to do all the talking, but it is her duty to organise the system of communication, designate appropriate channels and ensure that correct information, or a least a consistent view, is agreed between all parties. This can be especially important if an excavation is operating in the sort of controversial circumstances which cause a media circus to descend *en masse*.

All of the above will involve a lot of time and effort, but site tours, displays and publicity need not be seen as a necessary chore which unfortunately diverts one from the main activity. Pryor (1989) has emphasised that a high level of academic understanding is a prerequisite of successful communication. Hence such work is not only good public relations but can enhance, rather than compromise, the archaeological integrity of a project. The large number of organisations producing such publicity, as listed for Britain by Crummy (1986), suggests that the profession as a whole is getting the message. The list includes material for use after the excavation has finished, a reminder that public involvement is an extended commitment. Using a combination of top-down approaches with formal publications and the setting up of computer websites, and the bottom-up, direct communication on site and through local media, we can publicise an individual project and promote the public's overall perception of the importance of archaeology to enhance our wider reputation. Yet we can also do our duty by our paying 'customers' into the bargain. Enlightened self-interest and moral requirements here point in the same direction.

Environmental facilities are the next requirement. Ecofactual material is clearly of great relevance in understanding past societies, whether in terms of general background environment (weather, river regimes, etc.) and more local conditions within parts of a settlement, its buildings or their specific rooms; in elucidating food supply and the exploitation of rural regimes; or in the use of animal and plant residues in other processes of production (bone artefacts, ceramic tempering, etc.). It is not surprising, therefore, to find that archaeologists have been interested in gathering material for the last 140 years (Steenstrup 1857, quoted in Orton 2000) However, it is only in the last few decades that even the potential of animal bones, probably the most common archaeological ecofact to be collected, has been fully appreciated, let alone that of carbonised grain or beetle wing cases. Thus, when the general research objectives of a project have been decided, and the level and types of survival on a site are known from evaluation, environmental scientists will help to construct a coherent sampling strategy. This will need to: designate the types of question to be asked of each sample type which is collected; define the type of site formation process, and thus strata, which might be considered relevant to each area of interest; decide on sample sizes and the approximate number of samples which might be expected; and think through the storage requirements and resources needed for subsequent processing.

Some of the work of collecting ecofacts can be done by site workers if they have been properly trained. Murphy and Wiltshire (1994) give full chapter and verse on the practicalities of the work, though publications such as Renfrew *et al.* 1976 and Dimbleby 1978 still have a useful role to play, both in increasing awareness of environmental evidence and in describing some techniques. However, if one is truly to fulfil the potential of archaeological science, specialists must be involved not only at the design stage but also when reacting to different situations as they arise during the work. Indeed, some specialists may insist on taking samples themselves and on seeing the site first-hand before deciding on procedures and possibilities, for example in archaeomagnetic work. In other cases there may have to be more interaction, for instance when processing a sample of residues from a certain deposit to decide whether a more intensive collection strategy is needed for similarly constituted strata.

Ideally, archaeological scientists should engage in discussions at the earliest stage of a project and then go through their reasoning processes with excavators at regular stages as they develop thereafter. In this way, by demystifying the process of scientific work, they can expand awareness and understanding amongst all site staff. This will have a twofold impact. First the potential of environmental work will increase, since excavators will be better able to recognise new sampling opportunities during their work and to raise them with appropriate specialists. Second, the site worker's own expertise will be developed – it should surely be an objective of every excavation project to extend its staff intellectually, and thus enhance their career prospects and personal fulfilment.

Such procedures need not be complex. For example, if the expert osteologist trains site staff in skeletal recognition before starting a long-term cemetery excavation, this will not only expand the expertise available to the project, but will also retain an excavator's interest when under pressure to uncover the seventh skeleton that week as the rushed schedule of the work unfolds. Subsequently, when the fieldwork is finished and the osteologist finds she needs an assistant for some months to gather metrical data from the bones, an interested site worker may come forward to do this. This avoids the need to explain to a newly arrived individual the background to the site work, and gives an extension to the contract of a valuable staff member who is already committed to the project.

The methods used in environmental sampling, and the facilities they require, are many and various, and may be limited by finances or by the physical constraints on the site, for example water supply for sieving/screening deposits (though even these problems can be circumvented with a little thought and ingenuity; see Ganderton 1981 for significant environmental work done with minimal sophisticated equipment). However, it is important not to make necessity into a virtue. Planning can often make things available which are unobtainable at short notice and for some types of process there simply is no substitute for the proper equipment. Further details of recovery procedures and sampling strategies are outlined below.

Finds processing systems must also be created at an early stage. Gathering 'clean' groups of artefacts in controlled conditions is a fundamental objective of many excavation projects, both to gain general knowledge of trade, technology and art, and to throw light on dating and function on particular sites or zones within them. Thus artefact study has been fundamental to much archaeological research from its earliest days. Not surprisingly, then, finds collection policies are needed on nearly every project today and a considerable range of expertise may be demanded in creating such a policy, sometimes requiring background research into previous published work beforehand in order to be fully productive. Gaining the appropriate knowledge places significant demands on any evaluation exercise and requires sufficient lead-in time.

Finds specialists will also be needed regularly during the excavation, both to process the artefacts and to advise on any changes in direction that the work might take as a result of what is being uncovered. For example, the unexpected discovery of *in situ* stonework associated with a standing building may need the advice of an architect to decide whether especially accurate recording is needed. Such action now may then avoid problems later when attempting structural reconstruction: here photogrammetry, though unnecessary the rest of the time, may become essential. If a building seems rather too large to be called a find, consider pot sherds used as dating evidence. Knowing the approximate date of a horizon during excavation, or of a particular feature, may affect the type of record made or even justify the abandonment of an area. Conversely, recognising the existence of particular sherds with a functional significance may lead to recording their position with more than the usual accuracy. Regular spot-dating and brief inspections of finds assemblages allow interaction with recording work on site.

Lastly, there is the issue of finds analysis post-excavation. Sometimes an excavation director may have only a very restricted assemblage to report on, and thus will study the finds herself. Or, even on a finds-rich site, the director may be the last great polymath and have plenty of time to spare before publishing the excavation, so take responsibility for all specialist work. However, back in the real world, different finds experts will be required to work on various artefact types. For reasons given above, such specialists are best selected during the fieldwork stage or, better still, chosen even earlier, when evaluation indicates that certain artefact types are certain to be recovered. This allows them to advise on sampling strategy and to see the types of features involved and the recovery conditions on site, saving a lot of time in explanations, and possible misunderstandings, at the post-excavation stage.

Specialist expertise is one thing, but the majority of finds processing will involve dealing with the more mundane, and for that reason more archaeologically important, materials such as lithics and ceramics. Designated finds assistants, or just the normal site staff, will be involved in a range of processes including cleaning, cataloguing, bagging, transporting and even appraising artefactual assemblages throughout the excavation project, before finally ensuring their proper storage. The demands involved vary greatly with the nature of the site, the type of finds recovery procedures to be adopted being covered in other specialist manuals, notably Orton *et al.* 1993. But provision of facilities to carry out this work – buying containers, labels and pens, obtaining furniture for laying out and sorting artefacts, organising drying facilities and storage racks, hiring transport, etc. – will be the ultimate responsibility of the site director.

The provision of **conservation facilities** is another consideration. Site evaluation may indicate that organic materials are likely to be preserved, that fragmentary materials such as fallen wall plaster will be encountered in a particular area, or that larger finds such as mosaic pavements will need to be removed from the site for study and future display. In such situations, particular conservation skills will be required, and the sooner the finances and organisation of the project provide for them, the better. Indeed, some of this work may be essential even before excavation begins, for example when the conservator has to check-up on the most acceptable procedure for treating a particular combination of materials, or to develop new techniques to deal with a specific problem which evaluation has forewarned (see, for example, Tarleton and Ordoñez 1995 on the merits of different methods used to stabilise textiles from anoxic sites). Even with the best pre-planning, not all will be knowable in advance and specialist help may be needed at very short notice. The unexpected discovery of unusual material can be very expensive, quickly decimating the budget of an otherwise accurately funded project. The only solution is to welcome the unexpected and hope that financial sponsors are equally impressed.

This is not the place to give detailed information on technical aspects of conservation. Manuals and reference books for those with existing expertise are available for even the most obscure or specific matters (for example Mora *et al.* 1984 on virtually all aspects of the conservation of wall paintings). For the excavator needing to increase her general awareness, Dowman (1970) gives some background and Sease (1987) makes important points about safety, the need for planning and sources of supplies before detailing the treatment of different material. For the rest, it is probably better to consult the experts than attempt to do too much oneself and risk unnecessary damage in the process. Specific techniques and even general principles are changing rapidly (compare Leigh 1972 and the updates, Watkinson *et al.* 1987, Watkinson and Neal 1998: note also that the last two are collaborative, rather than individual works, and come with more practical plastic binding and cleanable pages, plus commercial advertisements – all a sure sign of the times, both good and bad).

At a practical level, the main role of the field director with respect to conservation may be simply to organise a workplace with special ventilation or to

Plate 10 A rudimentary tank, erected on site, for short-term preservation of water-logged timbers which were *en route* either to full recording before discard or, if merited, to proper conservation facilities followed by museum display.

provide secure storage for dangerous chemicals. On the more technical side, a system of sprays may be needed on site to protect *in situ* timbers until they can be lifted and fully treated, or stored in more controlled conditions such as a tank of water (Plate 10) or wrapped in clingfilm and placed in a dark, cool room. Other methods of stabilisation in the field, for example chemical impregnation (Dougherty 1988) may then be required. Finally, the presence of a conservator on the site demonstrates a concrete concern with conservation and thus increases general awareness amongst excavators. More care will then be taken with artefacts, both in the ground and after their excavation.

Concerning **computer systems**, it has been calculated that the information generated by society in the second half of the twentieth century is one hundred times greater than that derived from the whole of human history up to that point, and archaeology has played its part in adding to this explosion with its complex and detailed data generated in the field. Computers will be needed to store information concerning the administration of the project, but also a wealth of descriptive and spatial information on stratigraphy and finds. The systems created must allow the latter sets of data to be input easily on site, together with appropriate checking procedures to enhance data-quality, but also to be manipulated in post-excavation analysis, both individually and in conjunction with each other (see Richards and Ryan 1985, though in this fast-changing field many of their specific discussions, particularly on hardware, have become outdated).

The data structures must be related to the specific objectives of the project, as this affects the structuring of the site record. So one will need time not just to buy hardware but also to modify existing software, or perhaps even produce new versions. Thus systems analysts and programmers may be required at the outset (Dibble and McPherron 1988). In an ideal world, packages might be created to fulfil the exact needs of each project. In reality, most excavations will use a combination of software off-the-shelf and modifications as appropriate (often with insufficient time to test out the programmes beforehand!). In the 1980s, in particular, commercial data-base management systems were adapted to create systems which were sufficiently sensitive to archaeological require-ments (Guimier-Sorbets 1990 and various papers in Ross *et al.* 1991, especially those by Burnard and Smith).

In the 1990s, emphasis moved much more towards relational data-bases which reflect, in a more meaningful way, the links between different data sets recorded on site (Richards 1998). Hence, for example, the system designed for the Scottish Urban Archaeological Trust allows finds and site context informa-tion concerning deposit descriptions, spatial position and stratigraphic rela-tionships to be manipulated in an integrated way (Rains 1995). At the same time, various groups have tried to mechanise the process of checking and drawing Harris Matrices (e.g. Herzog 1993 and the Bonn programme, below Chapter 9), though these will always be of limited use until one can fully incor-porate plan information. This has led, in turn, to the establishment of excava-tion archives which allow the user to move between different record sets, whether these are stored as text or as images. Thus a researcher can access data in the way in which the logic of the particular work demands, rather than as the field-workers produced it, or even meant it to be used. Ryan (1995) and Agresti *et al.* (1996) provide good examples here, with the Heslerton excavation perhaps the most well-rounded project of its type to date (Powlesland 1991). Such developments have a clear resonance with post-processualist views on how the study of the past should be approached.

Whatever methods are used to computerise site records, the staff who will input the data will need to be trained at the start of the project. In addition expert personnel may be needed at later stages of the work to remove the bugs which inevitably arise. More significantly, recording requirements often change during any project, no matter how good initial site evaluation, and it is impor-tant that someone then makes modifications and additions to the computer system. If not, there is a danger that the more developed record will only appear on paper, or that such innovations will not happen because the computer system does not 'allow' it. Finally, it has been necessary on some projects to remove initial fear of computers amongst the workforce (Richards 1986).

Having computer expertise on hand during the process of work can help develop people's confidence here, though current trends in education have meant increasing computer literacy amongst archaeologists. Hence, fortunately, such suspicion has now become much more a thing of the past.

Yet another consideration in need of early planning is **photographic coverage**. Today, photographs of an excavation are seen as an integral part of its archaeological record, including shots of general site conditions and activities, overviews of archaeological horizons and details of specific features. This requires some background knowledge, perhaps scientific expertise, and certainly the appropriate equipment (Dorrell 1989: see also White 1990 for discussion of present practice and perceptions of the role of photography for site recording in the fieldwork profession).

However, photographic coverage should not just start when excavation work is in full swing. General shots will be needed from a very early stage – setting-up activity such as machines breaking-out concrete or excavators de-turfing the site; or personalities, academics and museum bosses visiting the project at the start of the process in the full glare of publicity (most never to be seen again, unless you turn up something which the media deem important!). To be able to use those 'before and after' photographs beloved by so many lecturers, one needs to record the pandemonium of the initial conditions to contrast with the archaeologically controlled, ordered situation later on. By the latter time the role of the photographic record in relation to the rest of the recording system must have been settled, which requires intellectual application, followed by organisational arrangements. Photographers will also need their own special equipment and consumables, either ordered specially or obtained through a centrally controlled system. Sometimes larger plant may be needed for overall shots. Thus, rather than the type of turret used previously, the generally cheaper and more adequate option is either to hire a 'Simon tower' for particular occasions or to use a fixed photographic tower on a continuous basis.

A **surveying system** will be needed on almost every excavation. Each site needs to be located in the landscape, in terms of either known field boundaries or natural features in the countryside, or streets and buildings of the town: only thus can it be tied into a national grid. Most excavations will also require secure points, accurately located, for planning and a number of benchmarks to be established for taking levels. Thus some surveying expertise and equipment is essential. If the project is of only limited duration, the site grid may be set up once and then left to run itself. However, if work is extended into new areas, a repeat performance will obviously be necessary. Also, if digging takes place over a period of months and involves deep stratigraphy, the grid points will have to be moved down as strata are excavated around them, necessitating repeated checking for accuracy. In a sense, this is a simple procedure, the fundamentals of surveying being only 'school trigonometry' writ large. However, it is really an attitude of mind, rather than technical skills, which is at stake here. Some people are more committed to getting the grid exactly right than others, so it makes sense to allocate this work to those particular individuals.

General books on methods of field survey have made the subject fairly accessible. Adkins and Adkins (1989) provide the easiest introduction, including a short bibliography. Hogg (1980) covers most of the ground, though sometimes using methods such as chaining which some would consider old-fashioned, and Bettess (1984) is more up-to-date. Reading about techniques is one thing; practical experience of working with a skilled surveyor is another, not least to learn all those little wrinkles which make the job more efficient and fulfilling (e.g. using old rubber tyre fragments to prevent slippage of tripod legs when setting up on difficult surfaces – Reyman 1978; this is the sort of trick known to the *cognoscenti*, but rarely publicised outside their coterie). All methods require some equipment, even if it only amounts to pegs, string and fibre tapes, and this must be thought through in advance. It is also worth remembering that, despite the use of electronic distance measuring machines (EDMs), etc. on sophisticated excavation projects, basic methods can be perfectly appropriate for much fieldwork, even if a little more time consuming. Farrar (1987), for example, espouses the use of the prismatic compass, especially for surveying earthworks, and this may still be the most practical and economic response to some isolated situations in which archaeologists find themselves.

Next we have the provision of **excavators**. Digging staff are mentioned last, not because they are least important, but because it is vital to have the support systems, both staff and facilities, in place beforehand to ensure their proper use. Diggers come in many types and from many sources, even by the standards of a discipline which itself embodies considerable diversity as a whole. Indeed, this diversity, it is to be hoped, will increase further as the base of undergraduate entry into university is broadened. Certainly a wider range of people gets some form of contact with the subject than even in the sixties, let alone pre-war, and they comprise a mixture of ages, sexes, social backgrounds and attitudes. Thus excavators may be local people, archaeology undergraduates, or schoolchildren, those with or without academic qualifications, with or without previous experience or expertise, and with or without long-term, sustained interest. Further one should expect no simple correlation between academic qualifications and expertise, still less between these and long-term commitment. The basis of their employment may range from full-time professionals, whether itinerant or fixed at one unit, to students obtaining experience on field schools during their vacations and volunteers who have responded to national appeals and newsletters of local societies, or simply individual interested members of the public who have turned up to help.

Whatever the source, background and ability of excavators, all will need training: a site manual may try to set out clearly what is required, but it is people who actually operate the system. Some years ago, Clarke wrote a 'cautionary tale' (1978) on site staff, seeming to argue for the use of professional archaeologists on the basis that volunteers were inherently unreliable in their ability to recognise the existence of, and thus retain, certain artefact types in the excavation process. The real lesson of this tale is rather that, if we are to get the consistency of data that modern archaeology rightly demands, all staff, professional or volunteer, need to be trained to similar levels and operate under a clear, and clearly understood, recording system. Perhaps safety and litigation concerns may still mean that volunteer labour cannot be as fully utilised today as in the past, although one would hope that any project would endeavour to provide the safest context for all work, independent of whether the staff involved are full-time employees or weekend helpers.

Of course, it will not be appropriate to train each excavator in exactly the same way, since people start at various levels and with diverse backgrounds, and anyway learn things in different ways and at different speeds. In addition, particular technical tasks such as driving machinery and transport vehicles, maintaining this plant, and being responsible for safety matters may rightly remain the province of a few. None the less, the majority of site work can be done by all excavators, and helping them reach a common standard can be achieved with simple techniques. The case for, and form of, standardised recording procedures is set out below, together with ways of achieving those standards. Thus the use on-site of a type-series of common stones may aid geological recognition in masonry foundations, and training in the field tests of the sedimentologist, plus a reference collection of soils, will help the accuracy of deposit descriptions. It is even possible, with a little effort, to develop expertise in more obscure areas, for example the recognition of slags (Backmann 1982). Training demystifies site recording systems, reduces the (self-)importance of the technocrat, and gives excavators a more fulfilling and effective working day.

Finally, the **archiving** of all material generated by the project will have to be planned in advance. This will include catering for: physical objects such as artefacts requiring museum storage, often at a designated cost for different types of find (Museums and Galleries Commission 1992); environmental samples, whether stored for future processing or as a long-term archive from the site; and the written and drawn record from the field (Institute of Field Archaeology 1994, Owen 1995, Murray and Ferguson 1997). It will also be necessary to include information about the setting up of the project itself and the conduct of activities in the field, and finally to produce a guide to the whole archive (SCAUM 1997). In planning for the long-term storage of, and access to, these outputs, it may be appropriate to approach local institutions first, as they are the most likely repository for much of our material and may have guidelines which any project will be expected to follow.

However, for computerised data, further considerations arise beyond those described above for the stage of data-capture. One must also plan for subsequent management and presentation of the data, and for its use by a variety of researchers, not least because the quickly changing world of computer technology means that its hardware and software constitute much more hazardous archive media than either paper or microfiche. Thus it will be necessary to guard against future inaccessibility by setting data standards in advance, and to account for any legal issues which may arise in relation to intellectual property rights, confidentiality, and the integrity and reputation of the data creators. It seems likely that most countries will soon develop and adopt general standards for data held in this way (see, for example, the work of the International Standards Organisation (ISO), the Open Archival Information (OAIS) and the International Council of Archives Committee on Electronic Records across the globe, the Commission for Preservation and Access in the US, and the Arts and Humanities Data Service in Britain). We will also see the creation of more advanced systems for holding such material (the National Archives and Records Administration in the US, the initiative for Preserving Access to Digital Information in Australia, the European Preservation of Information Centre, and the Public Records Office in Britain). Individual systems will have to conform with such standards, and link to these major institutions, to ensure that their data are widely available.

4.3 General site safety

As argued above, a safe site is the first priority of any excavation director and must be created from the very start of a project. Formal recognition of this fact became essential with the professionalisation of the workforce (Fowler 1972b), though inevitably many of the more technical and legal matters discussed then have been overtaken by subsequent legislation. The SCAUM 1986 Health and Safety Manual seeks to show that such matters continue to be taken seriously by unit managers in Britain. Many things go to making a safe working environment, of which one of the most important is the attitude of the staff. This is not to say, however, that if a humble volunteer carries out unsafe work and is injured, then they are to blame and 'should have known better'. People get their attitudes towards safety through the training they receive and their perception of how such matters are regarded in the rest of the organisation. Thus the person(s) in direct charge of the project and their superiors have the final responsibility to ensure that their staff do not act in unsafe ways whilst at work, and that the standards, equipment and practices followed on the project create appropriate working conditions.

Crowded and complex archaeological sites are dangerous places at the best of times, and so present special difficulties for safety provision (Plate 11).

Plate 11 A typical scene on a complex urban project, with controlled archaeological excavation proceeding in one area amongst processes of demolition and reconstruction elsewhere on the same site.

However, some principles can be recognised and a series of reminders will be outlined below. There is no room for complacency in this area, whether one is part of a big, governmental operation such as the Corps of Engineers, the National Park Service, the Forest Service in the US, or a large commercial fieldwork unit in Europe, or just a member of a small, 'one-man band'. Failure to take safety matters into account can lead to personal tragedy, as shown by the death of an archaeologist in York some years ago following the collapse of an unshored section face. In losing the services of Jeffrey Radley, archaeological knowledge and expertise in the city was dealt a severe blow – our discipline can ill afford such events.

Even where the impact is less severe, non-compliance with regulations can be financially expensive, as shown by Niquette's report (1997) on a project working on the floodplain of the Ohio River near the state boundary between Ohio and Indiana. Here an unexpected inspection from the Indiana Department of Labor's Occupational Safety and Health Administration turned up serious violations concerning the wearing of safety helmets, lack of proper egress arrangements, unretained spoil heaps lying too close to trench edges, too steep a slope to trench sides, and workers screening soil directly above others engaged in excavation. These, plus less serious violations concerning inadequate safety documentation, resulted in a hefty fine, though this was reduced during subsequent discussions with IOSHA. This employer, at least, seems to have learnt the lesson. Investment in staff training has now increased awareness and technical knowledge of safety matters, and ensured that structures such as weekly meetings and daily, documented inspections of staff clothing have been put in place. What this example shows is that lack of knowledge is in no way a defence against negligence. Hence projects will need to have made themselves aware of legislative provisions, whatever country they are working in; to have carried out some form of risk assessment before the start of the project; and to have created systems to monitor developments thereafter.

Aspects of **legislation** which relate to archaeology in general will, of course, vary around the world but are usually quite accessible, given the will to seek them out. O'Keefe and Prott 1984, a reference book which brings together current regulations in over 400 separate political jurisdictions, provides a useful general starting point here and can be dipped into to check specific points. Of course, by its very nature, such a work is quickly out of date. In addition, a series of regulations will exist in every country which relate more specifically to safety on archaeological sites. In the US, for example, the provisions of the Occupational Safety and Health Act will be the main starting point but, as the papers brought together by Akerson (1995) make clear, one must then take into account the peculiar conditions which may pertain on urban archaeological sites, in the laboratory as well as the field, and on both research projects and the more frantic conditions of salvage work occurring as part of cultural resource management.

In Britain, the equivalent of OSHA would include the Construction Site Regulations (1961–6); the Offices, Shops and Railway Premises Act (1963) and, most important, the Health and Safety at Work Act (1974). Sections 2 and 3 of the latter Act outline the responsibilities of the employer in general terms, with this duty of care being defined more explicitly under the Management of Health and Safety at Work Regulations 1992. These require that the employer 'make a suitable and sufficient assessment of (a) the risks to the health and safety of employees . . . and (b) the risks to the health and safety of persons not in his (*sic*) employment arising out of, or in connection with, the conduct by him of his undertaking'. The best way to fulfil these requirements effectively is to implement a coherent process of risk assessment before any work starts, on a project-by-project basis. This will involve identifying hazards, assessing the risk involved and deciding who is likely to be affected, deciding on what control measures are needed, and then setting up procedures for maintaining a safe working environment. A 'suitable and sufficient' risk assessment must:

> identify foreseeable significant risks
> be appropriate for the level of risk
> enable the assessor to decide on action to be taken and priorities to be established
> be compatible with the activity
> remain valid for the period of work
> reflect current knowledge of the activity.

The technical knowledge to perform this task has been facilitated by the Department of the Environment writing a series of pamphlets, issued by HMSO, on Safety in Construction Work for Demolition (DoE 1973) and on Excavation (DoE 1974), together with a basic statement of rules for Safety and Health at Work (DoE 1975). The good advice which these publications contain means that they should be consulted by all archaeologists working on sites whether part-time or full-time, on a large project or in a small trench (in fact, it is often the small trenches that are the most dangerous). Remember that legislation covers all persons working on the site, volunteers and paid workers alike, and also most visitors, regardless of their status or the nature of their visit. It is also quite clear that the law requires, *inter alia*, employers of site archaeologists to issue a safety policy document, which should be reinforced by a safety manual translating broad principles into action. Copies of the latter must be kept on site, and be accessible to all concerned with safety (i.e. everyone).

Having made a risk assessment and put in place the necessary provisions, it will then be necessary to maintain these safe working conditions. Circumstances change substantially during any excavation. Quick alterations such as the emptying of a large pit to create a deep, dangerous hole may be readily recognised as hazards, whereas the more gradual enlargement of the same feature is more insidious, and thus even more dangerous. However well-informed and careful the precautions were initially, the pressure to work in difficult situations to tight deadlines can mean that safety matters are quietly forgotten later on. And even the most experienced archaeologist cannot anticipate every problem, let alone create solutions. Regular visits from an independent safety consultant will solve many of these problems, promoting greater awareness among staff and noting, with an external eye, potential dangers which those working on the spot have missed. In addition, any project director will struggle to keep up with new approaches to safety matters, and with the appropriate legislation, whether local and national or, increasingly, continental (e.g. European directives) and international. A safety expert can provide a more informed perspective here, both on what is legally demanded and on what it would make good sense to implement anyway.

Finally, it is necessary to consult with all members of the workforce and ensure that they are not too intimidated to draw attention to potential hazards. By operating in conjunction with an organisation such as a trade union, project directors will promote involvement of all staff and also allow technical information on safety from this source to be incorporated into working practices. This also creates a system which is independent of the hierarchy of the employer, allowing complaints to come to light more easily and be acted upon. Given that three heads are better than two, regular visits to inspect site facilities and conditions are best undertaken by site director, union representative and an independent safety expert. Production of a written report by the last-mentioned after each inspection clarifies what is expected, with a copy sent to the central administration and another left on site listing necessary action: knowing that the consultant will be back again before long is a great incentive to check that all recommendations have been acted upon

All excavation projects will need to be covered by some form of **insurance**, minimally third party, personal accident and employers' liability. In Britain, the system set up under the auspices of the Council for British Archaeology is appropriate in many cases, but more long-term projects and full-time units will probably arrange cheaper and better cover via the umbrella organisations to which they are attached, such as museums, local authorities or universities. It is important to remember that responsibility for the workforce may include transporting them to and from the site, and that this is not normally covered by private motor insurance. When working abroad, arrangements will obviously vary greatly but can be even more vital, notably in medical insurance because of the increased risk of catching a disease as a result of reduced natural immunity and the much higher cost of medical treatment in many countries, plus the occasional need to transport personnel out of a region which lacks the necessary medical resources.

The most common hazards which archaeologists encounter on site are tetanus and leptospirosis (Weil's disease from rats' urine, or Hardjo from cattle: see the leaflet of the Health and Safety Executive). Thus all excavators should have current tetanus jabs to cover the former, and proper on-site washing facilities will go a long way to avoid the latter. However, new dangers continue to come to light, for example the recent recognition of Hantavirus Pulmonary Syndrome caused by contact with rodents (Fink and Zeitz 1996). In addition, when starting an excavation, especially in a modern urban area, **live services and**

recently deceased materials must be taken into consideration (see the Control of Substances Hazardous to Health Regulations of 1988, commonly known as COSHH in Britain, MSD in the US). For example, ducts or cables carrying electricity, gas, sewage or storm water may be encountered. A check must be made beforehand with appropriate local authorities and other providers of such utilities.

Some areas may be particularly hazardous because of previous activities there affecting ground conditions – chemical plants, munitions factories, sewage works, etc. Others may have used special materials, notably asbestos (and not just the blue variety – other forms are less dangerous but still a hazard). Asbestos will need expert removal, and then testing to see that this has been effective, before archaeological work can commence. See *Asbestos Dust: The Hidden Killer* issued by the Health and Safety Executive. Such work will often be monitored by government agencies who will also offer specialist advice. However, they must be reminded that archaeological excavation involves disturbing the ground beneath buildings and that we are in direct contact with the soil during this work. So safe levels for substances which have percolated into the ground may have to be much lower for the digger on her knees than those required for the machine driver working in a cab: our work takes place in what is an abnormal context, as far as many authorities are concerned.

The provision of proper **staff facilities** is an integral part of site safety. General tidiness on site is important, not only to remove specific dangers but because of the general attitude it develops towards safety matters. Thus working areas should be clear of obstructions, grid pegs marked to stop people tripping over them and their points covered when they are not in use. When certain areas are known to be dangerous, they must be railed off, or at least surrounded with bunting and clearly marked. Ensure that these safety signs, once erected, are not obscured by parked vehicles, whether the expensive, new car of a site volunteer, the second-hand car of the excavation director, or the dilapidated, highly unsafe bicycle of the average digger. Similarly, first-aid boxes should be not only provided but marked and signposted as such, with their position known to everyone. They should contain only the designated items (tablets for headaches, for example, are not specified) and their contents should be checked and augmented regularly by an appointed individual.

Other personal matters include clothing in general, and safety helmets in particular (see Construction (Head Protection) Regulations). Best practice for the latter is to ensure that they are suitably adjusted to individual head size, less than four years old, and of an agreed standard (e.g. in the UK those marked with British Standard BS5420). The conditions requiring helmets to be used may change by the minute, so it is best to err on the side of caution by designating only particular zones as non-helmet and expecting them to be used everywhere else. Shoes or boots with steel toe-caps are now common and gloves and ear-defenders may be needed in particular circumstances. Weather conditions, either hot, with the problems of sunstroke, or cold with consideration of wind chill and even frostbite, must be catered for as far as possible. Covering the excavation area not only provides a more controllable, and so potentially safer, environment in which to work but can also increase efficiency because of lack of hold-ups due to inclement weather. Adovasio and Carlisle (1988), with the arctic weather port, provide a good example of what is possible when operating with limited resources.

Allowing for regular breaks in work so that each person may get away from the extremes of the climate is important but it is equally essential then to have somewhere appropriate to go. So the provision of a staff room or its equivalent and changing, washing and toilet facilities of some sort, together with a supply of fresh drinking water, must be fed in at an early stage of the planning process. All facilities should be available whenever work on site is envisaged and heating them may require the use of portable gas heaters. LPG cylinders must be stored externally, with spares in a separate place, as required by recent government regulations. If petrol is used on the site, it will also need proper containers and an outside store marked appropriately and with no-smoking signs, etc. Site huts, whether heated or not, should contain fire extinguishers which are regularly checked and refilled or replaced as necessary and all huts and stores should be lockable, except for emergency exits. Finally, individuals suffering from the excesses of drugs or drink or from illness or general fatigue should be prevented from working no matter how capable they feel themselves to be. They are a danger to others as well as themselves.

Consideration of **access and movement** of personnel is vital for site safety. Moving about archaeological sites can be a hazardous business, especially if people are allowed to run or jump in and out of deep trenches. Walkways should be clear of obstructions, well lit if necessary and non-slippery. If used as barrow runs, boards of sufficient strength (e.g. Youngmans) should be used, set at a shallow angle (less than 1 in 6) with battens fixed across them to prevent feet from slipping. Planking, staked in place, should incorporate barriers to stop wheelbarrows dropping into lower areas, and the barrows should be well maintained with properly inflated wheels. Where ladders or towers are in use, they must be firmly anchored. Special care must be taken to use ladders of aluminium or unpainted wood (paint covers emerging cracks) which have been set at the appropriate angle (4 in 1) and secured with strong rope at both ends. They should also protrude sufficiently at the top to enable safe access (at least four rungs), and be placed at regular intervals throughout a large trench. Ladders should be used mainly for personal movement, not lifting heavy spoil out of the trench on any scale (see below for the preferred alternatives). However, excavators will still be climbing up and down, their hands occupied with a variety of small equipment, so the protruding rungs can be vital when moving safely onto the level ground up above the excavation trench.

The use of **plant and machinery** on site brings with it particular safety problems. As with all equipment, it is important that it is appropriate for the job in hand and in a good state of repair and being used by suitable people. For machinery, this may mean checking to see that there is an up-to-date test certificate, designating and training certain authorised operators, ensuring that safe levels of load are not exceeded, etc. Such matters become more vital as the size of plant increases, though even small machines can do considerable damage in the wrong hands. Outside work hours, machines should be immobilised to guard against theft or simply unwelcome and damaging drivers. Similarly, tools should be in a locked store, not least to prevent their use to break into offices, etc. Expensive equipment such as survey gear and computer hardware will have to be treated especially carefully, perhaps marked and any serial numbers noted in case of theft.

One piece of potentially lethal equipment which deserves special mention is the chain saw, particularly useful on sites sampling for dendrochronology but very dangerous, even in experienced hands. It is vital that the saw is in a good state of repair and that operators are proficient in its use. Suitable clothing will be needed, especially gloves and goggles but also ear mufflers and specially lined over-trousers which can resist the effect of an out-of-control saw blade. If a large number of samples are required, it is better to find someone who is experienced in using chain saws on a regular basis rather than a willing member of the site staff. However, one accident on a single sample creates dire consequences, and where only a few samples are required these may be better taken by hand than going to the trouble, expense and danger of using a chain saw.

Finally, no matter how safe a site is, accidents will still occur on occasion. Then it is important not only that qualified first aiders and appropriate facilities are available immediately, but that such incidents are recorded in the **accident book**. For some more major injuries this is a legal obligation (see the Health and Safety at Work Act for the British situation). Also, some seemingly minor accidents may turn out to be major (the ankle turned over on the barrow run is, in fact, broken and requires several weeks off work) so the more that is written down, the better. Finally it also makes sense to record dangerous incidents (i.e. near-misses or accidents 'waiting to happen') so that such situations can be recognised in advance and their causes eliminated.

4.4 Special safety situations

Safety is such a wide-ranging matter that what has been outlined above can only be an indication of the relevant considerations, and experts should be consulted for advice in particular situations. Indeed, each site may provide a need to deal with special circumstances. Thus work in desert regions might need to avoid dehydration, sunburn leading to skin cancer, bites and stings from virulent local insects, or a particular virus either in the soil or derived from local rodents. Equally, arctic conditions may mean guarding against frostbite. However, even some of the more common excavation contexts will merit especial attention and can be predicted as potentially dangerous in advance.

On **'watching briefs'**, excavators monitor commercial building operations but are not allowed their own, controlled access, so this work requires the greatest vigilance. Conditions are changing by the minute and archaeologists are only one of many groups of workers on site who may be using a great variety of plant, each with their own working practices, objectives and deadlines. Safety helmets are nearly always essential, and one's presence, location and intentions should always be made known to all relevant people. Nobody must work alone and, if the work is out of sight of the rest of the team, for example in a deep trench, someone must be acting as a 'banksman', monitoring activities on the surface and warning others of the presence of those below.

Excavating within buildings creates particular difficulties (Plate 12), though each with its counterpart in the open air. Lighting will obviously be required, not just for seeing the site to excavate, photograph and record it, but also on walkways, stairs and access points. Halogen lighting of 1,000 watts on a 110v system is better than festoons of light bulbs, and a properly installed system is obviously preferable to endless coils of cables, with their tendency to trip people or get cut by tools during the excavation process. Generally, 110 volts is safer than 240 volts just in case an electric shock occurs, though this does require the use of a transformer, which may be prone to failure or overloading. It therefore makes better sense to have a back-up system, especially for lighting which, if it fails, may halt work entirely. Enclosed conditions can create problems of ventilation, especially if non-electrical machinery is being used, and may exacerbate noise and dust. Masks and ear defenders can be essential here, though of course are not precluded in outside work. However, bear in mind that excluding unwanted noise means that normal forms of verbal communication may be correspondingly impeded.

Working on **human burials** brings its own problems, and not just in terms of legal requirements concerning the necessary permissions (Garratt-Frost 1992) or protecting the sensibilities of the public. Certain sites, especially recent ones, may have 'good' organic preservation. Plague pits or church crypts are obvious cases in point, but even work in open graveyards can encounter well-preserved burials in lead coffins or involve contact with human hair, skin, etc. (McKinley and Roberts 1993). If these must be dealt with, specialist advice should be sought. The provision of disposable gloves, special overalls, etc. should be the responsibility of the organisation rather than particular excavators, together with washing facilities. A good example of the problems of burials and working

Plate 12 Working inside a tunnel in the City of London. Walls and surfaces associated with the Roman forum of London are seen here being recorded in section.

inside coming together was the excavations within the crypt at Christ Church, Spitalfields (Plate 13). Here, apart from the archaeological problems of stratigraphic relationships between each coffin, some of which were standing on end, the site director had to consider lighting difficulties and numerous health and safety problems of excavating well-preserved and recent burials, including lead levels and even psychological problems for excavators dealing with the bodies over an extended period of time (Adams and Reeve 1987). If problems can be overcome in such a situation, there can be no excuse for working in hazardous situations elsewhere, in which the threats may be less obvious but the consequences of a mistake just as serious.

Plate 13 The crypt of Christ Church, Spitalfields, before formal excavation began, with coffins of all shapes and sizes, each with well-preserved contents, distributed at various angles. Such sites create huge challenges for the excavator, both physically and psychologically.

5

EXCAVATION IN PRACTICE:
PREPARATIONS ON SITE

Introduction

With the intellectual and practical foundations outlined in the preceding chapters correctly laid, one is next ready to start detailed preparations for digging the site. Of course, every excavation brings its own, particular logistical problems at each stage of the work but all projects have certain things in common and these are considered in order below. Thus each site requires some preparation of the selected area before excavation proper can start, even if it is only the removal of turf (see Site clearance – **5.1**, below). Most planning systems used to record the spatial arrangement of features on the site utilise some form of site grid (surveying – **5.2**). Excavation involves the controlled removal of deposits, inevitably generating material which must be then discarded (spoil removal – **5.3**). Digging into the ground creates a hole, of whatever shape and size, whose sides may collapse without support (shoring – **5.4**) and, in some circumstances, the depth of excavation creates problems of flooding (de-watering – **5.5**). Finally systems must be set up to gather finds from the strata as they are excavated, ranging from simple hand recovery to wet and dry sieving/screening and more exacting forms of environmental sampling (finds retrieval – **5.6**).

5.1 Site clearance

When starting an excavation, one may have to engage in activities which are anything but archaeological to reach the point where 'the real archaeology' begins. The removal of overburden, whether the substantial buildings or concrete slab that cover an urban site, or the turf covering a green field in the countryside, is an essential preliminary. Exactly where overburden stops and archaeology starts can be difficult to assess, and depends in part on the research objectives of the project. Whatever its definition, the removal of overburden on any scale usually involves machines, which may also be used later to remove spoil from the site and reinstate it at the end of the project.

Archaeological use of earth-moving equipment goes back some way (Nichols 1954, Petch 1968). Recent technical developments in plant have made it more economic to employ machines in a wider range of site activities and they have now become fairly central to any major excavation project. Pryor 1974, though a little dated, gives a basic account of the types available and their pros and cons. For major earth-moving, especially at the start of an excavation, three main types are worth mentioning. The bulldozer or grader with a fixed blade can skim off successive levels of overburden quite accurately, especially in the hands of a skilled operator. However, it does require level ground to operate effectively and may need a lot of clearing up afterwards by hand. Its use can also have a disastrous effect on fragmentary remains underneath owing to compression and earth tremor, burials being at particular risk. The bull-dozer's main role is on those extensive rural sites where it has been decided largely to ignore the top soil as an archaeological horizon. In such situations the top of the 'natural' stratigraphy is usually the point at which archaeologi-cal strata are deemed to start, the cultural deposit being the fill of any features intruding into it.

A second type of machine is the Hymac or Poclain, named after the main manufacturers, which is a tracked vehicle with a single arm and shovel with 360 degree arc of operation, making it highly manoeuvrable. The use of different types and sizes of bucket give it considerable flexibility, a bucket without teeth being the least damaging from the archaeological point of view. It is, however, quite expensive to hire and must be delivered on a low loader, which is not allowed on all sites at all times of the day, so such a machine tends to be used in the main for once-off large-scale clearance at the start of an excavation. If used for lifting heavy objects, it must display its 'Safe Working Load' (SWL) and not exceed this mark.

Third, for smaller-scale work, the tractor with bucket and back-acter (the 'JCB', in common British parlance, or 'backhoe' in the US) is usually employed. It is less versatile than the Hymac, in terms both of the positioning and manoeuvrability of the machine and of its reach. It also needs to lower hydraulic legs at the back end to work, which can damage underlying strata. However, being wheeled rather than tracked, it can be driven directly to the site and is cheaper to hire than the Hymac. Both Hymac and JCB can be fitted with a breaker to remove concrete slabs or modern stanchions, and even to carefully take out archaeological features such as substantial walls in the course of exca-vation (Plate 14).

Of course, accurate work can only be done with great control, and with a good driver who knows exactly what the job entails. When machining, the golden rule is to realise that, though drivers rarely have to deal with archaeol-ogists, they do spend most of their working day at the controls of the machine and will have been required to do a variety of site work, both delicate and rudi-mentary. Having explained your objectives clearly, plus any specifically archae-ological limitations ('try not to drive on our newly cleaned area'), it is then best to listen carefully to how the driver thinks these can best be achieved and follow his advice, rather than to try and instruct him on how it should be done.

For more detailed clearance one can use 'micro-excavators' (Adkins and Adkins 1983), which have the advantage that site workers can operate them effectively with practice and they are cheap to hire, so can be left on site during

Plate 14 Breaking out concrete in the crowded conditions of a typical urban excavation. A pneumatic breaker (*right*) is fitted to a JCB/backhoe and the resulting rubble is loaded immediately into a waiting lorry by the 'Hymac' (*left*) for dumping off-site. Organising the efficient integration of these activities can be a major headache but failing to do so means that expensive plant will then stand idle, wasting scarce financial resources.

the initial stages without running up a huge bill. Past this point, it will be necessary to return to the traditional hand-operated plant such as drills or jackhammers. If the latter are driven by compressed air, great care must be taken with air lines and couplings. If a joint fails, the whiplash of the lines can be dangerous and should be approached only after switching off the compressor. Hence, for safety, it makes better sense to use the less robust, but more manageable, electric breaker of the 'Kango' variety, which comes in various sizes and so can be adjusted to the job in hand. In either case it will be essential to work in steel toe-capped boots, gloves and goggles, and probably to wear ear-defenders as well.

5.2 Setting out a site grid

When any initial clearance has been completed, it will be necessary to survey in the position of the site with respect to the surrounding area and set out trenches within this. It is then possible to establish a site-specific grid to aid planning, and insert bench marks related to the Ordnance Datum for taking levels on plans. Failure to do this at the earliest possible opportunity can mean that the recording of the uppermost stratigraphy may be less rigorous than the layers below, which is obviously undesirable (unless it is an explicit objective of the project to be more summary with later levels). Thus it makes sense to create the site grid and locate it with respect to a National Grid at one and the same time, also noting the methods used to set it up for future reference. If one does this by relating the site to nearby extant features, it is essential to ensure that the latter will remain after redevelopment: it is no good knowing the exact position of a trench with respect to a road frontage or hedge line if these are then swept away in major rebuilding on the site. Alternatively, and more accurately, one can use electronic positioning via satellites, for example the Global Positioning System (Spennemann 1992) or the LORAN-C system developed more recently (Gould 1995), using hand-held receivers.

The mechanics of establishing fixed points in a grid across the site have been covered in many publications and do not need extensive repetition here (Bettess 1984: chapters 2 and 5, and Adkins and Adkins 1989: 63 plus refs.). It can be done most accurately with a theodolite or, better still, an electronic distance measuring machine (EDM): virtually nothing can go wrong, unless you inadvertently kick the tripod or ignore regular maintenance of the equipment by qualified personnel. If such apparatus is not available, metal or fibre tapes can be used. Metal tapes cannot stretch and thus remain more accurate than fibre ones through time. However, they are affected by temperature variations, so it is necessary to incorporate the manufacturer's correction factor into any calculations. If only fibre is available, use a new, unstretched tape, checked previously for accuracy against a standard.

The setting out of a grid requires the initial creation of a base line, preferably up the middle of the site. Then, working outwards, insert points at regular intervals at right angles to it to create a number of grid squares. The easiest way of doing this is to establish right-angled triangles along the base line using Pythagoras' theorem. Most people use triangles whose sides are in the proportion 3–4–5. However, it is worth remembering that other combinations also produce a right angle, for example 8–15–17 or 20–21–29. These may be more convenient if grid squares with sides of 15m or 20m are required. My personal preference is to use 5–12–13 shaped triangles, making it easy to insert a grid square with a side of 5m. Also the total of the sides adds up to 30m, the length of a standard surveying tape. Using the whole length of the tape, and thus maximising the size of the triangles used in the setting up operation, increases the accuracy of the grid produced (Figure 6).

Of course, when establishing the grid, all tapes must be held horizontally. This is especially important on a sloping site. If possible, it is best here to move down the slope as you measure-in each grid point, using a plumb bob where the ground is lower to ensure that the location then marked on the ground is exactly vertically below the appropriate point on the tape. If the slope is considerable, and/or the distances are great, use a line level to ensure that the tape is truly horizontal. In addition, you will need to take a greater number of

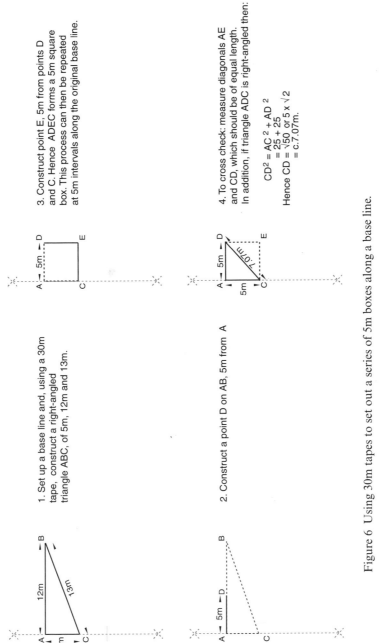

1. Set up a base line and, using a 30m tape, construct a right-angled triangle ABC, of 5m, 12m and 13m.

2. Construct a point D on AB, 5m from A

3. Construct point E, 5m from points D and C. Hence ADEC forms a 5m square box. This process can then be repeated at 5m intervals along the original base line.

4. To cross check: measure diagonals AE and CD, which should be of equal length. In addition, if triangle ADC is right-angled then:

$$CD^2 = AC^2 + AD^2$$
$$= 25 + 25$$
$$Hence\ CD = \sqrt{50}\ or\ 5 \times \sqrt{2}$$
$$= c.7.07m.$$

Figure 6 Using 30m tapes to set out a series of 5m boxes along a base line.

cross-checking measurements before the job can be considered finished. Thereafter, it will be important to ensure that site drawing in the course of excavation (whether using triangulation, offsets or drawing frames: see below) proceeds using equipment also set up in a horizontal position.

If safety or practicality on a severely sloping site make it impossible to hold a tape horizontally, a last resort can be to measure along the ground, and then calculate either the angle of decline using a theodolite, or the drop in slope between the end points of the tape using a dumpy level. One can then use either the cosine function available on most calculators ($Cos^1 x° =$ adjacent $\div$ hypotenuse; hence 'horizontal distance' = 'distance measured on ground down the slope' multiplied by '$Cos^{-1} x°$') or Pythagoras' theorem (horizontal distance $= \sqrt{((\text{distance on ground})^2 - (\text{vertical distance})^2)}$). However, if one has a theodolite available, or better still an EDM, it is probably easier, quicker and more accurate to use it to create the grid in the first place, rather than tapes. And if it is too dangerous to measure in the grid using tapes, why are you excavating there anyway?

Having set up the grid boxes, it is important to verify their accuracy, either to iron out cumulative errors or simply to correct mistakes. This is especially important when working on undulating or sloping ground (i.e. on the vast majority of sites in the real world) and is quickly achieved by checking whether the diagonal measurements in each grid square are of equal length. It can be helpful to remember certain square roots here, in particular that $\sqrt{2} = c.1.414$ and $\sqrt{5} = c.2.236$. Thus a triangle with equal sides of 10m should have a diagonal measuring c.14.14m, and one measuring 10m by 20m a diagonal of c.22.36m. It takes only a short time to check these distances at the start of an excavation and at regular intervals thereafter, but much longer to work through the whole grid when an inaccuracy suddenly appears at an inconvenient moment during the excavation.

Where the grid is placed on the site need not matter too much, as long as the original points are established in positions which can be easily relocated and will not need to be moved during the subsequent work. Other things being equal, it may be advantageous to set the grid parallel to an edge of the excavation area as defined by an independent factor such as a modern street frontage. Alternatively, it can be aligned roughly parallel to known or suspected archaeological features on the site, thus aiding planning accuracy. Of course, such alignments often vary between different structures and periods, so a compromise will be necessary; or they may be simply unknown, though hints from the evaluation work can help here. However and wherever the grid points are set up, each will need to be made as solid as possible and its position monitored regularly in the course of the excavation. One useful way to avoid too much grid movement and to set up permanent bench marks for levelling is to use the tops of the sheet metal piling which surrounds some sites. However, remember that the sheets are seldom driven with complete accuracy, so a point established as part of the grid on the top corner of the sheet before excavation started is unlikely to be exactly above the corresponding edge 6m down in the excavation.

If fortuitous, immovable features such as sheet piles or standing buildings are unavailable, it will be necessary to use wooden pegs to mark the grid points. First establish the approximate position, to within about a centimetre, and hammer in the peg. The exact position can then be measured and marked by a nail driven into the head of the peg but protruding for about 5mm to allow the end of a tape to be attached. If minor adjustments to the position of the nail are needed, they can usually be achieved by hitting the ground beside the base of the peg on one side in order to move it fractionally across at its head. This is preferable to pulling out the peg and starting again, which merely results in a loose peg and inaccurate planning.

Having set out the grid, it is necessary to decide on a co-ordinate system for the site. Here a simple numerical system is better than a combination of numbers and letters. Define a point towards the south-west limit of the site and number this as 100/200 (i.e. 100m east of, and 200m north of, a theoretical 0/0 point – Figure 7). This ensures, first, that you will never get the wrong side of that zero point, so can avoid the difficulties of dealing with negative values; and second, with the bias in the numbers selected, that eastings will tend to be in the 100–200m range and northings in the 200–300m range, so the two can be more easily differentiated (Biddle and Kjolbye-Biddle 1969). Of course, if the site is large and extends over more than 100m, then a suitable adjustment to the numbering of the initial south-west point will be required to retain the numerical distinction between eastings and northings.

Recording the site in a vertical dimension requires the establishment of a series of bench marks within, or at the edge of, the excavation area using a theodolite or dumpy level. Ideally, this should be done using traverses of less than about 50m from the nearest bench mark related to the national Ordnance Datum. Failing this, or if there is insufficient time at the start to connect up the site to a known datum, an arbitrary level can be established at some point on site and used for all work. Picking a large enough number, say 10m, as the level of this arbitrary point then avoids the problem of working with negative levels (assuming the site is less than 10m deep). All site-specific levels can then be related to the national Datum at a later time. Sufficient bench marks should be established to ensure that at least two are visible from anywhere on the excavation to allow crosschecking wherever the dumpy level is set up and at whatever depth. Once established, the height of each bench mark should be marked indelibly on it and its position and height recorded on a central site plan (Figure 7).

Salvage operations ('watching briefs') present particular problems in planning and levelling and it may be impossible to establish a proper grid and bench marks along the lines suggested above. One solution here is to position observations in plan in relation to nearby upstanding features such as modern buildings or field boundaries for which an accurate drawing exists, perhaps that obtained from the site engineer, agent or architect, and tie the two together

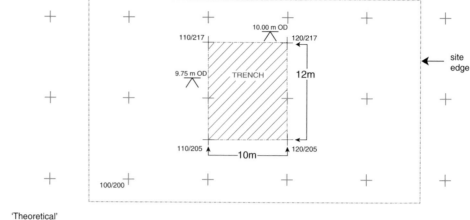

Figure 7 Defining a site grid and labelling Temporary Bench Marks before the start of excavation. A trench of dimensions 10m × 12m has been laid out in the centre of the site. By labelling a grid point as 100/200 towards the south-west limit of the site (i.e. 100m east of, and 200m north of, a theoretical 00/00 point), the corners of the trench can be noted (e.g.110/205, etc.). In addition one can set up Temporary Bench Marks (e.g. 9.75m OD) to take levels within the trench, marking their positions on this base plan.

retrospectively. By the same token, measurement of depths can be taken from the modern surface, for example a pavement, to obtain relative heights, and then calculated as an approximate absolute height at a later date. However, it is essential to check beforehand the accuracy of the drawing being used. Equally, if positions are recorded by triangulation from standing buildings, etc., which is often simplest and quickest, be sure to plot these points promptly and use extra cross-checking measurements. Often this can be done during those many times in such salvage work where the archaeologists are not allowed access to the trench for safety or other reasons. Mistakes can then be rectified at an early stage by remeasuring critical points.

Similarly, when monitoring commercial test pits being dug in apparently carefully specified positions, one can plot archaeological features on the associated, accurately drawn architect's plan. But beware! The objectives of the contractors in digging the pits are not the same as yours. They may simply require very general information on approximate level and character of natural and of overlying 'fill', so may not be unduly worried about accurate pit positions. Yet for the archaeologist, measuring the exact line and position of an

exposed substantial masonry foundation may be vital. First check the positioning of the contractors' pits, both for internal consistency and, if possible, in relation to surrounding features. In these situations it is virtually impossible to have
too many cross-checks.

5.3 Spoil removal

Virtually every excavation involves the disturbance of the ground and hence the
creation of loose soil. Some of this material may be kept as finds and various
sorts of samples, but much will be thrown away after being processed (the decision on what is kept and what discarded, and the processes which the material
passes through before being discarded, need not concern us here). The digging
tools used to create this spoil will vary from site to site, depending on the levels
of recovery required and the types of soil involved – chalk, limestone, clay,
gravel, rock and sand require different techniques and different degrees of
expertise, both to discriminate between successive strata and to excavate. Turf
cutters, spades, shovels, forks, picks, even crow bars may all be needed for heavy
work and hand shovels, brushes of various sorts, spoons, and even dental tools
for more delicate operations. However, the trowel remains of central importance and will be discussed in detail below (12.3).

Whatever tools are used in its creation, the spoil produced must be catered
for from the very start of an excavation. The initial logistical issue of storage
can be solved by attempting a rough and ready calculation of its expected
volume, guided by pre-excavation evaluation, to gauge the scale of the problem.
This then allows one to decide whether spoil should be stockpiled for the
course of the excavation and used as trench backfill at the end, taken away at
regular intervals, or removed on a continuous basis. If spoil heaps are to be
used, they will need to be accessible using safe routes from the site and to be
stable or securely retained. They should not cover areas where access to services
may be needed (e.g. water taps or electricity junction boxes) or where future
excavation is envisaged: the tales of covering the most important part of the site
with the spoil heaps are legion, if mostly apocryphal, and this is easily avoided
by doing some deposit evaluation below a proposed siting before any dumping
takes place. Finally heaps should be positioned with a view to ease of removal
from the site, if appropriate, or for machine access when the site is back-filled
with its own spoil. For work inside standing buildings, spoil can be a particular problem. If it is dumped inside, be aware that most internal walls are
designed to take a vertical, not a lateral, load and so cannot safely cater for a
large build-up of weighty soil against their faces.

Whether the decision is to remove spoil at regular intervals or to store it in
one place for the whole of the dig, arrangements must be made to get it from
the point of excavation to that holding area. Usually this has meant filling
buckets on site and emptying these into wheelbarrows, which are then wheeled

away. Here it is merely necessary to ensure the availability of sufficient equipment and a proper organisation of barrow runs set at an appropriate angle. As with any lifting of heavy objects on site, it must be remembered when barrowing spoil that only manageable weights must be attempted, and then with attention to posture – straight back, bending at the knees, with a firm hold and wearing steel toe-capped boots to minimise the damage of any slips. For heavier work of a greater volume, small equivalents of the large excavation plant – mini excavators or 'bob cats' – can be employed, perhaps being craned down onto a site that otherwise has limited access and removed when finished. However, these machines can also damage the archaeological deposit if used carelessly and involve a lot of clearing up afterwards, so are best employed when required over an extended period of time.

With larger excavations, particularly those which proceed to a considerable depth, problems may be encountered when raising the spoil out of the trench and/or taking it to a heap some distance away. Various lifting mechanisms might be employed and most will be subject to the Construction (Lifting Operations) Regulations, 1961, which require, amongst other things, weekly logged inspections. Hoists at the edge of the trench employing manual methods will usually be too slow or strength-sapping for extended use, so a diesel or electric hoist is often preferred. The former, the barrow hoist, is cantilevered out over the excavation with a counterweight and a full barrow is attached to it via rings on its handles and a hook at the wheel end. This is then raised and swung round at the top of the trench to be wheeled away to the spoil heap. Electric hoists are usually set across the top of the trench with a self-contained motor and winch which moves along a beam. They need a more sophisticated arrangement to be set up than the barrow hoist and are probably more expensive to run. On the other hand they have advantages in avoiding noise and fumes, and in their increased safety of operation: barrow hoists have a tendency to produce pinched fingers and, all too often, to allow badly attached, laden barrows to fall back into the trench below. Whatever type is used, there must be a marked SWL and an agreed signalling system for their safe operation.

For larger-scale operations still, conveyer belts or cranes might be considered. Here it is even more essential to create an agreed system of signals by a designated individual whilst the machines are in use (a 'banksman') and to employ qualified operators. Conveyer belts move spoil either up into a skip placed at the edge of the trench or directly into an appropriately positioned dumper truck (Plate 15). They are less versatile than the crane but easier to run and cheaper to hire. Cranes can be manually or hydraulically controlled, of which the latter is certainly less tiring but needs fuller maintenance. Electrical starting is much to be preferred to a manual system, barked knuckles being almost universal on sites employing starting handles for diesel cranes. Most cranes come with purpose-built skips hauled directly from the site and deposited into a dumper truck. It is best to keep to vertical lifting and avoid the unsafe manoeuvre of dragging a loaded bucket by crane for a distance across

Plate 15 The use of a micro-excavator, driven by regular, but suitably trained, site staff, and a conveyor belt to remove soil from extensive excavations and deposit it into the waiting dumper truck. The most efficient method is to designate an area within the trench for stockpiling spoil, then to transfer it at regular intervals. This also avoids unnecessary fumes from idling machinery.

the site. Also driving the crane to the spoil heap with a full bucket hauled up to the top of its jib is not recommended. This is not only dangerous but also very time-consuming because the machines are very slow and only operate effectively on level ground immediately adjacent to the excavation. Even quite small pot-holes can make them unmanoeuvrable, so prepare the ground beside the trench in advance and use the crane only for lifting the spoil, coupled with a dumper truck for moving it elsewhere.

It is important to ensure that there are enough skips on site before starting any craning operation. Also it is usually more efficient to have a 'production line' of skips to make onslaughts onto temporary spoil heaps at regular intervals using several people, rather than to fill a single skip and then wait around whilst it is emptied into the dumper truck, leaving the diesel crane idling yet belching out fumes into the trench in the meantime. The minimum amount of spoil needed in the temporary area is that required to fill one dumper truck, so that empty skips can be refilled whilst the truck is being driven to the main spoil heap. Cranes can also be used to lift particularly heavy artefacts such as timbers or masonry from the site, provided these do not exceed its SWL. However, remember that stonework can be difficult to attach for hoisting without proper slings, and that timber may need reinforcing by strapping modern planks to it, together with the use of suitable padding to prevent damage during the removal operation.

Dumper trucks, as mentioned above, are often needed with other lifting gear if the process of transporting to the spoil heap is not to hold up the other parts of the spoil removal process. They will require regular inspections, especially of any hydraulics, a qualified driver, and are not allowed to take passengers or, usually, to go on to a public road. Edge boards should be fitted to the trench top where they are working to prevent any overshoot, otherwise the dumper will suddenly join the diggers in the base of the excavation. Finally, with all of this plant working at the same time, there may be a build up of fumes in a deep excavation or even more with an inside excavation. Air quality within the trench may therefore have to be monitored to check on carbon monoxide levels.

5.4 Shoring

Excavations, by definition, lower the level of the ground surface within the trench and, if the reduction is greater than 1.2m, its sides must be shored. Dangers in shoring trenches occur mainly when inserting or removing the supports but any system will require regular inspections in between, especially if conditions change radically, for example as a result of a downpour, or if the standing walls which form one side of the trench are part of a building which contractors are busy dismantling round your ears. Some more specialist aspects of shoring will require the expert advice of a qualified engineer and here help-in-kind from developers of the site may become extremely useful. Of course, it is vitally important that you get the right people for the job, not just those said 'to know a bit about the subject'. But by explaining your archaeological problems and encouraging them to put their expertise at your disposal, it may also be possible to promote their interest in archaeology at the same time (Ross 1971).

One way to shore a trench is to batter the sides at the top and step in the trench at a lower level, the angle of batter being a function of the nature and stability of the material being dug into. This method obviously has the disadvantage of producing a smaller excavation area at the lower levels of the trench, but as long as this is known in advance and is catered for in deciding initial trench dimensions, it can be quite effective. Another basic approach is to prop the sides of the trench with scaffold boards against the section faces supported by internal raking braces, usually 'Acro' props, attached to them. This, though simple, has the disadvantage that the props intrude into the excavation area and thus complicate work. It is also very difficult to extend such a system as the excavation proceeds downwards.

Given the above difficulties, it is more useful to insert a vertical framework in small trenches, held in place by cross-members and extendable downwards as the work proceeds. Various systems are available to perform this function, utilising both timber boards and metal sheets. Some of the members which would otherwise revet the trench sides can even be omitted to allow section drawing of stratigraphy at the trench edge at vital points, as long as the safety of the system is not compromised by doing this. As an alternative, a cumulative section can be drawn at the base of the trench of its baulks before lowering the shoring to a new, lower level (Plate 25). Thus, although the sheets may eventually totally obscure the trench sides, one does not lose what might be a vital aspect of the record. As a trench deepens, it is important that ladder access is provided. It can be dangerous to use the framework to climb in and out since this is designed for a lateral, not vertical load.

When a large area must be spanned, difficulties with using such frames will arise. Then it may become necessary to invest in the expense of sheet piling the perimeter of the excavation (Plate 16). Here interlocking sheets are driven into the ground with a piling rig (make sure that there are no services in the area below beforehand!). This can be a time-consuming and messy business, so site staff may have to have other work available during the driving operation. If excavation proceeds to a sufficient depth within the sheet piles, it is usually necessary to insert a subsidiary walling within the trench, either perpendicular cross-members or diagonal braces, to hold the sheets in place. This is even more difficult to organise within an ongoing excavation because piling contractors are used to doing such work on level ground, which archaeological sites rarely are, and to having uninhibited access to the area inside, rather than having to avoid trampling on, or driving over, delicate stratigraphy. It is also a process which is difficult to plan in advance; contractor's work requires advance warning with a 'lead-time' of several weeks, but reaching exact depths in the stratigraphic sequence can be difficult for the archaeologist to calculate with corresponding accuracy.

In such cases the qualified engineer becomes vitally important, being able both to take on board the archaeological considerations and to consult with piling contractors in language which they understand. For example, it may be possible to design the positions of wailings crossing the site to fit along the lines of robber trenches or other linear cuts, thus minimising archaeological damage when they are inserted. When well-organised, sheet piles can give a safe, clear and dry trench in which to excavate. Indeed, with water-logged sites, they may be a prerequisite of any work being done, especially if the most important levels are at the base of the excavation. Of course, in excluding water, piles also seal water in, so surface run-off from adjacent areas and rain will have to be catered for.

5.5 De-watering

On some sites, ground water can be a great problem, limiting the adequacy of recording and greatly increasing the risks of injury during the work, or even preventing any excavation. In such cases, pumps operating from an appropriate

Plate 16 The sides of a large excavation area are revetted using sheet piles, with extra internal supports added at a later stage (*top*). This allows a dry, well-ordered excavation to proceed. However, the system can only be set up using a large piling rig imported onto the site. This must be organised in advance and is worked by non-archaeologists. For smaller areas (*bottom*), a similar system can be inserted using a JCB/backhoe, then tensioned using hydraulic pressure on the internal struts. Thereafter, by selectively releasing that pressure, sheets can be driven down manually as excavation proceeds inside. It is important to realise that subsidiary struts are built to cater for horizontal forces, not vertical loads and should not be weighted with large containers of spoil (occasional finds bags or bits of drawing equipment, as here, should not pose any threat to the integrity of the structure).

sump may be required (Fasham 1984). A sump can be specifically dug for pumping out, or located within a convenient excavated archaeological feature, for instance a well or deep rubbish pit. In either case it may be necessary to shutter its sides to prevent collapse and clogging of pumps during operations. It should also be remembered that pumping can affect the stability of the surrounding area, so qualified engineering advice may be needed before implementing a system.

For small excavations, electric pumps with a motor in a submersible head can be used. However, for work on any scale, they would be needed in some numbers. A better solution then is the separate, wheeled engine, set outside the trench, with a 2 in. or 3 in. (50mm or 80mm) capacity pipe. However, this does have the drawbacks of creating noise and fumes and needing regular maintenance checks and someone to be designated as responsible for keeping it filled up with fuel. These pumps can be as difficult to start manually as dumper trucks or cranes, so an electric starter motor is to be preferred. If fitted with a timing mechanism, this can also be set to begin pumping before workers arrive in the morning so that they begin with a dry(ish) site. The alternatives are to spend the first hour paddling around and getting wet for the rest of the day or to assign someone the unenviable task of arriving on site at an ungodly hour to start the pumps. The ideal situation is to use the two methods in concert: high-capacity, diesel pumps to empty most water from the site before work starts, then small electric pumps to continue de-watering during the day without the noise and fumes.

Water from pumping can be removed using nearby drains or, if convenient, a river or the sea, large-scale de-watering being mostly necessary on waterlogged sites, which are usually close to standing water for obvious reasons. However, using waterways in this way may require permission from river authorities and, where existing storm drains are to be employed, care must be taken not to clog them with silt from the site.

5.6 Finds retrieval

Many projects now display a need to use finds retrieval systems other than old-fashioned hand recovery at the point of excavation. Indeed, for certain types of ecofact, hand recovery may be not only inadequate, but entirely misleading when interpreting the assemblages derived from the project. Recovery methods can range from the rudimentary – the person wheeling the barrow away monitors the spoil for artefacts beforehand while waiting for it to be filled – to the highly sophisticated, such as paraffin sieving/screening for fish bones. In some situations, for example on sites with limited stratigraphic distinctions, it may be possible to create an integrated approach to the excavation of soil, its removal from the site, and sieving for the finds which the soil contains (van Horn *et al.* 1986). Otherwise, the two most common finds recovery techniques used on most sites comprise the use of detectors to recover metal, and perhaps some organic, artefacts; and of water or dry screening. These will be discussed below.

Using metal detectors on site can still raise eyebrows in some quarters because of the long, and often stormy, debate about the activities of private detectorists (Gregory 1986, Dobinson and Denison 1995). However, the machines themselves are simply that – machines. It is the context of their operation which counts, and there is a big difference between finding artefacts for personal profit to sell on the international antiques market (which is *not* what most amateur detectorists are doing anyway) and recovering designated artefact types from controlled, stratified excavations. Metal detectors may be used to screen for *in situ* artefacts pre-excavation by simply checking over a deposit before its removal and tagging the position of any signals. In this case, all that is needed is the right equipment and the expertise to use it. The latter might be best imported from the local 'amateurs', who know the pros and cons of different machines and how difficult they are to use. It can also form the basis for collaboration to heal some of the aforementioned rifts.

Alternatively, screening may take place after excavation by monitoring soil kept in stratified groups beside the trench. Although any find recovered in this way lacks an exact spatial position, the stratigraphic unit to which it belongs can still be known. In this case, a suitable area will be needed which is free of underlying metal, large enough to spread out soil to a common depth and located as near as possible to where the material will be discarded after screening. If site staff are still worried about being seen as merely glorified treasure hunters, it may also be necessary to separate off this work area from visitors (however, in my experience, these matters seem problematical for the upper echelons of archaeological management, rather than the site workers actually involved in the detecting, or the public who watch them). Suitable equipment will be needed by those operating detectors, including non-steel toe-capped shoes. Also bear in mind that this work, though mundane, can be very tiring, so a rota-system may be advantageous. Not everyone may want to be involved: some find wearing headphones and working in such an unreal atmosphere difficult and this should obviously be respected, apart from the fact that they will not be working with the efficiency and commitment of an enthusiastic operator.

Secondly there is sieving/screening for finds. In some cases, especially with small environmental material, this will often take place off-site under controlled laboratory conditions, whether during or after the dig. However, in others, it may be desirable to get feedback on what is being recovered with minimal delay or to sample on a scale which makes on-site work essential. Mostly this will mean sieving rather than sorting residues, especially since the latter may require equipment such as microscopes. If sieving is to take place, preparations of equipment, clothing, water supply, etc. will have to be arranged

Plate 17 A concrete mixer being used to separate soil from the more robust finds, with residues then tipped onto meshes below to be sorted – crude but effective!

beforehand. Some requirements can be met with fairly rudimentary equipment (see Fitzgerald 1985 for one approach, and Jones and Bullock 1988 for another – a concrete mixer!! Plate 17). Exactly what is needed here depends entirely on one's research objectives and how these are followed through in finds recovery systems (below, 12.1 and 12.2). As with metal-detecting, staff with different aptitudes and attitudes will have to be accommodated.

6

A STRUCTURED APPROACH TO RECORDING

Introduction

The recording process which takes place during excavation is, in principle, a straightforward matter. The objective of the exercise is to split the site into its component parts – its stratigraphic units, however defined – and then remove them in the reverse order to which they were deposited, recording their physical, spatial and stratigraphic properties in the process and collecting finds from them to agreed sampling policies as one proceeds. A number allocated to each unit enables its various attributes and the artefacts and ecofacts derived from it to be tied together for the purposes of later analysis.

In Chapters 4 and 5, it was suggested that a structured approach to site organisation pays dividends and the same applies when tackling the intricacies of stratigraphic recording: there is a logic that can be applied to the order in which the work is done. One way of ordering these tasks is outlined below. Such a systematic approach becomes particularly important when a large number of people are involved in site recording, with resulting need to integrate their work. Indeed, if time pressure requires the implementation of shift systems to allow work to continue twenty-four hours per day, it will then be commonplace for one excavator to start the recording cycle and another to complete it. Here a set procedure will obviously be vital. Yet professional, full-time field-workers need set ways of doing things, to common standards and in an agreed order, even to cope with the normal dislocations of site work caused by illness, vacations, etc.

In any recording process, one should only start the sequence of operations after the limits of the stratigraphic unit being dealt with are known (see **6.1**). It is also necessary to design beforehand a numbering system for labelling each unit (**6.2**). With these in place, the process of recording each unit can follow a set sequence of work (**6.3**). Such an organised approach can be reinforced further by the use of pre-printed recording sheets to store the resulting data (**6.4**).

6.1 The limits of a stratigraphic unit

The first, albeit obvious, point to make about site recording concerns the position of the unit to be excavated in the stratigraphic sequence. Excavations progress by taking away the latest unit first so, before starting to deal with any particular unit, the excavator has to be certain that it is not overlapped by another – in fact to be certain that this *is* the uppermost unit. Also its limits must have been defined on all sides in order to record its complete extent in plan. Thus the excavator should not start the process of recording until a unit is provably unsealed on every edge. If this seems a trivial point, it is only necessary to remember the number of times one has been tempted to start to record a layer at one end, and so begun planning, levelling and describing it, while studiously ignoring the fact that, at the other end, its relationship with a second layer still needs to be sorted out. Unfortunately, ignoring the latter problem does not make it go away. Things get worse when one finds that the first deposit not only continues below the second, but that the latter is itself cut by a pit, which is stratigraphically earlier than a wall, which is abutted by all the extant stratigraphy on the rest of the site . . . The excavator is then in the middle of dealing with a unit which may not become completely unsealed stratigraphically, and thus cannot be completely recorded, until many months later.

This need, to be sure that a stratigraphic unit is unsealed before starting the recording process, should not be confused with another, common situation, that of uncertainty as to the exact limits of a unit. For example, a soil layer may merge gradually with underlying deposits at one or more of its edges. Two points can be made about this. First, such degrees of merging are an important aspect of the stratigraphy, so a way of registering them must be built into the written or drawn record: plan conventions for indeterminate edges are the best solution (see below, 8.1). Second, if making stratigraphic distinctions is difficult owing to the character of the soils, nature of construction activity, etc., yet vital for the adopted research design, it will be necessary to develop techniques of enhancement which make such distinctions more apparent. This might involve simply spraying an apparently homogeneous thick soil deposit with water, to enhance colour differences. Alternatively, at the other end of the spectrum, one might use special photography, chemical treatment or even thin section analysis of carefully selected samples by a micromorphologist to distinguish between deposits (Carter 1993: 63). Each of these applications would need planning in advance.

Neither the need to consider enhancement nor the occasional inevitability of some degree of indeterminacy of edge can justify excavating one unit before another which is provably later than it. The only situations in which working out of stratigraphic order can be legitimate are: for safety reasons (for example dismantling the uppermost, dangerous elements of an early wall which is protruding from below later stratigraphy); because a later feature is to be preserved *in situ* (for example to be part of a permanent site display after the end of the project); or if the latest element is awaiting specialist treatment (for example a structural feature requiring photogrammetric recording, or a timber needing conservation, where one does not wish to stop all other work in the meantime).

These, of course, are intentional actions based on a secure knowledge of the sequence, rather than the excavator not having bothered to clean up a difficult and confused part of the site.

Sometimes, even with enhancement, it can be impossible to be sure of stratigraphic distinctions. Then one may be forced to abandon full stratigraphic methods and excavate using an arbitrarily imposed spit system (see below, 11.5). The decision on whether to take refuge in spit excavation requires balancing the resource and time implications of developing, then using, an effective system of enhancement against the needs of the project to recover stratigraphic and structural information, together with properly constituted finds groups. The further difficulty arises when one can define stratigraphic distinctions easily at certain points in the sequence, but this is impossible at others. Then one is forced to change regularly from one approach to another. Part of the sequence will be excavated using stratigraphic distinctions drawn on the basis of the physical properties of the deposits concerned, the remainder by spits. It is not the fact of changing systems or of employing different techniques for different situations that is problematical, but of failing to acknowledge that the change has occurred. Some formalised system of defining 'recovery levels' (Carver 1986), and noting when one moves between them, then becomes essential.

6.2 Numbering systems

The issue of 'What is a site?' has been discussed above (Chapter 2) and will have to be decided for each project on the basis of its research objectives and the cultural or natural boundaries which they define, set beside its present-day context and the physical and legal limits within which the excavation takes place. Thus the former may define chronological limits within which the excavation will fall ('We are intending to investigate the medieval levels but will be leaving all of the earlier features alone'), and the latter may dictate that the position of the trench ('Set right up against the modern street at the northern end, and as far as possible to the south given the limitations of time and resources on the project').

The site thus defined must be given a unique name, particularly if the organisation undertaking the work is running several projects at once. Any referencing system can be used for site codes, as long as it is clear and extendible without confusion. Letter codes (thus 'Ashcroft' for the site in Ashcroft Road) can be cumbersome and can only be listed alphabetically. A numerical system is simpler and indefinitely extendible (thus '1995.25' – the twenty-fifth site started by the organisation in 1995) but it does not contain such a useful *aide-mémoire* as the letter code. Here the best compromise may be a combination of the year in which the work started and a letter abbreviation (thus 'ASH95' for the above). Whatever is chosen, it should be simple and not too lengthy.

Remember that the chosen name will have to be marked onto hundreds of labels, and maybe thousands of small artefacts.

The stratigraphic units into which any site is split must also be coded according to a system which is simple, logical, easily readable and retrievable, yet flexible and capable of infinite extension. Since most sites contain more than twenty-six stratigraphic units, numbers are much to be preferred over letters. If all units have the same status on site, it is best to use a single numbering system for them. Some excavations reserve certain numbers in advance, either for particular features ('All skeletons will be in the range 5000–5999'), or according to a defined area ('Trench A is 0–999, Trench B 1000–1999'). This does have the advantage of being able to identify 'all the skeletons' or 'all the Trench A layers' quickly and allow them to be stored together.

However, there are corresponding disadvantages. One may turn out to have too many numbers for certain purposes and not enough for others, because size of the number blocks needed cannot be defined accurately in advance. Then gaps in the running sequence can occur. These will make it difficult to decide whether a number was never allocated or if a real stratigraphic unit was indeed identified, but the information from it later went missing. Also double numbering can easily happen, which is not only very confusing but also disastrous if finds from what are really different units have become amalgamated. Finally, the supposed advantages – that the records of a whole trench, all the burials or whatever, can be stored together – are less important today, when modern systems of computer retrieval allow listing, etc. of particular attributes to be quickly accomplished. On balance, therefore, it is preferable to allocate a number to each stratigraphic unit as necessary, i.e. as it becomes the uppermost surviving unit and is about to be drawn, described and removed.

On some sites a hierarchy of types of stratigraphic units is recognised during the excavation. Thus several fills are recorded as belonging to the same pit, which receives a feature number; and a collection of walls, pits, floors and deposits will be recorded on site as belonging to a building. Certain organisations who operate with such a hierarchy have stuck to a single numbering system, on the grounds that this system then gives site directors the latitude to use as they wish (Jefferies 1977). However, in reality, this supposed freedom means that there is no real structure to the data-base at all: a number may refer to an environmental sample, an artefact, a deposit, a feature, a building or even a whole site. Being all things to all people, such a 'system' ends up meaning nothing to any of them.

If one wishes to create a site record in which different classes of stratigraphic units are nested within each other, then it is essential that the numbering system explicitly reflects these hierarchical relationships. Thus each level will deserve its own numbering system (e.g. Stratigraphic Units 1–n, Features F1–Fn, Buildings B1–Bn, etc.). The hierarchy of numbering will need to be interrelated and cross-referenced as part of the recording process and this in itself can be quite a complicated business. Unless evaluation has been very full, and the system is very rigid, not all layers will belong to a specific feature and not all features to a building. Furthermore, buildings may thus contain not just features (i.e. units of the next level down) but layers not allocated to features (i.e. units below the level of features). So, before employing these hierarchically related units, and labelling them during the excavation process, it is necessary to think very carefully about their expected role in post-excavation analysis.

The alternative is to number only the basic units during the excavation and leave higher-order groupings to a later stage. Thus one would employ a single numbering system, starting with 1, and expect no gaps or duplication between it and the number allocated to the final unit. This approach has the clear merit of simplicity, though necessarily puts greater emphasis on stratigraphic analysis post-excavation (see further discussion below, Chapter 13).

6.3 The process of recording

In all excavations, but especially in those with large numbers of people operating in open areas which one is trying to excavate 'in phase', it is difficult to control the activities of excavators, particularly under pressure of tight deadlines in a variety of ever-changing situations. To keep up morale and efficiency, it is vital for everyone to know where they are at all times. The best solution is to designate a process which should be followed in recording each individual stratigraphic unit. The order in which the tasks are done, and especially the emphasis given to each, will obviously vary between projects. Also unexpected changes in excavation conditions within a specific project may require exceptions to any rule. However, as argued previously, working away from the known to the unknown is much to be preferred. Whatever order is chosen, it is vital that it controls site activities in a way which guarantees that the excavator produces data in every sphere deemed necessary by research design. The itinerary outlined here (Figure 8), though certainly not the only one possible, is that which I have found to work in a variety of situations in the past. It also creates an order for the discussions of the following chapters.

It has already been mentioned that, unless she is sure that the unit to be recorded is the uppermost surviving on that part of the site, the excavator should not start the process of recording. This requires that the area be clean enough for such certainty, and in particular that the limits of the unit, together with its degrees of merging with underlying units, are understood (*Step A*).

It is only at the point when the unit is known to be uppermost that it becomes relevant to allocate a number to it from the designated sequence, in order to avoid those problems, flagged up previously, of starting the recording process of a stratigraphic unit out of sequence. However, once a unit *is* ready for excavation, it should be labelled immediately so that this number may appear on all

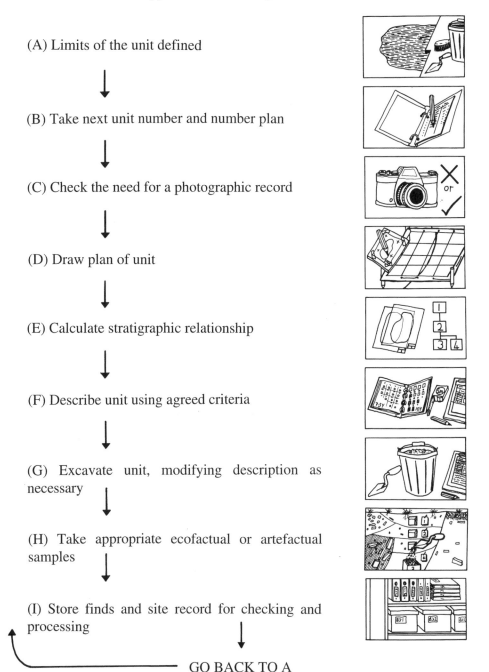

(A) Limits of the unit defined

↓

(B) Take next unit number and number plan

↓

(C) Check the need for a photographic record

↓

(D) Draw plan of unit

↓

(E) Calculate stratigraphic relationship

↓

(F) Describe unit using agreed criteria

↓

(G) Excavate unit, modifying description as necessary

↓

(H) Take appropriate ecofactual or artefactual samples

↓

(I) Store finds and site record for checking and processing

↓

GO BACK TO A

Figure 8 A flow diagram for recording a single stratigraphic unit.

photographs, plans, descriptions, samples etc. Numbers should be 'signed out' by the recorder, the simplest method being a series of pre-numbered sheets placed in a 'for site use' file, with a note on the final numbered sheet reminding the person who removes it to number the next fifty. As each sheet is taken, the recorder fills in an index book giving their initials and noting the type of unit concerned, the date etc. (*Step B*).

The time when a unit has been cleaned and its limits identified is often the best point at which to take photographs, before it gets trampled on in planning, partially dug away, or affected by sampling procedures (*Step C* – see Chapter 7 for a discussion of photography). All stratigraphic units have a spatial dimension, either in plan or in elevation. This must be recorded before any of the material is excavated (*Step D* – see Chapter 8 on the spatial record). Next the stratigraphic relationships of this new unit are best established before any of the evidence of its extent and character is removed from the ground. However, on sites of any complexity, this cannot be done easily before a plan has been drawn. Hence calculating its stratigraphic relationships with overlying units is best done after planning but before any excavation takes place. Underlying relationships can be recorded by a simple cross-referencing process at a later stage (*Step E* – Chapter 9 discusses the mechanics of this operation). With the spatial and stratigraphic records in place, the physical characteristics of the unit can be recorded, or at least a preliminary description produced. This will require close inspection of its surface and field tests of its component parts according to agreed criteria and procedures (*Step F* – the descriptive record is discussed in Chapters 10 and 11).

With this basic record of spatial, stratigraphic and physical characteristics in place, the excavation of the unit can begin, using the correct tools. In the process, the original description of the unit may be modified as appropriate (*Step G*). During this time it will also be necessary to operate the correct sampling procedures for artefact and ecofact recovery. These may range from basic methods such as sorting finds from soil in the wheelbarrow, to taking detailed samples in plan and elevation for the micromorphologist to elucidate the formation and transformation processes of the deposit (*Step H* – discussed with G in Chapter 12). Finally, the finds and samples derived from the unit must be sent for further processing or storage, and the record of its spatial, stratigraphic and physical characteristics checked for accuracy and then stored (*Step I*).

At any one time, assuming no errors of stratigraphic judgement, each excavator should be working on no more than one unit. Hence, with fifty people, no more than fifty plans and unit description sheets should be booked out. Numbers are unlikely to be allocated but unused, as excavators are forced to follow through the complete recording of one unit before they go on to the next. Using a single numbering system and the ledger, the director can book numbers in and out, thus monitoring the progress of every unit on the site: each number represents either a finished unit which has been checked back in, or a stratum under active investigation, or is yet to be allocated. Even the most complex excavation involving tens of thousands of layers and employing many excavators of a variety of experiences can be closely controlled and the status of any unit from the start of work to that moment in time calculated immediately. In this way stratigraphic analysis (Chapter 13) and other post-excavation procedures can be started immediately the excavation ends (or at least after a well-deserved holiday).

What has been described is a cyclical process. Thus recording one unit, *and being sure of its complete removal*, involves knowing simultaneously the character and limits of underlying strata. Furthermore, in the process of excavating an overlying deposit, it is usually possible to define the stratigraphic relationships between those strata beneath, if one is excavating cleanly and with proper attention to detail. Hence, if one is certain that the end of one unit has been reached, it should be possible to go straight on with the next one (*Step J –* essentially, go back to Step A).

6.4 A recording sheet (see Figures 17, 19, 22 and 24)

Not long ago stratigraphic units were recorded in site notebooks with descriptions written out on successive lines and sketches done on graph paper opposite. Now the process of recording has been taken one logical step further by putting all the information for each unit on a single pre-printed sheet. This is both methodologically more acceptable and practically more appropriate (worries about individual sheets of paper flying away in the wind can be solved by using clip boards to hold all records). Similarly, it is common to plan each unit on a single drawing using either drawing film with pre-printed grid squares of a standard size to ease archiving or, where unavailable, plastic film cut to size on clip boards covered with an underlay of graph paper to enable accurate planning.

From an organisational point of view, individual description and planning sheets also allow many individuals to record on site simultaneously, and create a record which is infinitely extendible, unlike the old site notebook. Only in the frantic conditions of a watching brief would a notebook come back into its own, but then probably as a basis for creating a proper account later, rather than as a final record in itself. Even here, the use of tape-recorders and cheap instant cameras may soon make the notebook as redundant as the back of the proverbial envelope or cigarette packet.

The design of a recording sheet will vary, of course, with the type of unit being dealt with. Examples of sheets for deposits, masonry and brick features, timbers, human skeletons and intrusive features are given elsewhere (Chapters 10 and 11). However, all such records will have certain core components in common. Hence it will always be necessary to note the *site code*, the *type of unit* involved and its *unique number*. There will have to be space for *descriptive information*, perhaps structured on the sheet in a way which automatically reminds the excavator of the project's recording system, and for references to drawings, site grid references, levels and other *spatial information*. Similarly, *stratigraphic relationships* must be noted and there will be ways of cross-referencing to the *photographic record*, the *artefactual record* (noting the finds present and a collection keyword, plus the recovery process used) and the *ecofactual record* (the type of sample, number of bags, reason(s) for sample). At the end of the recording procedure in the field, bureaucratic niceties must be observed by allowing the recorder, and the person who checked their work, to *sign and date* the sheet. Finally, either at this stage or later in analysis, it will be necessary to add *other notes and interpretation*, together with any *phasing decisions*, to that record. These should also be duly *signed and dated by the interpreter(s)*.

7

THE PHOTOGRAPHIC RECORD

Introduction

The photographic needs of any site should be expressed in an overall photographic policy based on a combination of the research agenda of the project, the nature of the stratigraphy being investigated and the resources available. However, there will be problems, both theoretical and practical, in implementing any such policy when a particular archaeological feature is being investigated. The theoretical problems derive from the fact that the decision as to when to take a photograph, and what to include and what to exclude, usually requires a higher order of interpretative decision than those involved in the rest of the recording procedure. For example, in order to produce a 'phase photograph' of a trench, it is necessary to have decided beforehand which features go together – 'these two walls, the clay floor with its industrial hearth in between them, and that external metalling are associated in a single phase of building'. Such decisions concerning correlations between stratigraphy, the functional interpretation of particular features, and the importance of particular horizons, are difficult to make with complete accuracy. And they are certainly different in kind from other, more basic decisions taken in the normal process of excavation, for instance that the deposit exposed in front of the recorder is the uppermost stratigraphic unit and thus needs to be planned, described and removed next.

It is not just these higher-order interpretative components which make the photographic record more complex to create than the drawn and written one. At the purely practical level, one must also make difficult decisions on the timing and exact content of the photograph and preparation for any shot will involve the integration of the work of a variety of individuals. Their activities have to be programmed so that the whole of a designated area is exposed at a pre-defined stage of investigation. Finally, if more technical methods such as photogrammetry are to be employed for particular purposes, the decision-making process as to what deserves such special treatment, when and how, creates even greater complexity.

The justification for producing a particular form of photographic record on an excavation is seldom discussed in detail, and even more rarely is it made explicit in the form of a clear policy. A common answer to the question 'Why do we need to photograph a site at all?' is that it produces a more objective account than the written or drawn record. The latter, it is suggested, is subject to biases of individual excavators as they decide what to plan, measure or describe and what to omit, whereas photographs are not prone to such prejudice. Yet this is rather a misleading conception. First, as argued earlier, every part of the recording process should be the result of a systematic approach to recording agreed by everyone, not a purely individual response. Second, photographs are no more 'objective' than other aspects of that record. When taking a photograph, someone still decides where to point the camera and from what angle, and on the content of the shot. That person also chooses to use a particular type of camera and film, including film speed, and employs specific processing methods, types of printing paper, etc. in developing the negatives. Hence it may be accepted that the importance of a photographic image derives from the fact that the camera does not edit or simplify the site – if the limit of a stratigraphic unit is tenuous on one edge, no matter how much cleaning and definition work takes place, this may be more apparent in the photographic record than in its drawn counterpart. However, any photograph is still attempting to translate colour and tone into monotone, or at best approximate colour equivalents, and to convert the shape, size and spatial configuration of real objects existing in three dimensions into a two-dimensional image. This process of translation and conversion is both a power and a limitation. Photographs, then, are a *different* aspect of the record but not an inherently more objective one.

The following discussion starts by outlining the different aims of site photography: recording details within particular units, the extent of whole deposits, the stratigraphic relationships between such entities, then 'phase' and 'daily record' shots (see **7.1**, below). This is followed by a description of the various techniques required to prepare sites for photography (**7.2**), finishing with a mention of various specialist uses, in particular photogrammetry, vertical photography of skeletons, and the use of video (**7.3**).

7.1 Reasons to photograph

There are a variety of roles which the photographic record might play in an excavation. Some of the more prominent are described below, moving from the particular to the general – recording details within an individual stratigraphic unit, the whole unit in isolation, the relationships between units or between groups of units thought to belong to a single period or feature, and 'daily record' shots.

The most specific photograph records detail **within a stratigraphic unit**. This can be a visual record of soil particles forming a deposit whose configuration elucidates site formation processes (for example the primary silting of a ditch); shots from carefully specified angles of the surface detail of a layer (for example to show wear patterns on an external metalling); or, most commonly, photographs of *in situ* artefacts or ecofacts to elucidate the position and status of a find in relation to its associated deposit (Plate 18). Such photographs can also

Plate 18 (*Top*) The articulated bones of small vertebrates found between larger leg bones associated with a human burial, suggesting that the corpse was exposed and the grave then acted as a deposit trap. (*Bottom*) Articulated cod vertebrae from Robert's Haven, a thirteenth-century site in Caithness, Scotland, implying an undisturbed deposit, here most reasonably interpreted as a midden. Such photographs not only record the stratigraphic context of bones but illustrate its significance for site formation processes and hence social interpretation.

arise as a result of specialist requirements, as with the need to record architectural features incorporated into a standing wall to aid future reconstruction. Of course, a policy of photographing every unit from every angle and at every stage of its excavation on the off-chance that it would yield such information would be inappropriate. What is required is to be alive to individual possibilities and react accordingly. Thus the decision on whether to take a picture, the best stage to do this, and the angle to take it from, will be a product of individual circumstance.

A second type of photograph is the vertical **record of a specific stratigraphic unit**, which can be planned in advance and thus operate within an overall policy. The *rationale* for photographing every unit is usually explained in terms of the need to record 'what each layer was like'. This means little in isolation, but what its proponents usually intend is that a record of the particular surface characteristics of each unit, which might otherwise be ignored, is retained. For example, most systems for plan drawing on site include decisions concerning the level of detail of surface inclusions to be drawn. Inevitably this means that the smallest elements will not be represented individually, but either receive schematic treatment or will not be recorded at all. A photograph, if used on a consistent basis, can fill this gap. Its most common use on site is for photographing individual skeletons, though recent developments in computer technology may take this approach to its logical conclusion, with traditional methods of planning being replaced by EDM to record layer outlines and digital camera surface detail. An added bonus *may* be that computer storage of the resulting pixels can provide a better long-term archive medium than hardcopy for photographic records.

A more general role for the photographic record is to register the **physical relationships between specific units**, usually in addition to the formal stratigraphic record rather than in place of it. On a site of any complexity, there will be an indefinite number of possible stratigraphic relationships which might deserve such treatment, so there will have to be a selection process to decide which shots to take rather than an overall policy for every unit. Two criteria can be put forward in deciding which relationships to treat in this way. First, those deemed *the most important* can be photographed. For example, during the process of excavation, one might know, or at least suspect, that a particular relationship will be of great significance for the interpretation of the sequence, either because of the nature of a specific feature or as a direct product of the research design employed. Thus if an excavation was set up to investigate associations between field systems, with a trench sited at the intersection of two boundaries as suggested by aerial photography, then the relationship between these features, when exposed, would be an obvious candidate for photography. Equally, if the objective was to get thermomagnetic dates from a series of hearths, then the proven stratigraphic relationships between the features might be selected for photography (Plate 19).

Plate 19 This shot of a medieval hearth, cleaned to a very high standard, shows the feature's material characteristics in a way which a drawing may never do. It also displays its relationship to an earlier feature in the foreground. A matrix diagram may show the stratigraphic sequence, but physical relationships of this sort may be obscured with single-context planning. Photography provides a corrective.

The second criterion is, in a sense, the exact opposite of the first. Some stratigraphic relationships are very difficult to determine, no matter how clean the site is and how able and experienced the excavator. A tenuous relationship may be known to be important at the time, or thought to be unimportant but become vital subsequently The abutment of two walls, the point at which one ditch system is cut by another, the partial sealing of a line of post holes by a later surface, or the time at which a particular structural division may have come into play in the sequence may all be potential candidates. In each case, it

Plate 20 The relationships between horizontal stratigraphy and structural divisions can be difficult to define, even after intensive analysis, and may have to rely on interpretation of stratigraphic asymmetries, rather than proven relationships. Here (*top*) the differences between clay floors to the left and to the right make it quite clear that a timber partition divided the two. With the trench-built wall (*bottom*), the different heights, texture and inclusions within the stratigraphic accumulations on either side of the stones suggest, albeit more tentatively, that the wall was in place when the deposit to the left formed. In the third photograph (*next page*), similarities in the surface detail of the clay floors to either side of the line of stones suggest that the latter were set into an existing surface, though one may never be absolutely sure.

Plate 20 (*cont.*)

makes sense to record such problem areas as fully as possible to aid later interpretation. Even if the photograph fails to help subsequently, it still helps to
show all interested parties why the stratigraphic relationship could not be
determined during the excavation, and thus why the record here remains necessarily equivocal (Plate 20).

At a more general level than particular stratigraphic relationships there is the
'phase photograph'. It is often possible to deduce, even during the process of
excavation, that a set of features go together and a photograph of a whole
period, or of a complete building, may then be appropriate. The decisions
involved are basically the same as those needed to decide to draw a phase plan
during the excavation process (to be discussed in Chapter 8), and thus will
employ some high-level interpretative reasoning which may be still open to
question. Nevertheless, the effort may still be worthwhile, even if later analysis
shows that the elements represented in the photograph do not really belong to
exactly the same phase or structure.

A related, though different, issue concerns the policy of taking a **'record shot'**
of the excavation at daily, or longer, intervals. This has essentially the same
rationale as the 'top plan' drawn at a certain point in the excavation and is thus
subject to the same reservations (below, Chapter 8): it records the process of
excavation rather than any past reality. Thus its role in any post-excavation
analysis must be questioned and, unlike the phase photograph, it does not even
have the status of a hypothesis which the analyst could test. None the less,
photographs which give general views of the site and of the work in progress,
the character of excavation, working conditions, etc., even if not part of the
basic record, can be very useful as an *aide-mémoire* during report writing and
to introduce specialists to the site before they do their work. They can also help

the reader of the final publication report to understand the process of excavation, and can present site interpretations in an informed and interesting way.

This brings up a final point about photography on excavations, going beyond its role within the formal site record discussed so far. Many people have contact with, and want to know about, the results of a project well before a weighty, published tome appears on the shelf (especially as the latter is usually available only several years after fieldwork has been completed). Sponsors, site visitors, museum exhibitions, etc. may need to use publicity shots of the work as it takes place, and to have some intimations of its main results, sometimes before any of the work has been properly completed (for instance to generate further funding), and certainly while the excavation is in progress. By the same token, audiences at conferences, academic institutions, etc. will become much more engaged with the project if lecture slides and other illustrative material can be provided at an early stage. So, as well as being part of the basic record, photographs are needed to fulfil these more general roles.

Some of this material can be produced by simply taking photographs as excavation proceeds, with a minimum of dislocation, but at other times it is necessary to set things up in particular ways. In either case, excavators at work in the shot not only provide a scale, but can also give a lighter and more vivid impression to the audience. After all, archaeologists are usually uncovering places which real people once occupied, so it can enhance understanding to include humans in any image. Finally, it should be remembered that the people working on the site also have an interest in seeing themselves and their fellow workers in action. Being a professional excavator does not mean that an ultra-serious atmosphere must pervade all activity. Indeed, a little levity can go some way to overcoming the difficult working conditions and the bad pay to which most excavators are subjected. Photographs of work in progress, then, have a variety of important functions.

7.2 Preparations and techniques

The most basic preparation for all photography is to create the necessary level of cleanliness in the area to be recorded. As discussed previously, deciding on archaeological grounds the exact point at which an overall 'phase photograph' should be taken, for example, is not only difficult in terms of archaeological interpretation, but also no easy task to prepare for at the purely managerial level. If the area to be photographed is large, the work of many people must be integrated to ensure that all are at the same point in the recording cycle and that different individuals have achieved the same standard of preparation. It is also essential that the work is completed at more or less the same time in different parts of the site. Furthermore, all cleaning must be done moving from the higher to lower areas and in a single direction. In deciding which direction,

Plate 21 The bones of a foetus and mother who died in childbirth from the medieval cemetery of St Nicholas Shambles, London. This shot, now famous for the detail it embodies, could be taken only after careful cleaning, with delicate tools, over an extended period of time

it is important to plan where the spoil resulting from the operation is to be deposited, otherwise it may become necessary to walk over finished areas to empty buckets, or one may, in effect, paint oneself into an archaeological corner. Site-wide images in particular represent a considerable investment of intellectual and human resources. Unless such resources can be committed in advance, the end product will be unsuccessful and thus represent a waste of time and money, not an addition to the record. Hence large-scale photographs should not be undertaken lightly.

The taking of any photograph is a selective procedure, and thus the degree of cleanliness required can only be judged in relation to what the photograph is aiming to achieve, rather than in terms of an absolute standard (Plate 21). However, the fact that the shot is aiming to convey a predesignated set of information does not mean that preparations should take the form of actively 'creating' a particular image, for example by carving away the edges of certain layers to make them more visible. After all, the degree of blending between contiguous stratigraphic units is an important part of the information content of the photograph, not something to be hidden or obscured, still less modified. Differential brushing or trowelling of surfaces may be another matter, as is spraying the site. Certainly there is nothing wrong or misleading about dampening an area then taking a photograph at a specific point in the drying process. Indeed, differential drying can be the only way of recording important stratigraphic boundaries, as sites such as Yeavering (Hope-Taylor 1977) and Sutton Hoo (Carver 1986) have so clearly demonstrated. Of course, when mechanisms such a spraying are employed in this way, it is important to note the method used as part of the site record. Usually the dividing line between 'cheating' and simply enhancing a stratigraphic configuration is easily drawn in practice, provided the director puts her faith in the integrity of the excavator.

The actual mechanics of taking a photograph need not be covered in any detail here. Dorrell (1989), *inter alia,* gives a convenient résumé, including such matters as the type of photographic scale to be used and its positioning. Bar scales are the least intrusive and give an appearance of a scientific approach when placed in an unobtrusive position parallel to the side or base of the frame. In addition, some archaeologists favour the use of a colour control insert in every photograph so that the degree to which real colour on the ground has been modified by the processing of the film can be assessed. As mentioned above, human scales can add interest to the shot, and may be essential if large areas are being recorded. If used, the people concerned should be working appropriately, not posing in a way which diverts attention from the archaeological features which must remain its central focus.

Once the photograph has been taken, it is important to set up a logging system incorporating each shot to ensure that no element of the record gets mislaid. In addition every image must be cross-referenced to the rest of the site record, preferably by means of the latter's most basic numbering system. This can be achieved by simply listing all photographs, and the date on which they were taken, in order in a notebook and collating this with negatives or contact prints when the film has been developed. However, things change with a site of greater complexity, where many photographs are produced and there may be some delay between the taking of a particular shot and its being cross-referenced into the main record; or a photographic team may be dealing with several projects and thus different sites may appear on the same set of negatives. Then it may be better to create a system which numbers each shot, accompanied by a photographic diary. To this can be added a method of placing a label in each photograph which gives the numbers of the stratigraphic units being recorded. Chalk on a board is the cheapest method, but plastic letters are now a more commonly used, and neater, alternative.

7.3 Specialist uses

Particular situations on site bring with them their own photographic problems. For example, when working within standing buildings, control and consistency of lighting may be difficult and flash may be necessary (Plate 22). At the opposite extreme, in the open air, it may only be possible to get high enough for an

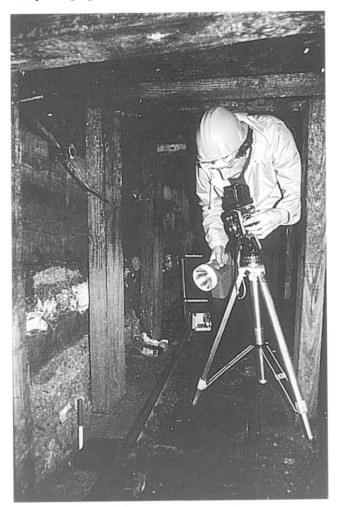

Plate 22 Photographic recording taking place in a tunnel for telephone cables running under Gracechurch Street in London, and thus right through the historic core of the Roman and medieval city.

overall shot of an extensive site by the use of an aeroplane, kites, or a specially constructed tower or bipod. In other cases, for example when working in deep and dangerous holes, or on the sides of high and precarious buildings, photography may be the only safe way of getting a visual record. Further particular specialist concerns include the use of photogrammetry for complex three-dimensional features, photography of skeletons and the use of video. These are discussed next.

Some commentators have recommended the employment of **photogram-metry,** on the basis that it produces a more intricate, and perhaps more sophisticated, record (Anderson 1983). Such a record could be created in isolation, or in combination with other, more traditional field methods (Cummer 1974).

The issue which needs to be thought through here is not how to attain the greatest degree of accuracy on the ground: photogrammetry, properly used, will clearly be better than conventional drawing. Rather the crucial question is how much accuracy is *needed* in a given situation. The decision to use photogrammetry to record part of a standing building, probably its most common application, is partially a function of the complexity of the feature under consideration. Hence the half-truncated remains of a stairway may require the full treatment, whereas a simple wall may not. But it is also a question of how one will need to utilise the data which result. What type of reconstruction needs to be created and how accurate must the record be to achieve this? Technical and architectural advice may be needed during the excavation to make an informed decision here, thus ensuring that the record is full enough, yet not increasing detail beyond what is strictly necessary. For instance, to reconstruct the superstructure of a medieval undercroft from the half-collapsed remains of part of its vaulted sub-structure, one may need expert advice beforehand and accurate recording of difficult angles in inaccessible places during the excavation. Here photogrammetry may be not just the quickest, safest and cheapest method, but perhaps the *only* way of getting the requisite degree of accuracy.

A second specialist area concerns the use of photographs, instead of a drawn plan, to **record human skeletons**. Creating scale drawings by hand on cemetery excavations can be very labour intensive and time consuming. A solution now widely adopted is to avoid drawing every skeleton, but to clean then photograph them instead. An exact drawing of the position of every bone, if this is later required, can then be created by overlaying plastic film on the developed photograph, blown up to the correct size, and tracing from that. For this to be successful, it is obviously essential that the skeleton is clean enough for all bones to be visible, or at least all to be visible enough for exact body placement to be deduced from their articulation (Plate 23). It is also necessary to tie in the skeleton to the site grid and to record its position in a vertical dimension. The latter can be done by taking levels at particular designated points on the skeleton, for example skull, sacrum and feet, plus any extra high or low points. The plan position can be recorded by placing spring-headed nails, perhaps brightly painted to aid visibility, at the extremities of the skeleton before the shot is taken and then recording their grid co-ordinates, or marking their position on the grave cut after lifting the bones. It is then a simple matter to rotate the photographic underlay to their exact, plotted position before the bones are traced off.

Lastly, some field-workers have recently emphasised the usefulness of **video** in recording the excavation process (Hanson and Rahtz 1988). They stress the advantages of high-quality colour image, instant playback and flexibility, though acknowledge that the cost of equipment and problems of storage of the record in archive may present difficulties. A more major problem, however, is that of how to achieve consistency for such a record. A video diary of an excavation could give useful information about the way in which data collection

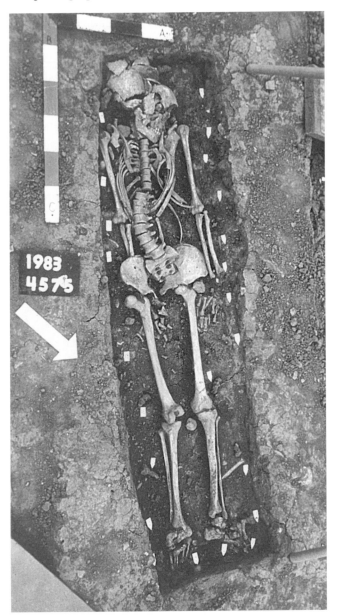

Plate 23 Photograph of a medieval skeleton, with year code and skeleton number, direction of view and coffin nail positions marked for future reference. Having been cleaned and photographed, it is ready for written recording and then lifting.

proceeded, the problems of recording at various stages, etc. As a hint or *aide-mémoire*, and one which produces moving images and thus gives a more rounded picture of the three-dimensional context in which work took place, video clearly has a potential role. However, if it is to be more than just a useful adjunct to the traditional excavation record, its application has to take place in a more structured way. To become part of the basic record of individual stratigraphic units which allows comparison between features in later analysis, the timing of shots, direction of view, etc. need careful consideration and consistent implementation. None the less, the wider availability of increasingly cheap equipment, and increasingly sophisticated computer storage of visual information, suggest that photography will have a continuing, and probably growing, importance in the site record.

8

THE SPATIAL RECORD

Introduction

All stratigraphic units have a spatial dimension, which can only be recorded in its entirety after a unit has become completely visible, and before any of it has been removed. Recording its position must therefore await its being defined as the uppermost element of the sequence but precede the start of excavation. Such spatial information can, of course, be gathered by purely informal methods, for example by the use of textual description ('The pit is about 2m across and lies 5m north of the building'). This approach may be adequate for initial survey work but greater accuracy is normally required in formal excavation and so a drawn element usually accompanies any written record.

In creating the drawn record, the usual practice is to start by setting up a grid system covering the site to which all drawings can be related. It is also necessary to decide at this initial stage on the techniques and equipment required, the latter being chosen with an eye to the future storage in archive (both issues discussed previously). The conventions to be adopted in the drawn record must then be decided (see **8.1** below). Next there must be an agreed policy on which elements to record in plan and which in section, and to what degree(s) of accuracy. Various types of approaches to planning can be suggested ('single context', 'phase' and 'daily' plans – **8.2**), and a variety of methods for producing such drawings can be used (triangulation, offsets or drawing frames – **8.3**), each with advantages and disadvantages in terms of speed and accuracy. Similarly, there are various types of sections and elevations (the recording of baulks at the limit of excavation, cumulative/running sections, and those laid out to solve particular stratigraphic problems or across intrusive or standing features to elucidate their character – **8.4**) and a variety of techniques can be used to prepare such surfaces for section drawing (**8.5**). Finally, as well as drawing complete stratigraphic units, particular circumstances may require recording the spatial position of individual finds within such units (**8.6**). Only when all these issues have been thought through will it be possible for the site worker, with the right equipment to hand and sufficient expertise in the hand, to complete any drawing.

Apart from knowing the conventions and having the right pencil and paper, there is another prerequisite for successful drawing on site – namely to have decided beforehand the limits of what you want to record. Only then can one ensure proper differentiation within, and between, drawings (Ford 1993). Some time ago a child, when asked how she approached her drawings, is reported as replying 'First I have a think, then I draw a line around my think.' This, to me, grasps the essence of producing technical drawings on site – they should be representations of decisions already made, not part of an evolving, individual thought process. Hence spatial aspects of the stratigraphy must be conveyed accurately, and in a way which is consistent with the activities of the other workers on site. The illustrator is concerned with graphics skills, not artistic inspiration.

8.1 Techniques, equipment and drawing conventions

In the near future, technical advances will reduce the amount of time taken up by planning. Spending many hours bent double over a drawing frame, plumb bob in one frozen hand and crayons in the other, will be a thing of the past. It will be replaced by the digitising of the periphery of a unit using a giant electronic pencil which transfers information directly to a computer in the site hut, storing only those points needed to produce an edge of unit to the requisite degree of accuracy dictated by the research design. Photographic techniques, most obviously digital cameras, will then be used to record the surface of the deposit without losing any nuances of detail (Stančič 1989) and the resulting image will be translated into pixels and draped by computer over the digitised periphery of the unit on screen when required by the archaeologist. Similarly, the position of each find will be recorded electronically and downloaded automatically (Plate 24). For the present, however, it's back to the drawing board.

It is not intended to discuss here the specific techniques required for archaeological illustration. Fortunately, it is easy to turn to far more accomplished illustrators in the field for advice. For example, the experience of Hope-Taylor (1966) is still relevant three decades later, even if the materials, especially the soft pencils which he recommends, have become outmoded (the use of plastic film – 'permatrace' – is *de rigueur* on most sites today). Barker's discussion (1977: 150ff) of the manual techniques involved is also very useful, together with his comments on the different proprietary brands of crayons which are available. Finally, Adkins and Adkins (1989: chapter 3) provide the most convenient, general discussion of the expertise required.

Similarly, the types of equipment, especially in relation to the long-term preservation of the record, are discussed in detail elsewhere. Adkins and Adkins (1989: chapter 2) look at mundane materials such as pencils and paper, plus some more technical equipment, and provide lists of suppliers. Arnold and Gersbach (1995) note the existence of a new machine for field drawing, the Kartomat, which has the advantage of not needing a power source. Finally, Kenworthy *et al.* (1985) give good general background on the horror stories that have arisen when archiving of the drawings which result is not properly

Plate 24 The use of an EDM to record the co-ordinates of individual finds, with data then downloaded directly onto computer. Here communication with the pole holder in the distance requires the use of walkie-talkie radio, held by an assistant to the right of the surveyor.

planned, and provide appropriate solutions. Other aspects such as the machine readable archive will no doubt be superseded as computer hardware and software are developed, though the principles which underpin their use will stay the same.

There remains the issue of the conventions to be used in drawing. Whether one employs a specialist architect for all site drawing (Dinsmoor 1977) or, as I would prefer, uses most site staff for producing the basic record but greater expertise for reconstruction and publication work, every site plan will have to incorporate a certain amount of standard information. Thus each should carry the appropriate site code; a plan number which either is allocated according to a running sequence or, for single-context plans, is the same as that of the stratigraphic unit drawn on it; a north sign and reference to the site grid which allows the plan to be related accurately to all other drawings; a place for the drawer to sign and the checker to counter-sign; and a space to add any relevant notes giving extra information, such as colour codes peculiar to that drawing. The use of pre-printed permatrace sheets is now widespread, ensuring that the appropriately sized boxes exist on each drawing to promote the completion of all this information. Such sheets also guarantee drawings of a consistent size, thus easing storage at a later stage. Finally, all drawings will have to be done to an appropriate scale, designated beforehand on the basis of the degree of accuracy demanded by the research design, with that chosen scale recorded on the illustration.

In addition to these common requirements, every site planner will have to adopt conventions for the edges of each unit and its surface details. When using plans to compare the extent of successive stratigraphic units in post-excavation analysis, two types of information concerning their edges are essential. First, the drawing must clearly show which edges represent the extent of a unit as it would have been when it was laid down, and which are arbitrary, constituting a limit where it was cut away by an intrusion or continued beyond the excavation: only edges of the first sort make statements about the 'real' boundaries of the unit, the others being evidence for what happened to it later. Hence if two adjacent floor make-ups have a common, real northern limit, this may be an indication that they abutted a wall line on that side. However, if their surviving edges coincide simply because both were truncated at this point by a later, linear intrusion, their corresponding edges need have no such implication.

Second, as mentioned previously, not all edges of a unit can be established with complete certainty and it is essential to record the *degree* of indeterminacy, as well as the fact of indeterminacy, on the drawing to aid the analyst using the spatial information later on. These uncertain limits should not be simply left open on the drawing. Even where they cannot be exactly determined, the edges may not vary wildly. Conventions to illustrate this degree of uncertainty are fairly straightforward. The most useful has proved to be a zig-zag symbol, whose width varies according to how uncertain the edge is.

Many excavations also record the distribution and type of inclusions incorporated into a unit, whether in its surface when drawing a plan, or in elevation in section. The level of detail required (i.e. the minimum size of inclusion to be drawn) will have to be designated in advance, bearing in mind the research objectives. Thus, if the distribution and size of cobbles in a road metalling is seen as essential to understanding the development of street topography, all such surface detail will have to be plotted accurately during the planning process. Equally, it will be important to relate any decisions on the size of inclusion to be included to the scale being used on the plan – remember that a sherd 2cm across at a scale of 1:20 is represented by a 1mm diameter dot. If surface inclusions down to this size are to be recorded usefully, more accurate, larger-scale drawings will be required.

A key to inclusion types will also have to be determined. Written abbreviations, noted adjacent to the detail on the plan, might be used when few inclusions are to be represented ('ch = charcoal, st = stone'). However, this method can become cumbersome on complex drawings and colour codes are now more common. By selecting a crayon close to the colour of the inclusion in the real world (black for charcoal, red or orange for ceramic tile, etc.), one can commit the conventions more easily to memory, removing the need to refer continuously to a correlation chart. However, when buying new crayons to colour in surface inclusions, always remember to reorder the same make: each company seems to produce slightly different shades and, if one is not careful, the orange convention for brick adopted at the start of the project begins to merge gradually with the red convention for tile over time, as office staff obey orders from their bosses to buy materials from whoever is the cheapest or most convenient supplier of the moment.

8.2 Types of plan

Drawings produced by hand are still the most common way to record the horizontal dimensions of a stratigraphic unit and here three types of plan can be distinguished – multi-context single-level plans, multi-context phase plans and single-context plans (Figure 9). Each has its advantages and drawbacks, the choice depending in particular on the depth and complexity of the stratigraphic sequence being recorded and its degree of integrity.

A **single-level ('top') plan** is a drawing of the extant stratigraphy, done at a designated point in the excavation process. Such drawings are the only form of planning recommended by some, a particular form being the 'daily trench plan'. Thus Joukowsky stipulates that 'all architectural features and objects must be plotted and recorded intelligibly on the daily plan' (1980: 214). Even if drawings are not produced on a daily basis, the method is still the norm on many excavations, and not just on sites with limited stratigraphy (Hammer 1992).

However, when dealing with complex sites, the problems of such a system become manifest. It is seen to be unsound in theory, and likely to produce incomplete records in practice. Concerning the former issue, any excavation aims to distinguish entities which relate to events which really happened in the past. Thus we record an area of clay as a distinct stratigraphic unit because it is believed to have once been a floor, a line of stones because it seems to have been a wall foundation, etc. However, the various units shown on a single-level plan, though they are viewed by the excavator on the site together at one time, do not purport to refer to a real, existing point in the historical development of the site. Indeed, they may be known to be of very different periods, even at the point at which the plan is being drawn.

For example, in the illustrated case (Figure 9), it is fairly clear, even at this stage, that the walls and floors at the base of the drawing are later than the two lines of post holes towards its centre. Equally the layer which overlies the corner of the wall on the bottom right, together with the pit which cuts into the metallings flanking it at the top right, obviously belongs to a later period(s). In sum, the only thing which the various units recorded on this top plan have in common, whether it was drawn at the end of a day, a week or an excavation

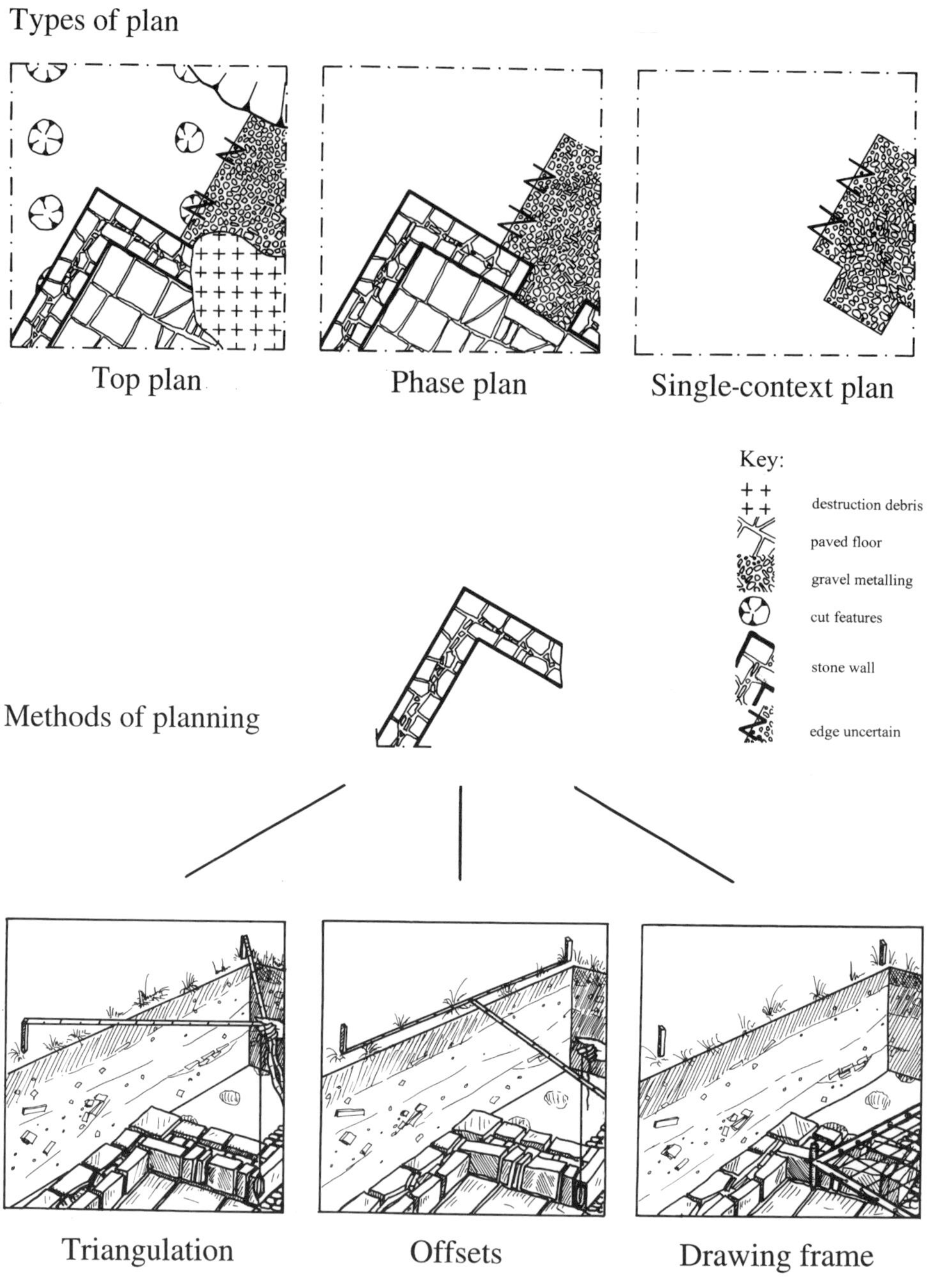

Types of plan

Top plan   Phase plan   Single-context plan

Key:

+ +
+ +   destruction debris

paved floor

gravel metalling

cut features

stone wall

edge uncertain

Methods of planning

Triangulation   Offsets   Drawing frame

Figure 9 Examples of different plan types and planning methods.

season, is that archaeologists happen to have exposed them at a single time. Thus the top plan method essentially records the process of excavation, the progress of the work, rather than the past reality which we, as field-workers, are trying to approach. This makes its production philosophically unsound.

Furthermore, there are practical problems. If the site includes superimposed stratigraphic units, then it is impossible for the full extent of each unit to be recorded on such multi-context plans. In the illustration, the probable doorway in the wall line is covered by a later layer. As a partial solution, the excavator might use dotted lines to show such sealed edges. However, doing so already represents a move away from the concept of drawing a single level and, because of the superimposition of units, such a plan is unlikely to record all of the surface detail of every unit: *lacunae* are likely to be embodied in the spatial record (Alvey and Moffett 1986).

A second approach, which gets round at least some of these problems, is to use **phase plans**, i.e. multi-context drawings of extant stratigraphy, created at a stage where the horizon exposed across the whole site is considered to belong to a single point in time in its development. Planning by phase is believed in some quarters to have 'long gone out of fashion' (Adkins and Adkins 1989: 77) but such plans are, in fact, still in widespread use within the field profession, at least in Britain (Hammer 1992). This is partly due to the influence of particular projects utilising the method, for example work in the 1970s in Winchester which trained a whole generation of field-workers and had a formative influence on stratigraphic practices in particular. Unlike the arbitrary 'top plan', this procedure at least has the merit of being based on a decision about an archaeological entity, the phase, which is purported to have actually existed in the past.

However, there are problems with the method and it has to be used with caution. For one thing, it suffers from some of the problems concerning incompleteness which were noted with the top plan: sealed, or partially sealed, units may be not recorded in their entirety, or may even be missed out altogether. A more fundamental difficulty concerns the status of the decision on phasing which forms the basis of the drawing. In one sense, of course, any decision taken on site to do a drawing is an interpretative act, as discussed above (the young girl's 'line around the think' mentioned previously). Thus the statement during an excavation that 'This is a single deposit of clay, and therefore will be treated as a single stratigraphic unit, rather than part of a larger clay unit or subdivided into several different sorts of clay' clearly embodies an element of interpretation. Yet the *level* and *type* of interpretation involved in this case are qualitatively different from those needed to justify the drawing of a phase plan: 'This clay layer, and those three underlying but partially exposed layers, fit with these two walls and the seven parallel post holes to form a building, flanked by those gravel metallings and their associated occupation layers and ditches.' The phase plan, then, embodies a different order of interpretation (though not nec-essarily a more risky one) than a basic decision on the extent of individual units. If this higher interpretation turns out to be wrong, then so is the plan. The latter is not, therefore, a record of primary data from the site.

Furthermore, the underlying stratigraphy which gives rise to that surface configuration is not fully visible at the point in time at which one decides to draw a phase plan. Still less is the stratigraphy fully understood, not least because firm information from finds on dating and site function will not be known for some time. Yet knowledge of sealed deposits and other specialist information are both required before phasing can be securely established. So, if this planning policy is applied across the board, the basic spatial record pro-duced in the field, in the form of a multi-layer drawing, will represent what can only be *preliminary suggestions* on site phasing. Its content may, and on a site of any complexity will, change as a result of later analysis post-excavation.

These problems with planning multiple layers on a single drawing have led to a third approach, the use of **single-context plans.** These are particularly prev-alent on deeply stratified sites containing stratigraphy truncated to different levels, where the identification of phases across the whole excavation area at one time can be impossible. The *rationale* for the single-context plan is straight-forward. The process of excavation involves splitting a site into its component parts and recording each unit in its own right. The record of the physical attri-butes of each unit defined in this way can be stored by writing on a single, pre-printed sheet. So, in the same way, its spatial attributes should be given their individual sheet – the single-context plan.

Unlike the single-level, multi-context 'daily' plan, this system ensures that the surface of every unit is recorded in its entirety and, unlike the phase plan, it does not require that decisions on correlations between stratigraphic units become embodied in the basic record. It also lends itself more easily to efficient work organisation, with each recorder responsible for all aspects of the record-ing process as applied to a particular unit. This avoids the hold-ups which occur when one excavator defines the extent of a deposit, then waits for the spe-cialist planner to produce a plan of the area, before returning to describe and dig the layer in question. Finally, single-context plans can be stored more easily, whether as hard copy or as digitised points in a computer.

However, there is a price to pay for these advantages. Some maintain that, with single-context drawings, 'planning errors are likely to occur' (Adkins and Adkins 1989: 76). I see no evidence of this, especially when a system of over-lays is then used to calculate stratigraphic relationships (see Chapter 9). More convincing, perhaps, is the claim that the standard of drawing falls when the site is split into these unconnected units. It is true that some of the most accom-plished site drawings in Britain, particularly coloured plans with a highly detailed record of surface inclusions, have come from sites recorded using phase plans, not individual-context plans: the archives from the Roman town at Wroxeter and the Lower Brooks Street sites in Winchester contain some of the most impressive examples. However, even these archives have their 'failures', in terms of graphics standards, so planning by phase is no guarantee of success. Also single-context planning has meant that a lot more plan information is being recorded than previously. Any fall in standards is more likely to be due to the increased workload and to its being spread around to less experienced, and thus less accomplished, planners. This is an argument for more training, not against the single-context method *per se*.

One thing that cannot be denied is that recording a site in this way makes each unit seem to float free of any of its associates and the main result of this is to place much greater emphasis on deciding phasing at the post-excavation, analysis stage, rather than on site. This has important implications for the procedures used at this later stage, one of the issues taken up in the final chapter. Whether the analytical work is made more difficult, easier, or simply different, is open to discussion.

8.3 Techniques of measurement

Various drawing methods can be employed to produce a plan, of which the mechanical methods of triangulation, offsets and using drawing frames are the most common (Figure 9). **Triangulation** uses tapes attached to two grid points (or three if one requires extra accuracy) to measure successive points around the periphery of the unit. The mechanics of taking the measurements involve holding the two tapes between thumb and forefinger and hanging a plumb bob in the angle between them. Then, standing to one side, it is possible to let one or other tape slide gradually through the grip while keeping both tapes taut and moving slowly backwards until the plumb bob lies vertically above the point to be measured, then reading off each distance. For accuracy, it is important to maintain an approximate right-angle between the tapes. If this becomes too sharp or too shallow, it will be necessary to move the zero point of one of the tapes to a new, known base point.

The points on the periphery of the layer are thus recorded as being a certain distance from each triangulation point and their exact position can then be plotted with a beam compass or, if necessary, a scale rule. Plotting can be done either at the end of a measuring session or by a second party as the person reading off the actual measurements moves to the next point. The latter is preferable, as points plotted off-site at a later stage tend to produce plans which look like 'join-the-dots' drawings, whereas someone plotting on site can look directly at the edge being represented and reproduce accurately the intricacies of its twists and turns between each measured point, either by eye or with occasional use of a hand tape.

A second method is to measure by **offsets** from a base line, each point therefore being recorded as so far along, and so far out from, that line. Once again this technique is best used with one person drawing and another measuring. The former individual is positioned beside the base line opposite the point to be measured, the latter directly above that point holding the zero end of a hand tape. When the hand tape lies perpendicular to the base line, the distances along and out from that line can be recorded. However, if necessary, the same result can be achieved by a single person, using a plum bob and a hand tape set at right-angles to a base tape as illustrated, noting the two measurements and then plotting the point out. Accuracy can only be ensured if the hand tape is exactly perpendicular to the base line. Fortunately the human eye can be extremely exact in judging right-angles but, if there is uncertainty, you can check by using the hand tape to describe an arc above the base line. When this reaches a minimum reading, the two tapes are perpendicular to one another. However, given the potential inaccuracies in the method, it is best not to offset over a greater distance than 2m. Setting out a series of parallel base lines at 4m intervals solves any problems.

Both of the above methods are effective for measuring the periphery of a unit, but can be cumbersome for recording surface detail. As this has become an increasingly important requirement of the drawn record, fieldwork has involved the greater use of **drawing frames.** These are relatively easy to make (Adkins and Adkins 1982) and comprise a wooden or, preferable since lighter, a metal frame which is strung with twine at set intervals. The interval chosen should match the scale adopted for planning. Thus, if drawing at 1:20, it is best to place the string at 0.20m intervals, each grid square formed by the string in the frame then corresponding to a 10mm square on the paper. By standing vertically above the frame, using a plumb bob if it has to be set far from the surface being drawn, the planner can then record the edge of the unit and most of its surface detail by eye. The size of frame used depends on the irregularity of the ground, greater irregularity requiring smaller frames. However, frames 1m by 1m cover most situations. Whatever its size, positioning the frame can be problematical. For accuracy, it has to be level and positioned as near to the ground as possible. A spirit level can be used to check the former, but the undulating character of many sites means that one corner may be much higher than another, and so the frame has to be supported precariously on bricks, pins, etc. Adjustable legs are an inexpensive way to ensure accuracy and stability.

Whichever method is used to create a plan, the drawing will have to record inclusions and undulations which form the surface details of any unit. The former may involve not only colour-coded different types of find, as discussed above, but also the delineation of areas of wear or increased compaction, some of which may be patterned and thus reveal important information about former occupation. The vertical dimension of the spatial record can be represented either by a combination of spot heights and hachures, which record breaks in slope on the surface, or by contours. Contour lines can be very effective but are time consuming to produce, although this will change if the data are held in computer, when the survey might be produced at the push of a button. For the present, spot heights remain the commonest method to record the vertical dimension on a plan. Their number and position depends on the degree of irregularity of the surface being recorded. Thus an exactly level unit covering the whole site (admittedly an unlikely event) requires a single spot height, whilst a small deposit with many peaks and troughs will need many readings, carefully positioned on its maxima and minima. Setting a rule requiring the taking of measurements every 0.20m, in the guise of being 'more scientific', is therefore misguided.

The taking of levels on site at these designated points used to be the reserve of the specialist site surveyor, using a separate 'levels book' with its own numbering system. This brought few advantages, merely cluttering up the plan with a mass of large, inconvenient numbers and the need to search for the elusive book, which was always being used by someone else on another part of the site when you most required it to hand. In fact reading and reducing levels is easily done by all site staff, requiring neither the special surveyor nor his special book. The best method is for the planner to mark spot height positions on the drawing and number them in a running sequence specific to that unit. When the set up of the levelling instrument has been checked, and a backsight and its associated bench mark recorded, the staff is then placed on the appropriate points whilst a colleague reads off the level and records the result on the unit description sheet. These readings can then be reduced to give the absolute level and the result transferred to the plan, the place where they will be needed in future analysis. The advantage of reducing the readings immediately is that any 'impossible' levels, usually the result of either reading the staff inaccurately or sloppy mathematics, can be corrected before any evidence is removed from the ground. This becomes particularly important if using a calculator to reduce readings, when it is also becomes even more vital to make a lasting record of the backsight and its bench mark. When employing manual methods, leave the calculation visible on the recording sheet, so that a rogue level appearing at a later stage can be investigated and, perhaps, corrected.

8.4 Types of section

Sections and elevations have long been employed to record the vertical dimension of stratigraphic units in various situations. They may provide an all-embracing record in controlled conditions, as with the trench edge drawn with great care and accuracy at the end of a long open-area project. Alternatively, the record may be rather more fragmented, though no less accurate, as with a detailed drawing of the thin, 0.25m wide strips of strata made visible by omitting some boards from the shuttering which supports the trench edge. At the other extreme, section drawings may be much less accurate, the result of work undertaken on the top lip of a hole which it is too dangerous to enter in a salvage operation, where sketches of the sides of the hole and a tape hung down to get approximate depths may be all that is possible. Even an outline idea of the level of natural strata and the character and the depth of stratigraphic accumulation on top can be a vital part of deposit mapping at the site evaluation stage. So the archaeological section has a role to play in a great variety of recording situations.

Whatever the mechanics of its production in the field, the use of sections in the controlled conditions of full-blown excavation can be rationalised into three broad areas. They can be used to record the stratigraphic sequence, along the lines promoted by Wheeler and taken up by many others since his time. Second, they can give information on the internal configuration of a particular deposit, for example to throw light on formation and transformation processes within the silting in a ditch, or on the relationship between units, for instance by recording the character of the interface between successive layers. Finally, sections can be used to solve specific stratigraphic problems on the site, for example the relationship between two inter-cutting pits, or between a trench-built wall and adjacent strata. Different types of section are necessary for these different roles. None the less, as I will argue below, better methods than the section exist today to record the stratigraphic sequence. Thus, I believe, sections are best employed in the last two cases, to elucidate deposit formation and for problem-solving.

The types of section which are available to the field-worker can be divided between that drawn from the trench sides or baulks at a specific time, usually the end of the excavation; that produced cumulatively along a predetermined line across the site in which the whole sequence is recorded eventually but never seen in its entirety at any one time; and that imposed on the site to resolve specific issues and removed once these have been sorted out.

The **section drawing of the baulks** exposed at the edge of a trench was seen by Wheeler and his followers as the fundamental record of the stratigraphic development of the site. Just as plans drawn in each box gave information on spatial configuration within it, section drawings of the sides recorded sequential development. When the intervening baulks between boxes were removed at the end of the excavation, the spatial record could be completed. Thus it was possible to reconcile two different aspects of the record. This system is still followed on many sites, at least to the extent of drawing the strata exposed at the limit of excavation when the site has been fully excavated within this. Where sheet piling obscures these standing sections, drawing can be done piecemeal as excavation proceeds, before the metal sheets are lowered (Plate 25).

Such a system may work well when the plan form of the buildings being investigated is fairly regular, as they were with Wheeler's excavations of Roman sites. However, when sites leaving more ephemeral, less symmetrical remains had to be recorded, recognising the plan form became more problematical.

Plate 25 Section of stratigraphy showing below the sheet piling of an excavation. The strata can be drawn on a cumulative section before the sheets are driven down to the extant horizontal stratigraphy and excavation continues to lower levels.

Here larger excavation areas were required, and stretching the distances between baulks exacerbated what had always been the problem with the box excavation – that not all of the units visible in plan appeared in the section at the trench edge.

One solution to this problem is to create intermediate **cumulative sections** across the excavation area using temporary, narrow baulks. These are not left in place to be drawn top to bottom at the end of the excavation, but are drawn in part then removed, to be reinstated when underlying stratigraphy needs to be added to the drawing. Thus a section through the entire sequence is created, though the latter is never seen in its entirety on the ground at a single point in time. The definition of the stage at which the successive elements of the section should be drawn varies. On some excavations it is done when one reaches the base of a major phase, recalling the philosophy (and problems) behind the use of the phase plan described above. On others, recording occurs when one reaches a distinctive stratigraphic unit which is easily recognisable on either side of the temporary baulk, guaranteeing success in connecting up the two sides. In others still, it is drawn simply when a deep or extensive horizon is reached on both sides.

Often, these three criteria are used interchangeably, though it should be

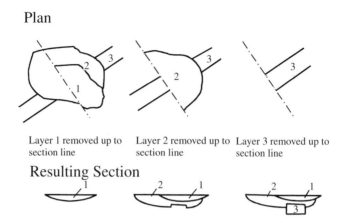

Figure 10 Creating a cumulative section.

noted that there is no guarantee that the top of a phase will be comprised of distinctive or large horizons, so there is a certain amount of confusion here. Given this, many excavators have taken the logical way out: the section to be drawn cumulatively is set up on a predetermined line and, whenever it crosses the position of any single unit which is about to be excavated, the line is strung out and one part of the unit is excavated up to that line. Its profile in elevation is then added to the section drawing and the section string is taken down. After this, the remaining portion of the layer on the other side of the line can be removed (Figure 10).

A major disadvantage of this solution is that one can never see successive units together in section. Thus investigating the nature of the interface between deposits, so useful in illuminating site formation processes, is automatically precluded. Furthermore, both section drawings of trench baulks and those created cumulatively within the excavation area have the important drawback that their line must be decided on, and imposed, in advance. Thus, in both cases, the section can cut into particular parts of the stratigraphic sequence only by chance, rather than by intent. On a site composed of small stratigraphic units, the likelihood of every unit crossing a predetermined line is slight. Hence such sections are unlikely to be able to portray the full sequence. Finally, their ability to elucidate the internal character of any deposit or the nature of the interfaces between contiguous deposits may be limited. For example, an arbitrarily imposed section line which happens to cross that of a linear feature such as a ditch or wall at a very oblique angle is unlikely to throw light on the nature of the feature itself, and may even create problems in understanding the relationship between it and adjacent stratigraphy.

These difficulties have produced a move away from using sections in set positions to record full sequence and promoted the idea of individually positioned sections which cater for particular problems. Thus, when two apparently inter-cutting pits are visible on the surface of the site, yet the relationship between them cannot be determined by the trowel in plan, a suitably aligned section might be used to help throw light on the problem (Figure 11). Similarly, care-fully aligned sections can be vital in elucidating matters when dealing with strata which have a vertical element in their mode of deposition. Tip lines within the fills of a pit, or the exact configuration of stones in a wall core, can be seen to best effect in elevation, using a standing section set carefully across the full width of the pit or perpendicular to the line of the wall. The increased use of open-area excavation has often been criticised for making insufficient use of the section as a recording tool. What is being argued here is that, with proper problem orientation, area excavations can make much fuller use of sections by focussing them on those aspects which they are best qualified to tackle, as opposed to just hoping that they hit the right spot by luck rather than judgement.

8.5 Preparation techniques

The techniques of preparing a section for drawing are fairly straightforward. The excavator should ensure that it is as vertical as is possible, using a plumb bob, then clean the surface **from top to bottom,** concentrating on difficult areas at each level before going on to those beneath, and working around any inclusions which protrude if they are too solid to be sliced through, as with stones, or too important, as with skeletons. Remember that, as with stratig-raphy seen in plan, differences in texture and compaction can be more vital than colour for stratigraphic distinctions, so concentrate on deposit definition during the cleaning. Indeed, if one leaves all such definition to the end, there is a danger of having a perfectly clean elevation but still not knowing where all the lines are to be drawn. Going back to reclean a problem area near the top then means that every other division below becomes dirty and thus obscured. When the surface has been cleaned as thoroughly as possible, it may be useful to spray with water to bring out slight colour differences. Differential drying, and even weathering if the section can be left for a while, can also indicate layer boundaries.

The mechanics of actually drawing the section are well known (Adkins and Adkins 1989: 81). It starts with the setting up of string to form a horizontal line at a known level across the whole section, the end points of the string being tied in to the site grid. The information on the datum level of string and its position at either end of the section should then be marked on the section drawing, together with the scale of the drawing. The best way to avoid errors in section drawing is to begin with the top and bottom of the section and the limits of excavation at the sides, then in-fill this frame with the main strata, followed by

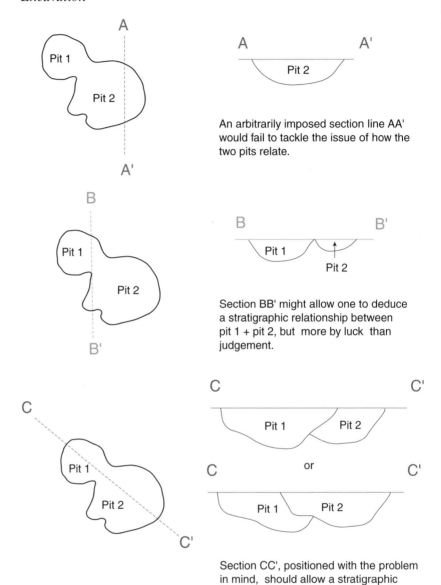

An arbitrarily imposed section line AA'
would fail to tackle the issue of how the
two pits relate.

Section BB' might allow one to deduce
a stratigraphic relationship between
pit 1 + pit 2, but more by luck than
judgement.

Section CC', positioned with the problem
in mind, should allow a stratigraphic
decision to be made.

Figure 11 Positioning a section line for problem-solving. A section imposed at
the start of excavation along the line AA′ might provide a convenient cross-
section of Pit 2 but would say nothing about its relationship with Pit 1. That
running from B to B′ *might* give some indication of the order in which the two
pits were cut but lies at such an oblique angle to the likely line of intersection that
this information would be obtained more by luck than judgement. In contrast, a
section deliberately positioned along the line CC′ stands the best chance of
allowing an informed decision.

the more complex areas. If some strata are particularly tightly packed, or detailed inclusions must be recorded, for example of the stones of a wall core, then a drawing frame hung vertically against the section aids speed and accuracy. When the drawing is complete, critical finds can be dug out of the baulk to give a rough idea of the dating of successive strata. If excavation in plan is precluded, and section recording is all that is going to be possible, it may even be useful to dig back behind its line at this stage to try to ascertain the alignment of any walls, etc. seen only end-on in the drawing.

Two issues which often arise in section recording are whether one should use continuous lines to delineate the boundaries of strata, and whether colour-coding of layers should be used. By matching drawing crayons with the real colouration, colours can then be blended together to reflect more accurately the merging of deposits when appropriate. The approach advocated by Pyddoke (1961: 120) is worth repeating here. The intention behind recording stratification is to provide information on events, the section providing either an intelligent interpretation of these or the information for such in the future. Hence it is important to show both the cases where layers clearly exist, and also areas of blending. For this a conventionalised section, with full use of the symbols indicating indeterminate edges where necessary, may be preferable to a naturalistic, coloured one.

A final point concerns the relationship between the section and the plan record. Every excavator is aware that they do not always match exactly. This can lead either to attempts to reconcile the two, which is not always possible, or to a battle over which element of the record should be accorded priority. Both solutions rather miss the point. The two drawings record the stratigraphic sequence in totally different circumstances. There is never a complete correlation, not because one is right and the other wrong but because they are trying to do different sorts of things. It is interesting, indeed it may be vital, to view the sequence in these two different ways. When the two correlate, this is important; when they do not, it is equally important and perhaps more interesting. But neither should be considered as inherently superior to the other and thus more likely to be believed.

The practical implication of this argument is that, because they represent two different views of the site, they should be created independently of each other. Thus each unit shown on either plan or section drawing should be given its own number and description, with a separate and individual statement of its stratigraphic relationships. It is important to construct the sequence as indicated by the section in a separate sequence diagram immediately the drawing is done, so that the illustrator can focus in on particularly vital relationships while the physical strata are still in view. Then, when a particular relationship is being used in a vital argument at the post-excavation stage, the analyst can be reassured by the knowledge that it was recognised as important at the time of recording and a decision reached which was as reasonable as was then possible.

Producing a full set of new descriptions for the strata seen in section, when one has only just excavated the adjacent, and broadly equivalent, material in plan, might seem like unnecessary repetition. However, it is not that time-consuming (and one need never run out of numbers for new units if they are allocated from a running sequence!). In addition, where correlations between plan and section are inexact, it will be necessary to have separate numbers anyway. Indeed, even when there is a one-to-one correlation, the case can be made much more succinctly if the two units have been recorded separately and shown to match after due consideration of all the evidence, rather than assumed to be a single entity from the start and appearing as such in the primary record. In the latter case, one cannot even begin the have the argument in analysis.

8.6 Measuring-in or piece-plotting finds

On most excavations, the stratigraphic unit is defined in terms of its physical composition and spatial and stratigraphic attributes. When these components have been recorded, the numbered unit is excavated and any finds from it are kept under its number. Thus the position of any find is known to the extent that it must come from that part of the site indicated by the plan or section of its associated unit. For small units this may be sufficient to tie finds down to a very small area, but for deposits which are either deeper or more extensive in plan, individual finds will obviously be tied rather less accurately. Then it may become desirable to divide a large horizon into arbitrarily defined sub-units (spits). A special case of this situation occurs when it is important to know the position of a particular find type with even greater accuracy: Hietala (1984) gives a variety of studies in which the analysis presupposes that the exact position of each artefact has been recorded in the process of excavation, for example.

In other cases, the measuring-in of individual finds may provide a way of reconstructing stratigraphic groups. For example, the 'blurring' of boundaries in alluvial deposits on a Bronze Age site at Runnymede (Needham and Stig-Sorensen 1988) required each sherd to be numbered and its exact position recorded. Consideration of the position and condition of individual sherds and of their interrelationships allowed the identification of the original surface of the settlement and elucidated post-depositional changes. Computer techniques such as 3DPLOT (Nelson *et al.* 1987) can speed up the processing of these spatial data in order to assess whether occupation levels can be recognised in deep sites lacking visible stratification, whilst other software packages can utilise evidence from joining sherds to elucidate both formation processes and post-depositional factors (Bollong 1994).

On sites with very few artefacts, it may be possible to measure-in all finds as a matter of course. However, on most excavations, a selection policy will be needed. Projects often decide to give such priority to the 'most important' finds, importance being defined for them in terms of the rarity of the find or its potential to provide accurate dates. Coins, for example, are often measured-in this way. However, these criteria can be difficult to justify. When a coin provides a vital date within a stratigraphic sequence, what really needs to be known is not its position to the nearest millimetre, but that the find was well stratified.

In general, the most important factor to be born in mind when deciding which finds to measure-in should not be the nature of the find itself, but the status of the relationship between it and the stratigraphy on site. In particular, we need to know more accurately the position of those finds which have not been redeposited, and which may relate to primary activities in the area. This requires establishing criteria for recognising the right kind of deposits and the right type of find in advance. Also, if distribution maps are to be created, the designated find must occur in sufficient numbers for statistical viability, but be sufficiently spread for meaningful patterns to emerge. Generally it is not eminently datable coins or prestigious gold jewellery which needs measuring in (though each of these may need separate treatment and numbering at a later stage for other reasons, for example to distribute to specialists or comply with a museum accessioning system). In terms of site activity, it is specified artefacts that occur in some numbers and from known primary contexts which deserve the extra accuracy which measuring-in provides.

Grave goods are an obvious case in which a primary context can be defined in advance. More mundane, but equally valid, are artefacts with a known structural function (door fittings, window glass) lying within, or at the base of, *in situ* destruction debris, thus providing vital structural information when plotted individually. Nor need it be only primary contexts which are important in this respect. For example, at the Billingsgate excavation in London, certain worked stones set within the core of a post-medieval foundation were clearly recycled from an earlier structure. Although in a secondary context, each stone was measured-in and, when analysed later as single artefacts, it proved possible to understand their architectural role in the original building. By comparing this with their position as found, one could understand the process by which one building (in fact a church burnt down in the Great Fire of London) was dismantled and a second (the merchant's house which replaced it) rose from its ashes. Obviously, if the number of finds involved is large, measuring-in every one can be time-consuming and thus prohibitively expensive. So, before embarking on such a policy, it is necessary to be very clear on how the information which may accrue fits into one's research strategy.

Some short cuts can be used when measuring-in finds. For example, rather than measure the position of each designated find straight away, a modern nail can be used to mark the point during excavation (different artefact types can be plotted by using differently painted modern equivalents if necessary). If there are too few nails to allow significant patterns to emerge when the layer is completed, they can simply be removed. If there are a large number, and their configuration seems significant, they can be planned or photographed, otherwise not. Of course, this does not avoid the difficult problem of deciding which patterns are significant. It must always be remembered that such patterns can be a positive indication with structural significance (e.g. lines of nails indicating planks of a timber floor), but can never be used as negative evidence. At the very least, marking positions in this way, then measuring several at a single time, is more efficient than dodging back and forth continuously between trowel and hand tape throughout the excavation of the layer in question.

Finally, when measuring-in large numbers of finds, the practical implications of this for their later processing must be considered. An EDM, for example, can enhance the speed with which individual co-ordinate points can be obtained (Plate 24) (Dibble 1987), perhaps linked via a computer to a numbering system related to the unit from which they came (2570/1 for the first object from unit 2570 and so forth). Thus it becomes possible to store the co-ordinates for hundreds, if not thousands, of finds quickly and efficiently, even printing out automatically a bar-coded label to accompany the measured find. But such recording may then play havoc with the finds data-base in the computer constructed on the basis of a different numbering system. It also requires that all finds processing and cataloguing at a later stage be similarly individualised. Knowing the exact position of every sherd may provide an exciting way of using the site's new piece of surveying wizardry, and be excellent news for the manufacturer of small plastic bags, but can be most unwelcome in the finds shed where each sherd must be individually marked with its unique number and stored separately – be sure that it is really worthwhile before committing the resources involved. None the less, when applied consistently and for good reason, there is no doubt that recording exact finds positions in this way can release vitally important contextual and structural information.

9

THE STRATIGRAPHIC RECORD

Introduction

Perhaps the most common justification for putting resources into excavations is that, in contrast to random digging for treasure, the work of the field archaeologist must take place in controlled conditions, allowing full recording of the physical character and spatial disposition of the stratigraphic units on a site. Such conditions do not merely allow better descriptions of site features and yield larger numbers of finds: they also let the excavator understand the latter's context of deposition and position in a sequence of development of the site. This allows excavated data to be interrogated in ways which are qualitatively different from that which would be possible using unprovenanced assemblages. If the expenditure on modern excavations is to be justified in such terms, then the drawn and descriptive elements of each unit must be set beside a third component – the stratigraphic relationships between units. Without these, deposits remain dissociated entities and every finds group floats with respect to all the others. Recording stratigraphic relationships is therefore a fundamental aspect of almost every excavation.

The types of relationships which might be encountered on any site come in two broad types. First there are general ones relating units which touch each other or are superimposed, i.e. essentially physical relationships. In addition there are the true stratigraphic relationships (both are discussed in **9.1**). Having decided on the type of relationships being recorded, the issues of how they are to be stored and represented graphically come to the fore, and here three broad approaches might be distinguished (**9.2**). Lastly the methods used to calculate how each unit relates to all others (which has been, surprisingly, little discussed in the literature) will be considered (**9.3**). The conclusion of this final section is that plan overlays are the most secure method of producing accurate stratigraphic information. This can only be done after a unit has been drawn and is best done on site before it is described and actually excavated: hence the discussion of stratigraphic relationships comes at this point in the manual.

9.1 Types of stratigraphic relationship

The relationships between units of stratigraphy can be classified into two broad types – physical relationships and, a sub-set of these, purely stratigraphic relationships. The physical relationships take a variety of forms, often recorded in terms of pairs of opposites – a particular unit overlies/underlies, cuts/is cut by, abuts/is abutted by another unit. They can also include more ubiquitous relationships, such as when one unit is recorded as touching/being touched by another.

There are several reasons why excavators might need to record such connections. For example, in order to identify the very existence of a truncation horizon within a sequence, it may be helpful to know all physical relationships of every unit (Yule 1992: 22). Alternatively, they may have a role when integrating finds information. For example, to understand cross-joins between residual pottery sherds in the fill from a pit and from adjacent horizontal stratigraphy, it will be important to consider those deposits which the intrusion actually cut. Knowing already that 'A is cut by B' will speed up analysis. Similarly, when analysing the structural development of the site after excavation, it can be very useful to be aware that a particular floor was laid against a wall. This implies that the latter continued in use, rather than the floor sealing its line and thus marking its demise as a structural division: knowing 'A abuts B' will be helpful. Finally, recognising that one unit actually touched another may help in understanding such matters as how an environmental sample from one deposit may have been contaminated by the percolation of a chemical compound from an overlying, contiguous deposit: a note of 'A touches B' is required. In such situations, therefore, a record of the physical relationships between units on the site can be vital.

However, in creating a system to register such relationships, two points should be remembered. First, deducing some of these physical relationships can be a very time-consuming business. A modern pit intruding from the top to the bottom of a complex sequence may truncate many thousands of other units. So its position and cut number will have to be labelled at all future stages of the excavation in order to make a complete record of the 'cuts/is cut by' variety, unless the recorder is content to have recourse to the chancy mechanism of individual memory. Similarly, when dealing with a horizontal layer, one might ask the apparently simple question 'Which other units were in direct contact with Unit X?' Yet if Unit X was extensive and only seen in plan, then it may prove exceedingly difficult to provide a completely accurate answer to the question. Of course, the fact that a relationship may take a long time to calculate is not a reason for failing to record it. But it is a reason for making certain that the question being asked is important enough to justify such an investment of time.

It is equally important to decide whether such relationships are needed for all units, and thus require systematic recording on site as a matter of course, or are merely important in particular circumstances, as in the examples given above. In reality, in my experience, there are very few occasions when the former is the case, raising the issue of whether they need to be part of the basic site record. If they are required for particular aspects of specialist work post-excavation, then proper use of the plan record should enable them to be deduced retrospectively one-by-one as required. Usually it is only after some analysis following the excavation, rather than at the data capture stage, that the reasons for wanting to know physical relationships can be assessed more accurately and fully justified in terms of the project's research objectives.

Second, it is important to realise this type of relationship is different from a *stratigraphic* relationship in the strict sense of the word. The latter is concerned not with the physical disposition of the units (which unit touched another), but with the chronological construction of the sequence, a record of the order in which the deposition of successive units took place. It is usually only relationships of this second type which must be recorded as a matter of course in excavation.

Even if one accepts that it is stratigraphic, not physical, relationships which should be recorded, there is a further confusion to be dealt with. Harris, in what was a seminal work, rightly made much of the above distinction between physical and stratigraphic relationships. However, when discussing purely stratigraphic connections, he suggests (1989: 36) that these can take three forms. Any two units might:

(A) 'have no direct stratigraphic connection'
(B) be 'in superposition'
(C) be 'correlated as parts of a once-whole deposit or feature interface'.

The first two types present no problems. If two layers have no proven link, as in (A), then they can be seen as 'potentially contemporary', or 'floating with respect to each other'. To call this lack of a stratigraphic connection a true relationship may seem a little strange, but the meaning is clear. Though not recorded directly on site, its existence can be recognised implicitly by the absence of any relationship of types (B) or (C). Equally clear is the meaning of type (B), commonly translated on the recording sheet as one layer being '(stratigraphically) earlier than' another and, correspondingly, of the second being 'later than' the first.

However, the implication of Harris' third category, (C), is less obvious. What does it mean for one layer to 'correlate' with another? Such correlations are usually translated as one unit being the 'same as' another but this phrase is open to a variety of interpretations. It could denote that two numbers were allocated in the field to what turned out, on fuller investigation, to survive as a single, continuous unit. But this does not mean that a new type of relationship has been conjured into existence, merely that an error has been made. It is better not to make the mistake in the first place than to invent a technique for representing it in a sequence diagram.

Yet it seems unlikely that this is what Harris has in mind. The figure which illustrates his case is a section drawing in which two units of similar character and level are shown to be cut by an intervening intrusion. Presumably, therefore, the implication is that two physically distinct units on either side of the intrusion are thought to have joined up. It is *interpreted*, then, that one unit was once the 'same as' the other. However, correlating stratigraphy on either side of a later intrusion is a chancy business. Two layers might be linked on the basis of their physical characteristics, their surface level, their position in plan, the date of the finds which they contain, or any combination of these, and other, criteria. Whatever the basis used, it clearly involves a higher level of interpretation than is needed to deduce the existence of an (A) or (B) type of relationship. Thus Harris' Type C should be acknowledged as being different in kind from the more fundamental relationships.

This discussion suggests that the true stratigraphic relationships which must be recorded for every unit as a matter of course can be reduced to the 'earlier than/later than' category, the second element being, of course, simply the converse of the first. Hence what is required of a system is that it can decide, for each unit, which other unit(s), excavated previously, are immediately later than it. Everything else then follows on. Some ways of doing this will be described in the final section but first the graphical representation of stratigraphic relationships must be considered.

9.2 Representing stratigraphic relationships

There are a variety of ways in which stratigraphic relationships recorded on site might be stored and represented. The information on an individual unit, of course, can be held in words on its associated description sheet – 'unit 2 underlies 1, and overlies 3 and 4'. However, the objective of stratigraphic recording is to see all such relationships interrelated, not just written on each recording sheet, so a diagram combining them is required for analytical work. The ways put forward by Carver (1979b) and Harris (1989) will be considered here.

The Carver approach is essentially a development of the sequence diagrams derived from the Wheeler system (see, for example, Kenyon 1964: figs. 13 and 14). In this 'Carver diagram', stratigraphic units are represented in boxes, either individually or collected together in a feature. Their position on the diagram reflects the position on the site, and the size of the box, especially its upper and lower limits, corresponds to the length of time during which each entity is thought to have continued in use: a building with a complex internal structure and a long life will occupy a wide and long box; a simple ditch which remains in use for an extended period of time will be contained in a tall, narrow box; and a pit dug, filled and quickly sealed will be drawn as a box of limited dimensions in both planes. Thus, although the diagram obviously contains stratigraphic information, it is essentially concerned with presenting interpretations of the sequence, of how basic units form higher-order groups (see discussion under 13.7) and of how long they were structured into the activities on the site, rather than recording basic stratigraphic fact. Such interpretations are vitally important but, it will be argued below, can be made with certainty only at the post-excavation stage. This suggests that, *as a method of storing fundamental stratigraphic relationships*, the Carver approach may be of limited use (its ability to present interpretative suggestions after analysis is another matter – see further in Chapter 13).

In contrast with Carver's approach, the Harris-Winchester matrix can be used from the start of excavation to record basic stratigraphic relationships and should not change its configuration as a result of analysis afterwards. The method is well known, having been clearly set out on several occasions by Edward Harris himself (Harris 1989 provides the most recent statement; Orton (1980: 66–73) also gives a particularly concise definition of the matrix, although he maintains that, strictly speaking, it is a lattice, not a matrix). The Harris matrix is, in my experience, the best, in fact the only, way of represent-ing the stratigraphic sequence on a site of any complexity, presenting a com-plete statement of the stratigraphic sequence which shows all relationships, rather than just those which happen to reach the baulk, as with section drawings.

The essential basis of the diagram is very simple. The number representing each unit is inserted in a consistent rectangular box. Unlike the 'Carver diagram', the size of this box does not vary as a function of how long-lived the unit is thought to be (though, as discussed in the final chapter, its shape may be changed after post-excavation work to indicate the different types of inter-pretative units – occupation layers, pits, walls, etc.). Figure 12 demonstrates the principle: if unit 2 can be shown to be earlier than unit 1, then a line is drawn between the base of box 1 to the top of box 2. If 3 is earlier than 2 a line is drawn from 2 down to 3 and so forth. Hence if 3 is earlier than 2, which is earlier than 1, then 3 is also earlier than 1. This is demonstrated diagrammatically by the fact that one can travel up the strands from 3 to reach 2 and then 1. Similarly, 4 is earlier than 2, and by implication earlier than 1. However, it has no rela-tionship with 3, and they are placed on different strands of the diagram.

This diagram shows that Unit 1 is later than Unit 2, and that Unit 2 is later than Units 3 and 4. These are both Type B relationships - that of being '*in superposition*'. Units 3 and 4 will have one of two relationships: either '*no direct stratigraphic connection*' (Type A); or '*correlated as parts of a once-whole deposit*' (Type C). Which of these types applies depends on higher-order interpretations based on the physical and spatial characteristics of both these deposits, and of others around them.

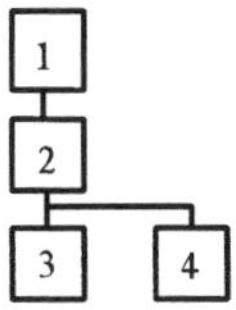

Figure 12 A simple Harris matrix.

In this way the stratigraphic relationships between any one unit and all the others on the site can be illustrated, however complex the sequence:

> if one travels from a particular unit via the strands running up from it, all units through which one passes are provably later than that unit;
>
> if one travels down, every unit *en route* is provably earlier;
>
> any unit which cannot be reached in one of these two ways has no proven relationship with the unit in question (i.e. the two units are potentially contemporary, an example of the Type A relationship discussed above).

For sites of all sizes it makes sense to put all of this information onto a single, site-wide diagram since every unit is part of a single sequence. However, on an extensive, complex site with many such units, this diagram can get very large. In practice, the only limitation is the size of the wall of the site hut (perhaps an argument for more palatial accommodation on excavation!). However, when thousands of units are incorporated onto a single diagram, it can be very difficult to find a particular number amongst a mass of boxes in order to insert a newly numbered unit below it. In this case, it is useful to divide the diagram into areas labelled by letter running across and numbers down it, like a street map. The square in which any unit lies is then written on its recording sheet and those wishing to add further boxes below it then know roughly where to look on the diagram.

Three further practical points might be mentioned. First, matrices are often drawn in which one line 'jumps' another. They can make a diagram appear overcomplicated and it is best to iron out as many as possible (indeed, computer software has been created to do this automatically – see Herzog 1993: 209ff). However, because a matrix represents three-dimensional stratigraphy in two dimensions, some jumps cannot be avoided. (Figure 13).

The stratigraphic situation represented below comprises a rubble foundation ⑦, overlain by timber sills ⑤ and ⑥, with each sill capped at one end with a levelling tile, ③ and ④ respectively, before these tiles were themselves overlain by another timber ②. These relationships are shown below diagrammatically using continuous lines. However if a second timber ① also overlay sills ⑤ and ⑥, its position in the matrix cannot be represented accurately without implying a false relationship with either ③ or ④. Here it is necessary to use a drawing convention to show one line 'jumping' another (seen in the dashed lines below).

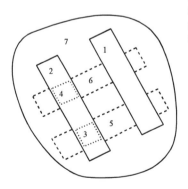
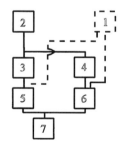

Figure 13 Dealing with 'jumps' in a Harris matrix.

Given that not all loops can be removed from a diagram, it is far more important to ensure that the diagram is clear and that the statements it makes are correct than agonising for hours on whether a loop can be removed by redrawing. A rough and ready, but essentially correct, record is much to be preferred at the end of the excavation, as opposed to a copied matrix which has minimal loops but embodies inaccuracies.

Second, a common source of error when constructing such diagrams is the creation of misleading 'H-shaped' relationships (Bibby 1993: fig. 7.2). These creep in when the lines drawn to the base of an overlying unit are not split but enter as single lines. Thus, in Figure 14, if 3 underlies 1 and 2, but 4 only underlies 2 and has no proven relationship with 1 or 3, then it is simply incorrect to have a diagram which shows 1 and 2 as both over 3 and 4.

Finally, it is important to finish off the matrix diagram clearly. At the end of the project, there will be some strands on the matrix whose lowest members hang in mid-air, lacking underlying strata. These should all be units which were the earliest encountered during the work. Such boxes should be drawn as overlying the limit of excavation (LOE) or above a point when no further excavation (NFE) took place. If there are then any remaining boxes hanging in mid-air, they represent mistakes, stratigraphic units which should have been linked back into the main sequence but have not been. The use of LOE/NFE elsewhere allows the ready identification of this, hopefully small, residue. The incomplete relationships must then be revisited and tied in before the matrix can be considered a finished record.

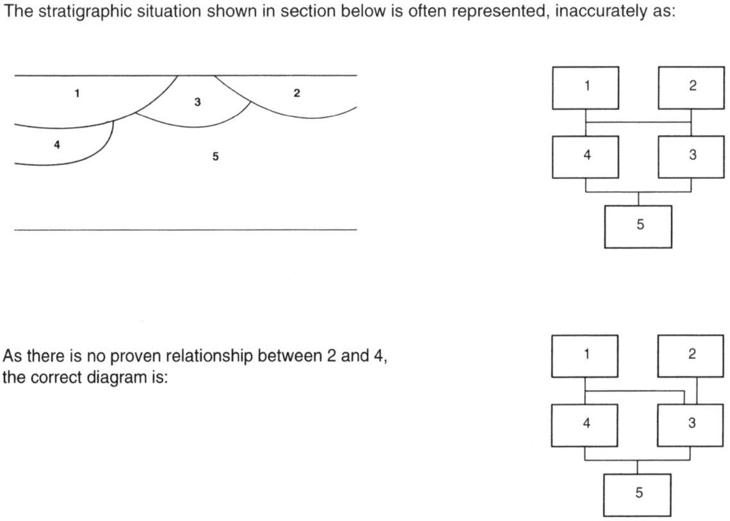

The stratigraphic situation shown in section below is often represented, inaccurately as:

As there is no proven relationship between 2 and 4, the correct diagram is:

Figure 14 Avoiding a common error in Harris matrix construction.

9.3 Calculating stratigraphic relationships

Although there has been a certain amount of discussion in publications on the best way to represent stratigraphic information, very little has been written on how the individual relationships are to be calculated and when this should be done. For example, Bibby (1993), in a chapter entitled 'Building stratigraphic sequences on excavations', argues strongly and eloquently for the need to record stratigraphy accurately and consistently, but then gives no insight into methods. Similarly, Pearson and Williams (1993), though recommending the super-positioning of plans to calculate relationships, then do not expand on how this is to be achieved in practice.

Of course, if the drawn section is used as the basic record of the site sequence, as was once common with the 'Wheeler method', then the relationships which it embodies can be abstracted in diagrammatic form at any stage. As was argued above, such stratigraphic decisions are best taken on site when the section is being drawn so that any inconsistencies or vital areas where relationships are not entirely clear can be recognised straight away and perhaps subjected to more cleaning and closer inspection to sort matters out. However, as also discussed earlier, recording sequence only in section has its problems. With large numbers of 'open-area' excavations, it is often the case that not all layers are visible in section, and alternative ways of calculating relationships are needed.

In many quarters, it is still assumed that the excavator will simply know, or can easily remember, what unit(s) overlay the one being dealt with at a particular time and can fill in the boxes on the recording sheet accordingly. Sometimes, especially on relatively shallow sites with limited horizontal stratigraphy and extensive layers, this will be a valid assumption. The excavator has very few units to deal with and it is usually a matter of knowing that B is below A when you have just finished the latter and are starting to record the former. However, in other situations, reliance on recent recollections can also be a recipe for disaster.

An area may not have been touched for some time and the memory fades, if only because the excavator may remember the character and rough position of any overlying deposit, but not its number. Alternatively, personnel in the area may have changed, and the new excavator simply has no memory of the overlying sequence to rely on. Third, excavators working in adjacent areas will be dealing with sequences which sometimes interdigitate with one another, so the memory of more than one person has to be called on. Finally, on sites of any complexity, especially when individual layers are small and discontinuous because they have been cut away by later intrusions, it is rare for one unit to be sealed completely by an overlying deposit and completely cover the next one down. Overlaps between deposits are much more common, and these may be only small but vital. Thus to remember that 'a deposit excavated two weeks before did, in fact, continue far enough south to overlap by 80mm the layer now visible in plan' is a chancy business. All of these difficulties increase as the work-force is enlarged and the professional field-worker, working in a large team on a complex site, requires formal mechanisms of stratigraphic calculation, rather than relying on informal guesses and individual memory. Methods which are impersonal and checkable (i.e. repeatable), yet simple, are the order of the day.

In the light of these problems, some have advocated the use of the computer programmes to monitor stratigraphic information. Thus the excavator writes down the relationships, presumably from memory, and feeds the result into a data-base. The programme then checks the information for internal consistency, and may even remove the loops in the sequence, flag up duplicated numbers, eliminate true but redundant relationships, and print out the resulting diagram in various colours. So, such programmes are clearly useful in terms of producing a tidy illustration, and in telling you that no data have been entered which imply the existence of the impossible relationship such as A is later than B, which is later than A. However, proving that a relationship is not impossible is not the same as showing it to be correct. After all, the information input from the site may create a diagram showing all units as being below topsoil and above the limit of excavation, but having no relationships with each other. Such a record is internally consistent (i.e. though unlikely, and certainly the product of a very boring site, it is not a stratigraphic impossibility). However, checking programmes cannot tell you whether there really were *no* relationships between *any* of the excavated units. The essential issue – the quality and accuracy of the original information – remains and here there are only two ways of creating a fool-proof system: labelling a stratigraphic unit in relation to all others as soon as any part of it appears during the excavation; or using the plan of a newly drawn unit to calculate relationships immediately before its excavation.

In the former system, underlying units are allocated a number and marked on the ground as soon as they are exposed following the removal of the overlying unit. These numbers are then entered onto the latter's recording sheet straight away. Thus the excavators remove topsoil, numbered 1, and twenty layers are distinguished below it. All are labelled on the ground, and 1 is recorded as being later than 2–21 inclusive on its recording sheet. As outlined in the initial discussion of this chapter, when these underlying units themselves interrelate stratigraphically, what is being recorded here is essentially the *physical* relationships between 1 and the other units – what the base of the topsoil actually touched – rather than its *purely stratigraphic* properties.

Certain practical problems arise with this approach. A complex site, on which each layer is labelled in the ground immediately any part of it appears, can quickly look as if it has been scattered with confetti as the tags proliferate.

Plate 26 Excavations at Winchester in the late 1960s, in which each deposit was numbered and labelled on-site as it was first exposed in the side of later intrusions. This had the big advantage of avoiding overreliance on the excavator's memory when calculating stratigraphic relationships. However, it meant that what was, in reality, a single deposit might be allocated many different numbers initially, all of which had to be correlated retrospectively. The excavation could also take on a confetti-like appearance in the course of the work.

Also the excavation of a major intrusion such as a pit may expose hundreds of other units, some of which may not be seen completely in plan, and thus will not be ready for excavation, for many months. In the meantime, nails can become dislodged, labels obscured or lost, etc. However, the solutions here – long nails, proper marking pens and careful excavation staff – are clear enough and present no barrier in themselves (Plate 26).

More difficult to solve are the problems derived from the need, in this system, to decide on underlying stratigraphic configurations immediately they are exposed. Consider the hypothetical example in Figure 15. On removing a layer of topsoil (1), several other deposits become visible and thus must be labelled. The dark silt layer (2) exposed in its entirety directly below the topsoil, which will be tackled next, presents no problems – 2 is stratigraphically below 1, and recorded as such on each sheet. But the clay layer seen in a 0.20m wide strip at the silt's west edge, and the superficially similar clay just appearing from below it at its east edge, will, presumably, each be given a new number, 3 and 4. If, on removal of the dark silt 2, the clays 3 and 4 are found to connect up, there will be two numbers for a single unit. This difficulty may reach enormous proportions. An extensive layer might appear in the sides of a hundred pit cuts and become visible beneath countless discrete and overlying deposits in the horizontal areas between the pits (Plate 26). The same stratigraphic unit will thus be given a different number many times. Of course, this is not an insurmountable problem. The numbers can be equated in post-excavation analysis, or even when the extensive deposit becomes fully exposed and is about to be excavated: the good thing about labelling units in a numerical sequence is that you can never run out of numbers.

Yet there is a third problem which cannot be overcome so easily. A particular unit numbered previously as a single entity, rather than being amalgamated with another layer, may on closer inspection in fact divide into two. This is particularly likely to occur when only a small portion of a deposit could be seen when it was first numbered and its relationship with an overlying unit recorded, as with the clay layer 4 mentioned above. Only when it is seen fully in plan does it become clear that a differently textured area at its eastern end is not a surface detail, as originally assumed, but really an additional, new unit which thus has no number. If this element is now allocated another number, 4a, and the remaining unit is called 4b, one cannot be sure that both 4a and 4b were covered by the original deposit 2. The only way to establish the relationship between 4a and 2 is to compare the extent of each in plan. This solution thus gives a clue to the other general method of calculating stratigraphic relationships. If it is necessary to refer to plans at this point to calculate the stratigraphic relationship, why not use that method from the start, in the process avoiding confetti on site and the making of long-winded correlations, and removing redundant, equated numbers, after the site has been dug?

If every unit is to be planned then the resulting drawings can be used to create a site-wide matrix during the excavation. The case for single-context plans was outlined in Chapter 8. Their usefulness for calculating stratigraphic relationships on complex sites provides, if anything, a stronger justification for their employment. The mechanics of calculating stratigraphic relationships using plan overlays are fairly obvious. The extent of the unit on the newly drawn plan is compared to that of another unit as represented on its plan, using the site grid to position the two exactly. If there is an overlap between them, the new unit must be earlier than the previously excavated one. By repeating this process for all the plans drawn thus far, one can establish the unique stratigraphic relationships of the new unit before any of it is removed from the ground.

Of course, the process of overlaying plans to calculate relationships can be

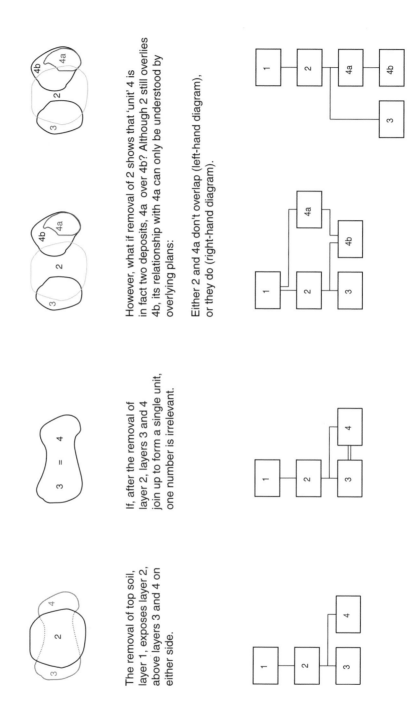

The removal of top soil, layer 1, exposes layer 2, above layers 3 and 4 on either side.

If, after the removal of layer 2, layers 3 and 4 join up to form a single unit, one number is irrelevant.

However, what if removal of 2 shows that 'unit' 4 is in fact two deposits, 4a over 4b? Although 2 still overlies 4b, its relationship with 4a can only be understood by overlying plans:

Either 2 and 4a don't overlap (left-hand diagram), or they do (right-hand diagram).

Figure 15 Problems in labelling stratigraphy ahead of its excavation.

done only after a unit is completely exposed and its full extent known and drawn up. Strictly speaking, this operation could occur at any stage thereafter, even when the excavation has ended (and sometimes this may be the only feasible time, most obviously with 'backlog' sites dug before matrices were in common use, or even thought of: Clark 1993). Yet there are some pressing reasons to carry out this overlaying process, where possible, at the earliest opportunity. First, any mistakes, either in planning or in overlaying, can be recognised straight away. Thus inaccurate plans – those drawn 0.20m too far west because the drawing frame was wrongly positioned; those rotated through 90 degrees due to the inexperience of the site worker – will usually be recognised straight away as being problematical because they do not match the positions of diagnostic features of overlying units (the edge of a later intrusion, the limit of excavation). These drawings can then be amended before the mistake formally enters the site record (incidentally, this mechanism constitutes one answer to the criticism of single-context planning, that it is likely to produce inaccuracies). Overlaying at this early stage also means that any small shifting of the site grid, which often occurs when large areas are being excavated over extended periods of time, can be recognised and taken into account. The process, then, is best done when the plan has just been drawn but before any of the unit which it represents has been removed from the ground.

There are still some problems with the overlay system to be considered. Calculating stratigraphic relationships on a large site can be a long-drawn-out process when it involves comparing the extent of a newly drawn plan with that of many thousands of previously excavated strata. Inevitably, for a site with complex stratification, the vital task of recording those relationships is bound to be time-consuming whatever system is employed (and even more so if only informal methods are used or if the work is left until after the excavation is finished). Fortunately, there are also practical measures which can be taken to make this workload more manageable.

First, with a new plan in hand, one should not simply check it against existing drawings in a random fashion. Because the site matrix is being created as the excavation proceeds, the relationships between all previously excavated strata will be recorded already on an evolving diagram. One can therefore start the overlaying process with the plan of a unit hanging at the base of one of its strands. Thus, on Figure 16, if the newly drawn unit 10 proves to underlie 9 when their plans are overlaid, and 9 itself has already been shown to be earlier than 6 and 4, there is no need to check for overlap between 10 and 6 or 4: whether or not 10 overlaps either in plan, it is provably stratigraphically earlier by virtue of the intervening relationship with 9. Of course, if no such overlap exists between 10 and 9, the plan of 10 must then be compared to that of units further up the sequence – 6, followed by 4, followed by 1 if necessary, until an overlap is established. If none can be found, 10 can float to the top of the sequence, alongside 1, and must await the excavation of underlying units to be pulled more fully into it. On a complex site, where many strands are in existence at any one time, tying a unit into one of these will not mean that all the others can be ignored. Each will have to be checked in turn before the relationships of the newly drawn unit can be uniquely established. None the less, starting with 'hanging units' can reduce the workload considerably.

There is a second way in which the process can be speeded up. While a newly drawn unit may *potentially* overlap *any* previously excavated unit, those units in other parts of the site entirely will never in fact do so. If this can be known in advance, the chore of overlaying is much reduced. One way of doing this is to draw plans within pre-ordained grid squares and file them by such squares. When a newly planned layer is contained entirely within a particular square, it can only relate to other units also in that square. Thus one can produce small-scale matrices interrelating the plans in each grid square, and only these have to be checked (using, of course, the 'bottom up' approach described previously). The new plan can then be added to the diagram when its relationships have been identified.

Obviously, if a unit falls within more than one grid square, it will have to be drawn on a second plan and this will have to be checked in its own grid square. The relationships deduced here can then be added to the first. Some of these will simply confirm the decision of the first square; others will be additional, the total relationships of the new unit being an amalgamation of all such calculations; others still will be shown to be true, but irrelevant since superseded by more critical relationships in the other square. When all plan matrices have been filled in, the relationships from adjacent squares amalgamated, and the true-but-irrelevant ones removed, the result can be entered on individual recording sheets and on the site-wide matrix. Computer technology now coming on stream will reduce such basic work of amalgamation to a minimum though, for reasons given above, will not remove the need to overlay plans to deduce individual relationships in the first place – only computer storage of the digitised periphery of each unit could allow this to take place automatically.

Thus, in Figure 16, if one deduced that unit 10 was earlier than 9 and 8 in one square and earlier than 2 and 9 in another, the repetition of 9 would mean a redundancy, the overall relationships being 10 earlier than 2, 9 and 8. But what if the relationship with 8 deduced from the first square was known from the second square not directly, but by virtue of 8 already being provably later than 9 there? Then the fact that 10 was earlier than 8, though true, would be irrelevant overall. Only the critically important relationships – that 10 was earlier than 9 and 2 – would be entered on each unit recording sheet and on the site-wide matrix. The relationship between 10 and 8 in the first plan matrix, though shown to be irrelevant overall, would be retained in that matrix because it might still be important in subsequent calculations of relationships for units confined to that square alone.

Clearly, when calculating the optimum size of grid square within which to

The plan of a newly drawn unit in a particular 5m square is checked for overlap against all previously drawn plans in that square, starting with the earliest units. In this case, in 110/220, 10 is found to underlie 9 (therefore it is not necessary to check 6 , 4, and 1) and 8. It has no overlap with 7 or 3.

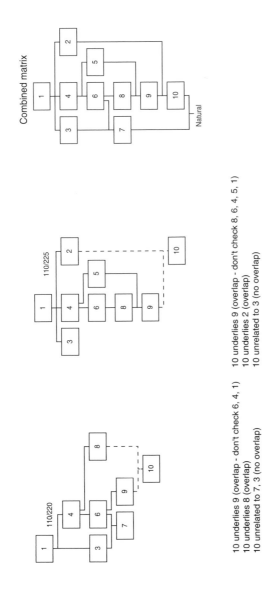

10 underlies 9 (overlap - don't check 6, 4, 1)
10 underlies 8 (overlap)
10 unrelated to 7, 3 (no overlap)

10 underlies 9 (overlap - don't check 8, 6, 4, 5, 1)
10 underlies 2 (overlap)
10 unrelated to 3 (no overlap)

By repeating this process for all plan squares (here 110/225), one can then amalgamate the results. Some relationships will be reproduced in each square (e.g. 10 is under 9 in both); some are additional (the relationship between 10 and 2 in 110/225 was not evident in 110/220); and others, though true of one square, are redundant overall because a more complicated route exists elsewhere (e.g. as 10 directly underlies 8 in 110/220 but 9 underlies 8 in 110/225, then the relationship between 10 and 8, though true, is not critical). A combined matrix represents the context relationships from all grid squares.

Figure 16 Using plan overlays to produce a Harris matrix.

construct these 'mini-matrices', there will be a trade off between the size of the squares on site and the number of plan matrices. If one chooses small squares, each plan matrix will be simpler and thus more quickly checked against each new unit. However, the chance of a unit occupying more than one such square is increased and the excavator is more likely to have to repeat the overlaying process for successive squares. Conversely, the larger the square, the more likely that a unit will fall completely within it, but also the greater the complexity of the individual plan matrices. The size of the grid square thus depends on the 'average' size of the stratigraphic units. On an urban site with truncated stratigraphy surviving only in discrete islands and comprised of small units often less than 2m across, grid squares of 5m may be appropriate. On an extensive rural site, where stratigraphic distinctions are difficult and the majority of units which can be defined cover much of the site, no subdivisions may be needed: the plan matrix is thus redundant, as it would be nothing more than an exact copy of the overall site matrix. Pre-excavation evaluation will help in making these decisions, also ensuring the most beneficial siting of grid squares, by positioning them along the lines of breaks in the stratigraphic sequence, for example where later intrusions cut it into discrete islands.

A final point about the method outlined above is that some commentators have seen this use of plan matrices as a move away from open-area excavation and back to Wheeler's methods of working within small squares or boxes (above, 1.1). In reply, it should be emphasised that using plan grid squares in this way has no implications for the excavation of the unit itself, which must still be described, numbered and removed as an individual entity. The plan matrices simply facilitate the process of overlaying plans, easing the complex task of calculating stratigraphic relationships by breaking it up into more manageable elements. Such a system ensures that a consistent, checkable method of calculating stratigraphic relationships can be implemented, with no need to be reliant on individual memory, or chancy estimations, in creating what should be a fundamental part of the excavation record of any site.

10

DEPOSIT DESCRIPTIONS

Introduction

The objectives of describing the physical characteristics of any stratigraphic unit are twofold. First there is the need to elucidate the formation processes which created the unit and any transformations which it has undergone in the ground subsequently: this requires a *detailed* description of its character and contents. Second, this record has to be created in such a way that every stratum is comparable with all others: this necessitates a *systematic* approach to recording. A great variety of types of stratigraphic unit may be encountered on site and an almost limitless number of aspects of each might be noted, so any record must select which are important on the basis of the research objectives of the project and site evaluation before full-scale excavation. The resulting recording system will then require the creation of field test procedures and the training of personnel in their use. Of course, even with such planning, any site can throw up the unexpected – a type of organic survival not anticipated, a method of construction not predicted – so the recording system will always be a development of the initial blueprint. However, the unexpected is best catered for by working away from an agreed method, rather than simply drifting towards a new approach because of gradually evolving circumstances. Certain broad but common categories of unit can be predicted and are discussed below.

Before any aspect of the written record can be produced, it is necessary to decide which personnel are to be involved in its creation and the stage of the excavation process at which they will do the work (see **10.1** below). Nowadays it is further necessary to design appropriate computer storage mechanisms for the data produced (**10.2**). Nearly every site will encounter different sorts of deposits, mostly sediment in horizontal layers. In recording these, archaeologists have drawn extensively on the methods of the soil scientist, though it is worth remembering that strata created by human agency are not the simple equivalent of those produced in nature (**10.3**). In general, field-workers will need to record the colour (**10.4**), particle size (**10.5**), compaction (**10.6**), inclusions (**10.7**) and the thickness and surface details (**10.8**) of each deposit. Stratigraphic units other than deposits – masonry and brick features, timber, human skeletons, intrusions and finds groups – will be dealt with in Chapter 11.

10.1 Who records and when?

There are two schools of thought on who should actually create the written record. Some maintain that it is best done by as few people as possible, a single person if this is practical, in order to achieve complete consistency. A 'site recorder' is therefore designated on many excavations. However, there are some arguments against this approach. On a site of any complexity it may prove either impossible to have all strata recorded by one individual or, if this is rigorously enforced, it can lead to considerable time wasting. Thus this specialist has to wait for the completion of planning before going to work, or the excavator sits idly by while the recorder modifies the description of the layer before excavation can continue. Second, anyone who does the same job for an extended period of time can get stale and start to miss things, especially if the work involves describing all units but rarely excavating them. Thus separating the two tasks of writing and digging may not guarantee a more accurate and consistent record. Finally, even if many trowel but only one writes, the diggers must still see what has been written down if they are to decide when to call the writer back in, for example to record some significant change in the compaction of the deposit, or in the proportion of the diagnostic inclusions in the mortar of the wall. Thus every team member must understand the whole recording system anyway in order to do her own particular job effectively, whether she actually does the writing or not.

Given these reservations concerning efficiency, accuracy and necessity of a specialist recorder, some projects have adopted an approach in which each excavator describes her own unit, the *rationale* being that this person is in the most privileged position to recognise the character of the deposit under investigation. For example, it is a commonplace amongst experienced excavators that many stratigraphic distinctions involve feeling tenuous textural differences between strata when trowelling, rather than those changes in colour or in proportions of inclusions readily visible to those with only indirect, physical contact with the deposit. Thus it is the person with the trowel in hand who decides when one layer has stopped and another has started because her knowledge is the most immediate and best informed. She is therefore best qualified to write about each stratum. Whichever system is chosen, my experience is that site directors, with many other pressing responsibilities, are seldom the best placed to produce an accurate and consistent written record, even though they do, of course, have responsibility for creating a systematic approach to recording.

Simply having a system is not enough: site personnel must be trained in its implementation. On any excavation, field-workers will start with different levels of experience and awareness, and everyone must be brought up to a common standard which is then maintained throughout the project, whatever the pressures of time. Initially it may be necessary to check the descriptions of newly arrived workers in their entirety, best done by their working beside an experienced co-worker to provide expertise directly and in a friendly and collaborative atmosphere, rather than delivering criticisms from on high. The work can then be handed over gradually to the new colleague as merited. Even here, do not forget that an excavator coming from elsewhere has experience to offer and may suggest vital improvements to an existing system, which the 'old lags' then ignore at their peril. What remains essential throughout this mutual learning process, and beyond, is making every attempt to demystify the job of recording. Clear rules, agreed procedures and proper training are the central ways forward.

Concerning the issue of *when* descriptions are produced, a preliminary record must be made before any excavation of the individual unit takes place. This may involve actions such as digging away and inspecting a small amount of a deposit, recording the external appearance of a wall, or noting the position of a skeleton in outline before proceeding more destructively. This initial judgement provides a basis for subsequent excavation, a sort of working hypothesis to be elaborated as necessary. It thus ensures that excavators do not fall into the trap of overreliance on memory – attempting to memorise every detail of the unit as excavation proceeds and writing it all down at the end will not provide the same quality of record. Of course, the written record produced at the initial stage will be incomplete as only surface details of any unit will be visible. For example, the numbers and distribution of diagnostic types of inclusion or soil compaction may change lower down a deposit and such differences must be recorded, using the same agreed criteria to allow comparability with the initial description. Thus the original description should not be seen as sacrosanct; nor, of course, do any amendments imply that it was badly done initially in failing to note what could only become visible at a lower depth. This 'evolution' of the descriptive record reinforces the point that, because the required modifications result from her own excavation work, it is essential that the excavator knows what was originally written down and how the description was worked out. An unnecessary division of labour between troweller and recorder serves merely to complicate this process.

10.2 Computer storage of record

As for how descriptive data are held, those old-fashioned media, pen and paper, are still effective for many purposes, though soft copy stored within a computer is now taking their place. Today many projects find themselves in an intermediate position, where the written record is produced on paper on site, but destined soon after for computer storage. This move towards using computer data-bases has succeeded in overcoming considerable inertia in the field profession, especially when the programmes were seen as constraining the diversity of the descriptive record (such worries, it must be said, were often a product of certain directors refusing to recognise the need for a systematised record, rather than an objection to computers *per se*). Even the notion that excessive use of key words limits flexibility in creating and using the record can be countered, as recent developments in software allow searching records for designated words, so that the distinction between key words and free text becomes increasingly tenuous.

Although objections in principle to the use of computers have been largely answered, creating an effective data-base for site records still needs thought to carry through effectively in practice. A fundamental decision concerns the number and type of descriptive fields which any data-base may need. This requires balancing three different factors. Which characteristics are common to the majority of a particular type of unit? Which are most likely to be needed for comparisons between units in post-excavation work? And which can be recorded on the basis of agreed criteria which can be systematically used on site? Only if a characteristic passes on all three counts will it be desirable, or indeed feasible, to designate it as a specified field. In fact, these three criteria really reduce to a single, essential consideration. Consider the example of recording the inclusions present in deposits. If manipulation of such judgements is needed in later analysis to allow analysis to correlate between islands of stratigraphy (the second criterion), they will have to be present in a significant number of cases for this to be feasible (first criterion). Equally, if these judgements are to be used with any validity, they must be capable of being recorded systematically on site (third criterion). Thus the requirements of post-excavation work – the 'analytical destiny' of the data (Carver 1991) – are the fundamental consideration here. The problem over computerisation, and therefore any solution, lies with the archaeologist, not the systems analyst, still less the designer of software.

The way in which data are put into the computer must also reflect the overall structure of the archaeological record and the order in which it is created on site. Thus, if there is a common numbering system for all stratigraphic units independent of their type, inputting this number will logically occur at the start of the process – it should be the first piece of information to be logged. If units are then divided into different types – for example the sixfold division between deposits, masonry and brick features, timbers, skeletons, cuts and finds groups used in the discussion below – then the data-base will follow these strands. If all units have certain aspects in common – for example the number of the plans or sections recording their spatial characteristics, their stratigraphic relationships, any samples taken or finds derived from them – then the programme will join back together to record these things.

Finally, certain safety mechanisms can usefully be built into any software so that some fields may not be passed without an answer, while others can be left empty. For example, all deposits have colour, so it can be arranged that one cannot proceed without recording something in the field 'colour'. In contrast, some layers have many inclusions, others none at all, so this field can be left open. Clearly, computer storage can greatly enhance the quality and consistency of the record. However, this can only be achieved within an appropriately designed data-base, and with sufficient speed of feedback between the record being created on site and its being stored. Thus, if one does not opt for hand-held computers at the work-face, the transfer of data to computer must take place nearby, and as soon as possible.

The most appropriate way to ensure a systematic approach to recording archaeological deposits is to enter the information about each onto a specially designed recording sheet (Figure 17). This will include sections holding information on colour, particle size, inclusions, compaction, thickness and surface characteristics, plus a variety of other bureaucratic and cross-referencing data such as stratigraphic relationships, plan numbers, finds recovered and environmental samples taken.

10.3 Deposit descriptions in relation to sedimentology and pedology

Deposits of various sorts are the most common type of stratigraphic unit encountered on archaeological sites, especially if one includes the individual fills of cut features such as pits and post holes. Examination of their composition, texture and structure can provide vital information on palaeoenvironments, former human activities and their spatial distribution, and site formation processes. Approaches to describing such physical characteristics have been borrowed from soil scientists concerned with natural formation processes. The most widely applied in British archaeology is that of the Soil Survey of England and Wales (Hodgson 1978), its US equivalent being the handbook on Soil Taxonomy. It is clear that an understanding of these natural processes is vital for all of those working on any archaeological site: hence our adoption of criteria such as texture, stoniness, structure and boundary form (Hassan 1978).

Soils react to a series of environmental factors, notably climate, organisms (including humans), the nature of the underlying parent material, the natural relief of the area and the passage of time. These factors can result in a variety of processes such as podsolisation, gleying, erosion and peat formation (Courty *et al.* 1989, which also demonstrates the need to integrate the efforts of micromorphologist and site recorder). Hence one will need to study the general physiography of the region and to note particular landforms and current land use before starting any project (see Waters 1992 and Birkeland 1984 for general background on archaeological soils and geomorphology). It may also be necessary to dig test pits into the parent material in order to understand fully the formation of archaeological strata above it.

To interpret formation processes accurately, it is often useful to distinguish human from natural phenomena. Consider the case of colouration. Reddening

Context type: *deposit/cut* (✔) site code:		Context number:
Descriptive Info: **Deposit** 1. Colour		**Cut** 1. Shape in plan

Descriptive Info:

Deposit
1. Colour

2. Composition
-particle size (>10%)
-inclusions   (<10%)
             frequent
             moderate
             occasional

3. Compaction

4. Thickness

5. Other information and
   comments

Cut
1. Shape in plan

2. Orientation

3. Corners in plan

4. Break in slope-top

5. Depth

6. Nature of sides

7. Break of slope-base

8. Nature of base

9. Other information and
   comments

Stratigraphic relationships

Context the same as:
Justify

Location
on matrix:

Spatial and photographic information
Plan Numbers (levels on reverse):   Other drawings (specify):

Photographs (tick when taken):   Photograph reference numbers:

Finds information

Artefacts:	Pot	Tile	Brick	Bone	Seed	Metal	Samples:	Bulk	Char.	C14	Dendr.	Other
✔ if present							✔ if taken					
collection key word- **A**ll, **S**ome or **N**one							no of bags					

Initials + Date: Checked + Date:

Interpretative information
Functional interpretation and other comments: _____

	Provisional date (give basis)	Phasing/grouping	Initials + date
cont'd over			

Figure 17 A recording sheet for deposits and cut features.

of strata, interpreted initially as the result of burning, might prove to be a product of natural agencies such as water-logging or iron pan; and black colouration, thought to be due to the presence of charcoal, or grey due to ash, may be related instead to the presence of manganese. The analysis of naturally formed soils may require particular sampling policies and procedures, or the use of simple chemical tests such as the use of dilute hydrochloric acid to test for calcium carbonate. Similarly, in particular cases, acidity may need to be measured via pH value to see why no bones survive on a site, or special Munsell charts to judge soil colouration. Here we are moving out of the realms of the 'normal' deposit description and into specialist analysis but suffice it to say that a certain understanding of these processes is required to describe archaeological deposits effectively.

Yet it is possible to take this focus on natural processes too far. For example, Pyddoke's *Stratification for the Archaeologist* (1961) mostly considers geological background and natural agencies; only in the last few pages do humans get a look in, and then mainly in terms of their effect on the natural environment. It should be remembered that archaeological deposits are created mostly by human, not natural, agencies. This is not just a contingent fact about such layers but a product of defining archaeology as related to the investigation of human action in the past – for an archaeologist, 'man is the proper study of mankind', albeit often in relationship to environmental factors, and we select our sites and their component parts accordingly. Hence the descriptions of archaeological strata will not be a direct equivalent to those of the sedimentologist, even if we have much to learn from each other. The description of deposits on site is usually structured in terms of colour, texture (particle size) and coarse components (inclusions), derived originally from geology, and the more 'archaeological' criteria of compaction, dimensions in plan and elevation, and types of surface treatment. These aspects are considered in order below.

10.4 Deposit colour

The colour of each stratigraphic unit has to be described using a defined language which is both diverse enough to be sensitive to individual characteristics, yet sufficiently constrained to enable useful comparative analysis later on. Thus calling all deposits either black, brown, grey or red will certainly be insufficient, but using a description such as 'dark blackish greeny-grey with a yellowy-orange tinge' is hardly likely to allow correlation between deposits. In most situations, one can construct a viable record in terms of tone, hue and dominant colour to reconcile the complexity of reality with the need for comparability: thus a deposit may be recorded as light (tone), greyish (hue) brown (dominant colour).

Two further matters need discussion. First, there is the issue of variations within deposits. Because human agency has a basic role in site formation processes, a single stratum often displays more colour variation within it, in either plan or elevation, than between it and other units. Thus recording it in terms of a single, 'average' colour will be of limited use. To argue, as was done above, that we should have a proper structure to the form of colour record is not to maintain that we must attempt to restrict the colour variations which an individual deposit may exhibit. Any colour judgement must accommodate this full variety.

Second there is the related issue of the use of specialist methods, notably Munsell charts, to aid colour comparisons between strata. Four points can be made here. First, if such charts are used, it is important to include not only the colour reference ('10 YR 7/3') but also the corresponding colour terminology ('dull yellow/orange') if these determinations are to be useful to a variety of audiences who may wish to use the site archive. Second, there is the practical matter of how long it may take to make each determination of colour using such a chart. A sample of each deposit must be moistened until it no longer darkens, then assessed against the chart. Further, if there are variations within the layer, as mentioned above, this process may need to be repeated on successive occasions, which all takes time. Finally it must also be remembered that, if working in artificial light, colour judgements will be affected, limiting comparison with records done in the open air and, if lighting is inadequate or varies within the site, even between strata in the same trench. Of course, the fact that using a chart is more time consuming is no reason to dismiss it out of hand, if it gives better results.

Next there is the question of whether such charts really do allow a more accurate and consistent colour record. Opinion here is divided. My own experience, for example in experiments with site staff at the major excavations at Wroxeter, is that there is as much variation between individuals in their allocation of Munsell colours as there is with using normal colour language and that, if anything, the latter can be more sensitive to the variations in hue and tone than the chart. However, other experiments have led to different conclusions (Booth 1980, 1983).

The third, and most important, issue concerns what one is hoping to achieve in recording the colour of deposits. Pottery specialists need colour determinations of their fabrics to allow comparisons between fabrics derived from entirely different assemblages, for example to see whether ceramics identified at one settlement come from the same production centre as those found at another. Similarly, soil scientists use their chart because they need to investigate formation processes over large areas and to make links between geological configurations in different regions. Thus, for both disciplines, inter-site comparisons are the order of the day. In contrast, site workers need, for the most part, to make comparisons within sites.

A descriptive language which allows accurate communication between all those working on a single project, but has limited value when making comparisons outside this, may be perfectly acceptable and not require the regular use of Munsell charts. Of course, Munsell numbers may become vitally important if one wishes to understand links between site formation processes on a much larger scale (the silting in the base of a disused stream bed, to allow comparisons with the riverine regime further downstream, for example). But in this case, a more accurate description of the soil itself will also be needed, moving us into the sphere of specialist sampling. Otherwise, the use of everyday language to describe colours seems, in my experience, to produce sufficient consistency for normal purposes.

10.5 Soil particle size

As mentioned above, the experienced excavator makes the most important stratigraphic distinctions by, literally, 'feeling' tenuous textural differences between strata when trowelling. Hence recording that texture, by estimating the particle size of the deposit concerned, is a basic element of the descriptive record of any unit. Some archaeologists do this by working with the soil science triangle (see, for example, the early system proposed by Prescott *et al.* 1934). Pure clay, silt and sand are situated at each corner of the diagram and soils can then be categorised in terms of three co-ordinates, depending on the combination of these components. Those in the centre of the diagram are usually designated as loams, with any deposit graded depending on where it lies within the diagram.

In order to operate this system, it is still necessary to define what actually constitutes the various key elements at the corners of the triangle. Various cut-off points have been put forward, but earlier schemes seemed to magnify sand unduly at the expense of silt and clay. Today it is commonplace to define clay as particles below 0.002mm, silt as 0.002–0.06mm and sand as 0.06–2mm (often subdivided into fine, medium and coarse), with larger entities (pebble, cobble, boulder, etc.) above this. However, making definitions in this way allows one the alternative of recording the character of archaeological layers by working out proportions between the various particle sizes ('60% silt, 20% fine sand and 20% medium sand'). I have found it much simpler to get consistency of judgement by classifying deposits in the latter way, without recourse to the triangle and a complex range of named soil types such as clayey loam, sandy loam, etc.

Of course, in post-excavation analysis, one has to accept that exact percentages may not be completely accurate when making correlations between strata and, especially, when denying them. For example, anyone wishing to maintain that the above deposit cannot link to a second described as 70% silt, 20% fine sand, 10% medium sand because of the differences in particle sizes is fooling herself, not least because there may be more variation in particle size than this within a single archaeological deposits. The accuracy of any description will depend on the expertise of the recorder(s) and, hopefully to a limited extent, the complexity of the deposit under consideration. Manipulating these data can only be done effectively with an awareness of these limitations.

Although one can legitimately expect fairly accurate estimates of particle sizes from the site worker, it is not possible to do this by sieving every layer for grain size in laboratory conditions (and such a sampling strategy would still fail to cater for the variations within deposits). So, to be useful in the excavation, any scale of particle sizes has to be translated into specific field tests. Generally, some form of hand-texturing is used to examine deposits in the field, the overall rule-of-thumb being that clay coheres, silt adheres and sand does neither. Hence some of the relevant physical attributes are that clay is sticky and plastic; silt has particles invisible to the naked eye and a soapy, silky and somewhat sticky texture and can be smeared on the skin; and the smaller sand particles have a visible twinkle and feel gritty when moistened, whilst the larger ones can be heard when ground between thumb and forefinger.

Perhaps the easiest way to differentiate between these different particle sizes is to create a cube of soil, about 25mm across, by moistening some of the deposit with water and kneading it thoroughly to give maximum plasticity. Then roll the cube into a ball and try to form a cylinder, or 'sausage shape'. If this is possible, further test its malleability by endeavouring to twist it into a complete loop. Pure sand particles will not hold their shape at all and, even when mixed with a minority of silt, will only form a sausage with cracks. Purer silt will form a cylinder proper, the smaller its diameter the finer the soil matrix. It may even give a u-shape if mixed with a little clay, but will break if one tries to complete the circle. Finally, pure clay will form both sausage and ring. This process of testing is best represented as a flow diagram which any excavator can follow (see Figure 18).

10.6 Compaction or consistency of deposits

The compaction of a deposit can vary because of formation processes, especially the nature of the material comprising the layer in question and its mode of deposition, or because of post-depositional factors, particularly its subsequent use. Soil scientists assess deposit compaction by employing a set terminology such as loose, weak, firm, strong, rigid, cemented, plus sticky and plastic on occasion. In my experience, it is difficult to get these terms used consistently when describing archaeological strata, whether due to excavators' lack of expertise or because of the different nature of the strata themselves. Perhaps for this reason, the degree of compaction of a deposit rarely provides a good basis for correlating between deposits across the site.

One way to assess consistency is to take a dry, or slightly moist, untrowelled

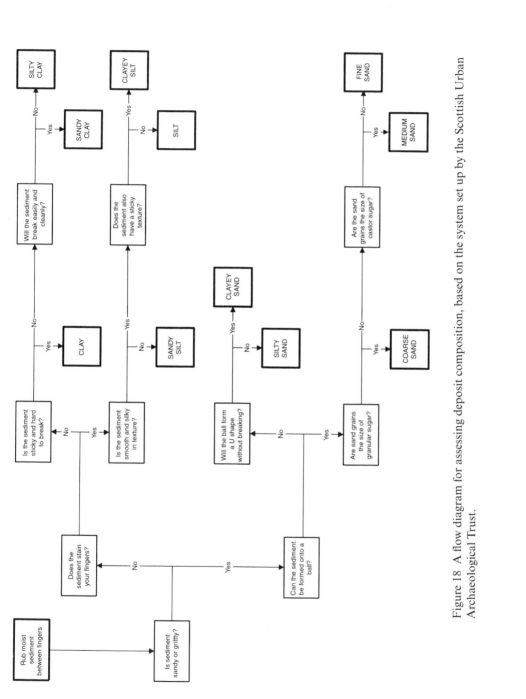

Figure 18 A flow diagram for assessing deposit composition, based on the system set up by the Scottish Urban Archaeological Trust.

cube of soil and crush it between thumb and forefinger. No resistance means a *loose* soil, low pressure a *friable* one, greater pressure defines it as *firm*, and, if it does not break up, it can be classified as *compact*. An alternative approach to recording compaction can be to note what it took to actually remove the deposit in excavation. Thus 'surface removed with point of trowel; remainder noticeably looser, removed with side of trowel' or 'this stratum needed much heavier use of pickaxe than overlying deposit' can be sufficient. As with estimating particle size, it is wise to make an initial assessment of surface compaction, then augment it as excavation proceeds.

Variations in compaction across the surface of a deposit can be vitally important for later analysis, so noting differences will be of greater importance than some bland average. Such differences can be recorded either in themselves ('the surface of the deposit is noticeably more compact at its north-east corner (see area delineated on plan)') or in relation to contiguous deposits ('surface noticeably more compact that overlying deposit 9325'). For example, the compaction of the surface of a deposit at a particular point may result from the insertion of a load-bearing wall 0.50m above it, a post-depositional factor. If so, the wall would be expected to affect the compaction of all similar intervening strata at this point. Conversely, the absence of compaction from layers in between would suggest that more local explanations might be considered, for example increased traffic on the surface of the layer in question at this point. Equally important will be differences in compaction between the surface of a deposit and its underlying components. For example, in a series of gravel dumps, the uppermost may be noticeably more compact at its surface than its base, whereas the two underlying dumps are loose throughout. This changed compaction may be the only indication that it once formed the surface of a road, for which the remainder of the sequence is merely preparatory make-up. In contrast, if each dump is compact at surface and loose below, one may have three successive, thin road metallings, not a single, thicker one.

10.7 Inclusions within deposits

As well as the basic soil matrix, all deposits contain inclusions. Before discussing how these might be recorded, it is necessary to remove a confusion about what constitutes an inclusion. Some excavators define inclusions in terms of the type of material, for example by picking out cultural, as opposed to natural, items: 'pottery fragments are an inclusion, sand particles are not'. However, archaeological strata nearly always contain a combination of cultural and natural materials, so it is inappropriate to define one as an inclusion and the other as part of the basic deposit matrix. The type of materials involved should not matter.

Others differentiate in terms of size, thus taking a lead from soil scientists who distinguish 'the soil' from the 'coarse components' within it. Hence an inclusion might be 'any entity above 50mm', or whatever. However, such an approach creates problems at the upper end of the scale. For example, the size of some tumbled bricks forming the primary destruction debris of a wall might be above the size cut-off point, yet constitute the majority of the deposit. Thus the 'inclusions' here would comprise more of the unit that the soil matrix which surrounds them.

It therefore seems better to base the definition of what constitutes an inclusion not on its character or size, but merely on what proportion of a deposit it comprises. As mentioned above, the ratio of variously sized sands to silt to clay in a layer can only be approximately determined. However, when these occur at less than 10%, any attempt at mathematical accuracy in the field can only give a spurious, scientific appearance. An inclusion can therefore be usefully defined as any element which occupies less than 10% by volume of the deposit. Within this band, it is only possible to sub-divide in general terms, for example between frequent, moderate and occasional inclusions. The first are those evident in considerable abundance but which, on careful consideration, do not seem to quite make it past the 10% deadline. At the other end, occasional inclusions can be recognised if one searches for them, but are few and far between. Moderate ones lie between these poles. Obviously, this is only a rough-and-ready guide, but any attempt at more rigorous estimates would require more time and expertise than is usually to hand. In any case, my experience suggests that this level of resolution is sufficient for most post-excavation work.

Alongside approximate proportions, the size of inclusions must also be recorded, the smaller ones split into categories such as flecks and fragments. The latter can be further divided between small and large fragments, perhaps using a division to either side of 60mm, thus fitting with the categories of particle sizes, of which these determinations are, in essence, an extension. For the largest inclusions, it is better to give real dimensions, either each measured on the ground if there are only a few examples, or as an average with maxima and minima if there are many. Mottles and patches within a deposit can be similarly treated, mentioning their material, what proportion of the layer they constitute, their size and distribution. Finally, any concentrations of inclusions within the surface of the deposit or in a vertical plane must be noted. This can be done in text or, better still, delineated on the plan. Carefully and consistently recorded, inclusions within layers can become the single most vital element allowing correlation between sequences during post-excavation analysis.

10.8 Thickness and surface characteristics

Lastly it is vital to record changes in thickness and surface characteristics of the whole deposit. The former, in theory, should be directly calculable using the spot-heights and hachures on successive plans. However, reconstructing this information is a laborious business, whilst recording this during the process of excavation is easily accomplished (e.g. the simple statement 'the layer was 50mm thick in the north, lensing out to zero in the south').

Surface characteristics are equally vital. For example, discontinuous lines of greyish brown silt on a clay make-up may be the only indication that an area was once covered by a plank floor, this material having found its way down between the cracks. Similarly, staining, if it shows a regular pattern, may be derived from contiguous fittings such as iron fixings or timber members, which were later removed. Such discoloration is best recorded on the appropriate plan. Undulations in the surface due to differential wear, perhaps indicative of access points, must be carefully noted, either in written form or, better still, on plan and/or by photograph. Equally, unworn sectors might indicate the former existence of features such as benches which covered the area and thus protected it from traffic. Recognition of differential wear is difficult as the processes involved may be insufficient to define depressions so that they can be planned. This places a premium on the correct positioning of spot heights on high and low points, and use of hachures. A complete record may only be possible with a carefully produced contour survey.

Similarly, patterning in the abrasion of surface inclusions can suggest that a deposit was subjected to wear, particularly if such material is pushed down into the layer. The converse can also be true. If inclusions protrude some distance above the level of the surrounding area, this may indicate that the deposit was not used as a surface but quickly covered. However it is also possible for such protrusions to be a result of other agencies, for example the later wearing-away of the surrounding soil matrix by water erosion. Here the roundness, orientation and inclination of any diagnostic, protruding items may be the only indication of formation process or subsequent wear patterns. Equally the nature of the boundaries between the deposit under excavation, and those encountered beneath it, is also important. How distinct is the change – sharp and abrupt, clear, or merely gradual and diffuse?

A last point is that, in all such deposit descriptions, a designated measurement system with tightly defined terminology is required. Some excavators have suggested that this measuring system should be chosen to fit with that used by the society under investigation but this is unacceptable. Hence the 'Roman foot' could be used to record a Roman site. But which Roman foot is to be used (it changed through time), and what system should be used to record the overlying medieval deposits? Apart from the fact that measurements may get conveniently rounded up to match the system, it is important for future researchers that data have been produced using an independent measuring system. Using 'Roman feet for a Roman site' makes almost impossible the task of anyone wishing to test the hypothesis that the society in question really did use a particular measurement module (yet another illustration of the important principle that we are trying to *impose* perspectives, and therefore measurement systems, on the site to investigate patterning, not communing with that society using their system as a convenient intermediary). The European standards provide the most widely accepted system here, their strength coming from the fact that they are provably irrelevant to most societies under investigation. Using metres and millimetres, with a cut off point either side of 10mm (thus 'stones were up to 0.12m across, though averaged 9mm') is much better than centimetres, and certainly better than employing feet and inches.

11

NON-DEPOSIT DESCRIPTIONS

Introduction

Although deposits form the majority of stratigraphic units on most sites, many excavations also uncover other types of entity such as masonry or brick walls, timber structures, skeletons and intrusive features of various sorts. Recording masonry and brick features requires knowledge of types of building materials and their articulation, and understanding the importance of their distribution within any structure, together with some special factors and procedures (see **11.1**). On sites with anoxic conditions, timbers may survive, so records of their dimensions, positions, condition and surface treatments, and the specialist joints which they incorporate, will have to be borne in mind (**11.2**). Another specialist area is the excavation of inhumations, raising matters such as position and orientation of the skeleton and its pathology, the classification of grave types, and particular considerations such as the spatial and stratigraphic records of the burial, and cleaning and lifting the skeleton (**11.3**). Recording 'cut features' on the same basis as one deals with the positive units on a site is now commonplace but raises issues of how one defines such intrusions and deduces their stratigraphic relationships, as well as the question of how to make a full record of their shape and size (**11.4**). Finally, in particular circumstances, a finds assemblage may be defined as a distinct stratigraphic unit in its own right, for instance when artefacts are broken *in situ*, when finds are recovered from spit excavation, or where material is derived from sieving or metal detecting processes (**11.5**).

11.1 Masonry and brick features

The investigation of standing buildings is an area of great archaeological potential which has not been always realised. It has been seen as a separate part of fieldwork, a sub-discipline in its own right (see Smith 1985 for a general introduction and Hutton 1986 on specific recording techniques). Yet, even accepting this somewhat arbitrary, and probably misleading, distinction between above- and below-ground archaeology, the site digger will still encounter various types of structural features in masonry or brick during her work. Walls, arches, foundations, etc. can act as upstanding structural features, or can constitute the lining of intrusive features such as cess-pits. Stone and brick can even be laid in horizontal layers, as in the example of a brick floor (for purposes of description, the last group therefore blends into deposits discussed in the previous chapter). Thus all excavators will need to know how to make a detailed record of masonry and brick features including, on occasion, specialist drawings.

In contrast with soil deposits, where stratigraphic relationships can usually be decided with some certainty before excavation, the use of underpinning and the existence of rebuilds within walls mean that initial calculations of relationships may need to be amended in the process of excavation. Indeed, some relationships can only be properly determined during dismantling. For these and other reasons, many organisations have found it useful to use a special recording sheet for masonry and brick features, at least as far as the descriptive and stratigraphic elements are concerned (Figure 19). When filling in such a sheet, the excavator should start with a description of building materials, including their finishing; then cover their articulation and the construction methods, employing technical terms where necessary; follow with a description of the bonding agent, usually mortar; and finish by looking out for specialist matters such as masons' marks, reuse of masonry and indications of contemporary ground surfaces associated with the feature. This is the order followed in the discussion below.

Any description of **building materials** requires identification of stone and brick types within the feature and their relative proportions. This may necessitate some knowledge of local geology, either by employing a geologist on the team (Rapp 1975) or by talking to a friendly expert. The information provided can then be communicated to the rest of the excavating staff by assembling a reference collection on site related to local needs. This collection will cover the majority of cases, and examples of the occasional unidentifiable stone can be kept as a sample until expertise is on hand. Similarly, with brick and tile, a reference collection of fabric types can be constructed by the ceramics expert and site workers trained in its use. More detailed description of this material may be needed on occasion, for instance measurement of complete faces of the best-preserved examples, but this is a matter for the artefact specialist.

It is important not just to recognise the simple presence and absence of different types of building materials, but to calculate their approximate proportions. This is easily estimated by putting each sort of stone into a different pile during dismantling and noting proportions at the end, though more accurate measurement will be needed for detailed analyses. In addition, different stones, or proportions of such, may be used in different parts of the feature, either for functional reasons such as their load-bearing capacity or weathering properties, or simply for decorative effect. Hence it is also important to note any differences in the use of materials between the core and outside of a wall or between its base and top, or concentrations at particular points along its length.

Context type: *masonry brick* (✔) site code:	Context number:

Descriptive info:

1. Materials, including sizes and proportion

2. Finishing of stone/brickwork

3. Articulation and coursing/bonding

4. Bonding material and mortaring methods

5. Other comments, including evidence for reused stones.

Stratigraphic relationships

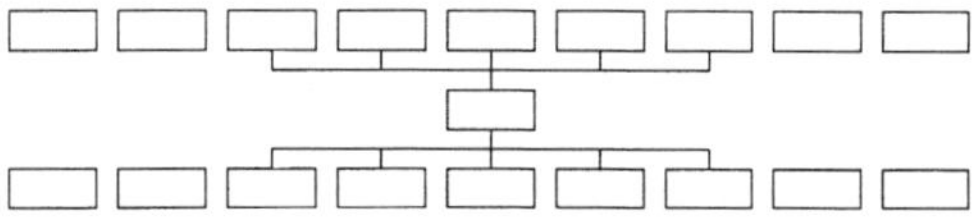

Context the same as/associated with: (justify)

Location on matrix:

Spatial and photographic information

Plan numbers (levels on reverse):

Other detailed drawings: (sketches on reverse)

Photographs (tick when taken):

Photograph reference numbers:

Samples: Petrological (✔) — No. of e.g.s | mortar (✔) — No. of bags | Regular bricks (✔) — (No. - usually 4) | Special bricks (✔) — No. of e.g.s

Interpretative information — Initials + Date: — Checked + Date:

Functional interpretation and other comments (include any thinking on contemporary ground surface, sources of any re-used elements and other structural components associated with this one):

cont'd over | Provisional date (give basis) | Phasing/grouping | Initials + date

Figure 19 A recording sheet for masonry and brick features.

Stone courses

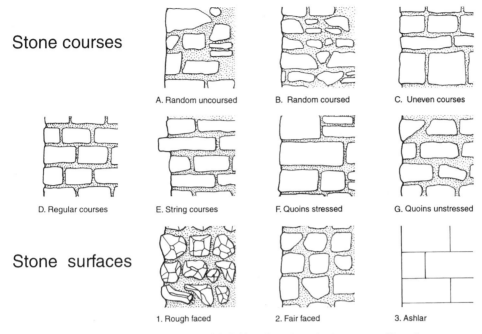

A. Random uncoursed   B. Random coursed   C. Uneven courses

D. Regular courses   E. String courses   F. Quoins stressed   G. Quoins unstressed

Stone surfaces

1. Rough faced   2. Fair faced   3. Ashlar

Figure 20 Stone courses and finishing, based on the Museum of London system.

How the stones are worked and their dimensions, and any patterning in these, are similarly important, as this influences whether they can be set to produce a rough or a fair face to the wall. In describing their working, one should distinguish, minimally, between rough-hewn, roughly squared and accurately squared ('ashlar') blocks (Figure 20). For the dimensions of rough masonry it will probably be sufficient to give the largest and smallest stones and degree of variation or an average, or better still both ('varying from 0.50m down to 0.20m across, but tending towards the latter with an average of 0.25m across'). However, when the building material has been more accurately made, as with some higher-quality masonry walls or, most obviously, with brick and tile, actual dimensions should be given. If these measurements suggest the use of a module in brick production, it may be useful to keep a sample of well-preserved examples to aid future research into building material production processes.

Having dealt with the basic materials, their **articulation** within the feature must be recorded (Figure 20). Masonry might be described in general terms, saying whether it was randomly placed or set in courses. If the latter, the courses may be uneven or more regular, and there may be differences between core and facing in this respect. In places the feature may incorporate a string course, whether for engineering reasons or for decorative effect, which uses either the same material as the rest of the wall, or a different one such as tile.

Lastly, the corners often embody different techniques from the remainder of the feature, to enhance load-bearing capacity at a critical point. In particular, it should be noted whether the quoins are stressed or unstressed. Finally, one must also record the depth of the courses. This is best done by taking at least four measurements and averaging the result, rather than trying to measure and write down each individual instance. Of course, variations in this depth may be indicative of quality of workmanship and must also be mentioned.

The orientation of elements within a brick wall can be even more complex than that of masonry features and thus require greater attention to detail. Most bricks will be placed on bed, but others may be on edge – e.g. for use in coping, sills, non-load-bearing features, floors because of increased wear resistance. Or they may be set on end – e.g. arch headings, decorative work or noggin (in-fill). Brick construction methods, including coursing and bond type, are used on repeated occasions, especially for walls, and one can therefore utilise a glossary of technical terms (Figure 21). These not only save time but also make the record more useful for the architectural specialist (especially an international audience which has neither the time nor the inclination to become absorbed directly in the intricacies of one's own recording system). Remember that it will still be necessary to provide measurement of the depth of courses in the way given for masonry features.

Brick bonds

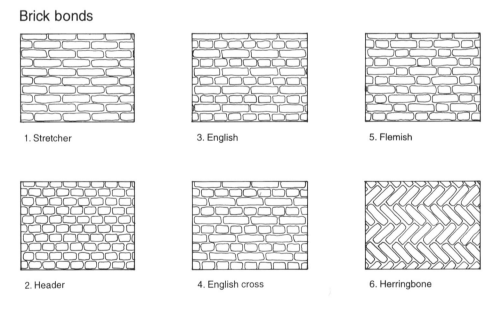

1. Stretcher   3. English   5. Flemish

2. Header   4. English cross   6. Herringbone

Figure 21 Common brick bonds, based on the Museum of London system.

However, when using names such as English bond or Flemish bond, it must be remembered that such terms are only shorthand and should be capable of clear translation into more basic characteristics in order to be used by site workers and to allow full integration with the rest of the site evidence. If not, there will be a tendency to gloss over significant variations by using a single technical term. It is far more vital to know whether or not a well-known method was actually employed in a particular feature, rather than roughly matching the configuration of its bricks. Remember that the exceptions are as important as the rules here, especially when such classifications are derived from architectural studies based on what was intended to happen, whereas excavated evidence tells us what really did occur. Recording a wall which is only *approximately* 'stretchers and headers alternating along each course' simply as '*Flemish bond*' is just not good enough. What might be important here is that the builders were attempting to copy a particular type of construction, but not quite managing it. Inattention to detail in recording masks the gap between theory and practice, intention and outcome.

Less problematical are the technical terms for detailed description of particular elements within a course. Some of the more common are given below:

> A **bed joint** is the horizontal joint between beds.
>
> **Galleting** involves the insertion of pebbles into mortar joints either as protection against the weather or for decoration. With pebble dash this continues over the whole surface of the wall.
>
> **Honeycomb** misses alternate bricks, either as part of a decorative scheme or for functional purposes such as ventilation in barns, access into dovecotes, etc.
>
> A **lacing course**, either of tiles or bricks, is used to reinforce a masonry feature and produce a level course. It may on occasion also be used decoratively.
>
> A **perpend** is the vertical joint between ends.
>
> **Rustication** refers to the use of chamfered joints.
>
> A **stopped end** produces a neat finish, usually with closers such as half headers set in the penultimate course.
>
> **Toothing** uses gaps or projections in alternate courses and is usually indicative of a return wall or buttress at this point, all other traces of which may have been removed subsequently.
>
> **Tumbling in** is where bricks are set at a diagonal angle to the remainder of the wall, usually to create a buttress against it.
>
> **Vitrified headers, glazed bricks** and **projecting headers** may be used as decorative devices, and the last also as support for an adjacent feature such as a floor.

The **mortar** bonding the feature must be carefully described using the same approach as for deposit descriptions, though with careful attention in judging its hardness, especially with respect to the mortar of adjacent features. Even minute proportions of different inclusions can be vital here, especially to provide the basis for suggesting correlations between walls which have no formal stratigraphic links. However, to do such work properly really requires designing a full sampling strategy for mortar in advance.

Methods of mortaring can be described in a variety of ways and can be vital in linking features or in elucidating construction methods, especially when deciding which side a wall was built from and which was its internal face. Some useful terms are:

> **flush**, in which the mortar lies flush with the end of the bricks;
>
> **pointing**, where a better-quality mortar is inserted into the end of the joint after raking out, either for decoration or for protection. Pointing would normally be done only on an exposed face and thus can be indicative of an external situation. Conversely its absence lower down can suggest the level of the contemporary ground surface.
>
> **raked out**, meaning clearing mortar to a depth of about 10mm, often for keying;
>
> **rubbed**, to remove excess;
>
> **scored**, where an exact line is scored with a straight edge to give the appearance of a good finish;
>
> **struck**, where the mortar is pushed in towards the base, usually indicating that the wall has been built from the other side with the mason leaning over the wall to lay the bricks overhand;
>
> **weathered,** where the mortar is pushed in at the top.

Other **specialist aspects** of wall recording include watching out for masons' marks; noting the reuse of stone (perhaps carefully measuring-in each recycled stone if they came originally from a single building to throw light on the latter's dismantling); and using extra-accurate drawing techniques, particularly photogrammetry, to give a more detailed record of complex elevations and thus aid structural reconstruction.

Finally, when dealing with a masonry or brick feature, estimating the level of the contemporary ground surface(s) associated with it can be essential, especially when phasing the site in later analysis (Plate 20). If these matters can be worked out on site, they should be mentioned under the 'notes' section, rather than the primary descriptive record, as they embody a higher order of interpretation. Hence, sometimes, horizontal layers can be clearly identified running up to the wall, which must then be later than it. On other occasions, it may be necessary to consider the character of the feature itself to decide such matters. Some structures suggest, of themselves, the level at which they were used, even when no other evidence survives, for example a hearth (though even here remember the possibility of sunken hearths). Alternatively, offsets built into a wall can indicate floor level (Plate 27, though beware because offsets can also be incorporated as a structural element, either to increase load-bearing capacity at foundation level, or above ground as a decorative device). The level of plaster rendering on a wall, or a quarter-round moulding related to it, can be similarly informative of floor position, so levels should be carefully recorded on it (though plaster would normally be considered as separate stratigraphic units from the wall itself). However, remember that plaster may not survive in its entirety, so its base as recorded only indicates the maximum height of any floor. Also wall renderings, or even associated floor mouldings, may be additions

Plate 27 Careful cleaning and recording of this wall, in particular the changed
methods employed below the offset level at its visible base, should allow
contemporary ground surfaces to be securely established.

rather than primary features of the wall and thus their base may be higher, or
occasionally lower, than the original ground surface associated with the feature.

A final indicator of ground surface concerns the finishing of the wall. Where
this becomes noticeably rougher, it can suggest the level at which the change
from foundation to above-ground wall proper took place. However, great care
must be taken with this judgement. Masonry above ground but at the base of
the wall can become rougher owing to later weathering, for example if in the
splash zone of water falling from the roof of the building. Conversely, walls are
often trench-built below the contemporary ground surface, using excessive
mortar to attach stones to adjacent, earlier stratigraphy and then filling in the
centre of the foundation. If pre-wall strata are then removed from around the
foundation, the excess mortar on the outside of the stones and squeezed from
between its stonework can look like a rough plaster facing, wrongly suggesting
that the wall was once visible at this point and thus seeming to imply a much
lower ground surface than was, in fact, the case.

Sometimes none of these methods can establish unequivocally the level of
contemporary use. Of course, in post-excavation analysis evidence such as
mortar spreads within adjacent deposits may help in deducing a wall's construction level. Or the analyst might note the point in the stratigraphic
sequences on either side of the wall-line above which correlations cannot be

made, and thus suggest that the feature must have been inserted at this stage. When a wall is partially or totally robbed and the evidence for any construction trench removed, such methods may be all that is left, together with important information derived from the character of the robber trench fills themselves. However, in order to use these 'higher-order' criteria to work out a sequence of construction, it is vitally important that the basic stratigraphic relationships, as recorded on site, have made no inaccurate assumptions about the relationship between the wall and adjacent horizontal stratigraphy. Thus, if a particular relationship is thought probable but still open to doubt when on site, it is better to make no definitive statement either way (let the units 'float' with respect to each other) rather than come down on one side and so create confusion in post-excavation analysis.

11.2 Timbers

Timbers survive on archaeological sites in a variety of conditions, from being on completely dry land, via water-logged settings, to lying entirely underwater. The types of associated structures are many and various, for example buildings, including walls, roofs, doors, drains and pit-linings; waterfronts, including stairs and piers; and still more unusual features such as boats, mills, tracks and bridges. Many of these timber features form special areas of study in their own right and one would need specialist advice to achieve a complete record (for example, the data needed to study boats varies depending on whether one is dealing with dug-outs, or carvel- or clinker-built craft). All that can be done here is to give the minimal requirements for the systematic gathering of data, in the hope that this can later form the basis for developing such specialist studies. Systematisation of timber recording has developed mostly in organisations facing large numbers of surviving timbers, for example archaeologists working on waterfronts in the City of London. Much of the following discussion draws on their experiences and expertise.

In some recording procedures, a distinction is made between wood, the material from which environmental information can be extracted, and timber, meaning worked wood which throws light on carpentry techniques, engineering practices, architectural methods, etc. Although we will be interested in the latter here, this is not meant to imply that the purely environmental evidence is any less important. Changes in timber technology can be vital in understanding past societies. For example, planks have been converted in most periods by splitting them radially from straight-grained trees fairly free of knots: hence oak was often used. More recent planks were produced by sawing through smaller, knottier trees. A greater investment in plant, using the saw, allowed wider planks to be created and the exploitation of a greater range of trees, for example elm which does not split well radially. Thus there is a complex relationship between woodland management, the technology used in timber conversion, and the structural requirements of the completed item. Only careful recording can start to elucidate this complexity.

When recording timber, it is important to follow a set procedure to ensure consistency and completeness. The use of a specially designed sheet once again enhances this (Figure 22). First one should give type of timber and its setting and orientation on the site, plus dimensions; then, when the timber has been dismantled and lifted off-site, one can describe its head, foot and various faces, the methods of timber conversion and working employed and any special surface treatment, as if it were an individual artefact; finally, any joints can be noted, together with the timber's condition. This order of operations is reinforced in the discussion below. Creating this record is greatly helped if the recorder has some knowledge of basic terminology, most of which refers to the role of the member within a structure.

The process of recording can be made even more consistent if the procedure is set out on the reverse of the record sheet, together with some reminders of conversion and common jointing methods (Figure 23).

Some of the more common terms are given below.

A **brace** or **shore** is a member, usually diagonally set, which props up a structure.

A **joist** is the base for a floor or ceiling, or both simultaneously.

A **plank** usually forms the external covering of a wall, revetment, boat, etc. (i.e. cladding a feature) or is part of a horizontal surface such as a floor.

A **plate,** either top plate or base plate, is a horizontal member for a structure.

A **post** or **stake** is a vertical member, the difference being either a matter of size, which should then be clearly designated in the recording system; or whether the timber was driven into the ground point first (a stake) or placed in the ground and packed with back-fill to hold it in position (a post).

A **tie-back** is joined to a plate or principal vertical member to prevent the movement of a feature forwards.

Wattle-hurdling or **wickerwork** is comprised of thin wattles woven around upright staves, forming a fence or similar when set vertically, or the base for a path or other foundation when laid out on the ground.

Turning, then, to the recording process itself, the **dimensions** of the timber should be measured first on site, using metres and millimetres and including, minimally, length, breadth and width (note whether the length measurement includes tenons protruding from the end of the timber, which are often invisible when the feature is seen *in situ*). Then describe its **position** and whether it was set horizontally, vertically or diagonally, and give its alignment or orientation in terms of the compass directions of the site grid. After lifting the timber, it is possible to describe its head, foot and then edges and faces (the face is the wider element in section, the other part being the edge). The 'best face' of a plain sawn timber is that most radial to the circle of the log from which it is taken. This is the face prepared first and the one from which other parts are then marked. The soffit is the underside of a timber.

Context type: *timber*	Site code:	Context number:

Descriptive info:

1. Type

2. Setting and orientation

3. Dimensions

4. Conversion and shape in X-section

5. Working and tool marks

6. Intentional marks

7. Joints and fixings

8. Other Comments (including conditions on site + when drawn)

Stratigraphic relationships

Context the same as/associated with (justify):

Location on matrix:

Spatial and photographic information

Plan numbers (levels on reverse):

Timber drawing number: (sketches on reverse)

Photographs (tick when taken):

Photograph reference numbers:

Samples: Dendro. (✔)   Species (✔)   Other, specify (✔)   (✔)

No. of e.g.s   No. of e.g.s   No. of e.g.s   No. of e.g.s

Initials + Date: Checked + Date:

Interpretative information

Functional interpretation and other comments (include any thinking on contemporary ground surface, sources of construction methods, repairs, other structural components associated with this one and any reused elements):

_____cont'd over

Provisional date (give basis)	Phasing/grouping	Initials + Date

Figure 22 A timber recording sheet.

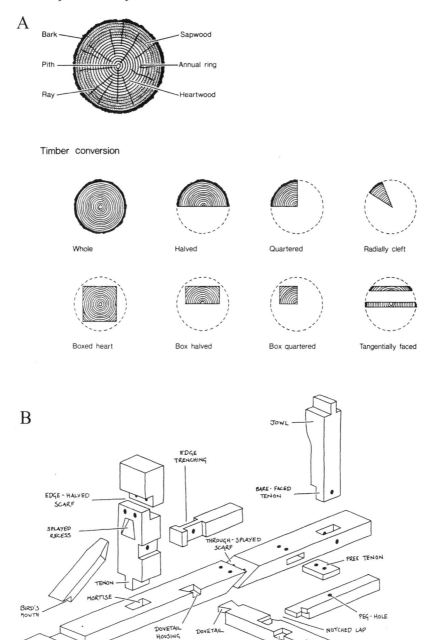

Figure 23 Diagrams of (A) conversion methods and (B) common carpentry joints, used as an *aide-mémoire* to enhance timber recording in the Museum of London.

Plate 28 Assembly marks on timbers from a medieval waterfront in London, here reinforced with chalk after a corresponding photograph had been taken without such enhancement.

Recording dimensions and positions leads to another aspect of the basic record, the **conversion** of the timber from its original condition as wood. Timber cut from a tree may be squared, halved, quartered, radially split or plain sawn. A living tree is composed, from the outside, of bark, sapwood (living cells and water conducting, so prone to decay), heartwood (no living cells and impregnated with tannins, so harder and more resistant) and pith (for storing food substance). Different proportions and positions of sapwood, heartwood, etc. will therefore indicate how the log was converted, which is best illustrated using a drawing of its shape in cross-section.

Next evidence of **timber working** must be considered by looking for tool marks derived from saw, adze/axe or chisel (admittedly, recognising the difference between these and natural ripples in some timber can be difficult). In addition, regularity of sawing can indicate the use of mechanical rather than manual methods of conversion, so the consistency of the marks is equally important. Usually tool marks survive best where protected from excessive wear by underwater currents or splash zones. When found, tooling is best recorded with a measured sketch or photographically in order to save time. 'Carpenters' marks' related to marking-out, batches or tallies, or the laying-out or assembly of the structure (Plate 28) may also be recorded at this point, together with any graffiti.

Another part of the record concerns **surface characteristics and treatment**. Any timber may show evidence of sooting, be burnt/charred or worn, subjected to insect attack, retain traces of paint, pitch or lime wash, or be carved or moulded. Such modifications should be described in text and on plan. Also important are colour variations on the surface, which can be indicators of former role within a structure, for example differential coloration of top and bottom of the timber owing to the latter having been covered at an early stage by a river foreshore. Other stains may indicate the position of former fixings set against the timber.

The final aspect of timber recording is one of the most technical, the description of any **joints** it displays. Timbers can be connected in a variety of ways and how this is done is fundamental to the understanding of the development of carpentry and may also influence engineering solutions and contemporary vernacular architecture. A record of the joints on each timber will include their type, number and dimensions. This may require detailed drawings and photographs when the timber is first exposed, during the process of dismantling the associated structure, and afterwards when it is recorded as individual member. With some types of complex joints, extra drawings at a scale of 1:1 may be needed to augment the normal 1:10 record described below.

Joints come in a variety of types, many very specialised, and they change through time and with local circumstances. The two most common are (Figure 23):

> the **mortise and tenon** in which a tongue fashioned in the end of one member is set into a slot cut into the edge or face of another;
> the **lap** which joins the end or face of one timber to the face of another.

Some variations on these basic themes follow.

> A **bare-faced tenon** has one shoulder rather than the normal two.
> A **chase mortise** has an inclined slot at the end to accept a diagonal tenon.
> **Edge trenched timbers**, not surprisingly, have trenches cut in their edges to accommodate other members.
> A **free tenon** is a tenon buried between two mortises to join them but attached to neither.
> A **half-lap** has wood removed from half the depth of each member to allow them to cross with a level surface.
> A **notched-lap** has a v-shaped notch to prevent withdrawal.
> A **scarf** is an end-to-end lap joint.
> A **secret notched-lap** has wood left on the outer face which obscures the internal notch, i.e. makes it 'secret'.
> A **squint-lap** is any lap joint set at other than perpendicular, i.e. on a squint.
> A **tusk tenon** protrudes through the mortise and is then pegged in place.

A good proportion of timber from one structure can be recycled in later ones and sometimes such reused timbers are the only record we have of certain types of feature. Therefore one should also note whether the joint was a primary feature of the timber as found, or whether it was redundant, thus indicating a different original role. When reuse is noticed, other similar timbers from the same structure will have to be looked at in this light: it was quite common to dismantle one structure in its entirety in order to incorporate it into another. In such situations the record of these now redundant features and relationships must be as full as that of the *in situ* positions of the members.

Timbers may be fastened together by means other than joints, such as wooden dowels. More popular in boats are trenails – dowels with an enlarged head created by deforming the wood at one end and a wedge of timber or fibre forced in at the other end to hold it in place. A variety of rivets, often with a washer (rove), nails, staples and bolts can also be used, especially when attaching plank cladding to a frame. As with joints, changes in such methods are vital indicators of building traditions in a certain area or of the work of a particular carpentry specialist. The gaps between cladding and frame can be filled with various plant fibres, moss, hair, tar, tarred hair, twine and rope as caulking. Similar materials can coat joints and external surfaces and, rarely, paint can also survive. Any indications of such substances should be carefully recorded and sampled for further analysis.

The above written record is usually augmented by a drawing of each timber, probably at a scale of 1:10 or larger, which includes the edge, face and end elevations of the timber and a cross-section to show the nature of its conversion and any rays (lines of thin-walled cells which run radially out from the centre of a log). It should also include knot holes and an indication, lightly pencilled to avoid obscuring other details, of how knotty or straight grained the timber was overall. These matters are vital in elucidating timber selection for particular functions and the relationship between such decisions and woodland management. Also the **condition** of the timber – complete, decayed, broken in antiquity or in excavation – must be recorded using the conventions _____, __z__z__, __.__ and __.____ respectively employed in 'normal' planning.

An important factor when measuring and drawing timber is the problem of shrinkage. When timbers are exposed initially they will have to be kept wet, or at least damp, by regular watering until they are ready to be removed from the site. This can be a time-consuming and/or technically demanding process, sometimes involving setting up spraying systems (above, 4.2). If this is not done, or if the timber is allowed to dry out after being lifted from the site but before recording takes place, considerable shrinkage can occur. Even more problematical, this does not take place evenly. The thinner the member is, the greater the amount of shrinkage, so a tenon will shrink more than the rest of the timber and a mortise will widen more. Hence a joint which was a snug fit when the timber was first discovered or even first dismantled, will appear to have considerable gaps when represented in the drawn record. The record would then suggest lower-quality workmanship than was in fact the case. So, when detailed drawing takes place, the recording conditions should be noted – whether the timber was dried and distorted or, hopefully, in the same beautiful state of preservation as when first exposed in the ground.

Having been lifted from the site and recorded, important timbers can be either stored in water, if tanks are available or have been constructed, or wrapped in cling film and kept in a cool dark place. The latter is obviously an easier option, but will not last as long. Whatever happens to the timber at this stage should be mentioned in the record – thrown away, sampled for dendrochronology, kept in its entirety for future conservation and display etc.

11.3 Inhumations

Burials have considerable potential for elucidating a great variety of issues of archaeological interest. The physical position of each burial on the site, and of the skeleton within the grave, is obviously of great importance. At a gross level, differences in orientation can relate to religious beliefs, for example the east–west orientation of some later Christian cemeteries and all Islamic ones. On other occasions even finer accuracy is required. For example graves may have been dug using the rising sun to obtain an east–west line. The sun rises in different positions during the year, so clustering of burials according to small changes in their alignment can suggest when during the year burial was most likely to occur, and thus presumably the seasonality of death.

Turning to the skeleton itself, we can gather information on demography, health and nutrition, physique and human diseases. Much of this work is, necessarily, specialist and occurs post-excavation but, for the specialist to be employed effectively, a certain level of recording is required on site (Bass 1992). Indeed, the investigation of human burial is an excellent example of the potential for collaboration between osteologist, environmentalist, even documentary historian and excavator (Bennett 1993, McKinley and Roberts 1993). Inhumations also provide excellent examples of primary contexts for artefacts associated with them, throwing light on aspects of dress, both clothing and footwear, and even, some have argued, belief systems concerning the afterlife (although it can be difficult to decide whether all finds within a grave are 'grave goods' in the strict sense). There is, therefore, plenty of justification for taking great care in the excavation and recording of any inhumation.

However, it should also be remembered that human burials have another potential, that of creating considerable political controversy, especially around the issue of reburial (see, for an introduction to some of the issues, Bahn and Paterson 1986, Dincauze 1986, Rahtz 1988 and Klesert and Powell 1992). A good example of what is at stake is the battle over Kennewick Man, found by chance in 1996 alongside the Columbia River near Kennewick City, Washington and initially thought to be the recent remains of a European settler on the basis of what some analysts have termed the 'Caucasoid' features of its skull. However, radiocarbon dating, supported by an associated willow-leaf-shaped spear point, suggested a date of before 9000 years bp, and the remains quickly became contested. On the one hand Native American tribal groups, notably the Umatilla Indians, argue for control of the skeleton under the North American Graves Protection and Repatriation Act and wish to rebury the bones and to prevent further scientific analysis such as more detailed measurements and DNA tests. On the other hand, some members of the archaeological scientific community have an interest in securing just such analysis, whilst still other groups such as the Asatru Folk Assembly, worshippers of pagan Norse gods, also claim Kennewick Man as an ancestor. The controversy continues, over both the exhumed bones and the site itself, which the Army Corps of Engineers, who control this section of the Columbia River, wish to cover with rocks for its 'protection', thereby precluding further investigation of the context of the find. The topicality of the issues involved is, perhaps, best demonstrated by the sheer size of the coverage by the local paper, the *Tri-City Herald*, whose website (http://www.tri-cityherald.com/bones/news/index.html) gives chapter and verse on how the debate has developed since 1996.

Although such a controversy does not, in itself, suggest that one should avoid such excavations, it must provide a great incentive for any excavation director to be aware of the pitfalls and remain sensitive to the impact which this work may have for the public at large. In addition, it is clear that problems may arise not only in the excavation process itself, but also during later analysis of the skeletal material in question. The fact that stories similar to that of Kennewick Man could be told about the African-American burial ground in Lower Manhattan, New York (Kaufmann 1994, Harrington 1996), the skeletons excavated at Jewbury in York, proposed as the site of a Jewish burial ground, and myriad Aboriginal sites in Australia (Webb 1987, Chase 1989) suggests that we may still have some way to go here. This section will consider the recording of the skeleton, any associated container, the grave cut, stratigraphic problems peculiar to burials and their lifting and storage. The discussion will conclude with other special considerations, notably concerning cremations and legal and safety matters.

It is commonplace today for information from burials to be held on a special recording sheet (Luke *et al.* 1996) (Figure 24). Before any such record can be made, overlying grave fills must be removed, using essentially the same process of recording as for the fills of any intrusive feature, and the skeleton cleaned *in situ*: work systematically from head to feet and avoid removing so much soil that the bones sit on a pedestal. A range of tools, more delicate than the usual trowel, may be used for this, including plasterer's leaf, spoon, paint brush, dental tools and, in the opinion of one expert veteran cemetery excavator of my acquaintance, the wooden stick of a lollipop. The hands and feet are particularly difficult areas and should be cleared only of the minimum of soil to allow planning or photography. Finally, sponging-off the largest bones and lightly spraying the remainder with water enhances photography.

When the skeleton has been fully exposed, the **spatial configuration** of the bones must be recorded by plan or photograph whilst they are still in pristine condition. Only then is it possible to describe the skeleton using a special form, and to record stratigraphic relationships, both within the grave and with respect to other burials. There has been considerable debate on whether burial position is best recorded by plans or photographs, but the majority now favour the latter, not least because of the time saved and the extra safety of not having to leave skeletons exposed, but unattended, on site overnight and thus subject to the threat of vandalism.

Production of the photographic record is straightforward. After cleaning, two coloured nails are placed at the skull and feet of the skeleton and their co-ordinates noted with respect to the site grid. A photographic scale and board with the skeleton's number and the direction of view are then placed with it and a vertical photograph taken. Levels taken on the highest points of the skull, sacrum and feet, together with any distorted areas, and on the base of the grave cut, record the vertical dimension. The skeleton can then be lifted immediately. Using the grid co-ordinates of the two nails and a developed photograph blown up to the correct scale, the position of the grave cut on the site, and of the bone detail within it, can be traced off onto a main plan of the whole cemetery at any later stage (Plate 23).

Obviously this method puts a premium on the photographs being correctly taken and developed, and it requires high standards of cleaning if all bones are to show up. After all, bones can be added to a plan as more become visible, whereas a photograph is a one-off shot and any elements obscured at this point will remain so no matter how good the photographic equipment, developing and printing may be. A related problem is that, although burials of single skeletons may be easily distinguished in a photograph, superimposed skeletons in the same grave or disarticulated bones from earlier graves complicate the picture (indeed, the distribution of the latter charnel may provide important information in its own right – Whyman 1996). Upper and lower burials can be delineated on a site plan, but not so readily in a photograph, particularly when dealing with juveniles and, especially, the fragmentary bones of neonates. So a fluid response will be needed, depending on the excavation conditions, time available for recording and complexity of the individual burials which one wishes to record. One can either revert to drawing bones in complex cases, or make extensive notes and sketches to allow distinctions later when tracing from photographs. Similar care will have to be exercised on the process of lifting superimposed and disturbed burials to ensure that complete skeletons are kept together.

Turning to the **written record**, the burial's approximate orientation should be noted, both in words with respect to the site grid north, and by means of a 'stick figure' in a field diagram (Figure 24). Its position must also be described in terms of whether it is crouched, flexed, extended, prone, supine, on right or left side. Similarly, the position of the head (facing to north or south, etc.) and of the legs and arms (to the sides, crossed on pelvis or chest, right over left or *vice*

| Context type: *skeleton* | Site code: | Context number: |

Descriptive info
1. Position: (e.g. prone, supine, LHS, RHS, crouched, etc.)

2. Orientation

3. Articulation of bones

Orientation

N

W --------+-------- E

S

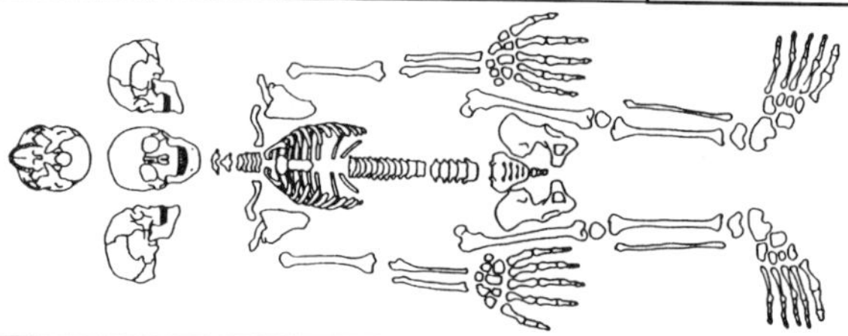

Stratigraphic relationships

Grave cut: Coffin: Fills: Location
Associated finds   Samples: on matrix:

Spatial and photographic information   **Field diagram**

Photographs (tick when taken and add reference numbers):

		Good	Mod	Poor
Preservation of bones	(✔)	☐	☐	☐
Collection quality	(✔)	☐	☐	☐

Co-ords. of markers: Levels:
   head-end   feet   skull   sacrum   feet

Interpretative Information   Initials + Date: Checked + Date:
Comment on body position (whether due to burial intentions or subsequent decay/disturbance) ; associated grave goods, residues, etc.
cont'd over

| Burial no. | Group | Provisional period | Initials + date |

Figure 24 A skeleton recording sheet.

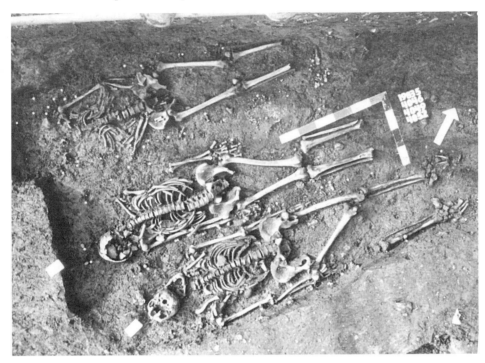

Plate 29 Detailed recording of the positions of the bones of the lower (4052) and
central (4049) skeletons during lifting should allow the excavator to decide the
order in which they were buried. Is 4049's slightly more haphazard disposition
due to disturbance by the adjacent burial, or because it was fitted into an existing
grave after 4052? Usually, such matters are best decided on the basis of
observations and notes made on site, rather than during later analysis.

versa, and so forth) can be written in. It is important to estimate at this point
whether the position of the skeleton in the ground is a function of how the
burial was laid out originally or the result of later decay or disturbance (Plate
29). However, any thoughts on these more interpretative matters must be kept
clearly separate from the basic record of its disposition as found.

In considering the bones themselves, obvious pathology can be noted,
together with a record of damage, both recent and in antiquity. The excavator
may lack sufficient expertise to recognise all pathological detail, but known
peculiarities, when seen, can be photographed *in situ* to flag-up their existence
to the bone specialist who may then be able to offer proper interpretation. What
is more vital is the representation of the presence and absence of all expected
bones. This is best achieved by colouring in a chart on which certain smaller
bones (phalanges, vertebrae, etc.) have been deliberately magnified to aid
clarity. Here, although a preliminary record can be made before removal,
careful searching may be necessary to ensure that certain bones are really
absent, for example teeth or the epiphyses of young children, rather than simply

not visible after the initial cleaning. Sieving of soil, especially from abdomen, chest and neck, may yield further osteological material, so be prepared to add to this initial estimate during the process of lifting the skeleton. On occasion, additional examples such as sesamoid bones from the hand or foot may turn up. For those unfamiliar with the human skeleton, it can be useful to have a life-size copy to hand or photographs of such hung up in the site hut (McMinn *et al.* 1987). When the colour chart for a particular skeleton has been finalised, any resulting absences can be commented on. Were some small bones lost accidentally in removing the grave fill or absent because part of the skeleton was cut away by later activity? Did they fail to survive because of adverse chemical conditions in the ground? Or are we dealing with the burial of a person with no lower legs (Plate 30)?

Next one must record the **type of grave** involved. In the case of certain inhumations, for instance multiple burials in barrows, this may involve what might be better described as a grave complex. However, even a single grave may be represented by anything from the plain hole in the ground, with or without a shrouded body, to those specially lined with a mortar floor or stone or tile cist, and/or containing a coffin of wood, stone or lead. Where coffins are well preserved and numerous, particular recording systems may be needed, including specialised approaches to decoration, coffin fittings, indications of preservation treatments for the body contents, etc. These situations are analogous to the masonry or timber sections mentioned above and can generate their own recording sheets accordingly. However, developing such a form can only be done with advice from appropriate artefact specialists, and any coffin number(s) generated here must still be cross-referenced to that of the skeleton, cut and fills of the associated grave.

Even when dealing with a plain grave cut, its exact shape may repay more detailed examination and recording than usual. Well-cut, vertical edges and a trapezoidal shape, carefully tailored to that of the container, may represent the only evidence for a former coffin. Less than right-angled corners and bowed sides might indicate decay of a former coffin, even when no wood survives. Even more convincing evidence for coffined burial can be provided by timber stains. Equally important are those cases where the shape of the cut is so irregular that it makes any form of rigid container unlikely, if not impossible. Deciding that the irregularity of a cut is significant negative evidence for burial container is a difficult matter, but such deductions are strengthened if exacting and similar standards have been applied to the description of all grave cuts. Finally, changes through time in the care with which graves were dug, as implied by the character of their cuts, can be vitally important for elucidating the relationship between central authority and mortuary practices. However, only large numbers of burials allow statistically valid deductions, which in turn may necessitate a long programme of excavation. So consistency of recording over an extended period of time becomes essential.

Plate 30 The incomplete assemblages derived from these two burials are obviously due to a later intrusion cutting away their lower bodies, but the physical anthropologist who receives the boxed bones later on may not have visited the site during its excavation and so may be unable to decide between alternative hypotheses: the bones were truncated (as is clearly the case here); they were not recovered properly and fully by the excavator; or the buried persons both lost their legs ante mortem. Stating the obvious is an important part of the recording procedure.

Recording the **stratigraphic relations** within each burial will usually be fairly straightforward: its cutting is followed by any bedding material, then the coffin, if there is one, and body, any material packed around it, and finishing with the grave back-fill(s). It will also be useful to record, and even discuss, other physical relationships, for instance multiple burials such as a mother accompanied by a foetus, or the sometimes complex relationship between grave goods, coffin and skeleton (Hummler and Roe 1996). In such cases, the difference between a burial inserted immediately after another, as opposed to after a lapse of time and following some decay of the original inhumation, may rest on the minor overlapping of just one or two minor bones at some point, or the disturbance of the earlier burial in a small but vitally significant way. Such information is easily lost unless recorded at the time.

Whenever inter-cutting or adjacent burials are encountered, it is important to consider in some detail the nature of their interaction and ensure that any implications are clearly stated in the notes and interpretations section ('the cut of this later burial was obviously modified at its northern end to avoid damaging the earlier burial 123 encountered when digging the later grave, suggesting some care in execution and an endeavour to keep disturbance of earlier burials to a minimum'). Yet any such interpretation, by itself, is of limited value unless backed up with an explanation of why such a conclusion was reached with reference to the primary record (in the above example, distortion in the shape of the later burial's cut, presumably) (Plate 29).

After the spatial, descriptive and stratigraphic records are complete, **lifting and storage** of the skeleton can occur. The right and left arms, legs, feet and hands should be lifted and bagged separately, as should the skull and lower mandible, pelvis, vertebrae and ribs (the fourth rib, if distinguishable, can be separated to help age assessment). The resulting bags should be fastened with a label inside and out and the whole placed in a box large enough to take all of the skeleton (the use of a box rather than large bag will prevent unnecessary breakages of fragile bones, as will the placing of the heaviest bones – skull, pelvis, long bones – at its base). Even with great care, it is often difficult to recover all the material by hand. In such cases, and especially for juvenile skeletons with unfused epiphyses, etc., dry sieving of lowest grave fills will be important and is easily organised. It will also allow the recovery of kidney, bladder, sinus and gall stones, which may be difficult to distinguish from epiphyses on site, and calcareous spheres which, to the tutored eye, can turn out to be cysts from the abdomen, thorax or cranium. The care with which the skeletal material was recovered ('collection quality') should be noted alongside an assessment of its level of preservation.

Once lifted, bones might be carefully washed or brushed, though opinions differ as to which should be preferred or even the desirability of either. Hence it may be best to avoid any processing until the osteologist to be employed on later analysis has been consulted and has agreed a coherent, up-to-date policy. Certainly it is unwise to clear eye, ear and nose orifices at this stage because of the 'interesting' residues which they may still retain. Similarly calculus, a concretion which forms on the teeth and can be indicative of the health and diet of the individual concerned, should be left *in situ*. Finally care should be taken to avoid removing any organic material associated with the skeleton, though this may require immediate conservation treatment, if not in the ground then straight after excavation, to retain its full information content or even to survive at all.

As bones are lifted, processed and conserved, records should be made at each stage, stating how well preserved they were originally, what site conditions if any affected the quality of collection (inclement weather, difficulties of working on a watching brief recovering skeletons whilst looking out for a machine looming over your shoulder, etc.) and any treatments applied by conservators – all of these things can affect subsequent analysis and the validity of the results derived from it.

Some types of burial require special consideration. For example, **cremations**, as opposed to the inhumations discussed above, pose particular problems, though very little has been written on the techniques of excavating and recording them (Gejvall (1963), for example, discusses only the problems and the potential of their scientific analysis – see now McKinley and Roberts 1993: 6 and their various references). If cremations are completely enclosed by a still solid container, it is best to lift the whole thing and carefully excavate the contents in the laboratory afterwards. If they lie within a simple hole in the ground, it is still best to bag the fill in its entirety and process it later in more controlled conditions. Fragmentation of cremated bone limits identification by specialists and can lead to misinterpretation of pyre processes, so must be avoided at all costs. Hence some consolidation of cremated, or even very fragmentary inhumed, bone may be required *in situ*, for example using spray foam to encase the pieces (Bement 1985). Such an approach will be essential with fragile infant bones (Dockall 1995), allowing detailed excavation and recording then to proceed off-site. However, pride of place here must go to the investigation of 'sand men' on the Sutton Hoo site (Plate 31).

Finally, the **law** poses particular problems for excavating burials (Garratt-Frost 1992). One must get permission in advance to exhume bodies from Christian cemeteries, in the process identifying a designated investigating organisation, and perhaps osteologist. It may also be necessary to screen off the excavation area and prevent photography of the process of exhumation by the public. After analysis, it may be possible to retain those bones exhibiting interesting pathology in the final archive, reburying the remainder by a designated time limit and on specified consecrated ground and/or the place of original burial. Extra safety considerations may also be relevant in the case of post-medieval bodies, particularly if there is good organic survival of body tissues or potential contamination from still virulent ancient disease. At the very least, special clothing and a system of proper laundering of it may be required. In some situations, for example the discovery of sealed lead coffins, such matters may even preclude any further investigation no matter how important and potentially exciting the contents, except under strictly controlled laboratory conditions. Such situations are fortunately fairly rare, though it then becomes

Plate 31 Intricate excavation of a 'sandman' at the Sutton Hoo site turns evidence which exists only as stains in the sandy soil into a recognisable, and so potentially interpretable, body disposition.

all the more important to watch out for them. Finally, the excavation of recent burials, especially those surviving fairly intact, can be psychologically, as well as physically damaging to some, especially if work continues unabated over extended periods of time. Moving people between different site activities is one possible solution here.

11.4 Cuts

Preceding sections have discussed both horizontal deposits and upstanding structures made from brick and masonry or timber. However, as well as stratigraphic units accumulating on its surface or protruding from it, most excavations include features which are cut down into the site. Graves, discussed above, are a special case of such intrusions, but a great variety of other types can also be encountered including ditches, foundation trenches, rubbish pits, wells and post holes. The shape of these 'negative' features needs to be recorded systematically, in the same way as their 'positive' counterparts.

The recording of cuts, as they will continue to be called here for convenience, has come especially to the fore after Harris' 1979 discussion of 'interfaces' of destruction, later reinforced in the second edition of his book which drew all aspects into a single chapter (Harris 1989: chapter 7). As he made clear there, the concept of an interface is derived from the two notions used in geology, those of bedding planes and unconformities. The former can be seen to exist when superimposed strata are discontinuous in character, the evidence suggesting that formation of one deposit has ceased and a second commenced: the place where the two meet is a 'bedding plane'. The equivalent for archaeology might be the interface between a floor make-up and its associated occupation debris, and an overlying phase of flooring and use.

More germane for present purposes is the situation where two sequences of geological strata fail to match with one another when viewed in adjacent elevations. As each sequence was a product of natural agencies acting extensively across areas, this discontinuity must be explained by an intervening action, such as erosion or the slipping of one set of strata with respect to the other. Thus the existence of an interface is implied by the existence of the 'unconformity'. However, when one looks for archaeological correlates of this second situation, problems arise, both in deciding whether such an interface exists at all, and in identifying its relationships with adjacent strata.

On the question of the very existence of an interface, the geological concept works because it can be assumed that the formation processes involved operated on a large scale. Such an assumption can be questioned on an archaeological site. Consider a layer such as a mortar floor which stops at a certain point and its place is taken by another layer, a gravel metalling. There is a clear discontinuity and it is possible that the mortar floor was cut away or eroded at this point, in which case this destructive action could be called an interface and labelled as such, in imitation of the geological situation. However, the unconformity could equally be due, not to destruction, but to the fact that one layer was deliberately laid up against another, for example on the line of a structural division, or for myriad other reasons. In short, unconformities need not be due to later modification ('destruction') of the archaeological record.

Clearly, the suggestion that a particular stratum, with a clear limit exposed in excavation, once continued further than this will often be open to doubt. Thus knowing that a proposed interface, or 'negative feature', exists *at all* requires a higher level of interpretation than is needed for the identification of positive features such as deposits, walls, etc. This is especially true of suggested erosion, which may be characterised by the oblique profile of the surface concerned but rests on the assumption that this was once regular and had been worn away in one place. Similarly, knowing that one has a single interface rather than many, with the surface of a layer worn away at this point, truncated at another, can be extremely difficult to calculate. Still more problematical is the secure identification of the limits of each interface, especially if proposed truncations are seen only in section.

It should be clarified here that I am not arguing that the concept of an interface is of limited use, merely that postulating the existence of this type of stratigraphic unit embodies a level of interpretation which is different in kind from, and of a higher order than, that involved with the other types discussed previously. This difference is readily acknowledged on excavations working with the 'layer and feature' system, where cuts are identified only at the feature level, but has become obscured with 'single-context' systems which treat the two sorts of stratigraphic unit as exact equivalents.

Cuts pose a second, related problem, even when the excavator can be sure of their existence. This concerns their stratigraphic relationships, specifically the identification of the exact point in the sequence at which the cutting or 'destructive' action is thought to have taken place. If one considers a trench representing the line of a completely robbed wall, then the fills resulting from the robbing activity will be later than the latest strata on either side of the feature. Similarly, the 'interface of destruction' related to that robbing will have intruded into these adjacent strata. However, further down the trench, the shape of its sides may be not a product of robbing, but formed by the construction trench of the wall. This is likely to be earlier than at least some of the layers beside the trench, for example a floor surface laid up against the original wall and the associated occupation debris on it. Thus, as one moves up the side of the trench, one cut, representing the action of construction, stops, and another, representing robbing, starts. The point at which this change takes place is vital for the creation of the stratigraphic sequence. Yet deducing where it occurs on the ground is usually extremely difficult, and may not be possible with complete certainty even after full analysis post-excavation. The best solution is to make no statement about the position of the cut(s) with respect to the adjacent horizontal stratigraphy, letting it 'float' below its fills and above the uppermost layer which clearly underlies any form of cutting action (Figure 25).

These problems of knowing that a cut exists and, if so, deducing its stratigraphic relationships, come even more to the fore with decisions on truncation horizons. As Yule (1992: 20) shows, defining such higher-order entities into existence requires looking beyond specific descriptions of individual units to more general configurations and may also demand recording the physical relationships of units, rather than just their more basic stratigraphic ones (see above, 9.1). On other occasions, it may be that truncation is entirely invisible in the site evidence but can be suggested by the configuration of pottery seriation diagrams (Carver 1980: fig. 52).

Similarly, when trying to deduce the level from which a feature has been cut,

When seen in section, the first matrix might seem to represent the sequence.

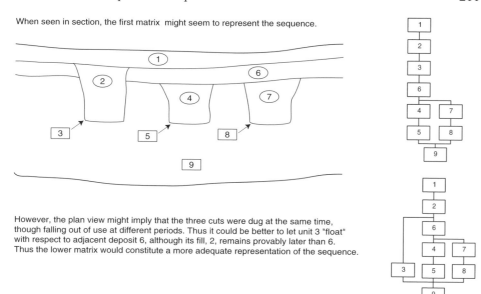

However, the plan view might imply that the three cuts were dug at the same time, though falling out of use at different periods. Thus it could be better to let unit 3 "float" with respect to adjacent deposit 6, although its fill, 2, remains provably later than 6. Thus the lower matrix would constitute a more adequate representation of the sequence.

Figure 25 Problems with the stratigraphic position of cut features.

it may be necessary to incorporate finds information which can only be fully known after artefactual analysis post-excavation. For example, one might find a concentration of pottery of a particular century lying, apparently, within an amorphous deposit which is dated, otherwise, to an earlier period. Yet if this concentration lies physically above a pit containing the same, late ceramics but whose existence was only recognised at a lower level, it may be suggested that the feature really was inserted from a ground surface within the upper layer. Alternatively, the pit may have been cut through the whole deposit but this was not recognised at the time (thus just a problem of inadequate stratigraphic control, insufficient enhancement of soil, etc.). Finally, it may even be that, though the pit was properly sealed, natural mechanisms such as bioturbation have disturbed some elements of its fill to a higher level (Hutcheson 1992: 24). In each case, later finds work has sounded the death knell for either pit or deposit being a proper, single stratigraphic entity. Overall, therefore, it becomes clear that processes of truncation, whether inferred on site, suggested after stratigraphic analysis or derived from finds work, have a different status from the other units of stratification discussed previously.

Whatever the specific solution to such conundrums, the physical characteristics of each cut must be recorded in order to achieve a consistent and usable record. Here the combination of information in the text and on the drawn record is more vital than ever. There is no advantage to giving a long-winded description of the irregularities of the side of a feature in words when this is covered far more accurately and economically by the hachures and spot heights on the plan, a section across its fills and a sketched profile in the opposite plane on the recording sheet.

Any written record must note the following elements, preferably working from top to sides to base as in the order given below and setting out the information gained on a dedicated recording sheet (Figure 17 – right-hand side):

> the feature's general shape in plan (circular, sub-rectangular, etc.), orientation and approximate dimensions, noting which are real and which are minima ('2.70m long north–south and at least 1.25m east–west, being cut away at its west end');
>
> the nature of any corners in plan, perhaps using particular terms for the angles (rectangular, rounded, sub-circular, etc.) rather than the pretence of exact measurement in degrees;
>
> the nature of the break of slope at the top: this relationship between top and sides can be vital for understanding the level of the contemporary ground surface, especially with features affected by an extensive horizontal truncation;
>
> the overall depth of the cut, together with variations in such, again remembering that spot heights on the plan and any sections or profiles will provide the more detailed record;
>
> the nature of sides, including the degree of regularity as well as estimates of slope: if variations and irregularities here are thought to be due to the character of the stratigraphy into which the feature was cut, this should also be noted, but under the 'notes' section rather than as part of the basic description;
>
> the nature of the break of slope between the sides and the base, which can indicate former function (the difference between a driven stake and an inserted post, for example) and/or the process of removing such structural entities;
>
> the nature of its base, again noting overall shape and, especially when dealing with a linear feature, whether it drops down regularly in one direction or another, plus local irregularities;
>
> any other information not covered in the above, often best backed-up by reference to associated drawings or to sketches added to the recording sheet.

If all of these elements are recorded, and no misconceptions are included which reduce the stratigraphic latitude of the cut to a greater degree than is really the case, then post-excavation analysis should stand the best possible chance of relating this cut to other, possibly contemporary features, and integrating it as accurately as possible into the overall sequence.

11.5 Finds groups

The discussion so far has focussed on the recording of stratigraphic units which can be defined on the site as physically existing, individual entities. In this situation, any finds derived from the excavation of a unit will be kept together as a discrete assemblage and given the same number as it. However, in particular circumstances, it may be necessary to label a finds assemblage in its own right, and not just because it was derived from a particular feature of the site. In particular it can be useful to distinguish groups of finds from a specified subdivision of a layer, whether defined in plan or elevation, or to keep finds in separate groups, although from a single unit, because they were a product of different recovery mechanisms. In both cases it may be simplest, bureaucratically, to label such groups with a number as if they were a 'proper' stratigraphic unit.

In theory, the objective of archaeological excavation in carefully controlled conditions is to recognise the individual actions – construction, occupation, destruction – which create the formation of a site. This is done by using changes in the physical nature of the strata which compose that sequence. Hence if a floor was laid down, was trodden on and then fell into disuse when the building in which it lay was destroyed by fire, we would expect to identify a make-up layer, an occupation layer and a layer of destruction debris, and to recover three distinct groups of finds from those contexts. However, sometimes things are not that simple. Artefacts pushed into a surface during its use may be difficult to distinguish in excavation from those lying completely within the floor make-up, especially if one is dealing with an earth floor. Similarly, the overlying destruction debris may include, at its base, finds related to the function of a room immediately before its demise, rather than only materials derived from the collapse of its walls. Yet it may be impossible in both cases to define an independent occupation layer. This is often the case with dumps of garbage, as well as with shell middens (Stucki 1993).

Of course, where physical distinctions are possible they should be followed in the normal way. But where they are not, it can make sense to impose a collection policy for finds which is not related directly to exact changes in the physical character of the deposits. Hence a distinct assemblage at the base of the destruction debris, especially if there is evidence of breakage *in situ*, may be kept together. Such *in situ* fragmentation may also require more detailed drawing and/or photography to record all relevant factors. Similarly the material derived from defining the surface of the underlying make-up, rather than lying properly within it, may constitute a valid group of material representing the occupation of the floor. At the most mundane level, the finds derived from cleaning across an area which has been left open for some time to prepare it for a return to controlled excavation are not completely unstratified material and might be usefully kept together under a single number. Of course, in each case, such finds do not constitute as water-tight a stratigraphic group as those derived from a physically defined unit and this fact should be noted on the recording sheet.

An analogous situation can occur when dealing with an extensive and/or deep and apparently homogeneous deposit. Here, for the purposes of finds collection, the layer might be divided arbitrarily and excavated in a series of spits. For example, the fill of an extensive ditch, though seemingly the same throughout, may reveal patterning along its length if artefacts are grouped as being collections from different parts of the feature (such arbitrary distinctions can also be useful in studies of joining sherds: Moorhouse 1986). Similarly, the 'dark-earth' horizon sandwiched between Roman and medieval stratigraphy on some British urban sites, often up to 1.5m deep, might be excavated in spits 50mm deep and the finds kept according to depth. Patterns may emerge later in the distribution, especially in date, of such finds which do not correspond with any physically definable change in the stratum (Plate 32). Finally, spit excavation of topsoil may be appropriate where evaluation showed that the whole of the over-burden was hopelessly mixed and contained no differentiation between strata which could be defined in terms of their physical characteristics in the ground, but might be reconstructed from the distribution of datable artefacts such as pottery.

In some cases spit excavation is an appropriate strategy even where stratification is visible. For example, the object of a project might be to study how successive foci of settlement occupation spread across the landscape. If the strategy adopted is to recover artefacts from known points in the landscape, it may only be necessary to record where material was in plan, not its level and stratigraphic context in the ground. Such a project might be criticised for asking inadequate, or at best tedious, questions (although it should be remem-bered that establishing the background noise of pottery use in a region may be a necessary prerequisite of asking more interesting questions in a nested research design). What we could not fault is the matching of the recording system to the research agenda which gave birth to the fieldwork.

Where spit excavation is planned, it must be approached systematically by defining the physical position and depth of each arbitrary unit accurately, rather than merely scooping-up finds from the surface wherever they are found. For example, when a large deposit is to be sub-divided for the purposes of finds retrieval, these might be grouped as being from the western, central and eastern thirds of the deposit, or from its top 0.10m, next 0.10m, etc. However, arbitrary units defined in this way will merge and move through time, and can be difficult to control on site. Thus it may be far more preferable to define the extent of each spit in terms of entirely arbitrary spatial entities, for example squares of the site grid and levels specified in terms of the site datum (25.10m down to 25.00m OD). The latter type of units can be imposed exactly and checked for accuracy simply at any stage of the work.

A final situation in which finds can be kept in arbitrary groups is where the same context is being subjected to a variety of finds recovery methods. It will be essential that artefacts derived using each method are kept distinct, both because such knowledge is vital to anyone quantifying and interpreting the assemblages later, and because such categories are needed to allow valid com-parisons between the efficacy of different recovery methods. Either the material can be allocated the same context number with a suffix added for each method of collection: 2570a means 'recovered by hand on site', 2570b 'the result of metal detection', 2570c finds 'sieved through the 10mm mesh', etc., with the

Plate 32 Spit excavation in progress at West Heslerton, North Yorkshire. The apparently homogeneous fill of this pit was removed in a series of arbitrary levels, with finds kept according to which quadrant, and which level, they came from. If artefact patterning became apparent in later analysis, it might be possible then to reconstruct stratigraphic distinctions within the fill, particularly if they matched divisions recorded in section but invisible when working in plan.

advantage of making the relationship between the groups immediately clear. Or a new number can be allocated to each finds group and these correlated under the notes on each context sheet. I prefer the latter since it retains the simplicity of the single numbering system and simplifies computer storage (a suffix can play havoc with an unsuspecting data-base unable to accommodate letters). Computer manipulation also allows lists of correlations between numbers to be easily organised, so that the advantages of having the same number and a letter suffix are now largely illusory.

12

EXCAVATING THE STRATIGRAPHIC UNIT

Introduction

When the photographing, planning, calculation of stratigraphic relationships and preliminary description of a unit have been done, its excavation can almost begin. However, before proceeding, it is essential to prepare for any samples to be taken, and for the recovery of artefacts and ecofacts likely to be encountered. At a simple level, this may take the form of labelling a finds bag in advance: an excavator has a greater incentive actually to recover artefacts if he has been reminded of their existence by fetching an appropriate container beforehand, and a greater incentive to keep them if it is there waiting to be filled, rather than available only by stopping excavation and trailing across to the distant finds hut. Also, having a container ready reduces the risk of leaving a small assemblage of vitally interesting, but unlabelled, finds on the edge of the trench at the end of work and failing to remember the next day the layer from which they were derived. At other times the recovery of artefacts and ecofacts may be far more complex than just filling a plastic bag or tray, especially if wet or dry sieving/screening is employed. The specific method used will result from the adoption of a carefully constructed sampling strategy (**12.1**), with each collection method carefully recorded (**12.2**).

How deposits are removed depends on the time available, the nature of the site and the type of information expected to be derived from it. Thus it may involve, at one end of the spectrum, working with pick and shovel and cleaning up roughly before proceeding to the next unit; or, at the other, careful dissection of the soil with dental tools or even finer, more specialist implements, for example when exposing burials or delicate artefacts. But the most common form of controlled excavation uses the trowel, both to define the extent of deposits and to remove them. Trowelling is therefore discussed below in detail (**12.3**). This is followed by a consideration of that vexed question: How does one decide during the excavation process that one unit has stopped and another is about to start? (**12.4**). After excavation is finished, it will be necessary to complete the record (**12.5**) by listing finds present, filling in sample sheets, noting recording conditions, adding in any information on provisional date and then signing and dating the recording sheet. Then another party can check the result (**12.6**), including the accuracy of plans, calculations of stratigraphic relationships and appropriateness of written description. After checking, each record can be booked back into the system as the excavator goes on to deal with the next unit in the sequence.

12.1 Sampling strategies for finds

Archaeologists have many reasons for collecting artefacts from sites. Some objectives relate to the find in its own right, independent of site context, for example study of pottery production techniques and developments in fabric and form. However, it is more common for artefact studies to be integral with the rest of the site evidence, for instance the analysis of industrial residues as indicators of site function, or the investigation of timbers to elucidate a particular aspect of structural development. Finally, other areas of interest might relate directly to the excavated sequence, as when using coins to give date ranges on deeply stratified sites, or artefact abrasion to elucidate processes of redeposition.

In the same way ecofactual evidence can be considered from a variety of perspectives. It may throw light on very general matters such as processes of zoological introduction or environmental and climatic conditions in a region at a particular time, allowing, *inter alia*, an understanding of the availability of natural resources. Alternatively the study of general economic data, most obviously food waste, can illuminate not only production, processing and distribution mechanisms but also matters such as health and artisan activities which utilise animal or vegetable products. Even ethnic affinities and religion may be accessible via diet, for example where a meat source is proscribed by a particular belief system. More site-specific behavioural information can throw light on function of buildings, rooms within them, or even the micro-environment in one part of a deposit, and this is often considered to be the most important aspect of environmental sampling strategies. Finally, further specialist matters such as dendrochronology can not just give absolute felling dates for timbers, but also use relative dates to elucidate chronological variations within and between structures, areas of primary versus secondary timber (re)use, dressing techniques, and even climatic change.

If any of these research areas is to be provided for effectively, it will obviously be essential to formulate a finds sampling strategy in advance of excavation (Orton 2000: chapter 6). The focus of such a strategy will be based on the particular types of research questions being asked, but must also take account of two other factors: survival characteristics of material on the site and transformations of the archaeological record.

Three, interrelated matters influence the first factor, each of which should have been elucidated, at least partially, by work at the evaluation stage. These comprise the existing general ground conditions on site, the presence/absence and abundance of an artefact or ecofact type, and the degree and type of preservation. However, knowing preservation details can be difficult, especially as they may vary at the local level – organics may not survive generally but exist in abundance in a particular well, carbonised materials may proliferate unexpectedly in a deposit, etc. Next, even with good survival, a deposit may simply be too small to give viable results, although sampled in its entirety, whereas on other occasions preliminary flotation may show that seeds exist in numbers which offer statistically significant data on, for example, crop imports. An informed judgement here must be based on the quick feedback of preliminary assessments and interpretations in order to modify the collection policy appropriately.

Research objectives and preservation conditions are not the only relevant factors influencing a sampling strategy. Between the time when an artefact was produced or a seed grown, and either item appearing beneath the trowel, each will have gone through a series of transformations. For a start, only a proportion of the finds which were produced, processed and distributed ended up in use. Subsequently, while they were circulating in society, a series of recycling and discard processes came into play which further bias the record. For example particular finds may have continued to be passed on as heirlooms, divorced from their initial function, or ceramic building materials may have been thrown away at the end of their useful life, to be then spread onto fields in the process of manuring. Even after final discard, other natural and human factors yet again alter the characteristics of any assemblage in the ground, perhaps ensuring its survival but in a very different form from how it entered the archaeological record. For example, soil may have been brought from one part of a settlement to level up another sector, or finds from one stratum on site redeposited into a later layer during pit digging. Not surprisingly, therefore, understanding the factors which influence the process by which sites are formed and transformed has been a major area of archaeological endeavour (see, for example, Schiffer 1987 and refs.).

The general implications of such studies will have been assimilated in constructing the initial research questions and relating them to particular finds groups. However, other issues cannot be taken on board at such a formative stage and require a more fluid response. These are concerned with the collection of material from the site (what is recovered), the selection of that material (what is recorded) and the derivation of data (the level of detail observed and the expertise and resources of the analyst, for example in terms of the availability of an appropriate reference collection). The following discussion relates mostly to the first of these, because the other decisions on selection and data derivation occur largely in post-excavation work (although the site director is still likely to be involved in these, if only at the level of resource allocation).

When considering the collection of finds on site, a central issue is the status of the relationship between the deposit and any material derived from it. Certain strata – the primary ones – contain material directly related to contemporary on-site activities and these may then get preferential treatment in terms of sampling. In contrast, artefacts derived from layers known to have been dumped in the area may have very little to do with the site itself but provide perfectly legitimate evidence of the general 'background noise' of artefact use in the whole settlement at the time.

Deciding what constitutes a primary relationship and what a secondary one is difficult, especially during the excavation process when not all relevant information can be to hand and underlying configurations of features are obscured. One solution to this dilemma is to 'over-sample', the theory being that it is always better to have more rather than fewer samples, then to throw away the irrelevant ones later. However, this is not very convincing as a proper strategy and, taken to its logical conclusion, would mean taking all of the site home to be dissected in the laboratory, which is neither practically feasible nor theoretically desirable. Some compromises, based on a well-considered evaluation pre-excavation, and perhaps ongoing evaluation exercises, provide a more coherent way forward.

In searching for primary contexts, hearths, ovens, pits, burnt floors (perhaps with sub-sampling of separate areas if these are extensive), middens, cess-pits, wells and drains might be expected to provide good sources. Occupation layers, non-diagnostic ditch fills and open areas might be less relevant, and make-up dumps and construction features such as walls still less useful. Of course, designing a sampling strategy based on such distinctions will only be effective if the different types of context can be recognised on site in terms of the fundamental physical characteristics of the units concerned.

Finally, the criteria of preservation and status have a complex relationship with each other, not simply a parallel existence. For example, charred remains of seeds, which throw light on crop production, might be redeposited but still retain this information value. Thus, if one is interested in cropping systems, the fact of preservation transcends the status criterion as a reason for gathering the material in question. However, the same material might have limited implications for detailed understanding of patterning in the distribution of crop processing within a settlement – if the material has been redeposited, it could have come from anywhere. In a second example, water-logged grain may include chaff which is very unlikely to survive redeposition. Thus the preservation of chaff in one layer may allow one to draw conclusions about the primary status of the context in question. Similar arguments arise with articulated bones, suggesting rotting *in situ*. Such considerations may influence not only recovery strategies but also the recording approach adopted on site and the care with which such material is handled in the process of excavation (see, for example, Chapter 8 on measuring-in finds).

By taking into account all of these factors, a sampling strategy reconciling research questions, general preservation characteristics and specific site context can be worked out in advance. It will also have to include some purely practical matters to ensure that the finds are not then damaged (Coy 1978 gives useful hints on the initial handling of animal bones, though her suggestions on discarding certain elements at an early stage in the recording process might not now be generally approved). In addition, for a large organisation which has responsibility for a whole settlement or even a whole region, such a strategy may have to be applied consistently between, as well as within, individual sites. Inevitably, it will be most successful when integrated with the excavation programme at the earliest possible stage, not seen as an added extra, a luxury to be used only if time and money allow.

12.2 Methods of collection

Having constructed a sampling strategy to define what types of finds are to be recovered from the site and in what proportions, it is then necessary to turn to the ways in which this is actually done. On many sites, the mechanics of soil removal will be fairly rudimentary. For example, those with limited stratigraphic distinctions, which are thus excavated in spits, might employ a mechanised process linked to a wet sieving/water screening system (van Horn *et al.* 1986). However, on most sites, one will remove soil with a pick, shovel or mattock or, for more stratigraphic control, the trowel. Yet even this last tool may be too destructive for certain material, for example carbonised seeds. Finally, recognising finds on site in the process of excavation and recovering them by hand may not be entirely reliable, yielding only a part of what was there, and then not a representative part. Indeed, some studies (Payne 1975) suggest that up to 85 per cent of certain finds may be lost using such approaches. Hence more rigorous approaches such as sieving, either wet or dry, and metal detecting may be needed.

Serious development of screening systems to recover finds came to the fore, perhaps not uncoincidentally, alongside the advent of 'New Archaeology' (Struever 1968 in the US; Payne 1972 in the UK). Although their adoption seemed open to question in some quarters initially (Barker 1975), the increased efficiency of recovery which sieving allowed meant quick converts and, since that time, much effort has gone into studying the comparative effectiveness of different methods (Weston 1976, Keeley 1978, Wagner 1982, Jones 1983, Van der Veen 1983) and into avoiding contamination (Keepax 1977). Others have developed further techniques such as the use of the seed blower (Ramonofsky *et al.* 1986) or taking columns of monoliths of soil to examine pollen and diatoms, with the convenient by-product of yielding larger, and perhaps more representative, finds samples (Castel 1976).

Obviously, the mesh size used directly affects the amount and character of the material recovered. However, this is not an even process because the numbers of large finds may not increase substantially if one employs smaller screens, whereas other, much smaller components such as fish bones may be entirely missed unless one is prepared to utilise close meshes. Experiments (see, for example, Muckle 1994) have begun to elucidate differential recovery methods for particular types of find, though the issue of screen size continues to be hotly debated (see, most recently, Gordon 1993, Dye 1994, then Gordon 1994). In addition, the essential, underlying issue of the complex relationship between increased finds recovery and enhanced provision of new knowledge (i.e. the marginal *information* yield of different methods for a designated finds category) has received little dedicated attention, dependent, as it is, on explicit, project-specific research objectives.

Dry sieves or screens, whether simple meshes held in the hand above a wheelbarrow or those set up in a variety of frames to cater for larger volumes of material, are probably the most common way to separate finds from the sur-rounding soil, particularly when the latter is loose and sandy. Indeed, if depos-its contain a profusion of cultural material, dry sieves are not only more consistent but faster than hand collection on site, which can otherwise intrude into the process of dissecting strata. Mechanical agitation of the screens can speed up the process considerably (Hunt and Brandon 1990), thus allowing staff to concentrate on more important recording work.

However, if the soil is at all clayey, or if small or carbonised items are required, it may be necessary to introduce water screening. One of the most rudimentary methods is to use a cement mixer to agitate deposit and water together and, when tipped out, allow the finds to be picked out more easily (see Plate 17; Jones and Bullock 1988). This seems to do less damage to the artefact and ecofact assemblages than might be expected and certainly makes it possible to deal with considerable quantities of deposit in a short space of time. Yet such methods are too basic for many purposes, in which case proper wet sieving is required. Various systems are available and the best can deal with considerable quantities of bulk-sampled soil, perhaps up to 100kg, to give evidence for mammals, birds, fish and marine shells, as well as the larger artefacts. If necessary, residues can be stored at this stage, the volume of the deposit having been much reduced, and sorted in the laboratory later, perhaps on a more selective basis, for example based on later interpretation of the deposit concerned ('traps such as wells, pits and drains deserve more attention than dumps' – see Rackham 1982).

At a more delicate level, flotation using a wet sieve with a 1mm mesh can yield not only carbonised material at the surface but identifiable bone and the non-floating carbonised material of larger plant remains, fly puparia, etc. in its residues. For still more detailed work, samples of up to 10kg in plastic bins can be sent to the laboratory and screened by paraffin through a 250mu mesh to get small weed seeds and cereal chaff, other water-logged plants, insects, mollusca, etc. Here it can be useful to take a small sample, process it immedi-ately to assess its potential, then modify the sampling strategy accordingly (Badham and Jones 1985). Such an approach demands careful collaboration with environmental specialists. Even if all appropriate deposits are sampled as a matter of course, particular concentrations of biological material such as individual plant remains or groups of articulated animal bones will also have to be catered for on an individual basis.

The more sophisticated sieving operations may need special supplies of materials such as chemicals, or of services such as electricity or fume cabinets, either on-site or, more likely, in laboratories later on. The former will be the responsibility of the site director and must be thought about in advance, in terms of personnel and safety as well as the facilities themselves. At the very least, wet sieving requires water, even if this is recycled by ingenious systems where supplies are scarce (Plate 33). Even in simple operations, it may be useful to use additives such as detergents to help break down clayey soils, or even sugar (Kidder 1997) to increase the specific gravity of the solution and thus enhance the flotation rates of carbonised materials. However, it may be necessary then to remove the sugar which will now saturate some of the archaeological material before it is further processed and analysed (Baker and Shaffer 1998, Kidder 1998).

Metal detecting can also be used to enhance finds recovery during the digging process. Perhaps the position of particular finds can be discovered and tagged on-site before excavation, to ensure their subsequent recovery and, if required, allow their careful measuring-in (Aostrom and Fischer 1987). Alternatively, the machines can be used to screen spoil heaps after excavation, storing deposits in their stratified groups if possible rather than mixing all soil together. Detecting equipment can even be used to register the existence of non-metallic objects such as leather and textiles, if one has suitable hardware and sufficient expertise.

Once recovered, most materials will be kept as bulk finds – pottery, plaster, tesserae, daub, brick and tile above a certain minimum size considered useful for analysis, etc. However, particular finds may be selected out and kept on an individual basis, for example decorated tiles, certain moulded stones, iron objects. This will occur for one of two reasons. If it relates to the nature of the artefact itself, it becomes an **accessioned find.** This decision usually depends on what is to happen to the item at the post-excavation stage in terms of future research or storage. In the case of the former, what experts are likely to be involved in the work? Which categories will they need access to? For the latter, are there particular storage requirements or conservation problems? Or is there a reasonable expectation of museum display? There is no reason why the selection of finds to be accessioned needs to take place on site. Indeed, there may be some reason to leave it to a later stage where it requires considerable background knowledge to recognise a type of artefact, or to decide what to do about composite objects whose conservation raises competing demands. Designating something as an accessioned find in the above sense may therefore not be of direct concern of the field-worker.

Plate 33 Wet sieving to recover carbonised material by flotation and heavier residues from within the tank. Where water is in short supply, a system which recirculates it can be especially useful.

This is not true of the second type of special find, the **small find**, where an artefact is set apart not through its own inherent qualities but because of its relation with the site from which it was derived. This happens most commonly because one is interested in the exact position of the find, rather than the simple fact that it came from a stratigraphic unit in an area of the site. Of course, if such spatial information is deemed important for all finds, then they will all become small finds and the appropriate action in recording will already have been taken (see above, Chapter 8, on measuring-in finds). However, in most cases, it is neither desirable nor practical to treat all finds in this way and an exact location will only be required for designated artefacts, as decided by criteria fitted within the research orientation of the excavation. For the most part this means choosing primary contexts, for example a burial, and recording selected artefacts with increased accuracy. The degree of accuracy required will have to be decided on, and made explicit, in advance. Hence, for an item to qualify as a small find, it will have to be a product of three criteria:

> being the right type of find ('dress fittings in the grave will count, other types of find will be ignored');
> having the requisite relationship with a deposit on site whose status can be assessed using criteria applicable **at the time of excavation** ('brooches lying on the shoulder of the skeleton are deemed important, those merely lying within the grave fill are irrelevant');
> the extra information concerning the position of the artefact which is needed to augment that of the rest of the assemblage has indeed been obtained – its absolute level, maybe its orientation, the exact co-ordinate position (the degree of precision here being a function of the questions asked) ('we remembered to mark the position of the brooch to the nearest centimetre, took a level, and noted which way up it lay').

Unfortunately, it is my experience that many artefacts which are kept as individual, special finds on excavations would not qualify as either accessioned finds or small finds according to the above criteria. For example, excavators are often tempted to deal differently with a particular coin because it supplies 'good dating evidence'. However, provided it remains related to the stratigraphic unit from which it was derived, the information value of the coin will not be enhanced by making it a small find. If conservation is a consideration, it must be treated appropriately when removed from the ground. Other than that, the coin is just another find which can be processed with the other metalwork and then sent off to the coin expert. Indeed, separating out particular items in this way can be a recipe for their getting lost, thus reducing not increasing their information value.

Finally, beyond small and special finds, certain artefacts or samples may require particular specialist treatment. Metalwork needing conservation has been mentioned already. Another obvious case in point is sampling for dendrochronology, the initial problem here being to decide what to sample. The existence of sapwood can be vital, with planks often being better than posts for such purposes. Next each sample requires a cross-section c. 50mm wide. Hence, if destructive sampling of boats and important structural features is unacceptable, this may limit what is possible (fortunately, using an increment borer which only removes a plug of 9mm, which can then itself be plugged to leave a negligible mark, can ameliorate the worst effects of sampling and, in the not-too-distant future, CT scan may make physical cutting unnecessary). Finally the resulting sample should then be bagged in a self-sealing or tied bag (not heat sealed or stapled, and without fungicide) and its bark, if present, taped onto it or tied with string to reinforce the sample. Of course, it must also be kept wet during initial exposure and afterwards. Gasoline-paraffin should not be used to stabilise charcoal and other charred timbers since this can obscure the counting of the rings. Similarly, paraffin and fungicides affect the possibility of using timber in C14 samples.

Not all finds can be kept, even as bulk finds. Just as recovering material from within a stratigraphic unit involves selection, so certain items may be discarded after being recognised. For example, this might happen immediately because of their stratigraphic context ('Unstratified, non-accessionable building material will not be kept' – in which case what constitutes an unstratified assemblage, and how this is to be judged on site, will have to be clear to everyone). Alternatively selection might be on the basis of the character of the finds themselves, either by date ('throw away all post-medieval bricks' (and earn the undying enmity of post-medieval buildings experts – the project director issuing this directive to site staff usually forgets to tell you this)) or by the nature of the find ('keep only stamped or decorated Roman tile'). Alternatively finds may be discarded after some quantification ('Measure complete sides of tiles and mud-bricks, thickness and number of complete corners, fabric type, and weight; then throw away'). Finally, only a proportion might be sampled ('Keep 10 per cent of all the ordinary Roman tiles, plus any others that seem interesting' (interesting to whom?)). In this last case, the retained finds must be recorded along the same lines as all other finds samples.

Having collected finds on whatever designated basis, it is then necessary to store them. Initially this may take the form of placing them in double bags, with one indestructible label placed between the bags and a second at the top, the whole then tied with non-rotting string (remembering to mark the number of the stratigraphic unit on each label using a spirit-based indelible marker). Alternatively, finds may be stored in plastic containers, similarly marked, though this will obviously be more expensive. Special storage situations may require particular approaches, for example in the case of articulated bones or pottery. Storage methods must also take place with an eye to subsequent finds processing, which itself will vary depending on the type of find, the facilities available and the volume of material involved. In addition one must take account of the ultimate destination of the artefacts, especially if they are to be lodged with a museum or similar institution with its own numbering system and rack sizes for acquisitions.

Lastly, approaches adopted to the mechanics of excavation, finds recovery methods, sampling procedures and storage mechanisms must be written onto the recording sheet. Only then can those using the resulting material be aware of what might be significant positive or negative evidence within the assemblage, rather than a product of the data recovery methods. As noted previously, a single stratigraphic unit can be subjected to different recovery methods and, though the finds must obviously be stored separately, material from what is essentially one site context must also be linked by cross-referencing within the numbering system. This becomes even more vital if some recovery processes are deferred for a time: if a coin turns up in the residue of paraffin flotation of a cess-pit sample in the laboratory several months after the excavation, it must still be investigated in the same light as the other coins from that fill recovered by hand.

12.3 Trowelling methods

Although a great variety of tools can be used on sites, the trowel is the normal excavation tool on the majority of projects. In fact, I would suggest that its use is still so important that an ability to use a trowel well in a variety of circumstances must be considered the *sine qua non* of archaeological excavation. After all, the production of good-quality drawings and systematic calculation of stratigraphic relationships can both be bureaucratically controlled on site and checked for accuracy before any damage is done. Whereas the correct use of the trowel when removing a stratigraphic unit, in the process defining the limits of those below, not only governs the ultimate adequacy of the data produced but also requires experience to perfect. Thus the necessarily destructive act of trowelling is the critical point at which the excavator interacts with the site and imposes the research design on it. If this is done badly, all of the other procedures, no matter what their standard, fall by the wayside. Hence, if I was asked to improve the standard of an excavation, after sorting out organisational matters, I would concentrate on finding the least accomplished troweller, raise the standard of her performance, then go on to the next least accomplished troweller and repeat the process.

Trowels are used both to define the extent of a deposit and to remove it in order to expose underlying strata. Although expertise develops mainly through familiarity, some hints on techniques can be outlined. The character of each deposit determines how trowelling must be used to define its edges and stratigraphic relationships. Particularly important is the decision whether to work along the lines of apparent differences or across them. For clayey and sticky deposits (i.e. those with a fine particle size), it is often best to trowel across the proposed line of intersection. This smears the material slightly but different layers will often break away from each other to give a clear distinction. If one works along the line, it is easy to merge elements of a more sticky deposit with one below it to suggest a division which merely follows the direction of the trowelling. For sandier, less cohesive material, however, working across the line simply mixes the units and produces no edge at all; here trowelling down the line may be required. In both cases the danger lies in creating unreal edges. Attention to cleanliness and working methodically from the known edges towards the unknown ones is the best way avoid this.

By the same token, when actually removing a unit, one must always work systematically backwards, pulling the excavated material onto the unexcavated part at one's knees rather than pushing it away onto the already exposed and

Plate 34 Trowelling properly, knees bent and putting weight on the tool for effective control.

clean underlying strata. Only by keeping the area in front clean can an excavator make sound stratigraphic decisions. Also the removal of one unit involves, *at the same time*, understanding the underlying configuration. There are not three operations – taking (most of) one layer away, then going back to check that it really has all gone, then working out the extent of underlying deposits and their stratigraphic relationships by further cleaning: these should all be part of the same process, because to know that one unit is finished is also to know that something different is now exposed underneath. Furthermore, in removing that overlying unit, it is usually possible to work out the relationships between the underlying strata (admittedly, the ease with which this can in fact be done, even given great expertise, will vary from site to site and from deposit to deposit).

Trowelling is an energetic process, not simply scraping away at the ground haphazardly. If the excavator does not find it tiring on the wrists, then it is probably not being done correctly. Such work also needs the weight of the body over the trowel to create the force needed to remove soil effectively. Therefore it is impossible to trowel efficiently whilst sitting down: you either have to squat or kneel (Plate 34). The sign of a badly run excavation, in my experience, is to see many people carefully excavating around themselves in a circle, piling the increasing amount of loose material under them until they sit cross-legged on their own little spoil heap. These self-made Buddhas will then wonder why trowelling is so very difficult and, becoming demoralised, quit the excavation

soon afterwards, leaving fieldwork to those who, apparently, have greater apti-
tude. Yet all that is needed is a systematic approach, the right trowelling position and some perseverance. Incidentally the amount of time that trowellers
can expect to spend on their knees is a cause for concern in terms of the long-
term effects on their joints. It is advisable for anyone who wishes to take up site
work seriously to wear knee pads as a matter of course to afford protection
from the damp and to avoid bruised knees.

The question of whether one uses the edge or the point of the trowel for
removing deposits is a difficult one, the choice depending on the compaction
of the material concerned, the depth of the layer and, to some extent, one's
priorities on the site. When removing loose, thin, tenuously defined deposits,
scraping away the overlying material with the side of the trowel can be the best
way to ensure that underlying strata are not cut into and makes it very much
easier to define their limits and relationships. However such an approach can
also be destructive of delicate finds within the deposit being removed, especially
if it is compacted and thus takes a lot of scraping to excavate. In such cases the
spoil derived from trowelling can be a pile of dust, with only the hardest materials like pebbles and better-fired clay surviving. Fragile pottery or carbonised grain, for example, can easily be destroyed.

A way to avoid this is to use the point of the trowel to remove soil from the
vertical face at the edge of the deposit. This allows the structure of fragile elements to be recovered whole as the partly broken down deposit is removed from
around them to leave the artefact or ecofact intact. However, chipping away at
the front of a deposit in such a fashion can all too easily lead to amalgamating
units by excavating more than one at a time, and missing the smaller finds. So
if artefact recovery is a vitally important aspect of the research design, yet stratigraphic distinctions are tenuous, it may be necessary to gather finds by other
means, ranging from water screening each sample to careful removal of deposits clinging to an artefact in a conservation laboratory. Even where such delicate methods are employed, it will still be necessary to ensure samples for
treatment are dug up in such a way that the contents survive to make the later
processing worthwhile. Clearly, therefore, there can be a trade-off between
control of the stratigraphy and preservation of contents. Fortunately it is
usually fairly simple to reach a compromise. If a unit is of any depth, the majority can be removed using the tip of the trowel maximising finds preservation,
with the base then cleaned away with the side of the trowel to control more
exactly the point at which underlying strata appear.

12.4 Making stratigraphic distinctions

When dealing with earth deposits, distinctions will be quite clear in some places
but edges elsewhere will merge together. Thus, when starting to remove the
uppermost deposit, it makes sense to work from the known to the less well

known. In addition it is vitally important for the excavator to be clear that she is removing the uppermost unit until something different appears, not simply following an underlying unit which was apparent at the edge of it and running beneath. If one simply digs down to that lower unit, problems will arise. First, what happens if it runs out and another earlier deposit continues? More importantly, if intervening units exist which were obscured at the time of starting these may also be amalgamated with the upper unit. So any troweller must be told to remove material of a certain type until they reach anything different, not to cut everything away to expose a particular underlying deposit (Figure 26).

There remains the problem of *how* different underlying soil has to be in order to be considered as a new unit in its own right. There can be no easy answers here, any decision being mainly a matter of experience. With greater familiarity, trowellers can manage, literally, to 'feel' the difference between strata which they were previously unable to distinguish. However the research objectives of the site should also be borne in mind when trying to make distinctions. Sometimes exact stratigraphic divisions are needed, at others rough assemblages of finds may be sufficient. However, if one is to alter the care with which distinctions are made because of the type of deposit involved, this must be clearly tied to the questions being posed. Thus if the research design demands that one differentiates between primary and secondary pit fills, great care will need to be exercised. If, however, initial evaluation shows that one is dealing with an apparently homogeneous stratigraphic accumulation and research only demands a large group of consistently recovered artefacts which are expected to be of the same date, then it may be quite legitimate to excavate in arbitrarily defined 0.10m spits, noting general tendencies for change within the deposit as you go.

Having said that, of course excavators must be fluid in their approach. If evaluation leads one to expect a lack of stratigraphic clarity between deposits, and one adopts a strategy appropriate to this but then encounters clear boundaries, it would be stupid to ignore them. In fact the ability to delineate clear limits would no doubt be most welcome. But it will be equally important to recognise that this will mean a change, in fact an important addition, to the potential of the site. If it can now answer a new range of questions, this means modifying, or perhaps totally rewriting, the initial research design and thus a new approach to recording.

An intermediate situation is more common than this 'all or nothing' position, in which certain deposits may be identified as of great significance for the questions posed and treated with great care in terms of stratigraphic distinctions and excavation, whilst others could be of reduced importance. Thus one may be very careful to distinguish between successive occupation deposits of very different dates, or between the primary and secondary fills of a pit, even when the distinctions are tenuous. However, when removing all of the material

View in plan

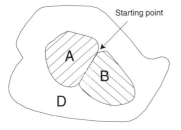

If one is removing deposit A because
it overlies all other visible stratigraphy, B then D,
then it makes sense to start the removal process
at the point where the distinction between the
two is most clear - as indicated.

View in section

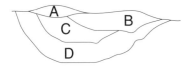

However, if one does this by adopting the rule
*"remove A by simply cutting away everything
until you reach B"*, problems can arise: What if
B soon stops and a third unit C, beneath B but
very similar to A, appears?

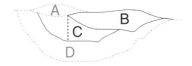

There is a danger of cutting down into C
and then the true extent of C will be
unknown, and most of its finds will be
amalgamated with those from A.

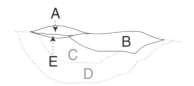

Equally, what if a new unit E distinct from, and
overlying B, appears under A? Removing all
deposit down to B, will amalgamate A and E,
with consequent loss of structural and contextual
information.

Thus the golden rule should be *"remove Unit A
until you get to anything that is not like Unit A"*.

Figure 26 Stratigraphic definition in trowelling.

slumped in from the side of that pit, or successive make-ups in the same
sequence of dumping, less care might be appropriate. In essence the arguments
here on deposit definition are essentially the same as those which arise when
deciding on recovery levels for finds.

Two problems must be acknowledged here. First, the criteria used to distinguish different types of stratigraphic unit must be clearly designated in advance
and related to the actual physical characteristics of the deposit in order to be

useful to the excavator. Thus if one wants to make differences in excavation pro-cedure for primary versus secondary fills, an occupation deposit as opposed to a dump, or slumped, as distinct from *in situ*, stratigraphy in the side of a pit, then one must be able to decide how each type can be identified on site.

Second, the decision to amalgamate units more readily in some situations than others will of necessity limit the comparability of the data sets in later analysis. In particular, if one has allowed higher-level judgements, for example whether a deposit is an occupation deposit or a make-up layer, to influence the amount of energy one puts into determining stratigraphic distinctions on the site, then this decision will be deeply embedded in the site record. It will there-fore be very difficult to assess the accuracy of such judgements at a later stage, and thus virtually impossible actually to test whether the inbuilt assumptions which go with it were justified. The role of preliminary studies on the site at the evaluation stage will be of paramount importance in setting up and justifying such an approach.

12.5 Completing the record

When the excavation of a stratigraphic unit has been completed, the recording sheet will have to be augmented with a variety of further information, entering the finds derived from it, completing any sample sheets, noting the recording conditions and, soon afterwards, incorporating information on its provisional date, before the sheet is finally signed and dated as complete (see spaces incor-porated into recording forms, Figures 17, 19, 22 and 24).

As the first part of this process, the **finds present** in the unit will have to be recorded. This can be simply done by ticking boxes on pre-printed sheets for the most common items such as pottery, types of building materials, bone, etc. and adding in any unusual things such as organic materials. However, on most sites, not all the finds derived from a unit will be retained for further study and it will be vital for a subsequent researcher to know whether she has a complete assemblage or only part, and if so which part. Even if no finds of a particular type were kept, though some were present (e.g. minute fragments of charcoal too small to allow identification of wood species), this should be noted, if for no other reason than to stop people searching in the stores later on looking for bags of finds which do not exist.

So there will also have to be a set of key-words giving a collection code in relation to each type of find, for example A for 'All' finds of the type kept, S for 'Some' and N for 'None'. Where only some finds have been retained, the ratio-nale for selecting these will, presumably, be given in the finds sampling policy adopted for the site, based on the character of the deposit and its date, and the research objectives of the project. However, it does no harm to repeat this on each sheet, if only in outline ('10% of bricks kept, as per building material sampling guidelines'). If specific units have been made exceptions to the normal sampling policy, it will be even more important to mention this on the appropriate recording sheet.

For environmental samples, it may also be necessary to fill out special **sample sheets**, giving details of the sample number, if a separate numbering system is used; the percentage of the whole deposit taken and what the resulting size of the sample should be; the reason for sampling, whether specific to that context (owing to its status as a primary deposit?) or part of the overall sampling strategy on the site; and the date when it was taken. If this sheet is to be later separated from the site recording sheet, it may also be necessary to repeat certain information held more fully on the latter. Thus one might mention the site code; where the sample was taken from, perhaps including its position marked on plan; the provisional date of the unit and how closely dated it might be; and the likely degree of contamination, whether from modern roots or other intrusive actions (for example because a deposit was not properly sealed), or from residual material, as in the case of dumped material. This record will help to inform those making a selection of samples at the later, processing stage.

This sheet can then be further augmented as it accompanies the sample on its journey through the laboratories of the archaeological scientists, to show the stage the sample has reached in its travels and to note other factors. For example, some deposit may be left unprocessed, either as a data bank or to allow a sub-sample for other analysis. Or it may go into storage to await further work for which there are presently insufficient resources, for instance when kept as an unsorted residue from wet sieving. Finally, the same sheet can also be used to contain information on the ultimate results of analysis.

Having noted finds and samples present, it will be useful to give an assessment, albeit somewhat subjective, of the **recording conditions** at the time of excavation. This is not so much an addition to the record as an assessment of its quality, giving later analysts some idea of the limitations imposed on the data. So comments on the weather (wet weather can produce a higher risk of intrusive finds) or the adequacy of lighting if working inside (this can reduce the certainty with which stratigraphic distinctions can be made) might be included. However, it would give a spurious sense of accuracy to pretend such matters could be usefully quantified, hence free text will be most appropriate.

Similarly it is often possible to make some assessment, during the process of excavation, of the degree of contamination of the finds assemblage derived from a deposit. Such contamination can take two forms, either later finds in earlier layers or material from earlier contexts redeposited into later strata. The latter is much the more difficult to recognise and often cannot be avoided, no matter how rigorous and careful the excavation is. Its existence is, therefore, in no way an indictment of data-gathering methods. Indeed, redeposition may only become apparent after considerable finds analysis. So recording the residual contamination is best not seen as part of the basic site record, even where it is seen as a strong possibility when on site because of the interpretation of the unit, for instance in the case of a proposed dump.

However, with careful control of cleanliness and exact stratigraphic definitions, one would hope to prevent later, intrusive material filtering into, or falling onto, earlier stratigraphy. Where this does not seem to be the case, for example because one is working under difficult salvage conditions, wet weather prevents close control, or the loose character of deposits invites later materials to fall down between underlying interstices, this fact should be mentioned on the recording sheet. The easiest way forward is to have a space to fill in the risk of intrusion, perhaps with a simple division between low and high because it is difficult to formulate any more useful categories than this. The majority of units will then be in the 'low' category, and for that small number where there is a high risk, the reason for this can be inserted.

At a later stage of the finds processing, it may be possible to suggest a **provisional date** for each stratum, for instance via 'spot dating' of its associated pottery assemblage on site soon after the completion of the excavation process. This information can then be noted on the recording form. However, such evidence must be used guardedly. First, the size of the assemblage employed may be very small, for example a few sherds of datable pottery. Next, ideas on dating can change, especially when it rests on the fabrics of one or two ceramic types which are not especially well known. Finally, one may have established the date of the material within this specific unit but the unit's true date may be provably later, for example when it contains mostly residual material and overlies strata which contain finds of a later date.

The most common reason for wanting to know such a provisional date, albeit only approximately, is that it may help in deciding future tactics on the excavation. For example, it is no good persevering with a research design focussed on the early medieval period when it is quite clear that all material of that date has been truncated and one is dealing with Roman buildings. However, for the reasons concerning residuality mentioned above, it is by no means an uncommon experience on deeply stratified, urban excavations to be digging pits yielding only Roman artefacts in the certain knowledge that they are medieval in date. So one must have sufficient evidence before changing direction so radically, especially if the change envisaged is to give up the excavation process entirely. Attention to detail in the evaluation stage should overcome many of these problems before the excavation proper starts.

Finally, an essential part of the record is for the excavator's role in its creation to be clearly acknowledged by **signing and dating** the sheet. In case of inaccuracy or other disagreement, this gives the supervisor a designated person, who has accepted responsibility, to check with. In addition it becomes possible, if desired, to compare the written record against individuals who created it. Does one person only use a certain type of colour language? This could be more than just an embarrassing, though interesting, exercise: it might also be an accurate way to test the adequacy of the record, or at least particular parts of it (e.g. the use of colour language in the above case) in order think up improvements or to implement further training, either of particular excavators or for all staff. Similarly, using the date, one might decide whether the standard of recording, as indicated by the number of errors, is less adequate at certain stages of the excavation owing to pressure of time. Dates can also be useful in working out such things as missing stratigraphic relationships. Thus, if a particularly vital relationship between two deposits has not been recorded, but the record of one unit was dated as complete one week before the other, one might reasonably suspect that this was the later of the two.

12.6 Checking the record

Once the excavator has said all she has to say about a particular unit, the sheet can be placed in a 'to be checked' file, from where it must be extracted to be scrutinised for accuracy and completeness by a second party, the sole way to maintain standardisation and to highlight errors. Only then can the unit be said to be finished and the checker sign to that effect. Such monitoring also indicates the general progress of work and can bring out any particular trends. For example patterns in provisional dates may show one part of the site is at an earlier level than the remainder and require an amendment of the research strategy or increases or reductions in numbers of personnel working in different areas to ensure one is excavating 'in phase'. Because of this potential for feedback to the excavation process and, more importantly, because some inconsistencies and gaps in the record can only be modified at an early stage of the work, such checking procedures must be part of on-site activities.

What form this checking actually takes is another matter. To some extent it can be just a bureaucratic process, ensuring that all necessary boxes have been filled in, cross-referencing has taken place, finds and sample sheets have been completed and related to a master sheet listing samples. Such matters take no great expertise, and in fact can be quite boring and thus perhaps a task best rotated. It does, however, still need someone who is committed to getting the basic record exactly right and takes pleasure in doing so, albeit a pedantic pleasure. The person(s) who will have responsibility for post-excavation analysis can often be relied on to perform such tasks well, as it is they who will bear the brunt of the problems if this has been done in a slapdash way. However, certain elements of the record, notably plans, stratigraphic relationships and physical descriptions, require particular attention.

For example, **plans** can be accurately drawn in themselves but mistakenly rotated through 90 degrees with respect to the site grid. They can also embody a variety of mistakes in administrative detail. Does the plan have the site code on it? Is the layer number correct and recorded in the right place? Is there a scale and the date of the drawing? Is it related to the grid using the co-ordinate system? Are the levels reduced and seemingly reasonable? Where a plan is drawn on more than one sheet, does its continuation fit? Are the conventions used in the correct form and are any exceptions noted on the drawing? All of this is usually simple to check at the time, but missing information is rarely recoverable after the excavation is completed.

Equally, the **calculation of stratigraphic relationships** may have to be checked carefully. The mechanics of how this is to be done in a rigorous way during the excavation, for example by the system of overlaying successive plans recommended above, should have been designated carefully in advance. However, critical relationships can still be missed, not because the job is excessively complex, more that the individual creating the matrix does not recognise the importance of the task. If the unique stratigraphic position of each unit is to be established accurately, the method used must be repeatable in order to be checkable. Having done the check, any redundant and confusing physical relationships can be deleted and any extra relationships added, for example with respect to unplanned units such as fills of known cut features. This checking of the matrix is a case *par excellence* where the one who can be relied on to produce the most consistent, complete records is the person who will do the stratigraphic analysis later. It is that person who will have the unenviable task of attempting post-excavation analysis on a site where matrix construction has been done inadequately.

Finally there is the vexed issue of checking the **written description** of each unit. If this information does not accurately reflect the physical characteristics of the unit when it was excavated, all the checking in the world will not correct this fault. For this reason some directors require that each description be checked at the point of excavation and/or that one person be responsible for writing every record. However, for reasons given previously, the excavator may be in the best position to make such decisions, having excavated the overlying strata, having defined the extent of the unit being recorded and having been in direct contact with it during its removal. Obviously training all site staff to the requisite standard is an essential preliminary here, but I feel it is better to put energy into this teaching than check everything on the site at the time.

Whether the excavator is trained and trusted not to mislead or checked up on by a colleague, there will still be a need to ensure that the description produced on site is then in the correct format, if only to facilitate its storage on computer. Has the frequency of all inclusions been recorded? Do the percentages of the soil matrix add up to 100? Has the correct terminology been applied? If the feature is a cut, is there a list of fills and presumed fills under the 'notes' section? These are often relatively straightforward things to do during the work on site or immediately afterwards, but very time-consuming to recreate retrospectively post-excavation.

When the record has been inspected for accuracy of planning and stratigraphic relationships, completeness of description, etc., and any problems are sorted out, any inconsistencies and incoherences should be not only noted and corrected, but recycled by bringing them to the attention of the excavator immediately. This is for two reasons. First, the site recorder may have had good reason to record a unit in this way and showing her the problem and discussing can be the only way forward. For instance, an overlap between plans may suggest a relationship between units to the checker which is not on the site matrix. Has this been simply missed by the excavator, or was it noticed but not considered entirely certain? If it is the latter, the excavator might be criticised for not noting her reasons on the recording sheet, but not for getting the matrix 'wrong'. Certainly the checker should not simply change things without consultation. In other cases, it may be that the recording system could not be fitted with the potential information which the excavator found on the ground and, rather than shoe-horn the stratum into the system, she stepped outside it. Thus there may be a good case for augmenting the approach to recording.

Second, if an element is simply missing from the record, for example the colour of a deposit, it is more likely to be accurately remembered straight away than at any later stage. Also excavators will never learn from such gaps and mistakes, and thus improve their performance in the future, without knowing of their existence. So any inconsistencies within the record, or between excavator and checker, must be discussed in a spirit of mutual desire to get things exactly right, and not used as a stick to beat inefficient excavators with or quietly modified, sometimes to the detriment of the record itself, and thus diplomatically swept under the carpet to give both parties an easier life.

After the unit has been excavated, the finds have been fed into the processing system and the site data have been checked, the record must be stored, whether in a computer or manually in a 'contexts complete' file. Where unit numbers have been allocated to strata before their excavation by signing them out in a book, that same book can be used to register completed and checked units before they are finally stored. By 'counting them out and counting them in' in this way, it is easy to verify which units are outstanding, presumably the ones under active excavation at the time. Thus, even on a site with complex stratigraphy and employing many excavators, the status of each stratigraphic entity should be knowable at the drop of a hat.

Of course, occasionally mistakes will arise. For example, the excavator may return to the site and decide that the apparently finished deposit in fact continued further north, so the plan must be augmented, and the stratigraphic relationships and description may need alteration. Here any such additions or modifications must be shown as just that – changes – on both plan and unit recording sheet, together with the date of change. No attempt should be made to conceal the alteration since the fact of having been altered can be as important as the modification itself. After this is done and the extra element removed from the site, all the data must go back into the 'to be checked' file and be recycled, fed back through the whole system as if it were entirely new. With such a systematic approach, there can be no excuses for 'losing' a layer on site, either during or at the end of the data gathering process.

13

STRATIGRAPHIC ANALYSIS

Introduction

If the spatial, stratigraphic and descriptive elements of each excavation unit have been recorded systematically, as described above, then the end of excavation work will allow the move from data collection to data analysis. The stratigraphic component of this analysis is a complex business involving, in the first instance, the interpretation of individual strata and making links both to adjacent units and to under- or overlying ones, i.e. ascribing function and phasing to every layer. Whatever system of classifying strata types and site phasing is adopted (to be discussed below), this information will have to apply to all of the excavated units – every entity, well understood or not, poorly stratified or otherwise, will have to be assessed and then make its appearance somewhere in the phasing structure, thence the report, of the site.

This apparently simple requirement – for a report to present *all* data, interpret them and justify that interpretation – is one reason why writing up a complex archaeological site can be more demanding than other forms of archaeological research, for example producing a doctoral thesis. The author of the latter can afford to select data carefully, dismiss what is clearly irrelevant, or even of marginal relevance, and stop when she has enough material. Whereas the field-worker, no matter how tightly the research design is focussed and how systematically the recording has been done, is always likely to recover some data which have been less than ideally recorded, are unexpected or simply perplexing. The best way to check that every stratigraphic unit has been slotted into the site's phasing structure is to create an index at the end of the process which relates each unit to a higher-order group. Only then can one be sure that all of the stratigraphic evidence has been considered. Such an index can also give basic interpretative categories for each unit (plough soil, fill, occupation layer, destruction debris, etc.) and thus facilitate access into the body of the report.

The challenges in writing up stratigraphy are not derived simply from requiring that every bit of data be understood to the same high level, which is plainly often impossible. There is the additional demand, to incorporate all of the evidence into a single narrative (assuming that this is what the site report endeavours to do, as opposed to telling the story of how the excavation took place, in the form of a novel: Hodder 1989). When some units can be interpreted to a high level but others are merely allocated basic functions and correlated across the sequence (and even then with differing degrees of certainty), the production of a single, simple story line is a demanding task.

Second, the production of a report requires not just consideration of site evidence but an investigation of finds and documentary material, i.e. it involves interdisciplinary processes. Thus a series of artefactual and ecofactual analyses must be organised and their results integrated, both with each other and with the site evidence. Such studies not only provide an absolute chronology for the sequence, as with a dated inscription from a specific deposit. More importantly, they can throw light on site functions, either at the general level (a profusion of coins throughout the sequence suggesting an emphasis on exchange, for example) or at the particular level (the biological remains found in samples from a specific deposit showing that dyeing of cloth was taking place on that part of the site).

In addition to the study of finds, documentary sources will have to be investigated in their own right and then related to the archaeological development of the site. On some occasions the two sets of evidence may contradict each other: here it is useful to remember that one source may be recording the intentions of law givers, whereas the other relates to the degree to which they were obeyed in the real world. At other times they may point in the same direction and have a symbiotic relationship, as where destruction debris on site can be linked to an earthquake recorded in a document. Thus the correlation of the site sequence with a documented event may provide absolute dates on which to hang the stratigraphy, and archaeological evidence may help to make anomalies in the written record intelligible. Hammer *et al.* demonstrate this two-way process for excavations in the Fleet Valley, London, where certain events known from the history of the area such as flooding and land reclamation provided 'safe milestones along the archaeological sequence' (1993: 17). Equally, the results of archaeological investigation were able to identify the line of a foreshore and an adjacent eyot whose position then explained a curious extension to a parish boundary in the area as seen in the documentary record.

Obviously, to discuss fully all aspects of post-excavation work would be very time-consuming and take us far beyond the confines of this book. These many, diverse and complex processes are, rightly, the province of another manual, as is the difficult issue of how such activities are to be programmed effectively. However, there is one analytical procedure – stratigraphic analysis – whose discussion cannot be postponed to a later stage, if only because its inclusion is demanded by the line of argument put forward thus far. Whatever one says about how such analysis should be approached after the end of the excavation – and it is likely to raise even more hackles than the approaches to site recording discussed already – nobody really doubts that this work is the logical next step for processing the site record and a necessary prerequisite of successfully integrating other specialist studies. There is only space here to suggest some broad principles and put in place some platitudes.

Before considering this topic in detail, there is the matter of tidying up and checking the existing record. In theory, if all the steps described in the first part of this book have been followed systematically, the photographic, spatial, stratigraphic and descriptive record should already be finished in its entirety as the last unit is excavated. In reality, even on the most carefully controlled excavation, and certainly in projects such as watching briefs, elements in each sphere are likely to need some final processing (considered below, **13.1**). In order to discuss stratigraphic analysis itself, it is important to raise the vexed issue of what role any interpretations reached on-site, during the process of data gathering, should play post-excavation (**13.2**). This has often raised more heat than light, in part because of a failure to distinguish between two related, but more importantly distinct, post-excavation procedures – correlating stratigraphy across a sequence, as opposed to assigning function to individual units and making vertical groupings (**13.3**).

Having set this straight, the reader will hopefully have agreed that on-site interpretation might usefully influence notions of formation processes and function, but should not be used to assume links between possibly contemporary strata. So, if one is not to employ such assumptions, it is necessary to put forward an alternative way of reconsidering any stratigraphic sequence if analysis is to proceed (**13.4**). Following on, in part, from the discussion of the representation of stratigraphic relationships in Chapter 9.2, various ways in which sequence diagrams can aid the process of analysis can then be suggested (**13.5**). Finally, the objective of this activity is to assemble individual units into groupings. Hence the defining characteristics of such higher-order entities must be discussed. This will be achieved via a résumé of the labels which have been attached to them – block, group, context series, period, etc. (**13.6**). The results of such analytical work can be presented, either initially to other specialists or, at a later stage, to the reader of a site report, by using sequence diagrams or transparent overlays above such (**13.7**). In order to illustrate all of these points, a single, simple stratigraphic sequence comprising only ten units will be employed (see Figure 27).

13.1 Tidying up the record

Although a complete excavation record should have been established as far as possible on-site, both time pressures and other practical problems, plus matters such as cross-referencing, mean that certain aspects will need to be finished after the event. The degree to which the basic record can be modified will vary, depending on which part of it is involved, and what situation pertained on the excavation as work proceeded. Most of the tidying and checking operation will be concerned not with adding to the record in any significant way, still less changing it, but with simply sorting out bureaucratic niceties. These might include making sure that the stratigraphic unit numbers form a running sequence – none is missing and none is double numbered; that all recording sheets have the correct site code; and that plan/section numbers, or sample and photographic numbers, if used, have been entered onto the relevant sheet(s). Doing this tedious job at this early stage saves a lot of time later, it being far better to sort the problems out immediately than to have to break off in the middle of some complicated stratigraphic analysis to look for an unreferenced plan. Also, after the pressure involved in the final phase of most excavation work, a fairly mindless task can be quite welcome, especially as the brain is about to be fully tested again in the analytical processes to come. Additions to, or modifications of, the basic record are outlined next.

In the **photographic record**, there is an inevitable time lapse between the taking of a particular shot and the development of the film and its filing. Hence, some photographs, if only the final ones, will need to have numbers of stratigraphic units and other basic information added – direction of view, object of attention, etc. This detail will need to be augmented for every shot with a hierarchy of captions covering the wide-ranging audiences using the photographic record, some of whom will require access when the site director has long disappeared to pastures new. These will range from the mundane cross-referencing needed for specialist site work ('layer 1534 abutting sill 1592'); via a more informative phrase which may be useful to the academic researcher ('debris from wattle and daub superstructure of Structure C collapsed against its western wall'); to that with widest appeal as required by the national broadsheet reporter ('Timber buildings destroyed by Boudicca ("Boadicea")') or headlines of the 'Queen Boadicea – phew, what a scorcher!' variety beloved by other, more popular newspapers. Obviously it is not possible to provide captions which cater for all users. The objective is not to write their text for them but to give them the wherewithal to do their job effectively and, as far as they and their editors see fit, accurately. As the start of this process, the most basic information can be written-in straight away and should be also cross-referenced into the rest of the site record, especially onto the relevant record sheet(s).

For the **spatial record**, there is rarely any aspect that can be legitimately augmented after excavation: in general, if the true extent of a unit has not been drawn accurately, very little can be done about it. Just occasionally the photographic record might be sufficient to allow real alterations to the plan. More common is the situation when the wrong convention is found to have been used, e.g. for the limit of excavation, and this can then be corrected. However, the site record should never be changed without very good cause, and then only with the original retained in some way for the future and the alteration described and dated.

Some archaeologists advocate more mundane 'tidying-up' of site plans after the excavation, for example by inking them in. However, this is a time-consuming process and rarely necessary if the originals are of reasonable quality. Also, it seems, graphite provides a more stable medium than ink, and thus is to be preferred in terms of a long-term archive. Better, therefore, to use a pencil of the correct type in the field (hard enough for accuracy but soft enough for legibility, including copying onto microfiche if that is intended) and then leave well alone. By the same token, if plans are drawn by triangulation, there is no need to rub out the resulting arcs in the interests of creating a more polished end-product. Indeed, leaving these points visible lets the analyst see how many were measured and their position, with implications for how accurate the drawing is likely to be. In short, to be useful, site drawings must be thorough and the method used in their production (frame, offset or triangulation) made clear. Other considerations, such as the aesthetic quality of the finished plan, must always be secondary.

Concerning the **stratigraphic record**, it is possible, in theory and assuming that the sequence is to be created using a system of plan overlays, to reproduce the same set of relationships at any stage during or after the excavation. However, as argued previously, it is better in practice to go through the overlaying process before each unit is actually excavated, rather than afterwards. Having done so on site, it is difficult to imagine what would be added by repeating this process a second time at the end of the excavation. In addition, if there are inaccuracies in the matrix record, these are likely to be picked up in later analysis. Computer programmes do exist which check whether matrices are internally consistent (Wilcock 1982). This is obviously an important consideration but, as discussed earlier, showing that there are no 'loops' in a stratigraphic diagram ('A is over B is over A') does not prove that it is correct, only that it is not obviously incorrect. Far better, then, to have a method of deducing stratigraphic relationships at the earliest possible stage which is all-embracing and checkable using the plans. This should mean that one is involved, later, only in cross-referencing missing relationships, not in deducing entirely new ones.

The **descriptive record** is also fairly immune from later modification: if the proportion of an inclusion in a deposit has not been noted, one is unlikely to be able to make a useful guess some time afterwards. Sometimes, usually soon after a unit has been excavated, missing aspects of a description can be suggested from memory. For example, the sedimentary texture of a deposit might be estimated belatedly, at least to the extent of being able to say that it was 'sandier than the underlying deposit' because different sandiness is recalled as the basis on which the distinction between the two was made when trowelling. However, where such gaps are filled from memory, it becomes equally vital to show clearly that the description was only completed retrospectively, not at the proper time. On other occasions it may be possible to add to a record sheet via information contained elsewhere. For instance, if the description of one deposit mentions that an inclusion within it is proportionately different from a second layer, this could be cross-referenced onto that second sheet. Or the photograph of an inhumation may clearly show more bone articulation than was recorded on site, so that record can be augmented.

Lastly, in order to prepare effectively for the next phase of work and, in the process, sign-off the preceding one, it can be very useful to have a '**debriefing**' (Malt and Westman 1992) at which all interested parties can compare the data collected, and the methods employed to do so, with the original research design. Even on the most organised project, objectives will have evolved during the fieldwork. Also, although considerable resources may have been expended on pre-excavation reconnaissance, practical problems encountered thereafter may have limited, or unexpected survival may have expanded, the data set derived from the fieldwork. Reminding oneself of the initial objectives of the project and how this was intended to structure data gathering, then seeing how both evolved when implemented, allows familiarisation with the total record. It thus gives one a feel for the overall coherence of its diverse elements recovered by different specialists, often over an extended period of time, and provides a good lead-in to the analytical phase.

13.2 The role of on-site interpretation in stratigraphic analysis

The objective of such analysis is to provide interpretations of every particular stratum. The process of doing this might be started at any time from when each was originally visible on site, and continue until the very last stage of post-excavation work, and even beyond. Such decisions must be noted on individual recording sheets and cross-referenced to the other relevant records. Space must therefore be allocated on the sheet for comments and any notes relating to the final phasing structure. Most recording pro formas reserve a section for such interpretations below that which holds the basic, descriptive information. It is important that not only the interpretation itself but also the *rationale* for it, and the degree of certainty with which it is held, are written down in that space. For example, if the excavator decides that a layer is a floor, then she should also mention whether this suggested identification is based on its physical composition, its compaction relative to surrounding strata, the wear on its surface, the nature of its interface with an overlying layer or some combination of these factors. Similarly, if one deposit is considered to be 'the same' as another, this may be due to physical similarity, stratigraphic position, absolute level of surface, or a variety of other criteria: the basis on which the conclusion is drawn is as important as the suggestion itself.

Of course, interpretations made during the excavation, in terms of either suggested function or correlation with other strata, often alter once underlying units have been exposed, thus requiring corresponding additions to the recording sheet retrospectively. This serves to emphasise their provisional nature and distinguish them further from the more basic data at the top of the sheet, which will not change (subject to the small provisos mentioned in 13.1). For example, the record of the physical character of a deposit or the plan of a timber base plate are clearly a more fundamental part of the record that the sentence which says that, together, they form the primary phase of a timber building. Even accepting that making interpretative statements is the most important objective of any excavation, because these eventually provide answers to the questions which stimulated the work in the first place, it is important to maintain this difference in status between data and interpretation.

The conceptual distinction noted above between the basic site record and other, higher-order statements leads onto a central issue of stratigraphic analysis – what role should on-site interpretation play in post-excavation work? There are two views on this matter, which relate, in part, to the dichotomy outlined at the start (Chapter 2) on total excavation versus problem orientation. Some maintain that issues such as site formation processes, assigning function to individual strata, making correlations between stratigraphic units and phasing the sequence should be worked out when the evidence is directly visible in the ground, i.e. during the excavation. Hence Lowe (1993) talks of a belief (for which no justification is actually offered there) that interpretation should be done in the field and thus that the 'preliminary testing of stratigraphic blocks, or context-groups, should also be undertaken at that time' (p. 23). Such blocks must necessarily be created on-site and 'none of this work should be jeopardised by the ill-considered desire to "do it all later"' (p. 23). In similar vein, McAdam decries the artificial distinction between excavation and post-excavation work, suggesting that higher-order interpretations, for example the grouping of basic elements of the record into larger units, should be used to allow 'the excavator to make explicit his *running interpretation* of the site' (1992: 7, my emphasis).

This conception is based on the assumption that the meaning of excavated data is directly understandable, that most interpretation can be worked out during the dig, if one is a good enough archaeologist, and that any failure to do this reflects badly on the director concerned. Hence post-excavation work involves the process of merely writing down 'what it all means', that 'meaning' having been decided when one was in direct contact with the material in question. If site data speak for themselves, as this view implies, then it is the duty of the field-worker not just to gather it but to listen and assimilate what is heard. If she is incapable of both recording and interpreting, through either inexperience or simple intellectual inadequacy ('bad hearing'?), simple division of labour should allow the field-worker to be responsible for the basic record, and the site director then to produce the clever interpretations during regular site visits.

However, there is an alternative view, one that has some distinct strengths. This stance maintains that creating interpretations in post-excavation analysis is essentially that – a later, analytical process, obviously linked to, but equally separate from, what went before. Thus Steane (1992a) talks of going back to the basic context descriptions to allow *re*interpretation of sites. Or, more strongly, Malt and Westman assert that giving a soundly based interpretation during the excavation can be 'little more than a glorified guess' (Malt and Westman 1992: 11) and thus maintain that phase plans (i.e. those drawings which express the spatial configuration of groupings of more basic stratigraphic units) 'ought not to be a matter of recognising what was already there' (p. 10, my emphasis) but reconstructed after the excavation has finished. Allowing ideas which developed while gathering data to influence final interpretations means relying on half-remembered – or mis-remembered – suggestions based on the one exposed unit and its partially obscured predecessors. Such speculations necessarily fail to do full justice to the more detailed, fuller record constructed by those out in the field. Further, on a site of any complexity, it is not practical to make all of the stratigraphic links between units as different individuals record and excavate different parts of the site. In essence, then, an excavation project involves data production, data analysis and data presentation as distinct stages in the research itinerary, and they should not be mixed together.

Those favouring on-site interpretation are strongly critical of the latter argument, considering it an admission of defeat on the part of the site worker, or an abrogation of responsibility by the site director. For example, when casting doubt on the central importance of on-site interpretation in the presence of an eminent Roman archaeologist, I can remember being told, in no uncertain terms, that once I was as old as him and had worked on as many sites, I would be able to do away with all the boring detail of the basic record and merely note the interpretation. Whilst accepting that the aim of excavation is to allow interpretation, and that some of this can be done on site, I still believe that those archaeologists have a point who maintain that providing *full* answers at the stage of data production is not only difficult but potentially misleading. To go beyond the apparent stand-off between the two views outlined above, we must recognise two things. First, there is clearly a complex relationship between data gathering and interpretation, not least because, in some sense, even the act of deciding the limits of a unit on site is an interpretative act. At the same time, *once defined*, data are conceptually distinct from their interpretation.

13.3 Correlating between units versus linking successive units

To make further progress, it is useful to distinguish between two important analytical processes – the making of correlations between different stratigraphic units, and the assigning of function to an individual unit. Of course, the two activities are interlinked, and both may be generated by ideas developed on site, just as both may be modified as a result of later work post-excavation. None the less, I wish to maintain that the first – making correlations – is best done initially without preconceptions developed in data production. Whereas the latter, assigning function, can legitimately build on interpretations developed on-site as a test bed, and indeed often must do so. I would further wish to suggest that the former type of work is more basic than the latter and should therefore come first in stratigraphic analysis. In both cases, the arguments put forward are based on empirical efficiency, not a matter of high theory.

In putting the above case, I take it as axiomatic that, where a sequence of stratigraphy exists, it makes sense to interpret it from the earliest elements upwards, in the order in which it has developed. This is to be preferred over analysing it from the top down, as it has been dug; or from any other point within the sequence going upwards, downwards and outwards, as would be the case if one started with a layer believed to be particularly important (important for whom and on what basis?) or a horizon which covered large parts of the site. Given such an assumption, I would argue for the following sequence of operations to be carried out, unit by unit:

> first comes the making of horizontal links across the sequence
> then, by incorporating provisional proposals on site formation processes, one blocks units together vertically and creates a phasing structure for such blocks
> finally one makes decisions on the function of each stratum in an ever-increasing hierarchy of interpretation (Unit 81 is interpreted first as 'occupation debris', then as 'an accumulation on Metalling 3', and finally as 'usage of the penultimate late-Roman street surface flanking Insula IV').

Initially, therefore, as each unit comes up for analysis, we must consider which other ones might link with it. This question comes in two forms: which units, out of the possibly contemporary stratigraphy, might be the same as a particular layer in question? Answers come from looking for horizontal links, discussed next. Then there is the issue of which of the unit(s), although immediately earlier in the sequence, might block vertically with it as a single event (discussed afterwards)?

Clearly the first matter, **correlations across the sequence**, is more fundamental than the second. Two deposits recorded in adjacent sequences, perhaps divided by a later intrusion, may be sufficiently similar to suggest that they once joined up and had been part of a single action on the site: this cannot be the case with two strata which are provably successive. For example, in Figure 27, 7 may correlate with 8, 9 or 10 but let us suppose that it has exactly the same composition and level as the last of these but is rather different in physical composition from either 8 or 9. Here analysis might allow the interpretation that 'Unit 7 is the same as Unit 10', meaning 'at a certain stage in the past 7 and 10 connected up as a single entity'. This constitutes the strongest link between two entities. In contrast, layers 3 and 7 in this same sequence were distinguished from each other in excavation on the basis of their different physical characteristics. At most they may be very similar in character, a product of the same type of site formation process and part of a single general activity on site. It is not possible for them actually to be the *same* stratigraphic unit.

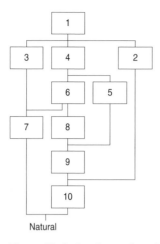

Figure 27 A simple stratigraphic sequence for analysis.

To make links across the matrix, one must start with the physical characteristics of the units in question. If these are nearly identical, the case for equating the two will obviously be stronger than when they are merely broadly similar. Following this general principle, it may even be possible to make correlations between strata using more formal, statistical methods, for example by quantifying attributes, such as particular inclusions, to generate more detailed patterns (Golemblik 1991). However, any patterning which results will be difficult to interpret or at least open to different interpretations. The degree of variation between descriptions which is deemed acceptable will depend, in part, on the type of unit concerned (i.e. its functional interpretation). Thus, although initial connections should be made on the basis of each written description, any suggestions may well require later modification in the light of other types of interpretation.

To illustrate the above point, consider the proposal that, as Unit 7 and Unit 10 have very similar descriptions, they were once a single entity. If 7 is a deposit thought to be an occupation layer and has some variation within it ('grey silt (60%) and fine sand (40%) containing frequent charcoal flecks in the north, becoming moderate further south'), then it may well correlate with 10 to its south ('grey silt and fine sand (50%/50%) containing occasional charcoal flecking'): the degree of disparity is small and some differences might be expected anyway given the proven variation within 7 and the formation process involved. Hence 7 = 10 would be strongly held. In contrast, what if Unit 7 is a mosaic pavement, cut away to its south but with sufficient area surviving to show that it has an entirely symmetrical pattern in its surface, and 10 is a second mosaic fragment further south set in the same mortar and with the same surface level, but with a slightly different pattern? Despite their considerable similarity, the two may be deemed unlikely to have once connected. 7 = 10 is stratigraphically possible but is improbable because the symmetry of 7's pattern would lead one to expect an *exact* correlate elsewhere, not just a similar mosaic fragment. Thus a degree of physical resemblance is necessary but whether it is sufficient will depend on other considerations, in particular the type of formation process (occupation build-up versus decorative floor construction in the above example) envisaged.

As well as the physical description of each unit, the analyst may use information contained on the drawings to suggest horizontal connections across the matrix – the absolute level at its surface, its extent in plan, concentrations of diagnostic surface inclusions, etc. However, this criterion is likely to be subsidiary to the first one. Surface levels can vary considerably within a single unit, yet successive layers may be very thin and have very similar levels. Hence making links across any distance on this basis can be questionable. Equally, if two units, though rather different in character, have a common alignment along one edge, one might propose that they were once the same deposit. Yet if their physical dissimilarity is considerable, they are likely to be linked only circumstantially, for example as two different floors in adjacent rooms laid down at roughly the same time and running up to the same boundary. Such a link is weaker than that proposed by saying that the two were '*the same*'. In short, assuming that one has no reason to question the accuracy of the written descriptions, plan data may strengthen or augment the descriptive evidence, but would rarely be preferred when the two appear to contradict each other.

Making connections across the sequence should be a first step in stratigraphic analysis whatever the type of site involved, albeit a quick and fairly unproductive process on a site with only shallow stratification. That said, we can now return to the previous debate concerning *when* connections should be made. One has to accept that formation processes, even if appreciated fully only post-excavation, can affect the process of stratigraphic correlation (influencing, for example, the degree of variation in descriptions acceptable in equating strata: see above on correlating occupation deposits or mosaic pavements). All of this work *could* be done after the fieldwork phase, using only the basic stratigraphic, physical and spatial characteristics of each unit recorded on site.

How would the alternative approach, using correlations suggested during excavation, facilitate this process? These suggestions can only have been put forward when the one unit was fully visible but at least *some* of its potential correlates were partially obscured, or even sealed entirely. Links suggested at one point in the site work may therefore change later on. For example, one might have decided, when both were exposed at a single time in the field, that deposit 7 (Figure 27) once connected with deposit 8. But what if a third element, 10, only revealed at a later stage below 8, is then seen to represent a link which is even more plausible? In this case the first suggestion would be wrong, or at least the less preferred option.

Those wishing to retain a role for on-site interpretation might accept that any suggested correlation might later be proved inadequate, but defend their position by maintaining that it was still useful as a 'working hypothesis'. If so, how is one to test that hypothesis during analysis? Consider the initial suggestion that 7 = 8. An obvious question to ask at the outset is 'Is a link between 7 and 8 stratigraphically possible?' If the answer is 'No', then the proposition is clearly wrong. However, even if proven *possible*, as is the case here, this does not make it right. On a site of any complexity, there will be at least several, and more usually many, connections which are stratigraphically possible (10, 9, 8, 5 and 2 could each be an exact correlate of 7, for example). Of these, a good number may be deemed fairly likely because of the superficial similarity of the physical characteristics of the units involved. However, which one is the preferred option, if such can be defined at all, will require taking on board a whole series of factors, not just the character of stratigraphy in question but its position in plan and surface level. More importantly, it will also include the interpretations of surrounding stratigraphy. Thus Unit 7 may be equally similar to both 8 and 10. However, what if 7 is overlain by diagnostic destruction debris 3, and 10 by very similar material 9 (i.e. 3 = 9), but 8 is overlain by 6, a deposit entirely different from both 3 and 9? Here 7 = 10 might be much preferred to 7 = 8, not because of the nature of 7, 8 or 10 but on the basis of another decision, that 3 seems to equate with 9 and not with 6.

In short, the process of making connections involves not only the interpretation of individual units, based on their specific properties, but also some conception of the whole sequence. By definition, the latter will not have been completely visible when any one unit was being recorded. Thus any correlation suggested on-site will be based, at best, on a partial understanding and provide a misleading starting point. Incidentally, this interlinked nature of stratigraphic evidence is also the reason why it is virtually impossible to analyse parts of a sequence in isolation, to start the process of analysis anywhere other than at its base, or to publish only part of it.

This last point, concerning writing-up and publication, provides a final nail in the coffin for the use of on-site correlations. The job of any site report is not only to present data and to suggest its interpretation but also to justify the second in terms of the first. Constructing the full case for a proposed connection will usually require drawing on a range of arguments which bring together far more aspects of the sequence than would be available at the point of excavation. Thus, paradoxically, even when an interpretation which might have been made on site turns out to be the preferred option after proper analysis, the case will be more fully justified and explained if the analyst has rehearsed all of the arguments by going through, and dismissing, all other possibilities, rather than having simply assumed the correctness of the original judgement. She will then be able to present a fuller, and usually clearer, line of argument in the report.

Having looked for horizontal connections, we can turn to vertical blocking, that is, deciding on the **association of stratigraphically successive units**. In part this can be done using only basic data, as with horizontal correlation, for example by suggesting the broad contemporaneity of two units on the basis of their similar inclusions or sedimentary composition. Thus a profusion of distinctive daub flecks in two superimposed strata might imply that the same activity occurred in each case. However, there are problems in drawing conclusions based solely on physical characteristics. The above, daub-flecked deposits *may* relate to a single event, for example the conflagration of a building, and thus be grouped together correctly. Yet they may result from very different formation processes which should be sharply distinguished. For example one may be primary destruction debris and the other an occupation deposit trodden above it, during which a significant proportion of the content of the earlier unit was disturbed and redeposited in the later one.

Thus, although it is possible to note gaps in a vertical sequence by focussing on those cases where a different and/or unusual attribute comes into play and suggest a significant change in land use (see Clarke and Hutcheson 1993: 67 for an example), the reverse does not apply. Where there is much in common between successive strata this need not mean that there is a close relationship between them and hence that they should be linked vertically. Similarity of description will be relevant to the argument but blocking of successive strata will only be fully justified when the units concerned have a common function: '8 is the fill of a pit, 9 and 10 below it have already been interpreted as earlier fills, so all can be grouped together' (Figure 27). Making such decisions requires going beyond the basic evidence and entering into a series of debates on site formation processes, including the incorporation of interpretations reached during the process of excavation and the results of non-stratigraphic analyses done during post-excavation. Thus the creation of vertical groups must have a dynamic relationship with decisions on **site formation processes** and **ascription of function** to individual units. This makes both different from, and potentially more chancy than, the suggestion of horizontal connections.

Making vertical blocks may involve the use of a wide range of other information including, where possible, micromorphological feedback, and certainly full artefactual and ecofactual information. Yet this does not mean that all suggestions must be put on hold until a later stage: indeed, one could slip into an endless, circular argument in trying to fulfil such a provision. For example, it is rarely possible for the micromorphologist to analyse all excavated deposits, so samples are taken on site because of the perceived significance of certain layers. Thus one might choose only those layers thought to be occupation deposits and/or those where a natural agency played a significant part in their formation. Next, if this policy results in too many samples for available resources, certain ones will have to be selected because of their proposed relevance to the understanding of the site. Hence initial ideas on the function of a particular unit, formulated during data production, influence whether a sample exists at all for future work and, at a second stage, some initial interpretation in post-excavation work is needed to select out those samples deemed especially important.

Similar issues arise with respect to finds analysis, which may have implications for the other site evidence in two broad areas: providing dating evidence, for example via pottery or coins; and elucidating site function, either in general or at the level of the particular activity associated with a specific unit of stratification. Concerning provision of dates, finds experts may *start* their analytical work, correctly, by looking at finds from each stratigraphic unit in isolation. Yet, in order to come to meaningful conclusions, they must view assemblages in sequence, and sometimes joined together into larger groups to give statistically meaningful results. Such amalgamation must be based, of course, on the phasing of the site. In other words, some stratigraphic analysis is a prerequisite of allowing finds dating to be fully effective. By the same token, when focussing on site function, artefactual or ecofactual material may be indicative of a particular activity, for example industrial residues such as hammer scale which suggests smithing. However, in order to decide how closely this relates to the site, one has to know whether or not such inclusions were redeposited. The suggestion that a find has a primary relation with its layer has to be argued for, not assumed by the specialist. This can only be done by referring to ideas on deposit formation deduced from work on-site, and in stratigraphic analysis post-excavation.

Thus it becomes clear that, in order to break into the interpretative cycle, one makes decisions on site which influence, *inter alia*, sampling procedures, and puts forward ideas on formation processes and deposit status both during and after excavation, in so far as this is evident from the basic record. The point is not that all of the arguments can come crashing down around the ears of the analyst by removing a single plank. It is rather that there is an interactive process, which starts off during excavation and continues, through reasoned collaboration, until a final (in the sense of most preferred) interpretation can be put forward. The question is not 'Who will have the last word?', as this necessarily comes at a much later stage, if ever, but 'Who kicks off the conversation, and on what basis?' To avoid circularity and engender a positive research cycle, two rules must be adhered to. First, the analyst must explicitly acknowledge that any initial ascription of function, whether during excavation or at subsequent analytical stages, is provisional in character and liable to be changed, hopefully for the better, as a result of further work. Second, as proposed earlier, she must ensure that the basis of any initial decisions and further emendations are clearly stated and justified. The latter starts with the filling-in of the 'provisional interpretation' box on the site recording sheet and continues throughout all later study.

Hopefully enough has been said above to suggest that, in their use of on-site interpretations, suggested correlations between possibly contemporary strata are different in kind from decisions on the function of a particular stratum and grouping it with earlier or later elements. One cannot know all about phasing as one leaves the excavation and any notions derived during digging should not be used to structure the first procedure in stratigraphic analysis, the making of the strongest horizontal connections. On the other hand, one can have some ideas on deposit formation which throw light on the functional interpretation of individual units and these provisional interpretations can be used in post-excavation work to suggest whether or not the unit now under investigation continues the processes assigned to an underlying stratum – i.e. to postulate that two successive units can be linked together (see 13.6 below on the grouping of 'actions' to form 'activities') – or represents an entirely new type of activity.

13.4 Stratigraphic nodes and critical paths

If one does not take, at face value, those connections across a sequence suggested on site when commencing stratigraphic work, how *should* one begin analysis? The case has been made for starting at the bottom of the sequence and working up. Yet what if there are several units at its base? And how exactly should one proceed thereafter if there are many strands? The following method provides one way forward and has been used successfully on several sites (see Dalland 1984 for another). It is predicated on three principles:

> that only basic stratigraphic relationships should be used when first looking at the strata;
>
> that the time to consider any individual, floating stratigraphic unit is immediately before one examines the unit above it;
>
> that, where there is a long sequence and a short sequence to be correlated, one is more likely to understand that shorter in the light of the longer than *vice versa*.

The practical application of these principles allows the definition of a route through the sequence, establishing a new order in which to look at the strata which utilises only the logic of the organisation of the diagram, not any pre-conceptions on links worked out previously. Thus the sequence represented in Figure 27 would be looked at in the numerical order 10 through to 1, the rationale being as follows: starting at its base, two units (10 and 7) directly overlie natural strata but 10 has less stratigraphic latitude than 7. Thus, although unit 7 and the sequence 10, 9, 8 have in common the fact that they are provably earlier than 6, it is likely (I would put it no stronger) to be easier to understand 7 in the context of already having some ideas about 8, 9 and 10 than *vice versa*. Hence it is best to look at these three, then 7, before going on to 6. By the same token, 5 could equate with 8, 6 and/or 7, but must come into play before 4. Finally, 3 has considerable stratigraphic latitude, but less than 2, which must be considered before 1.

If a sequence is rather complex, for example 1,000+ units, then it may be necessary to define a series of nodal points within it, a node being any particular unit which draws together many others underneath it. The units provably below the head of the group can then be lifted out and this smaller sequence ordered using the above principles and the process repeated for other groups. Some of these groups will be separate from each other, others successive. By treating each group as a higher-level entity in its own right, interrelationships between groups can be represented diagrammatically on a matrix. Then, by repeating the same principles, one can define an order in which each group is to be looked at. With an order for the groups as a whole, and a route within each of them, one can navigate a way through a sequence, no matter how complex, which allows every unit to be looked at afresh.

Two further points need to be mentioned here. An alternative way of analysing the sequence is to define the longest route through it, then to fit in all floating units at a later stage. Thus, in the above example, one would consider 10, 9, 8, 6, 4, and 1 in that order, then go back to 5, 7, 3 and 2 (see Pearson and Williams 1993: 96ff for a fuller statement of the method). Although perfectly logical, the disadvantage of this approach is simply that, before looking at the 'floaters', one will have interpreted every unit on the main strand up to the latest and written notes on each justifying that interpretation. Yet some of these, provably, *cannot* be contemporary with the unit considered next. For example, using this method, the central strand between unit 10 and unit 1 would have been read through and provisionally interpreted before looking at 7. However, 7 cannot equate with 6, 4 and 1, whatever its relationship, if any, with 8, 9 and 10. Thus those units most immediately in the mind of the analyst are known not to correlate directly with the next one to come under the spotlight. Far better, I suggest, to look at 7 immediately after all of the units of potential relevance to it – i.e. 10, 9 and 8 – have been considered.

The final point is rather more important. It must be remembered that this new order in which to look at a sequence is just a means to an end, not a thing in itself which might dictate any particular form of interpretation. Units on the longest route through the matrix, though definable mathematically, do not necessarily represent the longest sequence of development on the site (this is the trap which, I feel, Dalland's concept of 'key sequences' (1984: 120) falls into). Nor does the fact that a unit has more stratigraphic latitude in the matrix than another mean that its relationships are less secure or that it is less important in the development of the site. Thus, in the above example, unit 7 will be considered after 10, 9 and 8. It may equate with unit 9, in which case the sequence of deposition would be interpreted as being 10, then 9 = 7, then 8. Or it may equate with none of them and come before 10, between 9 and 10, between 9 and 8, or after 8: its position with respect to other units must be argued for. If this is true of its relative position, it is even more the case when considering its position in absolute time. For example, it is quite possible that 7 not only came into existence before 10 but continued in play long after 8 (see below, 13.7, for the representation of such situations).

13.5 Employing stratigraphic diagrams in analysis

The preceding section suggested an initial way forward in stratigraphic analysis using the configuration of the sequence diagram to define critical paths through it. The process can be aided further by adapting such diagrams in order to display information beyond the basic stratigraphic relationships. This includes illustrating the methods used in excavation and the shorthand representation of aspects of spatial data, especially boundary types, stratigraphic latitude, and descriptive criteria such as deposit types. Each will be discussed below.

First, when making use of any set of data, it is important to take into account the different **methods of data collection** which it may embody. For instance, if some work was done on a less-than-ideal watching brief and other records were derived from excavating in carefully controlled conditions, the former information will probably produce less reliable conclusions than the latter. By the same token, if some strata were recorded in section and others in plan, this may influence interpretation: tip lines in a pit may be simply distinguished in section but impossible to find in the plan record, whereas wear patterns on the surface of road metallings, seen in plan, may be invisible in section. Here, it is not a matter of different degrees of reliability, rather of finding an easy way to illustrate which data came from which source. The use of differently shaped boxes to indicate changed data-recovery conditions can ensure that the analyst compares like with like (Figure 28). The case study by Davies (1993: figs. 11.1 and 11.3) takes this whole process one stage further, distinguishing in diagrammatic form between the evidence derived from documentary sources, from the standing fabric of a structure, and from its subsurface components.

Second, when using the matrix diagram and unit description sheets, one might forget to refer to the full intricacies of the plan information. Indeed, a common criticism of the stratigraphic matrix, in its usual form, is that it presents all relationships in a 'cut-and-dried' way and fails, for instance, to exhibit **fuzziness of stratigraphic boundaries** (Adams 1992: 14). This does not seem, to me, to be the deep metaphysical problem which Adams suggests, and it must be remembered, anyway, that the strength of the diagram derives from its simplifying matters by reducing the stratigraphy to its essentials. None the less, the degree of blending at deposit edges is something usually incorporated into the plan record but rather obscured by the neat box drawn around every unit on a Harris diagram. It is relatively easy to create a notation which seeks to demonstrate this fuzziness diagrammatically. Of course, it would be necessary to systematise the degrees of blending in some way, as is done already in planning the extent of, and describing, soil layers. However, with a little ingenuity and by designating a north sign for the diagram, one could indicate the position and degree of such blending (Figure 28).

Next, it can be useful during analysis to see, at a stroke, the **degree of stratigraphic latitude** which each unit incorporates. One way of deciding which

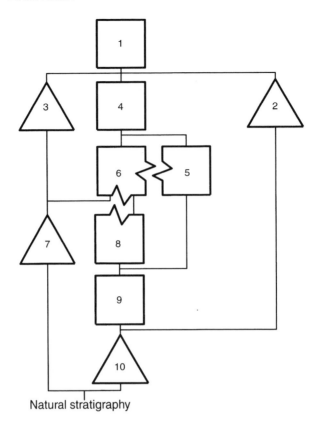

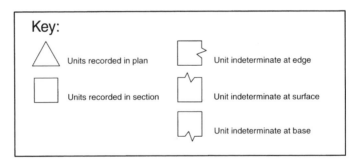

Figure 28 A Harris matrix amended to remind the analyst of different recording contexts (plan versus section record) and blending of the edges of certain strata.

entities to look at first, and which to leave for later, has already been discussed above in terms of the definition of critical paths (13.4). If one wants an alternative convenient method to display the potential correlates for any one unit, or, having made a phasing decision, to check that a proposed link is stratigraphically possible, then the 'Dalland diagram' (Dalland 1984) can also be employed.

Finally, and most important, **different types of strata** might be represented in terms of their basic physical constituents – for example types of wall coursing, of grave orientation, or of flecking within deposits – to aid analysis. Such information could be conveyed by changing the box shape, as suggested for recovery techniques. However, the descriptive information for each stratum is quite complex, especially deposits which include the nature of their basic soil matrix, types and frequency of inclusions, colour, compaction, etc. Unless one is prepared to utilise a great variety of box types, which can be cumbersome graphically and difficult to use visually, there may be a dangerous tendency to reduce such complexity to a few simple types and thus fail to make full use of the basic record. This would be especially unfortunate when trying to correlate across the sequence, where the appearance of a single diagnostic inclusion in two deposits might provide the vital clue which allows different stratigraphic strands to be fitted together.

A far better solution is to use colour on the edges of the box around each unit, employing the coding used on site. Thus a box coloured brown with grey line along its left side and across some of the top, replaced by green for the remainder, with a double cross in pencil on the right and three small black dots and one larger red dot along the base might be shorthand for '*brown* (box colour) *silt, 70%* (LHS and top) *and clay, 30%* (top), *moderately compact* (RHS), *containing frequent flecks of charcoal and occasional small fragments of tile* (base)'. Although colour would be expensive to publish, this would rarely be necessary: the objective is to have quick access to the information in visible form at the analytical stage. It should be remembered, however, that all of the techniques outlines above are a means to an end, *aides-mémoires*. There is no substitute for the careful reading of each description, close perusal of each plan and great attention to the stratigraphic position of each unit

13.6 Grouping stratigraphy

The process by which stratigraphic connections can be made across the sequence, uninfluenced by on-site notions of linkage, has been outlined above, as has the more complex procedure by which strata are blocked together vertically. As a result of such analysis, basic units will be allocated to higher-order categories. This raises the question of how such groups are to be defined – what is the point where one stops and another begins? Should there be a single type of group or a whole hierarchy of such entities? How should each be named? Or are the potential configurations so diverse that it is impossible to make useful comparisons between sites?

This issue has been approached by a variety of specialists who have produced different schemes and terminology. To some extent the differences are a function of the great variety of sites with which they are dealing, and are thus entirely legitimate. Equally, they come, in part, from merely giving a different name to the same concept (Barber 1993: 1). Thus one commentator calls a 'block' of stratigraphy just that (Lowe 1993: 23), others see it as a 'context series' (Pearson and Williams: 1993, 95) and a third as a 'sub-group' (Shepherd 1993: 3). By the same token, at the next level up, some use the concept of a phase of 'land use' (Steane 1993); others talk of 'groups' and, somewhat mysteriously, of an 'inter-group discussion' (Pearson and Williams 1993: 95); and some are prepared, in certain situations, to define full 'periods' (Shepherd 1993: 7). This profusion of terminology is to be expected, given that thoughts on such matters are at a very formative stage, and it is probably right to retain some diversity in any case, given the variety of sites and associated stratigraphic sequences, and types of analytical procedures applied to them. However, I feel that certain of these concepts embody dubious ideas about the process by which stratigraphy is grouped, hence it may be worth outlining the problems and putting forward alternatives. I hope this clears the air, rather than muddies the waters.

The three most common names for the lowest order blocks are 'text sections', 'sub-groups' and 'context series'. They are all meant to represent the next stage up from the individual unit, a group of strata which cohere closely and are unlikely to be broken apart as a result of further analysis. 'Text section', as a description of such an entity, does not seem very helpful at the outset (I say this as someone who has recommended its use previously!): it merely describes the way in which a set of data is to be presented in publication, without letting us into the secret of how we decide what is to be included in one part of a report and what excluded. The term 'sub-group' suffers from the obvious implication that its existence can only be defined satisfactorily in terms of a coherent definition of a higher-order entity, the group. However, it does have the advantage of an explicit definition – a set of units which have a 'direct stratigraphic link on a single strand' of the matrix and 'relate to a single action' in the history of the site (Shepherd 1993: 3). These two defining characteristics, which also seem to be embodied in the notion of a 'context series', will therefore be considered next.

Unfortunately the first seems to involve a misconception, that two strata on a single stratigraphic strand are, by definition, likely to link more closely together than those on different strands. In reality, two units appearing on different routes through a sequence may still be closely associated and thus need to be grouped together. To clarify this point using a sequence represented above (Figure 27), Unit 2 has more stratigraphic latitude than any other in the sequence but the interpretation that it once joined up with Unit 9 may be a cast-iron certainty given the character of the two, for example if both are fragments of a floor with very diagnostic surface design. In contrast, two successive elements such as 4 and 6, though directly linked stratigraphically, may be much less certainly related in interpretation, for example a concrete floor dated to *c.*AD 300 and an overlying, amorphous layer of dumped material mixed with a proportion of occupation debris, which could be the result of using the floor or a much later deposit of the medieval period long after the floor's demise, or a combination of these two formation processes. Thus the analyst may end up feeling fairly uncommitted on whether 4 links with 6 and 3, or belongs in a much later group with 1. Clearly the decision to block two units together, whether vertically or horizontally, is one which incorporates its spatial position and physical characteristics, and sometimes these may override simple stratigraphic relationships such as that of 'being on the same strand'.

The second part of Shepherd's definition, which talks of 'a single action', runs into another problem: How can a set of strata defined in this way be distinguished from the more basic stratigraphic unit recorded in excavation? It is the latter, after all, which many excavators describe as representing a single event – an action – in the history of the site. The notion can be rescued, perhaps, by using the concept of an 'activity' (the definition of context-series in Pearson and Williams 1993: 95). Thus a particular unit relates to a single action and will have a function ascribed to it ('occupation layer', 'pit fill', 'dump'). If it is part of a sequence of similarly interpreted actions – occupation layer 10, followed by occupation 9, then occupation 8 – these may be grouped into what I would like to call 'blocks' (the word block has the advantage of being fairly neutral in terms of any stratigraphic links or of the structure of any text, and the bonus of leading easily to the notion of blocks being built, on occasion, into higher-order entities). Thus a block constitutes a single activity taking place during the development of the site and is comprised of successive actions.

This seems a useful starting point: stratigraphic units represent 'actions' and blocks represent longer-term 'activities'. However, in using this distinction, it is important to remember four interrelated points. First, a unit may be designated as belonging to such a block, not just on the basis of its stratigraphic position and other basic characteristics, but also via deductions derived from artefact studies, micromorphology, etc. The stratigraphist endeavours to create such blocks to start off the process, but the final statement, even at this very low level, will be a product of all evidence as this becomes known. Thus, in Figure 27, one may decide initially that 'the site descriptions of 6 and 3 show that they are the same layer, a fourth-century concrete floor', but also that, 'although 4 could be a patch of dumped make-up going with 1 in the latest phase and thus of fourteenth-century date, it seems more like occupation debris mixed with churned up concrete from the underlying fourth-century floor $6 = 3$. I will therefore put it in the same block as them.' The implication here is that 'if finds analysts show later that 4 contains medieval pottery, it would not break my heart – I will happily put it with the later activity. However, if they show that we have got post-Roman pottery within 6, that really would confuse my phasing.'

Second, as implied above, although several units may be designated as being part of a particular block, they may not all belong to it with the same degree of certainty. For example, units 6, 4, 3 and 2 may be deemed part of the penultimate group; 6 and 2 may be the defining members of it, 3 probably belonging, and 4 placed there because it does not fit easily with 1 in the final group (of course, if 4 really did not fit at all with either 1 or 6 *et al.*, it should presumably be allocated to a block of its own).

Third, it is *empirically likely* that the decisions established using the basic characteristics of the units within each block will tend to be more certain. Hence the blocks thus created are less likely to be broken apart by later analysis than higher-order groupings. However, importantly, this is *not true by definition*. For example, evidence of pottery joins, or links with structural developments recorded in documentary sources, may provide a sounder basis for grouping stratigraphy than the site evidence, even at its very lowest level.

Finally, and in similar vein, the lowest-order groupings – blocks – are not always more definite and watertight than the higher-order ones, for example periods. Indeed, on occasion, things can be entirely reversed. Thus one may be absolutely certain that a set of stratigraphy all falls within a particular, broad period but remain very unsure about which units are members of which blocks, and even less sure of whether a specific unit actually joined up with an adjacent one or not. In saying that one must move across, then up, the sequence and must build from the lowest-order, interpretative elements to the highest, this does not mean that you are always passing from the more certain to the less certain. With these provisos, the concept of grouping basic actions into higher-order activities seems useful.

The above discussion brings us on to consider whether it is desirable, or even possible, to attempt to define any category above that of 'the activity'. Here I would wish to recommend that, where one can identify broad patterns of activity which cross the whole site, this should be explicitly acknowledged in the phasing structure. Hence, for present purposes, being 'site wide' defines a 'period'. Knowing that such a period exists in analysis requires that a line can be drawn across the full width of the sequence and there is an argument for *every* unit on the site, whether related to its specific characteristics or more general considerations, that it lies above or below that line. Thus no unit can belong to more than one period and, if one period can be successfully and usefully created, then every unit will belong either to it or to another period which, by definition, precedes or follows it.

This call for analysts explicitly to recognise periods where they exist is not based on abstract reasons but in relation to the character of most research design. One of the most significant questions to answer on any site concerns how widespread and coherent any particular activity might be. Thus it is important to contrast a situation in which structural development at a particular time took place across the whole of the area under investigation ('Buildings A, B and C were all knocked down and replaced immediately by D and F'), from one in which a more piecemeal process occurred ('A and B were demolished in the west, to be replaced by D and F, but C was retained in use further east'): the first situation would embody period distinctions, the second not. Of course, the smaller the extent of a site, the more likely such site-wide coherence will become. Conversely, large sites are likely to have fewer, more widespread periods (i.e. broader bands on the matrix). But then we would expect the structure of grouping to change with the width of perspective allowed by excavations of different physical extent.

If one accepts the above concept of site-wide activity of a 'period' at one end of the spectrum, and a single 'block' of basic units at the other, is there any need to define intermediate groupings? Several attempts have been made, none entirely successfully. For Pearson and Williams, such an entity is 'the group', whose defining characteristic is to come at a 'discussion point within the text' (1993: 95). Just as with the notion of a 'text section', such a concept only defers the question of definition to the next stage – how is one to decide when to insert such a discussion? Shepherd talks of these groups being 'a single land use element' (1993: 3), which is also the basis on which Steane recommends the construction of 'land use diagrams'. But how would such a concept differ from the idea of a single activity, which was put forward as the basis on which lower order 'blocks' were formed?

Rather than try to define a type between block and period with a relevance to all stratigraphic sequences, I would prefer to let each analyst decide if such are necessary in their own situation and, if so, what form they should take. Thus, on some sites, it may be possible to define only blocks whereas, on others, blocks may then group together into periods. Still other sequences may be more complex, defining blocks of all units, some of which can be amalgamated into successive 'buildings', a middle-order entity on a site with no periods which run right across it. Finally, analysis may allocate all stratigraphy to blocks but these may not all represent equally watertight groups – some could be stratigraphically narrow groups, others 'dustbin categories' containing units with great stratigraphic latitude or with uncertain phasing: the possibilities are endless. What can be maintained is that all sequences will produce blocks to allow the move from 'action' to 'activity', and that periods of site-wide activity, where such exist, should be recognised and then made explicit in structuring the sequence. Further categories must remain a function of individual circumstances.

13.7 Presenting stratigraphic interpretations diagrammatically

Having endeavoured to establish horizontal correlations between strata, made suggestions concerning formation processes and the functional interpretation of each stratum, thought about how long each may have lasted, and created a phasing structure to impose on the sequence, these decisions will have to be presented to other audiences, in the first instance those specialists who are working on different aspects of the project. To some extent, these people can work from indexes listed on computer screen: unit number cross-referenced to summarised aspects of its physical composition, functional interpretation, phasing, date and/or date range, etc. However, finds specialists may need to go further with dating information, or the more informed report reader may require extra detailed information or justification for the interpretations of the site. Their needs may be better provided for by representing decisions diagrammatically.

Thus, after establishing links across the matrix, the **strengths of correlation** can be shown by a series of lines connecting proposed contemporary units (Kobylinski 1993: fig. 4.4). Three strengths of horizontal connection (Figure 29) might be suggested:

> 'A = B' meaning that the two units originally joined up as a single entity. This would be the strongest form of statement which could be made, as in Figure 29 when destruction debris 8 is interpreted as once having physically joined up with debris 5.
>
> 'A–B' meaning that the two units have similar interpretations and were forming at roughly the same time, as with two occupation layers 9 and 2 on different parts of the same floor surface 10.
>
> 'A opposite B' meaning that the two are not strongly connected, but circumstantial evidence suggests that A is more likely to be contemporary with B than with any other unit. This is the weakest form of connection and is evident in the case of occupation deposit 7, placed opposite 9/2 and probably broadly contemporary with them, but not securely linked to the floor 10 which both of the others provably overlay.

It should be remembered in each case that the strength of link being represented does not equate in a simple way with the degree of stratigraphic latitude of the units concerned, nor with the level of the interpretation used in the argument to justify it. For example, A = B may be based on the results of some micromorphological analysis, not the basic site descriptions of the units concerned. Or A–B may be suggested by the site evidence for the process of structural development, as reconstructed in the light of some proposed correlations with documentary research and bearing in mind knowledge of contemporary carpentry practice and engineering knowledge. Obviously lines linking units across the matrix, deduced in analysis, are different in kind from the more basic relationships running up and down from unit to unit, established on site. This distinction between proven, vertical stratigraphic fact and suggested horizontal connection can be shown diagrammatically by using two colours, or by making one line thicker than the other. Better still, one can use the basic sequence diagram as an underlay and represent the suggested links across the strata on a transparent overlay.

In addition to horizontal links, the **types of interpretative unit** can be indicated diagrammatically, for example to differentiate between occupation material, construction dumps and destruction debris as an aid to the pottery analyst; or to distinguish primary from secondary fills of a cut feature for the

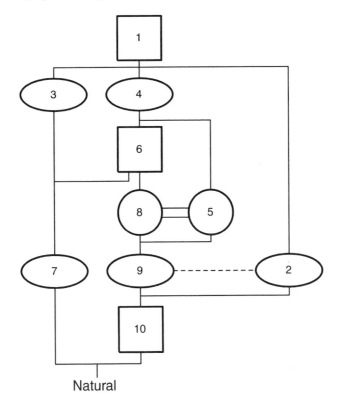

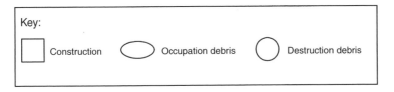

Figure 29 The box shapes in a Harris matrix amended to show interpretative types of strata, also indicating different strengths of linkage between strata.

snail specialist. Ideally, this could be done using colour coding. However, if the end product is to be widely disseminated in a final publication and cost is a factor (and when is this not the case?), then an appropriate alternative is to use differently shaped boxes, which can then be published cheaply (Figure 29; see also Paice 1991, Bibby 1993 and Hammond 1991).

Having indicated the type of unit involved, it may be possible to make explicit proposals on how long it remained in use, either until an overlying unit came into play or with respect to adjacent components of the sequence. Some suggestions might be based on site evidence, such as the character of an occupation layer formed over an extended period of time or a wall being in use with a whole series of floor surfaces; others might be derived from other information,

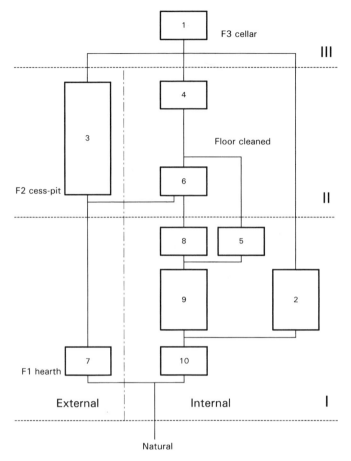

Figure 30 The Harris matrix can be 'stretched' to show relative time in diagrammatic form.

for example that obtained by pottery seriation. Carver's sequence diagram (Carver 1979b) can be particularly effective in showing longevity of both specific strata and higher-order entities such as structures or middens. Here (Figure 30), estimates of the **length of life** of each unit are represented diagrammatically by 'stretching' the length of the box enclosing the number of the appropriate stratigraphic unit. In addition, period divisions I–III and feature numbers allocated in the course of analysis have been added to the diagram, together with interpretative labels ('F1, hearth', etc.). Third, gaps in the sequence are noted and explained (the absence of build up on floor 6 whilst cess-pit F2 was in use was due to the floor being kept clean initially, though occupation layer 4 does accumulate at the end of Period II; thus if finds specialists were to find a big difference in date between 6 and 4, it would not come as a shock to the stratigraphic analyst). Finally such diagrams can be used to characterise different types of land use, for example the 'external' and 'internal' settings

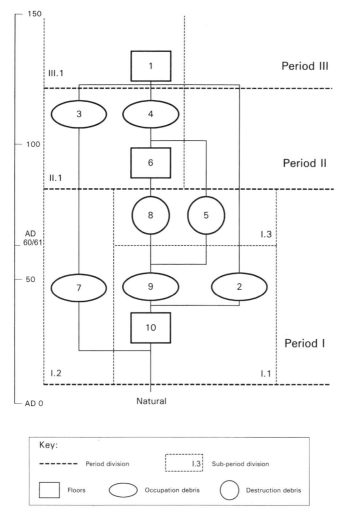

Figure 31 A Harris matrix adjusted to indicate absolute time, with phasing decisions imposed on the sequence (here period and sub-period) then added to the diagram.

noted here in Periods I and II, which no longer apply after the insertion of cellar F3 in Period III.

Finally, when the **phasing structure** for the sequence has been decided by defining higher-order units of blocks, periods or whatever, the content and extent of each of the latter can be indicated. This might be done by noting periodisation beside the sequence diagram (Brown and Muraca 1993: figs. 10.1 and 10.3) or, more usefully when the phasing structure is complicated, as a transparent overlay above it. The latter method has the added advantage of retaining the distinction between basic units and blocks of such units accompanied by suggested interpretations. Thus, in Figure 31, the sequence has been split into three periods (I–III) and the first of these in turn embodies three subdivisions (I.1: floor 10 and initial occupation 9/2; I.2: occupation debris 7, broadly contemporary with I.1; and I.3: destruction debris 8/5 marking the end of the period). I.1 and I.2 may have extended over a long period of time, hence employ elongated boxes, whereas I.3 is a short event in a thinner box. Once absolute dating evidence has been incorporated into the sequence, it is possible to set up a time scale on the left from AD0 to AD150 and to mention any relevant documented events (here AD 60/61, the date of the Boudiccan destruction of several Romano-British towns). Hence the reader can assess the relationship, if any, between such dated episodes and the sequence recovered in the field.

In this way, sequence diagrams presenting information on the nature of each deposit, its duration and its correlation with other deposits, and with absolute dating and documentary history, can summarise a wealth of interpretations at a great variety of levels and present them to different audiences in a convenient graphic form. It must be re-emphasised that decisions made during stratigraphic analysis, then represented diagrammatically, are not the final word on such things, only a means to an end. Yet they are vital to convey information to other specialists by making clear statements on what the stratigraphist considers to be the preferred interpretations at that time, on the basis of the limited but essential information available to them. They also indicate the degree of certainty which is believed to obtain when making such judgements. Clarity of argument and unequivocal expression of conclusions are needed to oil the wheels for the next stage, the integration of results from other analytical work. Diagrams allow the debate to proceed effectively, to move to more complex and conflicting matters – the stuff of archaeological research which gives individual field-workers the will to carry on, and the discipline as a whole the impetus to progress.

14

FUTURE PROSPECTS

Introduction

This book has been, first and foremost, a record of how archaeological excavations are carried out at the present time. However, in conclusion, it could be useful to suggest some ways in which this process might develop in the foreseeable future. In doing so, I am acutely aware that I will be offering many hostages to fortune and that, whilst I may get a few things 'right' (whatever that might mean in this particular context), I will certainly get the majority 'wrong' (unfortunately rather more easily defined). It is necessarily brief, as there are only so many such hostages that one individual can be expected to deliver. My general message is that it is possible to flag up some of the issues and debates which will continue to occupy, or perhaps dog, archaeological field-workers in the future. Yet the outcome of arguments which thereby arise – what they actually mean for practice in the field – is dependent on forces which not only are well beyond my own intellectual grasp, but are played out beyond the discipline itself, in the wider material context within which archaeology is practised.

In order to structure the discussion, I have employed the same broad conceptual divisions used in the opening chapter of the book. Thus intellectual matters are mentioned first (**14.1**), followed by a more lengthy consideration of technological developments both within and outside archaeology (**14.2**), and ending with some brief thoughts on the organisational, and more general social and economic, context in which archaeological excavation might take place (**14.3**). However, as also noted in Chapter 1, the secret to understanding development in excavation work, and for that matter elsewhere, is not based on what happens within each category, or even in how one defines their relative importance. It lies, rather, in understanding the complex interaction between these spheres.

14.1 Ideological factors

A quick glance at any recent book on archaeological theory will show that the perspectives employed today are radically different from those in circulation twenty-five years ago when the foundations for the present profession were being laid (compare Trigger 1989 or Hodder 1986 with any of Ucko 1995,

267

Preucel and Hodder 1996, Whitley 1998 or Johnson 1999; see also Hodder 1991 for some views on how such matters have been articulated across Europe during this time). At that time, hypothetico-deductive approaches were seen as central to the discipline, with an emphasis on research design to define projects in the field. However, even at this formative stage, much archaeological work was slow to acknowledge any theoretical dimension in its operations, and in some cases explicitly rejected the idea that there should be such a dimension.

In the last decade commentators have moved beyond processualist interpretative frameworks and, in their place, we have a sustained critique of the whole endeavour to portray the excavator as gathering data on site and then analysing them to arrive at 'scientific' conclusions. Two works by Shanks and Tilley (1987a and 1987b) were formative in developing this argument, though I think it would be fair to say that most field-workers have yet to face up to the challenges which these two authors issued. In a sense, many excavators may feel that, just as they were beginning to adjust to the idea of a progressive research agenda, the very notion itself has been rubbished, reinforcing the division between 'academic' research and 'practical' fieldwork which we had started to overcome. Hence it is only in very recent years that published works, for example Hodder 1995, have explicitly tried to link post-processual theory with practice. Here I wish to suggest that the two areas where further development might be expected in the future concern landscape archaeology and contextual studies.

One result of the post-processualist challenge has been the creation of a new approach to landscape studies, which may provide a more exciting structure for much of our fieldwork (Ucko and Layton 1999, Bender 1993). Previously the landscape had been seen by many excavators as simply the physical place where we carry out preliminary reconnaissance to 'find sites' (see Chapter 1 on defining 'the site'). In contrast, rather than being simply the environmental context for human action, it can now be portrayed as a cultural construct. As such, it is dependent on human perceptions and can only be understood by cognitive analysis. The influence of the *Annales* school (Bintliff 1991) on how such research should be conceived is already important in certain regions such as Greece (Bintliff and Sbonias 1999), and could equally be extended to other parts of the world. Some might even argue that the idea of a phenomenology of landscape (Tilley 1994) should influence how landscape projects are defined and put into operation, not just employed in the interpretation of their results. At the moment, however, such projects seem to consider the distribution of material remains in the landscape as an investigation in its own right, with its own particular ends. I find it difficult to see how these perspectives will affect the specifics of excavation methodologies.

Second, all fieldwork, but especially excavation, will need to respond to the call for contextual archaeology (Hodder 1987) to facilitate fuller social explanation. For example, gender archaeology has been virtually brought into existence in the last decade, Gero and Conkey (1991) setting a snowball rolling which has now gathered enough mass to allow the production of a reader in the subject (Hays-Gilpin and Whitley 1998). A variety of writings have brought together studies from different periods and regions (Moore and Scott 1997, Nelson 1997), whilst others have focussed on a specific aspect of society, for example Gilchrist's (1994) consideration of religious women in medieval England. What most of these studies have in common is the demand for detailed, contextualised information from excavation projects to allow similar studies to be even more effective in the future. This will require levels of resolution which the field-worker will have to work hard on site to achieve.

If we are to produce studies which integrate artefactual, ecofactual and stratigraphic analyses effectively, site formation processes in particular will have to be theorised and then investigated with greater rigour than has been the case previously. Thus whether, with Shott (1998), one characterises 'formation theory' as a general theoretical stance in its own right, or sees it only as subsisting within higher-order theoretical positions, it seems certain that we will be much occupied with integrating site deposit descriptions with the work of the micromorphologist and, for that matter, masonry or timber descriptions with the understandings of the architectural historian or carpentry specialist. Yet, even here, it is worth noting that the origins of work on deposit formation and on the analysis of standing structures antedates the development of post-processualism. Furthermore it continues to be carried out by specialists who adopt an explicitly scientific approach to archaeological research. In this sense, some of the more superficial approaches of so-called radical archaeology, setting up a straw man of 'scientism' to burn it down, may have militated against, rather than facilitated, collaboration between theory and practice.

Beyond the definition of cognitive landscapes and a call for contextual studies, the influence of post-processual ideas in excavation practice has been hard to find and, I feel, will continue to be so. Pleas to see the process of excavation as 'theatre' (Tilley 1989) have not been well received in many quarters, not least amongst professionals trying to defend archaeology against conflicting interests when managing the resource. Even if used only as a metaphor, characterising fieldwork in this way may not help one's case when competing with the site engineer or architect for more time or resources. Equally such an image is unlikely to persuade any commercial construction company to finance archaeological work beyond the bare legal minimum – the tax-avoidance schemes available to a rich property developer seem more likely to be invested in the real Arts, rather than their muddy 'counterpart'. Hence it will be some while before we see hospitality suites set up to overlook a cast of excavator-actors as they commune with the past on our archaeological sites – and a good thing too! By the same token, requests for those working on excavations to see themselves as 'experiencing' the past (Shanks 1992) have generally fallen on deaf ears, and demands for an interpretative archaeology (Thomas 1996) which are underpinned, in the end, by the same theoretical constructs seem destined for the same fate.

Such reactions might be seen by the above authors as an indictment of the untheorised nature of fieldwork due to a lack of intellectual commitment by its practitioners, or simply because the profession has sold out to Mammon. However, if one of the challenges of contemporary archaeology (Barrett 1995) is to relate new theory to old practice, then we have to look at the 'theory' that one is being told to apply. If, as I believe, much of the recent development has only very limited implications for how fieldwork is approached and carried out, then that is a significant comment on that theory, whoever is seen as setting the agenda in archaeology (Yoffee and Sherratt 1993).

Finally, in order to avoid the accusation of being an old fogey rejecting the relevance of all theory to archaeological practice, I would wish to make two points. First, post-processual, or radical, archaeology has itself been subject to much critique, raising issues about the internal consistency of its philosophical foundations, alongside adverse comments on its attempts to use these approaches when actually studying material culture in detail (see Watson 1990 or Hawes (forthcoming) for two of the more withering examples here). Second, one should note the intellectual origins of post-processualism, an archaeological offspring of the more general post-modernism which today constitutes mainstream social theory. The latter is itself closely connected to the premise that we now live in a post-Fordist, perhaps even post-capitalist, universe. If, as is argued below (14.3), this assumption does not actually correspond with the real world in which field-workers find themselves, it is not surprising that they find it hard to see their excavations as, first and foremost, performances to be watched. Nor would I expect them to want to describe the reports which they then write on the output of this work as 'novels' which essentially record just the process of discovery, from the start of digging to the end (Hodder 1989). For a start, most such discoveries do not take place with the trowel in hand anyway, but afterwards. Additionally, and more important, it is one thing to say we must put a particular excavation project in its social context, quite another to suggest that this is all, or even mostly, what one can achieve in carrying out that fieldwork.

14.2 Technical factors

Turning from the intellectual context within which research objectives are constructed to consider how technical developments will influence archaeological excavations, it seems fairly easy to project some current trends forward. There is little doubt that advances in information technology will be the key influence on archaeological fieldwork in the coming decade (see Richards 1998 for a convenient summary of the present IT position, to which the following account owes a considerable debt). Within this broad trend, I suggest that the *leitmotif* will be increased integration and accessibility of data. This will be evident at all stages of any fieldwork project, from reconnaissance and evaluation, to gathering data by excavation and analysing it, and then archiving this output and disseminating the results by various means. These discrete points in the fieldwork cycle are therefore used to structure the following discussion, cross-referenced to the earlier point in the book where the corresponding issue was first raised. However, I do not believe that these technological advances will reduce the need for intellectual endeavour in carrying out archaeological work in the field, rather the opposite, which is reassuring for those who wish to remain excited by our discipline.

When undertaking initial **reconnaissance**, we will see much more ready access to information on known sites and previous excavations (see 3.5 for earlier discussion). Much time and many resources have already been expended on the construction and validating of data-bases of existing information on sites by national statutory agencies with responsibility for managing the resource. Thus, for example, an enhanced Sites and Monuments Record (SMR), gathered on a county-by-county basis and stored by computer, can now be consulted before any fieldwork takes place in most parts of the UK. Equally the National Parks' National Archaeological Data Base (NADB) in the US allows archaeological investigations there to be made accessible through the Internet (http://www.cast.uark.edu/other/nps/nadb/). When last consulted, 240,000 reports on archaeological planning and investigation, mostly of limited circulation, were available from this source. This 'grey literature' represents a large portion of the primary information available on archeological sites in the US. The system can be queried by state, county, worktype, cultural affiliation, keyword, material, year of publication, title and author. Graphical applications make maps available as soft copy showing distributions of cultural and environmental resources across the US by state and at county levels. A similar undertaking (the OASIS project) being set up in partnership with English Heritage by the Archaeology Data Service (ADS) in the UK (http://ads.ahds.ac.uk/) will provide on-line indexing of corresponding literature here.

Although these databases were devised by agencies who are first and foremost concerned with planning for, and protecting, archaeological remains, they obviously provide a research, as much as a management, tool. Of course, when used for academic purposes, the fact that the creation of such systems was resourced by modern nation states raises issues concerning standards, data validation, and comparability across regions and national boundaries. As the papers in Larsen (1992) show, we will require solutions at a continental (in that case European) level in order to exploit their full research potential, or at a global level for other purposes, as shown by the various papers edited by Reilly and Rahtz (1992).

Perhaps the most interesting innovation here has been construction of Geographical Information Systems to manipulate and present such data. As Savage (1990) notes, early GIS development in the US took place in the context of Cultural Resource Management, to allow the integration of archaeological data and administrative information. From this Kvamme (1990), amongst others, has developed models which attempt to predict where sites will be found by taking into account fairly basic factors such as soils, climate, water and terrain. The same approach was then taken up in the Netherlands (Brandt *et al.* 1992). It is easy to see how these systems will greatly aid planning decisions, especially when dealing with large impacts on the landscape such as mineral extraction, or long linear intrusions through it such as pipelines. Thus statutory archaeological agencies will need to continue to invest in GIS development, and hopefully then to relate their work to that of cognate organisations. Most obviously, lists provided by those concerned with the protection of the natural environment (for example, Sites of Special Scientific Interest in the UK) will be linked to places with purely cultural significance. In addition, the latter will come to include a wider range of archaeological records beyond the simple SMR and thus constitute what are now termed Historic Environment Information Resources (HEIR).

However, given the simplistic character of the environmental factors being incorporated into these models, it is more difficult to see how they can enhance the study of the 'cultural landscapes' which, as mentioned above, are so central to recent theorising. Indeed, the whole concept of predictive modelling could be seen as a product of an outmoded processualism, in particular where it is underpinned by the concept of 'carrying capacity' which recent writing on archaeological theory would clearly criticise as inappropriate. Thus the role of GIS, at least in the form developed within resource management, may have limited impact as a more general research tool (but see further below).

It seems likely that a second sphere of reconnaissance, the use of aerial photographs (3.1), will continue to grow unabated. First it will remain necessary to overfly regions on successive occasions, and in different weather conditions and times of the day and year, to enhance our database. Furthermore, frenetic changes in modern agricultural regimes, evident across the globe, will mean that land use will alter at an increasing rate. Hence areas previously inaccessible (e.g. parts of former rainforest) or once registering no response (e.g. fields laid down to pasture in earlier centuries, before being disturbed by modern ploughing) may now yield up their secrets. We might hope to see greater international collaboration in this sphere and many others, for example extending the recent research between the UK air photographers and Czech archaeologists. Finally cheaper air transport, plus wider availability of satellite data independent of any national rules on overflying (for example data from Soviet 'spy' satellites, which Russia now makes commercially available over the

Internet), will ensure that we never run out of data. Initiatives are underway in the UK to make catalogues of present photographic holdings available over the Internet, and to ensure coverage of the whole country in a National Mapping Programme.

Of course, none of this increased density of coverage, sophistication of image and accessibility of material will avoid the need for human endeavour in the basic identification of features on the photographs, even with image processing (Pelfer1999). This, the critical *archaeological* activity, will continue to require local knowledge of settlement forms and features from a variety of periods, together with background understanding of settlement dynamics in those periods and experience of technical aspects of the air photographic record. However, once features have been recognised, technological development will allow more speedy and accurate plotting. For example, the development of Haigh's AERIAL programme (1991) has already aided rectification of air photographs in economic terms (Haigh and Ipson 1994). By further extending the system to allow digital terrain maps and consideration of surface topography (Haigh 1993), there will be potential to link into the more incisive approaches to landscape analysis noted previously. The hoped-for lesson, then, is that advances in IT will take some of the drudgery out of the aerial photographic work but, in the process, will increase, rather than diminish, its intellectual interest.

Having identified a site in any region, I would suggest that many of the basic principles of archaeological **evaluation** will continue as now in the short term. No doubt the hardware used in ground-based remote sensing (3.6) will be enhanced, not least because this sphere of development is promoted outside archaeology, for instance in commercial prospecting for minerals or water, or in monitoring degradation of standing buildings and other features such as oil and water pipelines. Here the greatest archaeological need will be to develop the surveillance of deep urban deposits, to parallel our relative success in the shallow, rural sites. Using geophysics in modern towns is complex, both because the upper layers are often sharply defined and difficult to penetrate whilst the lower strata embody diffuse boundaries, and because the characteristics of the whole deposit alter as a result of hydrological changes. Hence techniques such as Ground Penetrating Radar have had only limited success. Near-surface features tend to dominate and useful data are not easily obtained from underlying saturated clays. Towns have proven equally difficult for magnetometry-based systems, whilst resistive techniques require probing. Recent work at York in collaboration with electronics engineers suggests that the sort of cross-section information from the deep subsurface obtained in the mining industry using acoustic and electromagnetic techniques in borehole-to-borehole systems might be usefully applied to urban strata, and that the near-surface might be characterised by the measurement of the ground impedance with non-invasive, tomographic arrays. As is generally the case with geophysics, by applying a battery of techniques to an archaeological problem we should be able to overcome previous shortcomings.

Whether using current hardware or that still to be developed, we should also see enhanced methods of manipulating and presenting geophysical data (see the various papers in Higgins *et al.* 1996 for a synopsis of where we had reached a few years ago; Peña *et al.* 1999 for a more recent example). Archaeological data are complex and 'noisy', and these problems increase greatly when linking data sets from different types of instrument. Thus we will need to develop dedicated software and modelling techniques and to test and validate them, first against existing data, and then against new data. This will demand collaboration with those at the cutting edge of electronics engineering in order to employ even established statistical tools and graphics routines, let alone then develop and enhance them.

The need to enhance data manipulation and to evaluate it statistically will be equally important with other aspects of archaeological evaluation. As Orton (2000) shows, general developments in sophisticated approaches to statistical theory could be applied with more rigour to the records derived from the distribution of field-walking finds (3.2), digging shovel test pits to find sites (3.3), chemical signatures from topsoil (3.7) or more focussed augering (3.8) and trenching (3.9) for evaluation. Similar developments might be expected later in the excavation cycle, for example when considering various finds retrieval systems (5.6) to assess their reliability, allowing us to quantify reservations about the inferences which can be drawn from different finds groups.

Finally, whether one uses an evaluation process to help in making a decision to preserve a site *in situ* or to facilitate further excavation work (see further discussion below – 14.3), it is to be hoped that the presentation of evidence from these exercises will be greatly improved. If the aim is to facilitate urban planning by guiding the design of appropriate briefs for projects with archaeological impact, we will need urban deposit models which are closer to the real characteristics and properties of material below ground. Critically, this information must be provided in a way which is accessible not only to archaeologists but also to engineers, architects and others from commercial organisations involved in urban redevelopment. Here we will need to build on the sort of work done by Miller (1996) on the deeply stratified deposits within the City of York (3.10).

Alternatively, if the objective of evaluation is to facilitate further research, the 'grey literature' which results from these preliminary studies can be made accessible to other archaeologists using IT developments, as noted already. In addition, techniques are being developed which can draw together different evaluation data sets to allow the director of a research project to visualise diverse evidence in an integrated way. For example work by Richards (1996) on the early medieval site at Cottam on the Yorkshire Wolds employed a GIS using

ARC/INFO to overlay data concerning the distribution of metal artefacts recovered by metal detectorists on those from aerial photographic coverage, finds recovered in field-walking, magnetometry and resistivity survey, and limited trial excavations. The ability to consider data sets in combination in this way, despite recovering each at different levels of resolution, will be a significant aid when designing a coherent research strategy were one to carry out major excavations at the site. Even these preliminary results can be set beside other, more wide-ranging evidence, for example that of crop marks and of the geographical extent of the manor of Cottam as indicated by the Domesday Book. This will aid regional research into Anglo-Saxon settlements in Northumbria.

Moving on to the issue of full-scale **site recording** following evaluation, some future trends will be generated from outside the discipline, but many purely from within. Thus it seems likely that any new approaches to initial preparations such as site clearance (5.1), and other practical issues which arise during excavation work such as spoil removal (5.3), shoring (5.4) and dewatering (5.5), will derive from the wider context of the construction industry, in the hands of non-archaeologists. No doubt the plant used will become bigger and quicker, partly because the scale of modern development in general demands its continuing improvement, and partly because archaeologists will be set increasingly tight deadlines for the completion of their work. Critically, however, archaeological decision-making itself will not become more mechanised. How it is decided, during clearance, where 'the archaeology' starts and thus machines must stop, will still be a complex product of the team's archaeological experience, the project's research objectives, and the available resources. In short it will remain the difficult intellectual and practical exercise which it is today.

When it comes to the records generated by excavations as a whole, it seems almost certain that computer storage (10.2) will take over completely from paper (Plate 35). Today a few projects already record directly onto a machine, though many others produce paper records which are later converted to computer storage. These positions will reverse quite quickly, even in more inaccessible parts of the world, as laptop computers become relatively cheaper and allow much greater storage facilities, and can therefore be used directly on site, or in conjunction with hand-held instruments allocated to each excavator (Ryan *et al.* 1999). In essence, then, proforma will be on screen, not pre-printed (6.4). More importantly, we will see further development of programs to check the internal consistency of that record while on site. However, the need for a structured approach will remain, or rather increase, with computerisation (although if excavators wish to retain a preference for note taking, and even sketching in place of accurate planning, this could also be accommodated – Ancona *et al.* 1999). In addition we will still need to make decisions about when the initial description is to be produced (6.1) and how labelling of stratigraphic units will take place (6.2), and to provide an explicit definition of the recording process (6.3).

Plate 35 An early example of recording context data directly onto computer in the field, from the 1986 fieldwork season of the Heslerton Parish Project. In the subsequent decade such procedures became increasingly common, though even now are by no means all pervasive.

The main challenge here will be to avoid allowing such computer programs to be 'fossilised'. In part this is a practical problem, trying to ensure that, in the rush to get work done and perhaps in competition with other commercial units, one does not take the easy option of just reusing the software which worked on the last project, and more or less fits the new one (see 14.3 below). However, underlying this is a more difficult intellectual problem – how do we balance the need to achieve consistency and comparability between the records produced by different projects, which then facilitates research across a region, with the demand to relate recording systems to individual research objectives and site specific conditions? Ultimately this becomes an issue of the level of generality at which any one research agenda is set.

Concerning particular aspects of the site record, it seems to me that the stratigraphic and spatial components will undergo the most substantial changes. Within the first sphere, the need for intellectual clarity on the different types of stratigraphic relationship which we might record (9.1) will remain, but graphical representation (9.2) will be enhanced. Various programs have already been created to store stratigraphic information, check its internal consistency, and draw up Harris matrices automatically (see various papers by Boast and Chapman, Desachy and Djindajian, and Herzog and Scollar in Lockyear and

Rahtz 1991). In addition, the Bonn Archaeological Software package, developed under the auspices of Irwin Scollar, and authored, in its latest version, by Hundack, Mutzel, Pouchkarev and Thome, seeks to allow efficient drawing up of the diagrams. It can be accessed at http://www.mpi-sb.mpg.de/~arche/. In similar vein, Nick Ryan offers gnet as a general purpose editor/browser for directed graphs on his website (http://www.cs.ukc.ac.uk/people/staff/nsr/arch/gnet/). This can be used as a tool for visualising archaeological stratigraphy, though is equally suited to a wide range of other applications.

The big problem with development up to this point is that such packages assume that stratigraphic relationships have been determined in some way or another. They then provide a speedy method of flagging up any impossible relationships and drawing the resulting matrix. However, as discussed earlier (9.3), only plan overlays can provide a proper system for calculating those relationships in a consistent way in the first place. Thus it is only when all plans are digitised that we can truly imitate the manual system by calling up two plans on the screen and seeing whether they overlap. Even here, although one might define such overlap mathematically, the calculation of stratigraphic relationships will not be completely automatic – we will still need a human eye, backed up by a human brain, to decide on what degree of overlap constitutes a proven relationship. Furthermore, this decision will not just depend on the definition of a measurement ('If the peripheries of two units overlap by at least 20mm, then assume one is later than the other'). One must also take into account two other factors: the type of unit concerned (a 20mm overlap between two mortar floors with exact edges may be considered certain, the same overlap between two discontinuous occupation layers with nebulous edges much less so); and the features to which they relate (for example when dealing with the fills of bell-shaped pits, or masonry underpinning added to the foundations of an earlier wall, which is thus stratigraphically later, but physically beneath, the main feature).

Both to aid stratigraphic calculations, as noted above, and for more general speed and accuracy, we will continue to see big changes to the form of spatial record derived from archaeological sites. The creation of the 'drawn record' has already been greatly enhanced in recent years by the use of sophisticated electronic surveying instruments (see, for example, Messika 1999) and it seems certain that grid pegs (5.2), plus drawing frames, tapes and pencils (8.3), will soon be a thing of the past. In addition, we will see better ways of storing spatial information so that, for example, when we decide to measure-in a particular type of find (8.6), individual co-ordinate points can be automatically downloaded and viewed in the field, and perhaps overlain by other information such as the distribution of features defined by geophysical prospection. The speed with which any patterns become available should allow the field-worker to decide whether to continue working in this detailed way on site, and to be more fluid in general when changing recording strategies in the course of the work.

However before those, like myself, with limited graphics skills get too excited, the really difficult decisions which any project faces will remain. We must still tackle the intellectual problem of how much detail to draw and why this should be done for a given set of research objectives, together with the practical issues of defining conventions (8.1), deciding when drawing should happen (8.2) and then archiving records in a consistent way to allow their preservation and accessibility in the long term. Underlying these approaches to drawing, we will need to remain clear on the advantages and disadvantages of changing levels of resolution in recording in the course of excavation, which allows one to be responsive to different conditions on the ground, but limits comparability through the sequence.

Another important development in this sphere is visible on the horizon, the convergence of the drawn and photographic records. Here cheap digital photography seems destined to have a huge impact (see Toca and Lavín 1999 for a small beginning). Soon such techniques might allow us to take images on site and manipulate them as required, for example by draping surface details of deposits onto outlines of their peripheries recorded by an EDM. Yet each project will still need to construct an explicit policy on photography in order to guarantee consistency (7.1) and to ensure that the hardware and software storage facilities which they employ give the levels of resolution which their research demands. In addition, regularly updated, digitised images downloaded to websites will be an effective way to communicate with those wishing to see work in progress and to view it from a variety of chosen angles. This would no doubt be welcomed by those who see the 'story' of the excavation as the main point of the work, but one does not have to be an inveterate postprocessualist to understand the advantages of publicising a project in this way to a great variety of audiences.

Finally, as noted previously, it is to be hoped that the influence of interdisciplinary work will enhance the purely descriptive components of the site record, particularly as we move away from the notion that excavations should be designed to rescue data for their own sake and towards the idea that the record generated must be a useful research tool for both archaeologists and others beyond the immediate discipline. Thus the soil micromorphologist will enhance our approach to deposit descriptions (10.4–10.8), and perhaps a tighter definition of extended soil sampling strategies will encourage sponsors to allocate more resources to the dissection of a larger number of critical deposits offsite in laboratory conditions, not just the present emphasis on human cremations. Corresponding changes might be expected to how we record buildings (11.1), timber (11.2) and skeletons (11.3) by responding to the interests, and employing the techniques and expertise, of architectural historians, specialists in the use and reuse of timber, and those expert in human pathology.

Turning next to **data manipulation** after excavation, there is a great need to sort out the concepts used in stratigraphic analysis – a glance at Chapter 13 shows just how far we have to go here in order to match the systematisation which has been developed in the production of the site record. For the most part what is needed is intellectual clarity in defining concepts and then labelling them. However, development of computer programs will then enhance the speed with which such analysis takes place, and in the process alert us to a wider range of possible interpretations. Two areas of development seem likely to be especially significant – data integration, and the recognition of spatial patterning.

Thus such programs will not only allow more effective manipulation of each type of data, but will provide links between different aspects of the record. Ryan (1992) provides an early example of an object-orientated data-base which aims to manage the variety and complexity of archaeological data in an integrated way. Andresen and Madsen (1996) have tried to take this one step further with their Integrated Database for Excavation Analysis (IDEA). As such packages are tested, then refined, we will be able to relate artefact studies such as ceramic typologies to stratigraphic work, and ecofact studies such as animal bone fragmentation indices to activity areas defined by the structural record. Of course, this analysis will be effective only if we have developed our understanding of the processes of redeposition and of deposit status more fully than is presently the case.

Finally, concerning integration of the spatial record, GIS have helped archaeologists to move away from flat file data-bases of individual sites to a consideration of landscapes (Plate 36). Our site data can now be manipulated and presented in terms of arcs and polygons, and investigated in terms of inter-visibility, rather than remaining just points in the landscape. Perhaps under the influence of the new theorising on landscape perspectives noted previously (14.1), the need to study cultural landscapes has been acknowledged by IT specialists (Boaz and Uleberg 1995). This has led, in turn, to a greater concentration on human perceptions of the landscape, as seen with the use of viewshed analysis in northern Mull (Ruggles *et al.* 1993) or cognitive analysis of the location of rock art in Scotland (Gaffney *et al.* 1995). Work by Zubrow (1994) studying Iroquois longhouse settlement patterns shows that the message is now being taken up in the US, moving beyond the use of GIS for purely management purposes.

Much less common in these new approaches to the integrated manipulation of spatial and descriptive data are dedicated studies at the intra-site level. A consideration of burial sites, as seen with an Iron Age cemetery in Murcia, Spain (Quesada *et al.* 1995), provides an obvious way forward here. In addition two Mesolithic sites in the Alps (Vullo *et al.* 1999) show interestingly different patterning in their artefact distributions, with possible implications for seasonality. In the same way, the Romano-British site at Shepton Mallett (Biswell *et al.* 1995) demonstrates the use of artefact scatters to periodise the site and elucidate discard behaviour and activity areas. These authors then seek to show

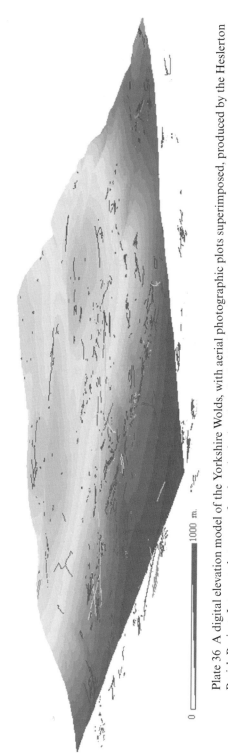

Plate 36 A digital elevation model of the Yorkshire Wolds, with aerial photographic plots superimposed, produced by the Heslerton Parish Project. Integrated storage of archaeological and geological information can be used both to manage the archaeological resource and to structure its academic investigation.

0   1000 m.

how these patterns can be linked internally to those of the structures and top-ographical features. Thus we already have some of the technology to make significant advances. However, the latter paper also offers a 'cautionary tale' of some of the problems of using GIS with salvage data, notably the way in which a lack of explicit and consistently applied sampling strategies on site will limit our interpretation of apparently blank areas. Even if this problem is solved, I feel we will still lack sufficient clarity on site formation processes and an under-standing of how these relate to finds distributions. We will be able move from finding patterning in the site record to social interpretation only when this is in place.

Next we come to the issue of **archiving** the output from excavations. Pressure on space, both physical and digital, when set beside the increased need for data accessibility by diverse interested parties, already presents important chal-lenges to our storage of archaeological archives and this will increase into the future. At the moment, paper archives are often stored by the excavation unit which produced them. If we are serious about the results of such work being available for future research, then this will have to be regularised. At one level, the solutions are not difficult to find. Most groups of artefacts can be stored in conditions which are openly acknowledged and not difficult to reproduce. More unusual finds, for example those made from organic materials, can be catered for on an individual basis. Finally, studies of degradation in stored soil samples should be able to define their shelf-life and thus allow us to decide on their fate in an equally informed way. Hence, although there is still the strug-gle to ensure that such facilities are made available, and no doubt over who should pay for this, the technical aspects of the resources which we should be fighting for either are known, or can be found out reasonably easily.

Rather more difficult will be material held as a digital archive and this will become even more problematical when the latter, as indicated above, increasingly involves the whole of the descriptive, photographic, spatial and stratigraphic record. Hence preservation of digital data is as significant for future research as the preservation of conventional finds and paper archives. The best solutions here will involve their storage and curation in an archive facility allowing remote access, with all holdings indexed to a consistent stan-dard to facilitate this. A good example of how the argument might go in the UK is apparent from the document recently issued by the ADS at http://ads.ahds.ac.uk/project/goodguides/excavation/. Their Guide to Good Practice in Excavation provides guidelines for those curating the resource, commissioning archaeological work, and carrying it out, not just for organisa-tions traditionally identified as archive repositories such as museums and government agencies. It supplies information on the best way to prepare and deposit digital material safely in an archive facility for future use. The guide also offers recommendations for the creation of a computerised index of archives, whether digital or not and, in the process, will no doubt stimulate debate on the development of a national digital archiving policy. Central to this strategy is short-term backing-up, refreshment, storage and documentation of data, coupled with data migration in the longer term. A second series of guides, on Managing Digital Collections, is concerned with the preservation of a range of other digital archives (http://ads.ahds.ac.uk/project/policy.html).

The Digital Archiving Pilot Project for Excavation Records (DAPPER: http://ads.ahds.ac.uk/newsletter/issue6.html#dapper), undertaken recently by the ADS, provides a further indication of future development. It aims to demonstrate the viability of the concept of digital excavation archives in order to inform the development of best practice in this emerging sphere. To do so, it makes available material from excavations at the Royal Opera House, carried out by the Museum of London Archaeology Service, and work at Eynsham Abbey undertaken by the Oxford Archaeological Unit. These projects were chosen because they were at their dissemination stage; had large, but quite different, digital archives to deposit; and contained raw data to which a community of scholars would want access. When the preliminary work has been evaluated, it should be possible to provide more informed guidance on the future structure of accessible digital archives.

Finally we come to **dissemination** of the results of analysis. The impact of new information technology is probably at its greatest, and most unpredictable, here. As noted by the editor in a recent issue of the journal *Internet Archaeology*, the possibilities raised form 'a microcosm of the debates taking place within archaeology everywhere – how can we better communicate our work to others, how can we represent the landscapes within which we work, how can we be multi-vocal and include a range of interpretations, viewpoints, and positions, as well as offer up our raw data rather than a single synthesis?' (Winters 1999). It seems likely that two particular spheres will be transformed – our access to underlying archives, as noted in the preceding paragraph, and second the very way in which we 'read' reports. Thus the detail which can be made available on-line will increase greatly, thereby blurring the previously central distinction between the formally published evidence and its interpretation, and the basic data beneath this held in archive. Second, it may no longer be necessary to read reports in a linear fashion. The reader will be given much more choice in how they approach the site, in particular the order in which they consider the evidence and in how much and how often they delve below the surface to test the validity of any conclusions.

Having taken a small step in some of these directions in the course of the 1980s, for example in the use of microfiche appendices containing detailed archive reports to accompany hardcopy publications, we have recently seen a further advance with site publication using either CD-ROM, on-line journals, or websites dedicated to particular projects. Some of the problems in these developments are already becoming apparent. CD-ROM publications might become inaccessible owing to changes in the hardware or software. For example, a reviewer discussing the CD-ROM *Excavating Occaneechi Town: Archaeology of an Eighteenth-Century Indian Village in North Carolina* (Bateman 1999) found that material written using the now outmoded technology of Windows 3.1 created teething problems when used with Windows 98. Clearly the onus here is on publishers to help their customers. In this case, the University of North Carolina Press offered a point of contact which provided a downloadable patch to solve the problem of mute video clips, which brought some of the best elements of the CD to life again. The difficulty lies in how one overcomes these problems in the longer term, as commercial publishers go out of business or are taken over by bigger brothers. Correspondingly, the actual CD may be equally transient. Discs have a shelf-life of only fifty years, and the hardware to read them may disappear more rapidly.

Equally writing reports to be published on either CD-ROM or the on-line journal/website will require new skills. For example, the report by Wickham-Jones (1999) of a Mesolithic site near Crail in Scotland started life as a traditional publication. She expected it simply to convert into an acceptable HTML form to allow dissemination through the journal *Internet Archaeology*. However, presenting the report in this new context required time-consuming processes of restructuring and re-editing. She concluded that it might have been easier to have started the whole thing again, rather than to work away from an inappropriate foundation. Clearly, if we are to make full use of the medium as a vibrant dissemination mechanism, we will need to acknowledge that it is different from the traditional report, because it serves different needs, and perhaps different audiences.

Websites can provide not only a source of newly recovered information, but also a context in which interested parties might discuss the findings. In order to do this, they obviously have to be internally organised for ease of navigation. Such sites have already become so numerous that they have created the need for indexes to web-based resources in archaeology. New ones still need to be accessible to potentially interested parties using either general or dedicated archaeological search engines. Gray and Walford (1999) suggest a need for 'structured site descriptions' defining particular items and their attributes (e.g. rubbish pits and their size or dates), which can be used to interrogate a great variety of sites. Once again we see the creative tension between systematisation of information, use of keywords, etc., and the demand that readers should be able to consume 'the text' in their own terms.

Further problems can be expected from the instant accessibility of the website. The fact that results can be made available much more speedily than before should obviously be welcomed. However, the status of many conclusions is likely to be only provisional, just as with the season-by-season 'interim reports' which some long-term excavation projects used to write for period or regional journals. Hence authors will either have to be guarded in their conclusions, to make it clear to the reader that interpretations may change in the future (though this is surely clear to most already), or have to be content to publish mainly undigested (and perhaps for some readers fairly indigestible) data. More generally, quality control of the data itself and of structured archives will remain an important issue, though one which the demand for consistent and explicit meta-data (Wise and Miller 1997) in relation to each report will go some way to solve.

One sphere which sees new approaches to information technology at their most creative, and seems destined to have the most lasting impact on our ability to communicate archaeological findings to a wider audience, concerns not the written word but the use of images. A good example of what is possible at the landscape level comes from work at Gardom's Edge in the Derbyshire Peak District, UK (Edmonds and McElearney 1999). Here the broad principle that different groups and individuals will need to access the output of the project in different ways is applied equally to the photographic record. Use of a Virtual Reality model allows viewers to change their viewpoint and to zoom in and out of images interactively. In addition, 'fuzzy viewsheds' and 'fly throughs' (admittedly still on a preordained path) give them a greater sense of reality, of what it actually meant to move through these landscapes. Such techniques have a clear resonance with new approaches to landscape archaeology in general.

Visualisation at the intra-site level also seems set to make giant strides in the near future. Originally developed as three-dimensional modelling (Reilly 1992), it then required huge computer time and so was dependent on more general hardware development. A good example of what was possible came from the modelling of the temple precinct at the Roman town of Bath using a Divided Object-space Ray-casting Algorithm (Woodwark 1991). This project demonstrated two things very clearly – the impact which reconstruction can have on archaeological interpretation and communication, and the commitment of those with IT interests to mnemonics (DORA here can be set beside OASIS, HEIR, AERIAL, IDEA and DAPPER mentioned previously, the second of these acronyms seemingly specifically designed to allow the originators to then make information available over the Internet in a package which can be called HEIRNET; I presume this is a spirited, and generally effective, attempt to counter criticisms that computer specialists lead humourless lives!). DORA has generated an offspring which applied similar techniques to the whole civic baths, but of course retained the humour (Daughter Of DOra – DODO).

Such modelling techniques are most effective when applied to above-ground, symmetrical buildings. Hence they have been used mostly for monumental Roman structures and medieval ecclesiastical buildings. More recently the emphasis has been on surface models, presenting a building as a series of two-dimensional flat surfaces rendered or lit in particular ways, especially useful for both research and resource management. Ray tracing has allowed more realistic creation of shadows, for example to show lighting in the Sacred Way, Athens

(Cornforth *et al.* 1992), or the effects of dust and smoke in Maltese tombs (Chalmers *et al.* 1995).

Mostly these reconstructions are relevant to organisations who have the graphics skills to exploit technical developments fully, not least because many younger viewers demand sophisticated images to retain their interest when set beside materials available to them elsewhere, whether as computer games or educational packages. None the less, archaeology is rising to this challenge, and displays of findings from excavations in progress have become an integral, and visually effective, part of most programmes presenting archaeology on television. In the process, these programmes have shown the provisional nature of such reconstruction, and helped their audience understand the process of archaeological reasoning which goes into creating them. In the future, further enhancement of desktop CAD systems will allow such work to come increasingly within the range of even small archaeological organisations.

A second sphere in which the results of graphics work can have a considerable impact is that of the museum display. A good example concerns the creation of a model of the Egyptian tomb of Sen-nedjem at Deir el-Medina using Virtual Reality Modeling Language (Terras 1999), which aimed to give context to associated finds held in the Egyptian gallery of the Kelvingrove Art Gallery and Museum, Glasgow. The author went through a process of contextualising the problem, design, initial modelling, refinement, testing and evaluation and the result allowed this structure to be made accessible to a variety of audiences. In the process, it reinforced the message derived from more traditional archaeological reconstructions, that these models are an excellent mechanism for pointing out what we do not know, either because the evidence does not survive or, more usefully, because we did not record in a particular way in the field (and thus might do so given a second chance in the future).

However, even with effective visualisations, some problems will continue to arise. For the Sen-nedjem tomb, insufficient development of the user interface meant that it was not sufficiently intuitive, interactive and informative to the viewer. Hence, in the event, the model was not used in the museum display. Furthermore, even if it had been, the creator of the model acknowledges that such a form of communication could never be all things to all people – some of the hoped-for learning outcomes required other approaches and mechanisms. Finally, at a more general level, the apparent solidity of the model, its being, virtually, an interpretation set in stone, may not sit easily beside the idea that there may be a multiplicity of pasts which we might present (Ryan 1996).

Personally I do not feel that this last point is a major problem. Once the shaky intellectual foundations of much post-processual writing on this topic are recognised, the issue is no different from that which comes with any attempted reconstruction, and indeed all archaeological interpretation. The archaeologist has a duty to ensure that the model fits the known facts, and that the viewer realises that it is only one view of how things might have worked.

Indeed, in the case of the Sen-nedjem tomb, one reason for not using the model straight away in the museum was that the user could not differentiate between areas based on archaeological evidence and those devised by the model's creator. As long as we, like those museum staff, are aware of our responsibilities, such reconstructions are just the sort of exercise that is likely to raise both the fact of debate, and its level, on what the tomb, or whatever, really looked like. Thus they are to be welcomed, not worried about.

More generally, it has been argued (Gaffney and Exon 1999) that making raw data available alongside higher-order interpretation, whether in text or as images, may well start to transform the relationship between the producer/author and the consumer/reader. This may be a welcome development, but will not be an automatic process. As Hodder (1999) notes, we may manage to cultivate networking between equals and so circumvent hierarchies. However, things could go the other way, with those trained in navigating their way around the data able to reinforce their powerful social position. The technology, in itself, does not dictate democratisation or the opposite: it only works in the hands of people, and they operate in a social context.

Second, to open up access and interpretation, rather than reinforce elitism, it will be necessary to increase the availability of computer hardware and to provide people with the skills to understand the data to which they now have access. For the immediate future, projects will have to use websites in addition to, rather than instead of, other mechanisms such as the more traditional displays and site tours. Having said that, if we are committed to the goal of accessibility for all, it may be quite easy to allow a new website visitor to understand the information presented to them. Hodder's idea (1999) of making the 'crib sheet' used to train site staff to establish appropriate deposit descriptions available on the website to aid such comprehension is a good example here. In addition, the same data sets can be wrapped under different 'front-ends' to facilitate access and usability by different audiences. This could include using digital excavation archives in Internet-based modules to facilitate teaching of archaeology, the final general area to be discussed here.

As noted above, when these new systems, standards and facilities are in place, developments in information technology can be used not only to tell people about archaeological findings, but to enhance programs which aim to teach them about archaeological fieldwork. Both would-be practitioners and just vaguely interested parties can already develop their understanding of sampling strategies by working, on screen, in the imaginary landscape of the humourously named Fugawiland (Price and Gebauer 1990), choosing which sites to excavate on the basis of a given set of research questions. At a more detailed level, an excavation simulation such as SYGRAF (Wheatley 1991), now updated and augmented in its offspring WINDIG by Sally Biswell and Sebastian Rahtz, can introduce them to the concept of recovery levels in excavation, working within budgets, deposit status and its effect on finds interpretation, and spatial analysis.

These sorts of detailed experiences must be set beside more general packages such as those developed from the UK's Teaching and Learning Technology Programme which introduce different periods of the past and explain techniques of archaeological, impact assessment, remote-sensing or faunal analysis. Present initiatives are seeking to extend this work by creating further teaching packages from holdings of digital archives. If properly resourced, these projects will allow us to do our duty by our various publics by informing them about findings and teaching them about how archaeology works. As a happy by-product, they should help to ensure that we have a larger proportion of the community on our side when arguing for increased resources for our discipline in competition with other demands.

14.3 Organisational factors

Near the outset of this book, I noted that the applicability and effectiveness of all technical development in archaeology depends on the particular way(s) in which archaeological labour is deployed, and the general context in which it operates. This point applies equally to the various potential improvements noted above. However, when it comes to predicting how the organisation of fieldwork may alter in the future, we are dealing with a sphere which already varies greatly across the world, and where any changes are dependent on forces almost completely external to archaeology. As outcomes are a product of struggles played out between groups of people with diverse and conflicting interests, they become impossible even to guess at. What I wish to do, in the place of prediction, is to finish on a more polemical note by giving my views on two of these contested areas – conservation versus investigation, and employer versus employee.

One debate which seems likely to continue bubbling in the course of the next decade, as it has for more than a century before this, concerns whether the primary duty of the field archaeologist is to investigate the past in the present or to protect and conserve its material remains for the future. In Britain, and much of Europe, the influence of environmental impact legislation, with its emphasis on mitigation strategies, in the 1990s has seen preservation *in situ* as the first option when responding to modern development. In the countryside this may mean diverting the route of a proposed development. In a town, it is more likely to involve creative engineering solutions for new building, for example by rafting above the archaeological deposit or using piling with minimal impact on the strata below. The effectiveness of the latter, urban measures in the longer term have been much debated, particularly in relation to the protection of deeply stratified, organic remains (Oxley 1998). Ultimately this is a question of technology coupled with political argument. If we win the debate over archaeological value, then either development will not be allowed, or the engineers will find a way forward.

Others, however, have questioned the preservation principle itself, arguing that the policy of non- investigation may be the death knell for archaeology as a vibrant discipline. This then leads to the alternative approach, as seen in the US and in many other countries beyond Europe, of investigating sites ahead of development. The rationale here is that the archaeological remains in question are of significance to the community, or at least some groups within it, and therefore must be rescued from oblivion. The use of the concept of significance, as opposed to value, is important here. It may be possible to suggest that a hidden, protected site has archaeological *value*, or at least potential value, even where there are no plans to exploit that potential. Whereas it is rather more difficult (though by no means impossible) to portray the same, invisible deposits as *significant* to sections of modern society.

In principle, I personally favour the second argument for intervention. If evaluation shows that a site is truly exciting, yet the reaction is to stop all work, our public is likely to be confused and our workforce increasingly demoralised. The general population support archaeology because it produces new knowledge about the past and this will be pushed into the background in the long term if preservation always comes first. Interested members of that public will want to know why, if a site is as interesting as we say, we refuse to dig more of it. Equally most practitioners came into archaeology because they wanted to be part of finding out original and significant facts out about previous societies. With the preservation option, the field-worker can only be pleased that evaluation has led to full excavation, and that their contract has therefore been extended, when the site concerned is considered to be of limited importance. Excavating only the second-rate sites is not a good way to stimulate a committed and creative workforce.

More important than my thoughts on this specific debate, I feel that the simple dichotomy put forward above misses what should be the central point underlying both positions. The archaeological value of a hidden site requiring *in situ* preservation derives from its research potential. Equally, the investigation of significant sites ahead of development is based on the fact that some communities see in them a real link with their own past which further investigation could elaborate. Thus, essentially, whether archaeological importance is defined in terms of significance or value, and whether it is decided to intervene now or to protect for the future, the judgement should be based on the academic importance of the archaeology under consideration. The real issue then becomes the question of who is to set this agenda, and at what level. This will define which groups have the incentive to ensure that research, rather than the short-term requirements of the modern world, drives our reaction to proposed development. In coming years, we will see competition for ownership of the past expressed in terms of international/continental, national, regional and local/ community agendas. How this debate pans out, itself an expression of the clash between forces for globalisation and demands for more local rights and inputs, will have radical implications for what our fieldwork is trying to achieve and thus how it is carried out.

The second area of debate concerns the economic position of excavators, in particular their conditions of employment. To enter the argument, it is important to note first that I do not expect the essential context in which most archaeological fieldwork takes place to change in the coming years – professional excavators are here to stay. Given the economic system within which we work, this means that they will be employed as wage labour. Furthermore, I find no evidence to suggest that we live in the type of new material conditions envisaged by the many post-modern writers who have influenced archaeological theory (above 14.1): a post-Fordist world of fragmented production processes and individualised consumer choice does not, and will not, exist. Hence most future excavators will continue to find themselves operating in a collective context, in teams or crews whose work-place, whether during excavation or in the process of post-excavation analysis, is separate from their houses. Very few will be dispersed, isolated individuals working from home, linked only by a modem, mobile telephone and conference networking. For that matter, I expect most archaeologists to inhabit the same sorts of housing estates and to shop at the same, increasingly large, edge-of-town hypermarkets as the rest of wage labour, not living a rural idyll, in a picturesque cottage serviced by the village shop.

Excavators, as wage labour, will therefore continue to experience a series of conflicts, whether open or hidden, in the course of their work. There will be severe pressure to lower standards of data gathering on site, together with attempts to ignore, or at least circumvent, adequate safety measures. In addition, in trying to get work done on time and to keep one's line manager happy, not least in the hope that one's own contract will be extended at the end of the project, there will be a temptation to take refuge in using tried and trusted recording methods, rather than developing innovative ones. Indeed, it might even be argued that we have already seen some such impacts in recent years. For example, the approach to systematised deposit description put forward in this manual was set out, in essence, in the late 1970s/early 1980s in the UK, along with the basis of the accompanying recording forms and organised approaches to recording stratigraphic relationships. These were almost entirely a product of the newly professionalised workforce. In the 1990s, when fieldworkers in this country have been subject to considerable pressures through the advent of developer funding and competitive tendering, I believe that methodological progress has been noticeably slower and, where it has occurred, is more likely to derive from a research project than from a commercial context. Paradoxically, at the same time as originality may be suppressed in the future, archaeological projects will be undertaken in the context of rapidly changing modern development, with objectives and timetables altered at ever increasing rates. Hence innovative responses will be even more necessary than before.

Financial resources for archaeology will always be tight, because we live in a world based on the need to make profits. Even where site work is adequately resourced, we will still need to struggle to support essential post-excavation analysis, to create proper archives and to make them accessible to wider audiences in the innovative ways mentioned above. The same will be even more true if we are to develop fully collaborative research with other disciplines. To take a parochial example, the UK has recently seen a drawing together of archaeologists working with below-ground strata and those investigating standing buildings. Many aspects of fieldwork methodology, for instance the concept of evaluation, is paralleled in both spheres, backed up by guidance from the government which applies the same broad principles to each. This is clearly to be welcomed, and one would hope the process will be extended to draw together field archaeologists, conservation architects and art historians. However, the resources to carry out interdisciplinary work will not be handed to us on a plate.

The above, rather bleak picture leads to a final, contentious point about who we turn to in trying to fight for more support for archaeology. Our own battles have their parallels in every other working context today beyond our particular discipline. It is essential that we recognise this larger sphere and identify with those engaged in campaigning for similar rights elsewhere. Otherwise, the unwanted alternative will be for each group to see all others as being in competition for the same pot of scarce resources, rather than having common ground to demand more resources for the whole of our endeavours. Hence, for example, interdisciplinary collaboration will be replaced with competition, with defending one's own corner at all costs. Ultimately, I believe that opening up ourselves and our discipline to these wider struggles will be more effective, in getting decent resources for the work, and wages and conditions for our excavators, than turning inwards. Winning more support for excavation in this direct way will also give archaeologists the confidence to continue methodological development. The alternative, introverted policy would mean excavators seeking to identify with the fellow, well-meaning archaeologist who employs them. This could be done only on the basis that the latter managerial intermediaries have real influence on those at the top of society, and that 'we all belong to one community' with exactly the same objectives. I do not believe either of these assumptions to be valid. Which way this argument goes will depend on political debate, but the outcomes will be of huge significance for our discipline in the coming decades. I am on the side of those seeking to develop real collaboration across the base of the subject. So I await the results of the debate with more than just abstract, 'academic' interest.

BIBLIOGRAPHY

Adams, M. (1992) 'Stratigraphy after Harris: some questions', in Steane 1992b: 13–16.

Adams, M. and Reeve, J. (1987) 'Excavations at Christchurch, Spitalfields, 1984–6', *Antiquity* 61: 247–56.

Adkins, L. and Adkins, R. (1982) 'How to construct a grid frame for drawing plans on site', *The London Archaeologist* 4(9): 214–16.

(1983) 'The use of micro-excavators on archaeological sites: a review', *The London Archaeologist* 4(10): 271–3.

(1989) *Archaeological Illustration* (Cambridge, Cambridge University Press).

Advasio, J. and Carlisle, R. (1988) 'Some thoughts on cultural resource management in the United States', *Antiquity* 62: 72–87.

Agresti, E., Maggiolo-Schettini, A., Saccoccio, R., Pierobon, M. and Pierobon-Benoit, R. (1996) 'Handling excavation maps in SYSAND', in Kamermans and Fennema 1996: 31–6.

Aitken, M. and Milligan, R. (1992) 'Ground-probing RADAR in archaeology: practicalities and problems', *The Field Archaeologist* (Bulletin of the Institute of Field Archaeologists) 16: 288–91.

Aitken, M., Webster, G. and Rees, A. (1958) 'Magnetic prospecting', *Antiquity* 32: 270–1.

Akerson, L. (ed.) (1995) 'The effects of OSHA requirements on archaeology', *Journal of Middle Atlantic Archaeology* 11: 1–2.

Alexander, J. (1970) *The Directing of Archaeological Excavations* (London, Baker).

Alvey, B. and Moffett, J. (1986) 'Single context planning and the computer', in S. Laflin (ed.) *Computer Applications in Archaeology, 1986* (Birmingham, Centre for Computing and Computer Science), 59–72.

Ammerman, A. (1985) 'Plow-zone experiments in Calabria, Italy', *Journal of Field Archaeology* 12: 33–40.

Ancona, M., Dodoero, G., Mongiardino, M. and Traverso, A. (1999) 'Taking digital notes in the field: the Archeo tool-set', in Barceló *et al.* 1999: 117–21.

Anderson, R. (1983) 'Photogrammetry: the pros and cons for archaeology', *World Archaeology* 14(2): 200–5.

Andresen, J. and Madsen, T. (1996) 'IDEA – the Integrated Database for Excavation Analysis', in Kamermans, and Fennema 1996: 3–14.

Andresen, J., Madsen, T. and Scollar, I. (eds.) (1993) *Computing the Past. CAA92: Computer Applications and Quantitative Methods in Archaeology* (Aarhus, Aarhus University Press).

Archaeology Data Service (undated) at http://ads.ahds.ac.uk/projetc/userinfo/deposit.html.

Arnold, B. and Gersbach, E. (1995) 'The Kartomat: a field drawing machine', *Journal of Field Archaeology* 22: 369–77.

Aspinall, A. (1992) 'New developments in geophysical prospection', in A. Pollard (ed.) *New Developments in Archaeological Science* (Oxford, Oxford University Press), 233–44.

Aston, M. and Rowley, T. (1974) *Landscape Archaeology* (Newton Abbot, David and Charles).

Åstrom, P. and Fischer, P. (1987) 'Metal detecting in Cyprus and Greece', *Antiquity* 61: 266–7.

Atkinson, R. (1953) *Field Archaeology* (London, Methuen).

(1963) 'Resistivity surveying in archaeology', in E. Pyddoke (ed.) *The Scientist and Archaeology* (London, Dent), 1–30.

291

Backmann, H. (1982) *The Identification of Slags from Archaeological Sites* (Institute of Archaeology, London, Occasional Paper 6) (London, Institute of Archaeology).

Badham, K. and Jones, G. (1985) 'An experiment in manual processing of soil samples for plant remains', *Circaea* 3(1): 15–26.

Bahn, P. and Paterson, R. (1986) 'The Last Rights: more on archaeology and the dead', *Oxford Journal of Archaeology* 5: 255–71.

Bailey, G. and Thomas, G. (1987) 'The use of percussion drilling to obtain core samples from rock shelter deposits', *Antiquity* 61: 433–9.

Bailey, R., Cambridge, E. and Higgs, H. (1988) *Dowsing and Church Archaeology* (Wimborne, Intercept).

Baillie, M. (1991) 'Marking in marker dates: towards an archaeology with historical precision', *World Archaeology* 23(2): 233–43.

Baker, B. and Shaffer, B. (1998) 'Sugar reflotation and curation', *Journal of Field Archaeology* 25: 369–70.

Balaam, N. and Porter, H. (1991) 'Phosphate survey in the interior of the hillfort', in N. Sharples (ed.) *Maiden Castle: Excavations and Field Survey, 1985–6* (HBMCE Arch. Rep. 9: fiche) (London, Historic Buildings and Monuments Commission for England).

Ball, J. and Kelsay, R. (1992) 'Prehistoric intrasettlement land use and residual soil phosphate levels in the Upper Belize Valley, Central America', in T. Killion (ed.) *Gardens of Prehistory: The Archaeology of Settlement Agriculture in Greater Mesoamerica* (Alabama, University of Alabama Press), 234–62.

Barber, J. (ed.) (1993) *Interpreting Stratigraphy* (Edinburgh, AOC (Scotland) Ltd).

Barceló, J., Briz, I. and Vila, A. (eds.) (1999) *New Techniques for Old Times: CAA98* (British Archaeological Reports, International Series, 757) (Oxford, Archaeopress).

Barker, G. (1975) 'To sieve or not to sieve', *Antiquity* 49: 61–3.

Barker, P. (1977) *Techniques of Archaeological Excavation* (London, Batsford).

    (1986) *Understanding Archaeological Excavation* (London, Batsford).

Barley, M. (ed.) (1977) *European Towns* (London, Academic Press).

Barrett, J. (1995) *Some Challenges in Contemporary Archaeology* (Oxford, Oxbow Books).

Bass, W. (1992) *Human Osteology: A Laboratory and Field Manual* (Missouri Archaeological Society. Special Publication 2) (Columbia, MO).

Bateman, J. (1999) Review of 'Excavating Occaneechi Town: Archaeology of an Eighteenth-Century Indian Village in North Carolina', *Internet Archaeology* 6 (http://intarch.ac.uk/journal/issue6/bateman.html).

Batey, R. (1987) 'Subsurface interface RADAR at Sepphoris, Israel, 1985', *Journal of Field Archaeology* 14: 1–8.

Bement, L. (1985) 'Spray foam: a new bone encasement technique', *Journal of Field Archaeology* 12: 371–2.

Bender, B. (1993) *Landscape, Politics and Perspectives* (London, Berg).

Bennett, K. (1993) *A Field Guide for Human Skeletal Identification* (Springfield, IL, Charles C. Thomas).

Bettess, F. (1984) *Surveying for Archaeologists* (Durham, Durham University Excavation Committee).

Bewley, R. (1993) 'Aerial photography for archaeology', in J. Hunter and I. Ralston (eds.) *Archaeological Resource Management in the UK: An Introduction* (Stroud, Alan Sutton), 197–204.

Bibby, D. (1993) 'Building stratigraphic sequences on excavations: an example from Konstanz, Germany', in Harris *et al.* (1993): 104–21.

Biddle, M. and Kjolbye-Biddle, B. (1969) 'Metres, areas and robbing', *World Archaeology* 1(2): 208–19.

Binks, G., Dyke, J. and Dagnall, P. (1988) *Visitors Welcome: A Manual on the Presentation and Interpretation of Archaeological Excavation* (Centre for Environmental Interpretation, Manchester Polytechnic, for English Heritage).

Bintliff, J. (ed.) (1991) *The Annales School and Archaeology* (London, Leicester University Press).

Bintliff, J., Davis, B., Gaffney, C., Snodgrass, A. and Waters, A. (1992) 'Trace metal accumulations in soils on and around ancient settlement in Greece', in P. Spoerry (ed.) *Geoprospection in the Archaeological Landscape* (Oxford, Oxbow Books), 9–24.

Bintliff, J. and Sbonias, K. (1999) *Reconstructing Past Population Trends in Mediterranean Europe (3000 BC–AD 1800)* (Oxford, Oxbow Books).

Birkeland, P. (1984) *Soils and Geomorphology* (Oxford, Oxford University Press).

Biswell, S., Cropper, L., Evans, J., Gaffney, V. and Leach, P. (1995) 'GIS and excavation: a cautionary tale from Shepton Mallett, Somerset, England', in Lock, and Stančič 1995: 269–85.

Bjelajac, V., Luby, E. and Ray, R. (1996) 'A validation test of a field-based phosphate analysis technique', *Journal of Archaeological Science* 23(2): 243–8.

Bleed, P. (1983) 'Management techniques and archaeological field work', *Journal of Field Archaeology* 10: 494–8.

Bloemker, J. and Oakley, C. (1999) 'The firebreak plow and subsurface site discovery', *Journal of Field Archaeology* 26: 75–82.

Boaz, J. and Uleberg, E. (1995) 'The potential of GIS-based studies of Iron Age cultural landscapes in Eastern Norway', in Lock and Stančič 1995: 249–60.

Boddington, A. (1978) *The Excavation Record Part 1: Stratification* (Northampton, Northamptonshire County Council).

Boismier, W. (1997) *Modelling the Effects of Tillage Processes on Artefact Distribution in the Ploughzone: A simulation Study of Tillage-induced Pattern Formation* (British Archaeological Reports, British Series, 259) (Oxford, Archaeopress).

Bollong, C. (1994) 'Analysis of site stratigraphy and formation processes using patterns of pottery sherd dispersion', *Journal of Field Archaeology* 21: 15–28.

Booth, B. (1980) 'Munsell colour charts – a waste of time', *Rescue News* 24 (December): 2.
    (1983) 'Recording soil colors in the field', *Journal of Field Archaeology* 10: 118–20.

Bossuet, G. (1980) 'La Reconnaissance archéologique des milieux urbains par les méthodes de prospection géophysique: l'exemple de la Charité-sur-Loire' (Mémoire de Diplôme d'études supérieures, Université de Paris I) (Paris, Université de Paris).

Bowden, M. (1991) *Pitt Rivers: The Life and Archaeological Work of Lieutenant-General Augustus Henry Lane Fox Pitt Rivers, DCL, FRS, FSA* (Cambridge, Cambridge University Press).

Brandt, R., Groenewoudt, B. and Kvamme, K. (1992) 'An experiment in archaeological site location: modelling in the Netherlands', *World Archaeology* 24: 268–82.

British Archaeologists and Developers Liaison Group (1986) *Code of Practice* (London, British Archaeologists and Developers Liaison Group).

Brown, G. and Muraca, D. (1993) 'Phasing stratigraphic sequences at Colonial Williamsburg', in Harris *et al.* 1993: 155–66.

Buck, C., Cavanagh, W. and Litton, C. (1988) 'The spatial analysis of site phosphate data', in S. Rahtz (ed.) *Computer and Quantitative Methods in Archaeology 1988* (British Archaeological Reports, International series, 446) (Oxford, Tempus Reparatum), 151–60.

Campbell, T. (1991) 'A structured evaluation of ground penetrating RADAR for archaeological use' (unpublished MSc dissertation, University of York).

Canti, M. and Meddens, F. (1998) 'Mechanical coring as an aid to archaeological projects', *Journal of Field Archaeology* 25: 97–105.

Carrete, J., Keay, S. and Millett, M. (1995) *A Roman Provincial Capital and Its Hinterland: The*

Survey of the Territory of Tarragona, Spain, 1985–1990 (Ann Arbor, Journal of Roman Archaeology).

Carter, S. (1993) 'Soil thin sections as an aid to stratigraphic interpretation', in Barber 1993: 63–4.

Carver, M. (1979a) 'Notes on some general principles for the analysis of excavated data', *Science and Archaeology* 21: 3–14.

(1979b) 'Three Saxon-Norman tenements in Durham City', *Medieval Archaeology* 23: 1–80.

(1980) 'Medieval Worcester: an archaeological framework', *Transactions of the Worcestershire Archaeological Society* 35(7): 1–14.

(1983) 'Forty French towns: an essay on archaeological site evaluation and historical aims', *Oxford Journal of Archaeology* 2(3): 339–78.

(1987) *Underneath English Towns: Interpreting Urban Archaeology* (London, Batsford).

(1991) 'Digging for data: archaeological approaches to data definition, acquisition and analysis', in R. Francovich and D. Manacorda (eds.) *Lo scavo archeologico: dalla diagnosi all'edizione* (Florence, All'Isegna del Gioglio), 45–120.

Carver, M. (ed.) (1986) *Bulletin of the Sutton Hoo Research Committee* 4 (Sutton Hoo Research Trust).

Castel, R. (1976) 'Comparison of column and whole unit samples for recovering fish bones', *World Archaeology* 8(2): 192–6.

Cavanagh, W., Hirst, S. and Litton, C. (1988) 'Soil phosphates, site boundaries and change point analysis', *Journal of Field Archaeology* 15: 67–83.

Chalmers, A., Soddart, S., Tidmus, J. and Miles, R. (1995) 'INSITE: an interactive visualization system for archaeological sites', in Huggett and Ryan 1995: 225–8.

Champion, T., Cuming, P. and Shennan, S. (1995) *Planning for the Past Vol. 3: Decision-Making and Field Methods in Archaeological Evaluation* (London, English Heritage).

Chase, A. (1989) 'Perceptions of the past among North Queensland Aboriginal people', in R. Layton (ed.) *Who Needs the Past? Indigenous Values and Archaeology* (London, Unwin Hyman).

Cherry, J., Gamble, C. and Shennan, S. (eds.) (1978) *The Rôle of Sampling in Contemporary British Archaeology* (British Archaeological Report British Series, 50) (Oxford, BAR)

Clark, A. (1990) *Seeing beneath the Soil* (London, Batsford).

Clark, J. (1978) 'Cadwallo, King of the Britons, the bronze horseman of London', in J. Bird (ed.) *Collectanea Londiniensia* (London and Middlesex Archaeology Society, Special Paper 2) (London), 194–9.

Clark, P. (1993) 'Sites without principles: post-excavation analysis of "pre-matrix", sites', in Harris *et al.* 1993: 276–92.

Clarke, D. (1978) 'Excavation and volunteers: a cautionary tale', *World Archaeology* 10(1): 63–70.

Clarke, P. and Hutcheson, A. (1993) 'New approaches to the recording of archaeological stratigraphy', in Barber 1993: 65–8.

Cleere, H. (1984) *Approaches to the Archaeological Heritage: A Comparative Study of World Cultural Resource Management Systems* (Cambridge, Cambridge University Press).

(1989) *Archaeological Heritage Management in the Modern World* (London, Unwin Hyman).

Cole, J. (1980) 'Cult archaeology and the unscientific method and theory', in M. Schiffer (ed.) *Advances in Method and Theory* 3: 4–33.

Coles, J. (1972) *Field Archaeology in Britain* (London, Methuen).

(1979) *Experimental Archaeology* (London, Academic Press).

Conyers, L. and Cameron, C. (1998) 'Ground-penetrating Radar techniques and three-dimensional computer mapping in the American Southwest', *Journal of Field Archaeology* 25: 417–30.

Conyers, L. and Goodman, D. (1997) *Ground Penetrating RADAR: A Primer for the Archaeologist* (Walnut Creek, CA, AltaMira Press).

Cornforth, J., Davidson, C., Dallas, C. and Lock, G. (1992) 'Visualising Ancient Greece: computer graphics in the Sacred Way Project', in Lock, G. and Moffett, J. (eds.) *Computer Applications and Quantitative Methods in Archaeology 1991* (British Archaeological Reports, International Series, 577) (Oxford, Tempus Reparatum), 219–25.

Courty, M., Goldberg, P. and MacPhail, R. (1989) *Soils and Micromorphology in Archaeology* (Cambridge, Cambridge University Press).

Cox, C. (1992) 'Satellite imagery, aerial photography and wetland archaeology', *World Archaeology* 24(2): 249–67.

Coy, J. (1978) *First Aid for Animal Bones* (Hertford, Rescue Organisation).

Cracknell, S. and Corbishley, M. (eds.) (1986) *Presenting Archaeology to Young People* (London, Council for British Archaeology).

Craddock, P., Gurney, D., Pryor, F. and Hughes, M. (1985) 'The application of phosphate analysis to the location and interpretation of archaeological sites', *Archaeological Journal* 142: 361–76.

Crawford, O. (1953) *Archaeology in the Field* (London, Dent).

Crummy, P. (1986) 'Presentation of results: the popular publication', in Mytum and Waugh 1986: 59–71.

Cummer, W. (1974) 'Photogrammetry at Ayia Irini on Keos', *Journal of Field Archaeology* 1: 385–7.

Dalland, M. (1984) 'A procedure for use in stratigraphic analysis', *Scottish Archaeological Review* 3(2): 116–27.

Daniel, G. (1975) *A Hundred and Fifty Years of Archaeology* (London, Duckworth).

Darvill, T., Parker-Pearson, M., Smith, R. and Thomas, R. (eds.) (1978) *New Approaches to Our Past: An Archaeological Forum* (Southampton, Southampton University Archaeological Society).

Davies, M. (1993) 'The application of the Harris Matrix to the recording of standing structures', in Harris *et al.* 1993: 167–80.

Deetz, J. and Dethlefsen, E. (1963) 'Soil ph. as a tool in archaeological site interpretation', *American Antiquity* 29: 242–3.

Dever, W. and Lance, H. (eds.) (1978) *A Manual of Field Excavation* (Cincinnati, Hebrew Union College–Jewish Institute of Religion).

Dibble, H. (1987) 'Measurement of artefact provenience with an electronic theodolite', *Journal of Field Archaeology* 14: 249–54.

Dibble, H. and McPherron, S. (1988) 'On the computerization of archaeological projects', *Journal of Field Archaeology* 15: 431–40.

Dimbleby, G. (1978) *Scientific Treatment of Materials from Rescue Excavations: A Report by a Working Party of the Committee for Rescue Archaeology of the Ancient Monuments Board for England* (London, Department of the Environment).

Dincauze, D. (1986) 'Public Archaeology Forum: report to the Society for American Archaeology on the Conference on Reburial Issues', *Journal of Field Archaeology* 13: 116–18.

Dinsmoor, W. (1977) 'The archaeological field staff: the architect', *Journal of Field Archaeology* 4: 309–28.

Dobinson, C. and Denison, S. (1995) *Metal Detecting and Archaeology in England* (London, English Heritage).

Dobinson, C. and Gilchrist, R. (eds.) (1986) *Archaeology, Politics and the Public* (York University Archaeological Publications 5) (York, University of York).

DOE (1973) *Safety in Construction Work: Demolitions* (London, Department of the Environment).

(1974) *Safety in Construction Work: Excavations* (London, Department of the Environment).

(1975) *Basic Rules for Safety and Health at Work* (London, Department of the Environment).

Dockall, H. (1995) 'Application of Bement's spray sealant technique to infant skeletal remains', *Journal of Field Archaeology* 22: 385–7.

Dorrell, P. (1989) *Photography in Archaeology and Conservation* (Cambridge, Cambridge University Press).

Dougherty, R. (1988) 'Problems and responsibilities in the excavation of wet sites', in B. Purdy (ed.) *Wet Site Archaeology* (Caldwell, NJ, Telford Press).

Dowman, E. (1970) *Conservation in Field Archaeology* (London, Methuen).

Droop, J. (1915) *Archaeological Excavation* (Cambridge, Cambridge University Press).

Dunnell, R. (1990) 'Artifact size and lateral displacement under tillage: comments on the Odell and Cowan experiment', *American Antiquity* 55 : 592–4.

Dunnell, R. and Dancey, W. (1983) 'The siteless survey: a regional scale data collection strategy', in M. Schiffer (ed.) *Advances in Archaeological Method and Theory* 6: 267–87.

Dunnell, R. and Simek, J. (1995) 'Artifact size and plowzone process', *Journal of Field Archaeology* 22: 305–19.

Dunning, N., Beach, T. and Rue, D. (1997) 'The paleoecology and ancient settlement of the Petexbatun region, Guatemala', *Ancient Mesoamerica* 8(2): 255–66.

Dye, T. (1994) 'Comment on Gordon "Screen size and differential faunal recovery: a Hawaiian example"', *Journal of Field Archaeology* 21: 391–2.

Ebert, J. (1984) 'Remote sensing applications in archaeology', in M. Schiffer (ed.) *Advances in Archaeological Method and Theory* 7: 293–362.

Edmonds, M. and McElearney, G. (1999) 'Inhabitation and access: landscape and the Internet at Gardom's Edge', *Internet Archaeology* 6 (http://intarch.ac.uk/journal/issue6/edmonds_toc.html).

Eidt, R. (1974) *Abandoned Settlement Analysis: Theory and Practice* (Shorewood, WI, Field Test Associates).

(1984) *Advances in Abandoned Settlement Analysis: Application to Prehistoric Anthrosols in Colombia, South America* (Milwaukee, Center for Latin America, University of Wisconsin–Milwaukee).

Ellis, L.(1982) *Laboratory Techniques in Archaeology: A Guide to the Literature, 1920–1980* (New York, Garland Publishers).

English Heritage (1995) *Geophysical Survey in Archaeological Field Evaluation* (Research and Professional Services Guideline 1) (London, English Heritage).

Farrar, R. (1987) *Surveying by Prismatic Compass* (Practical Handbooks in Archaeology 2) (London, Council for British Archaeology).

Fasham, P. (1984) *Groundwater Pumping Techniques for Excavation*, Institute of Field Archaeologists Technical Paper 1, Birmingham, Institute of Field Archaeologists).

Fasham, P. *et al.* (1980) *Fieldwalking for Archaeologists* (Andover, Hampshire Field Club and Archaeological Society).

Feder, K. (1984) 'Irrationality and popular archaeology', *American Antiquity* 49: 525–41.

Fink, T. and Zeitz, P. (1996) 'Hantavirus Pulmonary Syndrome and field archaeology: guidelines for risk reduction', *Journal of Field Archaeology* 23: 469–76.

Fitzgerald, J. (1985) 'Building non-commercial soil-separation equipment', *Journal of Field Archaeology* 12: 483–8.

Fladmark, K. (1978) *A Guide to Basic Archaeological Field Procedures* (Burnaby, BC, Simon Fraser University).

Ford, D. (1993) 'The nature of clarity in archaeological line drawings', *Journal of Field Archaeology* 20: 319–33.

Fowler, P. (1977) *Approaches to Archaeology* (London, Black).

(1980) 'Tradition and objectives in British field archaeology, 1953–78', *Archaeological Journal* 137: 1–21.

Fowler, P. (ed.) (1972a) *Archaeology and the Landscape* (London, Baker).

(1972b) *Responsibilities and Safeguards in Archaeological Excavation* (London, Council for British Archaeology).

Frink, D. (1984) 'Artifact behaviour within the plow zone', *Journal of Field Archaeology* 11: 356–63.

Gaffney, C. and Gater, J. with Ovenden, S. (1991) *The Use of Geophysical Techniques in Archaeological Evaluations*, Institute of Field Archaeologists Technical Paper 9, Birmingham, Institute of Field Archaeologists.

Gaffney, V. and Exon, S. (1999) 'From order to chaos: publication, synthesis and the dissemination of data in a Digital Age', *Internet Archaeology* 6 (http://intarch.ac.uk/journal/issue6/gaffney_toc.html).

Gaffney, V., Gaffney, C. and Corney, M. (1998) 'Changing the Roman landscape: the role of geophysics and remote sensing', in J. Bayley (ed.) *Science in Archaeology: An Agenda for the Future* (London, English Heritage), 145–56.

Gaffney, V., Stančič, Z. and Watson, H. (1995) 'Moving from catchments to cognition: tentative steps towards a larger archaeological context for GIS', *Scottish Archaeological Review* 9/10: 41–64.

Gaines, S. (1984) 'The impact of computerised systems in American archaeology: an overview of the past decade', in R. Martlew (ed.) *Information Systems in Archaeology* (Gloucester, Alan Sutton), 63–76.

Gallant, T. (1986) '"Background noise", and site definition: a contribution to survey methodology', *Journal of Field Archaeology* 13: 403–18.

Ganderton, P. (1981) *Environmental Archaeology: Site Methods and Interpretation* (Vorda Research Series 2) (Highworth, Vorda).

Garratt-Frost, S. (1992) *The Law and Burial Archaeology*, (Institute of Field Archaeologists Technical Paper 11, Birmingham, Institute of Field Archaeologists).

Gejvall, N. (1963) 'Cremations', in D. Brothwell and E. Higgs (eds.) *Science in Archaeology* (London, Thames and Hudson), 379–90.

Gero, J. and Conkey, M. (eds.) (1991) *Engendering Archaeology: Women and Prehistory* (Oxford, Blackwell).

Gilchrist, R. (1994) *Gender and Material Culture: The Archaeology of Religious Women* (London, Routledge).

Golemblik, A. (1991) 'Modelling the processes of stratification in medieval urban deposits', *Laborotiv Arkeologi* 5: 37–45.

Gordon, E. (1993) 'Screen size and differential faunal recovery: a Hawaiian example', *Journal of Field Archaeology* 20: 453–60.

(1994) 'Reply to Dye', *Journal of Field Archaeology* 21: 392–4.

Gorman, M. (1985) 'Beowulf in 3-D – soil-sounding radar surveys at Sutton Hoo', *Seismic Images* 8: 24–9.

Gould, R. (1987) 'Archaeological survey by air: a case from the Australian Desert', *Journal of Field Archaeology* 14: 431–43.

(1995) 'Archaeological survey by air: an update for the 1990s', *Journal of Field Archaeology* 22: 257–61.

Gould, S. (1978) *Ever Since Darwin: Reflections in Natural History* (London, Burnett Books).

Gray, J. and Walford, K. (1999) 'One good site deserves another: electronic publishing in field archaeology', *Internet Archaeology* 7 (http://intarch.ac.uk/journal/issue7/gray_toc.html).

Green, J. (1990) *Maritime Archaeology: A Technical Handbook* (London, Academic Press).

Gregory, T. (1986) 'Whose fault is treasure-hunting?', in Dobinson and Gilchrist 1986: 25–7.

Guimier-Sorbets, A.-M. (1990) *Les Bases de données en archéologie: conception et mise en œuvre* (Paris, Centre National de la Recherche Scientifique).

Gurney, D. (1985) *Phosphate Analysis of Soils: A Guide for the Field Archaeologist* (Institute of Field Archaeologists, Technical Paper 3, Birmingham, Institute of Field Archaeologists).

Haigh, J. (1991) 'The AERIAL Program, version 4.1', *Aerial Archaeology Group News* 3: 28–30.
   (1993) 'Practical experience in creating digital terrain models', in Andresen *et al.* 1993: 67–74.

Haigh, J. and Ipson, S. (1994) 'Economical possibilities for the rectification of digital images', *Archaeological Computing Newsletter* 38: 8–13.

Hammer, F. (1992) 'Excavation and post-excavation recording methods in British archaeology today: an investigation of strategies pursued by 70 archaeological units and projects during the 1980s' (Unpublished MPhil thesis, University of York).

Hammer, F., McCann, W. and Elsden, N. (1993) 'Does the history match the archaeology?', in Barber 1993: 15–22.

Hammond, N. (1991) 'Matrices and Maya archaeology', *Journal of Field Archaeology* 18: 29–41.

Hampton, J., Palmer, R. and Clark, A. (1977) 'Implications of aerial photography for archaeology', *Archaeological Journal* 134: 157–93.

Hanson, W. and Rahtz, P. (1988) 'Video records on excavations', *Antiquity* 62: 106–11.

Harrington, S. (1996) 'Bones and bureaucrats: New York's great cemetery imbroglio', in K. Vitelli (ed.) *Archaeological Ethics* (Walnut Creek, CA, AltaMira Press).

Harris, E. (1989) *Principles of Archaeological Stratigraphy* (second edition) (London, Academic Press).

Harris, E., Brown, M. and Brown, G. (eds.) (1993) *Practices of Archaeological Stratigraphy* (London, Academic Press).

Haselgrove, C., Millett, M. and Smith, I. (eds.) (1985) *Archaeology from the Ploughsoil: Studies in the Collection and Interpretation of Field Survey Data* (Sheffield, University of Sheffield).

Hassan, F. (1978) 'Sediments in archaeology: methods and implications for palaeoenvironmental and cultural analysis', *Journal of Field Archaeology* 5: 197–213.
   (1981) 'Rapid quantitative determination of phosphate in archaeological sediments', *Journal of Field Archaeology* 8: 384–7.

Hawes, D. (forthcoming) 'Beer cans and bits of pot, but not a lot of bottle', *Journal of Theoretical Archaeology*.

Hayfield, C. (1980) *Fieldwalking as a Method in Archaeological Research* (London, Department of the Environment).

Hays-Gilpin, K. and Whitley, S. (1998) *Reader in Gender Archaeology* (London, Routledge).

Herzog, I. (1993) 'Computer-aided Harris-Matrix generation', in Harris *et al.* 1993: 201–17.

Hesse, A. (1978) *Manuel de prospection géophysique appliquée à la reconnaissance archéologique* (Dijon, Centre de Recherches sur les Techniques Greco-Romaines).

Hester, T., Heizer, R. and Graham, J. (1981) *Field Methods in Archaeology* (Palo Alto, CA, Mayfield).

Hester, T., Shafer, H. and Feder, K. (1997) *Field Methods in Archaeology* (Mountain View, CA, Mayfield).

Hietala, H. (ed.) (1984) *Intra-site Spatial Analysis in Archaeology* (Cambridge, Cambridge University Press).

Higgins, T., Main, P. and Lang, J. (eds.) (1996) *Imaging the Past: Electronic Imaging and Computer Graphics in Museums and Archaeology* (British Museum Occasional Paper 114) (London).

Hinchcliffe, J. and Schadla-Hall, R. (eds.) (1980) *The Past under the Plough* (London, Department of the Environment).

Hirst, S. (1976) *Recording on Excavations I: The Written Record* (Rescue Publication 7) (Hertford, Rescue – The British Archaeology Trust).

Hobsbawm, E. and Ranger, T. (eds.) (1983) *The Invention of Tradition* (Cambridge, Cambridge University Press).

Hodder, I. (1982) *The Present Past: An Introduction to Anthropology for Archaeologists* (London, Batsford).

  (1986) *Reading the Past: Current Approaches to Interpretation in Archaeology* (Cambridge, Cambridge University Press).

  (1989) 'Writing archaeology: site reports in context', *Antiquity* 63: 268–73.

  (1995) *Theory and Practice in Archaeology* (London, Routledge).

  (1999) 'Archaeology and global information systems', *Internet Archaeology* 6 (http://intarch.ac.uk/journal/issue6/hodder_toc.html).

Hodder, I. (ed.) (1987) *The Archaeology of Contextual Meanings* (Cambridge, Cambridge University Press).

  (1991) *Archaeological Theory in Europe: The Last Three Decades* (London, Routledge).

Hodgson, J. (1978) *Soil Sampling and Soil Description* (Oxford, Clarendon Press).

Hoffman, C. (1993) 'Close-interval core sampling: tests of a method for predicting internal site structure', *Journal of Field Archaeology* 20: 461–73.

Hogg, A. (1980) *Surveying for Archaeologists and Other Fieldworkers* (London, Croom Helm).

Hope-Taylor, B. (1966) 'Archaeological draughtsmanship: principles and practice', *Antiquity* 40: 107–13.

  (1977) *Yeavering: An Anglo-British Centre in Early Northumbria* (Department of the Environment Archaeological Reports 7) (London, HMSO).

van Horn, D., Murray, J. and White, R. (1986) 'Some techniques for mechanical excavation in salvage archaeology', *Journal of Field Archaeology* 13: 239–44.

Howell, T. (1993) 'Evaluating the utility of auger testing as a predictor of subsurface artifact density', *Journal of Field Archaeology* 20: 475–84.

Hudson, K. (1981) *A Social History of Archaeology* (London, Macmillan).

Huggett, J. and Ryan, N. (eds.) (1995) *Computer Applications and Quantitative Methods in Archaeology 1994* (British Archaeological Reports, International Series, 600) (Oxford, Archaeopress).

Hummler, M. and Roe, A. (1996) 'Sutton Hoo burials: reconstructing the sequence', in Roskams (1996): 39–53.

Hunt, W. and Brandon, J. (1990) 'Using agricultural grain cleaners to mechanically screen earth', *Journal of Field Archaeology* 17: 116–21.

Hutcheson, A. (1992) 'Interpretation of the formation processes of one context on the North Downs in Kent', in Steane 1992b: 23–36.

Hutton, B. (1986) *Recording Standing Buildings* (Sheffield, Sheffield University Press).

Imai, T., Sakayama, T. and Kanemori, T. (1987) 'Use of ground-probing RADAR and resistivity surveys for archaeological investigations', *Geophysics* 52(2): 137–50.

Institute of Field Archaeologists (1994) *Standards and Guidance for Archaeological Excavations* (Birmingham, Institute of Field Archaeologists).

Jefferies, J. (1977) *Excavation Recording: Techniques in Use by the Central Excavation Unit* (London, Department of the Environment).

Johnson, M. (1999) *Archaeological Theory: An Introduction* (Oxford, Blackwell).

Jones, A. (1983) 'A comparison of two on-site methods of wet sieving large archaeological soil samples', *Scientific Archaeology* 25: 9–12.

Jones, A. and Bullock, A. (1988) 'Mix and mesh', in *Archaeology in York Interim* 13(2) (York, York Archaeological Trust), 11–16.

Jones, S. (1987) 'Archaeology – the preserve of the over-40's', in S. Joyce, M. Newbury and P. Stone *Degree, Digging, Dole: Our Future?* (Southampton, Southampton University Archaeology), 62–80.

Joukowsky, M. (1980) *A Complete Manual of Field Archaeology* (Englewood Cliffs, NJ, Prentice-Hall).

Kamermans, H. and Fennema, K. (eds.) (1996) *Interfacing the Past: Computer Applications and Quantitative Methods in Archaeology, CAA95* (Analecta Praehistoria Leidensia 28) (Leiden).

Kaufmann, E. (ed.) (1994) *Reclaiming Our Past, Honoring Our Ancestors: New York's 18th Century African Burial Ground and the Memorial Competition* (New York, African Burial Ground Competition Coalition).

Keeley, H. (1978) 'The cost-effectiveness of certain methods of recovering macroscopic organic remains from archaeological deposits', *Journal of Archaeological Science* 5: 179–83.

Keepax, C. (1977) 'Contamination of archaeological deposits by seeds of modern origin with particular reference to the use of flotation machines', *Journal of Archaeological Science* 4: 221–9.

Kelley, J. and Hanen, M. (1988) *Archaeology and the Methodology of Science* (Albuquerque, University of New Mexico Press).

Kenworthy, M., King, E., Ruwell, M. and van Houten, T. (1985) *Preserving Field Records* (Philadelphia, University of Pennsylvania).

Kenyon, K. (1964) *Beginning in Archaeology* (London, Dent).

Kidder, A. (1924) *An Introduction to Southwestern Archaeology* (New Haven, Yale University Press).

Kidder, T. (1997) 'Sugar reflotation: an alternative method for sorting flotation-derived heavy fraction samples', *Journal of Field Archaeology* 24: 39–45.

(1998) 'Sugar reflotation and curation: a response to Baker and Shaffer', *Journal of Field Archaeology* 25: 370.

Kintigh, K. (1988) 'The effectiveness of subsurface testing: a simulation approach', *American Antiquity* 53: 686–707.

Klesert A. and Powell, S. (1992) 'A perspective on ethics and the reburial controversy', *American Antiquity* 58: 348–54.

Klindt-Jensen, O. (1975) *A History of Scandinavian Archaeology* (London, Thames and Hudson).

Kobylinski, Z. (1993) 'Polish medieval excavations and the Harris Matrix: applications and developments', in Harris *et al.* 1993: 57–67.

Krakker, J., Shott, M. and Welch, P. (1983) 'Design and evaluation of shovel-test sampling in regional archaeological survey', *Journal of Field Archaeology* 10: 469–80.

Kunow, J., Giesler, J., Gechter, M., Gaitzsch, W., Fullmann-Schulz, A. and von Brandt, D. (1986) *Suggestions for the Systematic Recording of Pottery* (Cologne, Rheinland Verlag).

Kvamme, K. (1990) 'The fundamental principles and practice of predictive archaeological modelling', in A. Voorips (ed.) *Mathematics and Information Science in Archaeology: A Flexible Framework* (Studies in Modern Archaeology 3) (Bonn, Holos-Verlag), 297–305.

Larsen, C. (ed.) (1992) *Sites and Monuments: National Archaeological Records* (Copenhagen, The National Museum of Denmark).

Leigh, D. (1972) *First Aid for Finds: A Practical Guide for Archaeologists* (Hertford, Rescue – The British Archaeology Trust).

Levine, P. (1986) *The Amateur and the Professional: Antiquarians, Historians and Archaeologists in Victorian England 1838–1886* (Cambridge, Cambridge University Press).

Lewarch, D. and O'Brien, M. (1981) 'The expanding role of surface assemblages in archaeological research', in M. Schiffer (ed.) *Advances in Archaeological Method and Theory* 4: 297–342.

Lightfoot, K. (1986) 'Regional surveys in the Eastern United States: the strengths and weaknesses of implementing sub-surface testing programmes', *American Antiquity* 51: 484–504.

(1989) 'A defense of shovel-test sampling: a reply to Shott', *American Antiquity* 54: 413–16.

Lilley J., Stroud, G., Brothwell, D. and Williamson, M. (1994) *The Jewish Burial Ground at Jewbury* (Archaeology of York 12/3) (York, Council for British Archaeology).

Lippi, R. (1988) 'Paleotopography and phosphate analysis of a buried jungle site in Ecuador', *Journal of Field Archaeology* 15: 85–97.

Lock, G. and Stančič, Z. (eds.) (1995) *Archaeology and Geographical Information Systems: A European Perspective* (London, Taylor and Francis).

Lockyear, K. and Rahtz, S. (eds.) (1991) *Computer Applications and Quantitative Methods in Archaeology 1990* (British Archaeological Reports, International Series, 565) (Oxford, Tempus Reparatum).

Long, B. (1974) 'Systematic planning in urban archaeology', in G. Jones and S. Grearly (eds.) *Roman Manchester* (Altrincham, John Sherratt), 173–83.

Lovis, W. (1976) 'Quarter sections and forest: an example of probability sampling in the Northeastern Woodlands', *American Antiquity* 41: 364–72.

Lowe, C. (1993) 'Data washing, the data-base and the Dalland matrix', in Barber 1993: 23–5.

Luke, M., Steadman, S., and Dawson, M. (1996) 'Death by computer', in Roskams 1996: 14–24.

Lyons, T. and Avery, T. (1977) *Remote Sensing: A Handbook for Archaeologists and Cultural Resource Managers* (Washington, DC, National Park Service).

Lyons, T. and Methien, F. (eds.) (1980) *Cultural Resources Remote Sensing* (Washington, DC, National Park Service).

McAdam, E. (1992) 'Discussion session: feedback mechanisms from post-excavation to excavation', in Steane 1992b: 7.

McKinley, J. and Roberts, C. (1993) *Excavation and Post-Excavation Treatment of Cremated and Inhumed Human Remains*, (Institute of Field Archaeologists Technical Paper 13, Birmingham, Institute of Field Archaeologists).

McManamon, F. (1984) 'Discovering sites unseen', in M. Schiffer (ed.) *Advances in Archaeological Method and Theory* 7: 223–92.

McMinn, R., Hutchings, R. and Logan, B. (1987) *The Human Skeleton: A Photographic Manual* (London, Wolfe).

Malt, D. and Westman, A. (1992) 'Assessment versus analysis', in Steane 1992b: 9–12.

Marsden, B. (1974) *The Early Barrow Diggers* (Aylesbury, Shire Publications).

Marsden, P. (1987) *The Roman Forum Site in London: Discoveries before 1985* (London, HMSO).

Maxwell, G. (ed.) (1983) *The Impact of Aerial Reconnaissance on Archaeology* (London, Council for British Archaeology).

Messika, N. (1999) 'Real time, *in situ*: computerized graphic documentation in archaeological excavation', in Barceló *et al.* 1999: 81–3.

Miller, P. (1996) 'Digging deep: GIS in the city', in Kamermans, and Fennema 1996: 369–76.

Milne, G. (ed.) (1992) *From Roman Basilica to Medieval Market* (London, HMSO).

Montagu of Beaulieu (1987) 'Opening address', in S. Joyce, M. Newbury and P. Stone (eds.), *Degree, Digging, Dole: Our Future?* (Southampton, Southampton University Archaeology), 1–12.

Moore, J. and Scott, E. (eds.) (1997) *Invisible People and Processes: Writing Gender and Childhood into European Archaeology* (London, Leicester University Press).

Moorhouse, S. (1986) 'Non-dating uses of medieval pottery', *Medieval Ceramics* 10: 85–123.

Mora, P., Mora, L. and Philippot, P. (1984) *Conservation of Wall Paintings* (London, Butterworths).

Muckle, R. (1994) 'Differential recovery of mollusk shell from archaeological sites', *Journal of Field Archaeology* 21: 129–31.

Mueller, J. (ed.) (1975) *Sampling in Archaeology* (Tucson, University of Arizona Press).

Murphy, P. and Wiltshire, P. (1994) 'A guide to sampling archaeological deposits for environmental analysis' (unpublished – teaching collection, University College London).

Murray, D. and Ferguson, L. (1997) *Institute of Field Archaeologists Archiving Guidelines* (Birmingham, Institute of Field Archaeologists).

Museums and Galleries Commission (1992) *Standards in the Museum Care of Archaeological Collections* (London, Museums and Galleries Commission).

Mytum, H. and Waugh, K. (eds.) (1986) *Rescue Archaeology: What's Next?* (York, University of York).

Nance, J. and Ball, B. (1986) 'No surprises? The reliability and validity of test pit sampling', *American Antiquity* 51: 457–83.

(1989) 'A shot in the dark: Shott's comments on Nance and Ball', *American Antiquity* 54: 405–12.

Needham, S. and Stig-Sorensen, M. (1988) 'Runnymede refuse tip: a consideration of midden deposits and their function', in J. Barrett and I. Kinnes (eds.) *The Archaeology of Context in the Neolithic and Bronze Age: Recent Trends* (Sheffield, J. Collis), 113–20.

Nelson, S. (1997) *Gender in Archaeology: Analyzing Power and Prestige* (Walnut Creek, CA, AltaMira Press).

Nelson, S., Plooster, M. and Ford, D. (1987) 'An interactive computer graphic technique for identifying occupation surfaces in deep archaeological sites', *Journal of Field Archaeology* 14: 353–8.

Nichols, H. (1954) *Moving the Earth: The Workbook of Excavation* (Greenwich, North Castle Books).

Niquette, C. (1997) 'Hard hat archaeology', *Society for American Archaeology* 15(3): 15–16.

Noli, D. (1985) 'Low altitude aerial photography from a tethered balloon', *Journal of Field Archaeology* 12: 497–501.

O'Brien, M. and Lewarch, D. (eds.) (1981) *Plowzone Archaeology: Contributions to Theory and Technique* (Vanderbilt University Publications in Anthropology 27) (Nashville, TN, Vanderbilt University).

O'Connor, T. (1986) 'But what shall we tell the press?', in Dobinson and Gilchrist 1986: 31–3.

Odell, G. and Cowan, F. (1987) 'Estimating tillage effects on artefact distributions', *American Antiquity* 52: 456–84.

O'Keefe, P. and Prott, L. (1984) *Law and the Cultural Heritage* (Abingdon, Professional Books).

Olsen, O. (1980) 'Rabies archaeologorum', *Antiquity* 54: 15–20.

O'Neill, D. (1993) 'Excavation sample size: a cautionary tale', *American Antiquity* 58: 523–9.

Orme, B. (1981) *Anthropology for Archaeologists* (London, Duckworth).

Orton, C. (1980) *Mathematics in Archaeology* (London, Collins).

(2000) *Sampling in Archaeology* (Cambridge, Cambridge University Press).

Orton, C., Tyers, P. and Vince, A. (1993) *Pottery in Archaeology* (Cambridge, Cambridge University Press).

Osbourne, P. (1983) 'An insect fauna from a modern cess pit and its comparison with probable cess pit assemblages from archaeological sites', *Journal of Archaeological Science* 10: 453–63.

Owen, J. (ed.) (1995) *Towards an Accessible Archaeological Archive. The Transfer of Archaeological Archives to Museums: Guidelines for Use in England, Northern Ireland, Scotland and Wales* (London, Society of Museum Archaeologists).

Oxley, J. (1998) 'Planning and the conservation of archaeological deposits', in M. Corfield, P. Hinton, T. Nixon and M. Pollard (eds.) *Preserving Archaeological Remains* in situ (Museum of London and University of Bradford), 51–4.

Paice, P. (1991) 'Extensions to the Harris Matrix system to illustrate stratigraphic discussion of an archaeological site', *Journal of Field Archaeology* 18: 17–28.

Palmer, R. and Cox, C. (1993) *Uses of Aerial Photography in Archaeological Evaluations*, (Institute of Field Archaeologists Technical Paper 12, Birmingham, Institute of Field Archaeologists).

Payne, S. (1972) 'Partial recovery and sample bias; the results of some sieving experiments', in E. Higgs (ed.) *Papers in Economic Prehistory* (Cambridge, Cambridge University Press), 65–81.

(1975) 'Partial recovery and sample bias', in A. Classon (ed.) *Archaeozoological Studies* (Amsterdam, North-Holland), 7–17.

Pearson, N. and Williams, T. (1993) 'Single-context planning: its role in on-site recording procedures and in post-excavation analysis at York', in Harris *et al.* 1993: 89–103.

Pelfer, G. (1999) 'The Via Aurelia in the Tarquinia area: new results from an aerial photograph study by the Matlab image processing program', in Barceló *et al.* 1999: 51–4.

Peña, J., Esquivel, J., Ramos, A., del Mar Osuna, M. and Rull, E. (1999) 'Data analysis of a magnetic survey to contrast the most common treatments of data procedures in shallow archaeological surveys', in Barceló *et al.* 1999: 41–6.

Petch, D. (1968) 'Earthmoving machines and their employment on archaeological excavations', *Journal of Chester Archaeological Society* 55: 15–28.

Petrie, W. (1904) *Methods and Aims in Archaeology* (London, Macmillan).

Phillips, P. (ed.) (1984) *The Archaeologist and the Laboratory* (CBA Research Report 58) (London, Council for British Archaeology).

Pitt-Rivers, A. (1887) *Excavations in Cranborne Chase near Rushmore, on the Borders of Dorset and Wilts* (London, printed privately).

Powlesland, D. (1991) 'From the trench to the bookshelf: computer usage at the Heslerton Parish Project', in S. Ross, J. Moffett and J. Henderson (eds.) *Computing for Archaeologists* (Oxford University Committee for Archaeology, Monograph 18) (Oxford), 155–69.

Prescott, J., Taylor, J. and Marshall, J. (1934) 'The relationship between the mechanical composition of the soil and the estimate of texture in the field', *Physique du Sol. Trans. 1st Comm. Int Soc. Sci.* 1934: 143–54.

Preucel, R. and Hodder, I. (1996) *Contemporary Archaeology in Theory* (Oxford, Blackwell).

Price, D. and Gebauer, G. (1990) *Adventures in Fugawiland* (Mountain View, CA, Mayfield).

Proudfoot, B. (1976) 'The analysis and interpretation of soil phosphorus in archaeological contexts', in D. Davidson and M. Shackley (eds.) *Geoarchaeology: Science and the Past* (London, Duckworth), 93–113.

Pryor, F. (1974) *Earthmoving on Open Archaeological Sites* (Institute of Field Archaeologists Technical Paper 4, Birmingham, Institute of Field Archaeologists).

(1989) '"Look what we've found": a case study in public archaeology', *Antiquity* 63: 51–6.

Pyddoke, E. (1961) *Stratification for the Archaeologist* (London, Phoenix House).

Quesada, F., Baena, J. and Blasco, C. (1995) 'An application of GIS to intra-site spatial analysis: the Iberian Iron Age cemetery at El Cigarrejo (Murcia, Spain)', in Huggett and Ryan 1995: 137–46.

Rackham, J. (1982) 'The smaller mammals in the urban environment: their recovery and interpretation from archaeological deposits', in A. Hall and H. Kenward (eds.) *Environmental Archaeology in an Urban Context* (CBA Research Report 43) (London, Council for British Archaeology), 86–93.

Ragir, S. (1972) 'Techniques for archaeological sampling', in M. Leone (ed.) *Contemporary Archaeology* (Carbondale, Southern Illinois University Press).

Rahtz, P. (1974) *Rescue Archaeology* (Harmondsworth, Penguin).

(1988) 'Archaeology and the dead', *British Archaeological News* (34): 33.

Rahtz, P. and Hirst, S. (1979) *The Saxon and Medieval Palaces at Cheddar: Excavations, 1960–62* (British Archaeological Reports, British Series, 65) (Oxford, BAR).

Rains, M. (1995) 'Towards a computerized desktop: the Integrated Archaeological Database System', in Huggett and Ryan 1995: 207–10.

Ramonofsky, A., Standifer, L., Witmer, A. and Standifer, M. (1986) 'A new technique for separating flotation samples', *American Antiquity* 51: 66–72.

Rapp, G. (1975) 'The archaeological field staff: the geologist', *Journal of Field Archaeology* 2: 229–37.

Reilly, P. (1992) 'Three-dimensional modeling and primary archaeological data', in Reilly and Rahtz 1992: 147–73.

Reilly, P. and Rahtz, S. (eds.) (1992) *Archaeology in the Information Age: A Global Perspective* (London and New York, Routledge).

Renfrew, A. (1978) 'Archaeology and society in 1978', in Darvill *et al.* 1978: 157–78.

Renfrew, J., Monk, M. and Murphy, P. (1976) *First Aid for Seeds* (Hertford, Rescue – The British Archaeology Trust).

Reyman, J. (1978) 'Two techniques for better theodolite and transit set-ups', *American Antiquity* 43: 486–7.

Reynolds, N. and Barber, J. (1984) 'Analytical Excavation', *Antiquity* 58: 95–102.

Reynolds, P. (1978) 'Archaeology by experiment: a research tool for tomorrow', in Darvill *et al.* 1978: 139–55.

Richards, J. (1986) 'Into the black art: achieving computer literacy in archaeology', in E. Webb (ed.) *Computer Applications in Archaeology, 1985* (London, Institute of Archaeology), 121–5.

(1996) 'Putting the site in its setting: GIS and the search for Anglo-Saxon settlements in Northumbria', in Kamermans and Fennema, 1996: 377–86.

(1998) 'Computer applications in archaeology', *Journal of Archaeological Research* 6(4): 331–82.

Richards, J. and Ryan, N. (1985) *Data Processing in Archaeology* (Cambridge, Cambridge University Press).

Riley, D. (1987) *Air Photography and Archaeology* (London, Duckworth).

Roskams, S. (1996) *Interpreting Stratigraphy 8* (Papers presented to the eighth stratigraphy conference at York) (York, University of York).

Ross, N. (1971) 'Archaeology and the engineer', *Arup Journal* September 1971: 8–10.

Ross, S., Moffett, J. and Henderson, J. (eds.) (1991) *Computing for Archaeologists* (Oxford University Committee for Archaeology, Monograph 18) (Oxford).

Ruggles, C., Medyckyi-Scott, D. and Gruffydd, A. (1993) 'Multiple viewshed analysis using GIS and its archaeological application: a case study in northern Mull', in Andresen *et al.* 1993: 125–32.

Ryan, N. (1992) 'Beyond the relational database: managing the variety and complexity of archaeological data', in G. Lock and J. Moffett (eds.) *Computer Applications and Quantitative Methods in Archaeology, 1991* (British Archaeological Reports, International Series, 577) (Oxford, Tempus Reparatum), 1–6.

(1995) 'The excavation archive as hypertext document?', in Huggett and Ryan 1995: 211–19.

(1996) 'Computer based visualization of the past: technical "realism", and historical credibility', in T. Higgins, P. Main and J. Lang (eds.) *Imaging the Past: Electronic Imaging and Computer Graphics in Museums and Archaeology* (British Museum Occasional Paper 114) (London), 95–108.

Ryan, N., Pascoe, J. and Morse, D. (1999) 'Fieldnote: extending a GIS into the field', in Barceló *et al.* 1999: 127–31.

Savage, S. (1990) 'GIS in archaeological research', in K. Allen, S. Green and E. Zubrow (eds.) *Interpreting Space: GIS and Archaeology* (London and New York, Taylor and Francis).

Sayer, A. (1984) *Method in Social Science: A Realist Approach* (London, Hutchinson).

SCAUM (1986) *Health and Safety Manual* (London, Standing Committee of Archaeological Unit Managers).

(1997) *Recording Information about Archaeological Fieldwork* (London, Standing Committee of Archaeological Unit Managers).

Schaffer, G. and Cole, E. (1994) 'Standards and guidelines for archaeological investigations in Maryland' (Maryland Historical Trust Technical Report 2, consulted at http://www2.ari.net/mdshpo/ops.html).

Schiffer, M. (1987) *Formation Processes in the Archaeological Record* (Albuquerque, University of New Mexico Press).

Schuldenrein, J. (1991) 'Coring and the identity of cultural-resource environments: a comment on Stein', *American Antiquity* 56: 131–7.

Schuyler, R.-L. (1978) *Historical Archaeology: A Guide to Substantive and Theoretical Contributions* (Farmingdale, NY, Baywood Publishing Co.).

Scollar, I. (1982) 'Thirty years of computer archaeology and the future', in S. Laflin (ed.) *Computer Applications in Archaeology, 1982* (Birmingham, Centre for Computing and Computer Science), 189–98.

Scollar, I., Tabbagh, A., Hesse, A. and Herzog, I. (1990) *Archaeological Prospecting and Remote Sensing* (Cambridge, Cambridge University Press).

Sease, C. (1987) *A Conservation Manual for the Field Archaeologist* (Los Angeles, University of California).

Selkirk, A. (1986) 'The future of rescue archaeology: the role of the independent', in Mytum and Waugh 1986: 111–14.

Shanks, M. (1992) *Experiencing the Past: On the Character of Archaeology* (London, Routledge).

Shanks, M. and Tilley, C. (1987a) *Reconstructing Archaeology* (Cambridge, Cambridge University Press).

(1987b) *Social Theory and Archaeology* (Cambridge, Polity Press).

Shennan, S. (1997) *Quantifying Archaeology* (Edinburgh, Edinburgh University Press).

Shepherd, L. (1993) 'Interpreting landscapes: analysis of excavations in and around the southern bailey of Norwich Castle', in Barber 1993: 3–10.

Shott, M. (1985) 'Shovel-test sampling as a site discovery technique: a case study from Michigan', *Journal of Field Archaeology* 12: 457–68.

(1987) 'Feature discovery and the sampling requirements of archaeological evaluations', *Journal of Field Archaeology* 14: 359–71.

(1989) 'Shovel-test sampling in archaeological survey: comments on Nance and Ball, and Lightfoot', *American Antiquity* 54: 396–404.

(1995) 'Reliability of archaeological records on cultivated surfaces: a Michigan case-study', *Journal of Field Archaeology* 22: 475–90.

(1998) 'Status and role of Formation Theory in contemporary archaeological practice', *Journal of Archaeological Research* 6(4): 299–329.

Showalter, P. (1993) 'A thematic mapper analysis of the prehistoric Hohokam canal system, Pheonix, Arizona', *Journal of Field Archaeology* 20: 77–90.

Smith, L. (1985) *Investigating Old Buildings* (London, Batsford).

Smith, R. (1974) 'Ethics in field archaeology', *Journal of Field Archaeology* 1: 375–83.

Spennemann, D. (1987) 'Experiences with mapping sites on aerial photographs', *Journal of Field Archaeology* 14: 255.

(1992) 'Archaeological site location using a Global Positioning System', *Journal of Field Archaeology* 19: 271–4.

Stančič, Z. (1989) 'Computer vision: producing intra-site plans', *Archaeological Computing Newsletter* 20: 1–9.

Steane, K. (1992a) 'Reinterpretation: thoughts from the backlog', in Steane 1992b: 40–2.

(1993) 'Land use diagrams: a hierarchy of site interpretation', in Barber 1993: 11–14.

Steane, K. (ed.) (1992b) *Interpretation of Stratigraphy: A Review of the Art* (Lincoln, City of Lincoln Archaeology Unit).

Steenstrup, J. (1857) 'Et bidrag til Gerrfuglens, Alca impennis Lin., nauturhistoire, og saerligt til kundskaben om dens tidligere' *Udbredningskreds Vid. Medd. nat. For. Kjobenhavn.* 1855(3–7): 33–116.

Stein, J. (1986) 'Coring archaeological sites', *American Antiquity* 51: 505–27.

(1991) 'Coring in CRM and archaeology: a reminder', *American Antiquity* 56: 138–42.

Stone, G. (1981) 'On artifact density and shovel probes', *Current Anthropology* 22(2): 182–3.

Stove, G. and Addyman, P. (1989) 'Ground-probing impulse RADAR: an experiment in archaeological remote sensing in York', *Antiquity* 63: 337–42.

Struever, S. (1968) 'Flotation techniques for the recovery of small-scale archaeological remains', *American Antiquity* 33: 353–62.

Stucki, B. (1993) 'Three-dimensional assessment of activity areas in a shell midden: an example from the Hoko River Rockshelter, State of Washington', in Harris *et al.* 1993: 122–38.

Sundstrom, L. (1993) 'A simple mathematical procedure for estimating the adequacy of site survey strategies', *Journal of Field Archaeology* 20: 91–6.

Tarleton, K. and Ordoñez, M. (1995) 'Stabilization methods for textiles from wet sites', *Journal of Field Archaeology* 22: 81–95.

Taylor, C. (1974) *Fieldwork in Medieval Archaeology* (London, Batsford).

Tealby, J., Oxley J., Campbell, T., Giannopoulos, A. and Dittmer, J. (1993) 'Analysis of ground-probing RADAR data, including polarisation effects, when used in condition assessment of Ancient Monuments', in Vogel and Tsokas 1993: 235–47.

Terras, M. (1999) 'A virtual tomb for Kelvingrove', *Internet Archaeology* 7 (http://intarch.ac.uk/journal/issue7/terras_toc.html).

Thomas, J. (1996) *Time, Culture and Identity: An Interpretive Archaeology* (London, Routledge).

Thompson, R. and Oldfield, F. (1986) *Environmental Magnetism* (London, Allen and Unwin).

Tilley, C. (1989) 'Excavation as theatre', *Antiquity* 63: 275–80.

(1994) *A Phenomenology of Landscape: Places, Paths and Monuments* (Oxford, Berg).

Toca, R. and Lavín, N. (1999) 'New procedures for tracing Paleolithic rock paintings: digital photography', in Barceló *et al.* 1999: 73–6.

Trigger, B. (1989) *A History of Archaeological Thought* (Cambridge, Cambridge University Press).

Ucko, P. (ed.) (1995) *Theory in Archaeology: A World Perspective* (London, Routledge).

Ucko, P. and Layton, R. (eds) (1999) *Archaeology and Anthropology of Landscape* (London, Routledge).

Van der Veen, M. (1983) 'Seeds and seed machines', *Circaea* 1(2): 61–2.

Vogel, A and Tsokas, G. (eds.) (1993) *Geophysical Exploration of Archaeological Sites* (Wiesbaden, Viewig and Sohn).

Vullo, N., Fontana, F. and Guerreschi, A. (1999) 'The application of GIS to intra-spatial analysis: preliminary results from Alpe Veglia (VB) and Mondeval de Sora (BL), two Mesolithic sites in the Italian Alps', in Barceló *et al.* 1999: 111–15.

Wagner, G. (1982) 'Testing flotation recovery rates', *American Antiquity* 47: 127–32.

Wagstaff, J. (1987) *Landscape and Culture: Geographical and Archaeological Perspectives* (Oxford, Blackwell).

Wainwright, G. (1978) 'Theory and practice in field archaeology', in Darvill *et al.* 1978: 11–27.

Wandsnider, L. and Ebert, J. (eds.) (1988) 'Issues in archaeological surface survey: meshing methods and theory', *American Archaeology* 7.

Waters, M. (1992) *Principles of Geoarchaeology: A North American Perspective* (Tucson, University of Arizona Press).

Watkinson, D. (ed.) (1987) *First Aid for Finds* (Hertford, Rescue – The British Archaeology Trust).

Watkinson, D. and Neal, V. (1998) *First Aid for Finds* (Hertford, Rescue – The British Archaeology Trust).

Watson, R. (1990) 'Ozymandia, king of kings: postprocessual radical archaeology as a critique', *American Antiquity* 55: 673–89.

Webb, S. (1987) 'Reburying Australian skeletons', *Antiquity* 61: 292–6.

Webster, G. (1974) *Practical Archaeology: An Introduction to Practical Archaeological Field-work and Excavation* (London, Adam and Charles Black).

Weston, P. (1976) 'In pursuit of prehistoric subsistence: a comparative account of some contemporary flotation techniques', *Midcontinental Journal of Archaeology* 1: 77–100.

Weymouth, J. (1986) 'Geophysical methods of site surveying', in M. Schiffer (ed.) *Advances in Archaeological Method and Theory,* 9: 311–95.

Whalen, M. (1990) 'Defining buried features before excavation: a case from the American Southwest', *Journal of Field Archaeology* 17: 323–31.

Wheatley, D. (1991) 'SyGraf – resource based teaching with graphics', in Lockyear and Rahtz 1991: 9–13.

Wheeler, A. and Jones, A. (1989) *Fishes* (Cambridge, Cambridge University Press).

Wheeler, R. (1945) 'Technical section: recording archaeological strata', *Ancient India* 3: 133–40.
(1946) 'Technical section: further notes on digging and recording', *Ancient India* 4: 311–21.
(1954) *Archaeology from the Earth* (Oxford, Clarendon Press).

White, K. (1990) 'Photography on archaeological excavations: a consideration of present practice' (Unpublished MA dissertation, University of York).

Whitley, D. (ed.) (1998) *Reader in Archaeological Theory: Post-Processual and Cognitive Approaches* (London, Routledge).

Whyman, M. (1996) 'Charnel and what to do with it', in Roskams 1996: 28–35.

Wickham-Jones, C. (1999) 'Excavation, publication and the internet', *Internet Archaeology* 7 (http://intarch.ac.uk/journal/issue7/wickham_toc.html).

Wilcock, J. (1982) 'Strata: the microcomputer version', in I. Graham and E. Webb (eds.) *Computer Applications in Archaeology* 1981: 112–14.

Willey, G. and Sabloff, J. (1974) *A History of American Archaeology* (London, Thames and Hudson).

Wilson, D. (1982) *Air Photo Interpretation for Archaeologists* (London, Batsford).

Wilson, R. (ed.) (1987) *Rescue Archeology: Proceedings of the Second New World Conference on Rescue Archeology* (Dallas, Texas, Southern Methodist University Press).

Winters, J. (1999) Editorial in *Internet Archaeology* 6 (http://intarch.ac.uk/journal/issue6/editorial.html).

Wise, A. and Miller, P. (1997) 'Why metadata matters in archaeology', *Internet Archaeology 2* (http://intarch.ac.uk/journal/issue2/wise_index.html).

Wobst, H. (1983) 'We can't see the forest for the trees: sampling and the shapes of archaeological distributions', in J. Moore and A. Keene (eds.) *Archaeological Hammers and Theories* (New York, Academic Press), 37–85.

Woodwark, J. (1991) 'Reconstructing history with computer graphics', *IEEE Computer Graphics and Applications* January: 18–20.

Woolley, C. L. (1930) *Digging Up the Past* (London, Penguin).

Yoffee, N. and Sherratt, A. (eds.) (1993) *Archaeological Theory: Who Sets the Agenda?* (Cambridge, Cambridge University Press).

Yule, B. (1992) 'Truncation horizons and reworking in urban stratigraphy', in Steane 1992b: 20–2.

Zubrow, E. (1994) 'Knowledge representation and archaeology: a cognitive example using GIS', in A. Renfrew and E. Zubrow (eds.) *The Ancient Mind: Elements of Cognitive Archaeology* (Cambridge, Cambridge University Press), 107–18.

INDEX